SAINTS
v
POMPEY

First published November 2004
Copyright © Dave Juson, Clay Aldworth, Barry Bendel, David Bull and Gary Chalk, 2004

Published by HAGIOLOGY PUBLISHING
170 Westbury Road
Bristol BS9 3AH

ISBN 0-9534474-5-6

Designed and typeset by Elizabeth Porter, www.porterlizz-graphic-design.co.uk, Bristol
Printed and bound in Great Britain by The Bath Press

SAINTS

v

POMPEY

A History of Unrelenting Rivalry

DAVE JUSON

with Clay Aldworth, Barry Bendel, David Bull and Gary Chalk

in association with

and

Daily Echo

For reasons explained in the introduction at page ix, the copyright of pre-1946 illustrations is often not known. What follows, therefore, by way of picture accreditation, is mainly restricted to the images reproduced from Chapter 11 onwards.

The *Southern Daily Echo* has been a major source of illustrations. Photos known to be from the *Echo* appear in this book at pages 159, 165 (both), 167, 168, 169, 171 (both right), 174 (top), 177, 186 (right), 192, 194, 198 (all), 213 (top), 214, 247, 258 (both) and the back cover.

We have also used, sometimes in part only, *Echo* cartoons by Ron Moody (xi, 2, 115, 136) or Orf (160, 162, both) and caricatures drawn for the *Echo* by Saints and Pompey centre-forward, Ron Davies (182, 183, 184 and 187).

We have additionally used OZ cartoons, mostly in part, at pages 163, 164 and 166, with the permission of the late Don Osmond.

Photos known to be the copyright of Southampton FC are reproduced at pages 200 (left), 205, 206, 209, 210 (both) and 213 (middle).

The photo of the 1922 match (at page 103) is from the collection of Richard Owen, the Official Portsmouth FC historian, while that of Jimmy Dickinson (at page 155), is from Peter Jeffs, with the permission of Mrs Ann Dickinson.

The *News*, Portsmouth, is the source of the cartoon at page 180 and of the photos at pages 213 (bottom right) and 216, while the M & Y Agency has supplied the images at pages 189, 200 (right), 217 and 253, as well as the front-cover photo.

The caricatures at pages 112, 116 (both), 130, 131, 133, 140, 148, 149, 173 (both), 203, 208 (both) and 239 are reproduced, with Barry Bendel's permission, from his *The Pride of Pompey*.

Programmes used as illustrations are from the collections of Hagiology members, mainly Gary Chalk.

Contents

Foreword
Alan Ball

The first thing to be said about the Saints-Pompey rivalry is that too few of the games between them have been played in the last 25 years.

I had three spells with Southampton – two as a player and one as manager – and two as a manager at Portsmouth. Yet I took part in only four of the 200-odd South Coast derbies charted in this exceedingly thorough book.

The first was a Hampshire FA Professional Cup game on 22 December 1981. Both Lawrie McMenemy and Pompey's Frank Burrows treated this as a first-team fixture: I had Steve Williams and David Armstrong alongside me and Kevin Keegan, Mick Channon and Steve Moran up front. That's because we'd already lost most of that month to some dreadful weather and, in those days, managers would rather have their top-players run around a wintry Fratton Park than head for the Med.

So Lawrie McMenemy could explain that a 2-1 defeat didn't matter: all he'd wanted was a competitive game without injuries and that's what he'd got.

If only post-match conferences were always that simple for managers! My first derby match as Pompey's boss was the 2-2 draw in the First Division in August 1987, which turned out to be one of those games that thrill the fans but bring the dug-outs to despair. In other words, the goals came mainly from defenders giving away crazy goals – 'nervous goals' I called them, at the time. But it was a good game *because* of the mistakes.

In the 'return' at The Dell, Portsmouth weathered a battering for the first 15 minutes and were fortunate to be drawing 0-0 when, totally against the run of play, they scored. The whole game changed: Pompey got more confident and got better and better, while Southampton lost their confidence and got worse and worse. My team finished up cruising and were very easy winners.

My only derby as Southampton's manager was the testimonial for Alan Knight in 1994. I have a high regard for Alan and, once the police had OK'd it, I thought taking the Saints there for him would be a way of trying to bring the two clubs and their fans together a bit more.

I started with most of the side that Matthew Le Tissier had led to that famous 'Great Escape' at West Ham three days before, while Pompey rang the changes on 21 players, the way teams often do in testimonials. Mind you, I came on as sub for half-an-hour, just to brighten the place up a bit more, although Dave Beasant stole the substitute show by playing, outfield, with his goalkeeping gloves on.

Southampton won 5-1 but, like Lawrie McMenemy in 1981, I can honestly say the result wasn't important: the important thing is that there was a wonderful turn-out for a wonderful person.

Since that get-together in 1994, the rivalry between Southampton and Portsmouth seems to have become more bitter. This bitterness seems to come from one team being in a higher League than the other, the lack of stability at one club while the other is riding high.

That said, I was surprised how fierce the rivalry was when I first came down to Hampshire in the late 1970s. I've been involved in three other local rivalries – the Merseyside and North London derbies as a player and in Manchester as a manager – and the feeling is as high, here, as anywhere. I think the best derby in the country, by far, is the Liverpool derby, with families going to the games together, where inter-marriage has meant couples and their children having mixed loyalties.

I think that's marvellous.

As this book demonstrates, there are fans of both sides who wish their neighbours well and who disown the bitter minority, whichever team they may be supporting. I am pleased to be associated with this book's attempt to represent the views of the majority of fans who want our game to be enhanced by loyalties, not tarnished by it.

Introductions

... from the editor

This book is the idea of **Clay Aldworth** and the creation, for the most part, of **Dave Juson**. When Clay approached Hagiology Publishing with the outline of a book on SAINTS v POMPEY, we very much liked the notion but felt it needed a more historical text. Enter Dave Juson.

Or, rather, exit Dave Juson, bound for libraries far and wide, as credited in the 'Sources' at the end of this book. He needed to supplement three kinds of material we already had: the reference books (notably those of Gary Chalk and Duncan Holley) noted in those 'Sources'; the Southampton FC minutes, which we had long since been permitted to photocopy (up until 1976); and material gathered for previous Hagiology publications, like his own historical record in *Full-Time at The Dell,* reports in *Match of Millennium* and interviews I had conducted for *Dell Diamond.*

We shall occasionally refer you to those sources but it would be tedious if we drew attention to each and every mention of a game reported in *Match of the Millennium.* Let's hope we've given you sufficient indication of the sources we have relied upon, without needing to footnote every insight as if this were an academic text.

Dave occasionally came out of the archives to conduct an interview or two – Fred Dinenage, Guy Askham and Michael Withers kindly agreed to assist him in his enquiries – and to report progress. After a while, I had the temerity to question the rate of progress: how could it take so long to research the meetings of two clubs who had spent a century *not* playing each other?

Not for the first time, I needed to be disabused. I had believed what I'd read in the papers about the 30 or so times Southampton had played Portsmouth and had no idea that the total was 206 – rising to 209 with the flurry of activity in 2003-04. The material Dave amassed was impressive: voluminous wasn't the word for it. But it needed to fit into one paperback volume and I have been the brute who saw to that, discarding gems unmercifully (while occasionally *adding* a line or two, mostly of a contextual nature).

So that explains the content of Part I of this book. But this was never intended to be a book devoted entirely to the derby matches: we wanted to reflect on a few other aspects of the 'rivalry'. Clay Aldworth had prepared a chapter on those who had 'played for both', drawing mainly on the Holley and Chalk *Alphabet of the Saints* and Roger Holmes's *Pompey Players.* Gary Chalk has helped him to expand upon that idea in Chapter 14, while my Chapter 15 is an attempt to collate information (as verified by Gary) about war-time variations on Clay's theme.

And, if only as a counter to the assumptions that rivalry means hostility, we felt we should hear from Saints fans who had gone to watch Portsmouth in their glory days. Hence Chapter 16 – although you will see that it has developed into something more than that. I am grateful to all of those who contributed to this chapter, with special thanks to David Hutchinson for access to his autographed scrapbooks and to Richard Ember for the photo of himself, in an extremely compromising position, that appears on page 246.

Which brings us to the question of what kind of Pompey perspective the book should have. If this was going to be a book about the two clubs, it needed some degree of *balance.* Addressing that problem involved us in two issues: content and the cover.

We contemplated approaching a Portsmouth FC historian, with a view to a *joint* publication, but decided that what we needed was a chapter or two, providing the perspective of a Fratton Park regular, mainly reacting to what we (or, more often, reporters) had said about Pompey and its fans. That's where Barry Bendel came in. He was researching biographical details for his exquisite compilation, *The Pride of Pompey,* and hoped I might be able to help him with Portsmouth stars who had also played for Southampton. It was very soon obvious that he would be ideal for our purposes and he would have time, once his book was published, to help us with ours. What's more, he came with a substantial portfolio of caricatures.

We offered him two chapters but he preferred to concentrate his thoughts in one. We have been helped by three other Pompey historians, occasionally in answering queries but mainly for photo research (of which more in a moment); but our main support, day-to-day, has come from Barry Bendel. He even chipped in with ideas for the cover, some of which we have used.

Cover design is seldom simple but this was an especially problematic and time-consuming one to produce. For a start, it meant we needed to vary our usual red-and-white cover by introducing a block of Pompey blue. That would have been easier if we had had, from the start, a photo or two that fitted a red, white and blue design. But we didn't.

We had hoped to balance the obvious photo for Saints fans – Steve Moran's winner in the FA Cup in 1984 – against the equally obvious Pompey pic: Yakubu Ayegbeni's winner in the Fratton Park derby of 2004. Unfortunately, the shape of these two photos made them difficult to juxtapose. But, then, the M & Y Agency kindly sent us a selection of images, among which our designer spotted the potential of the photo you see on the front cover. Wedded as most of us had become to the idea of having goals on the cover, we soon came round to her view.

I hope you can see why. The photos of those two goals are, of course, in the book. You may well feel that they should have been presented more prominently in their respective match reports.

So do I, but I'm afraid the shape of a photo sometimes obliges us to reproduce it smaller than its significance says it should be. Other photos will appear inappropriately small because of the quality of the original. Conversely, some may appear unduly large, but this will always be the case in a book that tries to match illustrations to the text in the way we have.

Whatever your thoughts on size, we hope that the illustrations help to tell the story – not least of matches played before they were routinely photographed, a problem exacerbated by the destruction, during the Second World War, of the *Echo* archive. Dave Juson has traced some cartoons (many more than could be employed) and otherwise we have relied, for pre-war photos and cigarette cards of Southampton players, upon Gary Chalk's collection (including the 1906 photo on page 46, acquired from Portsmouth fan, Alf Harris).

Duncan Holley's collection has been the main source of post-war photos of the Saints. Where these are known to be *Echo* photos, they are credited as such on page iv and have been used on the generous terms agreed with Stewart Dunn and Ian Murray. Many of the more recent photos are the copyright of Southampton FC, having been taken by Mike Atkelsky and retrieved for us either by James Philpott at the club or by Nikki Saunders and Mark Bratcher at Cedar, the printers of the matchday programme.

Barry Bendel has helped us hugely in tracing Portsmouth photographs and in allowing us to use caricatures from his *The Pride of Pompey*. Most of the pre-war photos are from his collection, but some of the very early ones are from Mick Cooper's. We have credited, on page iv, the photos supplied by Pompey historians, Richard Owen and Peter Jeffs; by the M & Y Agency, through the good services of Mike Walker and Pat Symes; or by the Portsmouth *News,* where Dean Kedwood and Deborah Croker were so helpful.

A few post-war, and most of the pre-war, illustrations are uncredited. As repeatedly explained in our prefaces, accepting photos from ex-players has often left us unclear as to copyright. And I fear that modern technology could be making this problem worse. When asked where a photo of him had come from, a former Pompey player told me he had 'no idea: somebody copied it off a website and sent it to me.' All of which means that we will have used photos unattributed and their copyright-holders may wish to contact us for appropriate recompense.

Some of the facts have been checked with Mike Davage, while Mike Swain has given the text the once-over in his usual conscientious and unstinting way.

Having assembled all this material, we depended upon Liz Porter to fit it on the pages that follow. We applaud her bravery in taking on this assignment as her first book and thank her hugely for the careful and creative way she has performed on her debut.

It should be self-evident why we asked Alan Ball to contribute a foreword and we are delighted that he agreed to do so.

David Bull, October 2004

... and from the lead-author

SAINTS v POMPEY: one of the most passionate and bitter rivalries on Planet Football! Wherever and whenever commentators discuss the great rivalries, be they Celtic and Rangers, Everton and Liverpool, Manchester City and United, Argentina and Uruguay, Arsenal and anyone in London, they cannot be taken seriously unless they draw parallels with the Solent derby. Can they?

We can dream. But let's be honest, the only time the rivalry excites much comment outside Hampshire is on the rare occasions, in recent years, that there have actually been games between the two clubs, when we are, at best, patronised. And even these meetings aren't taken as seriously by the national press as the derbies of the 1900s, when both clubs were in the Southern League.

There is a good reason for this: Pompey and Saints were sharing an equally lofty status at the time. The Southern League's standing faded – for reasons discussed often in the early chapters that follow – as did the fortunes of the two clubs. Then, in the 1920s, with both clubs in the Third, then Second, Division, any significance was purely a local matter. After Pompey rose into Division I in 1927, derby games ceased to be an event of much interest even around the Solent. Then they just ceased.

It wasn't until the 1960–61 season that the clubs met again to contest League points, in Division II. At which point, Pompey's fortunes were turning to dust, while the Saints, Division III champions, were most definitely on a rise. That short, and often turbulent, reunion ended in 1966 when Southampton were promoted to Division I. Thereafter, with the Saints having spent all but four seasons in the top flight, the respective supporters have seldom had the opportunity to give the 'other lot' a good deal of thought, except on those rare occasions when they have actually got to play each other, at which point there is most certainly something at stake: the banter at work for the next week or two can be somewhat exacting for those on the receiving end of the triumphalism – we're informed.

Unfortunately, there is a small minority in both cities, and around them, for whom it is axiomatic that support for one club demands pure, blinding hatred for the other; though it is comforting to report that when the Northam Stand choir render *Sit down if you love Pompey...* the vast majority of those in St Mary's keep their bottoms firmly in place.

Discussing the recent 'hate-hate' phenomenon with older supporters, and inquiring as to the roots of the problem, one is met with bemusement. Saints' fans of the 1940s and '50s clearly regarded Portsmouth as so out of their league (and they were) that the idea of a real rivalry was out of the question – more than enough of them, as you will read in Chapter 16, happily journeyed to Fratton Park when the Saints were away. And as for Portsmouth's fall from grace in the 1960s, and beyond, longstanding Pompey supporters seem more inclined to hold those running Portsmouth FC culpable. What did Southampton have to do with anything?

Rival ports?

Reasons for animosity are cited – the most common being the famous dock strike in Portsmouth, which was broken by the South Coast Union Men of Southampton, giving us the much-used acronym, SCUM.

There are many variations on this yarn, but the most problematical factor, in authenticating it, is that nobody disposed to believe it can actually agree when it took place. The April/May 1996 edition of the fanzine *Frattonize* places the incident before World War I, whereas interviewees in the *Observer*, in August 2003, claimed it was in the 1950s and... well, other dates, every bit as vague, are offered, which doesn't give the diligent historian much to go on.

Research for this book uncovered no references to a labour dispute in Portsmouth involving strike breakers from Southampton – and, even if the story were true, it seems somewhat extreme to hold a festering grudge against more than 200,000 people for the actions of a few dozen, at most, individuals.

Which begs the question: excluding urban myth, are there any historic reasons for animosity between Southampton and Portsmouth?

It can be confirmed that armies from the two towns have never faced each other across the River Meon, nor, as far as I am aware, has Southampton ever borrowed

Portsmouth's lawn mower and refused to return it, but history does point to the occasional frictions.

Southampton was almost certainly the first urban conurbation in Saxon Wessex. Archaeologists have now established that the population was in excess of 4,000 (possibly much larger) by the early 8th century, and the area around it was known colloquially as 'Hampshire' from that time. For all processes of law and government, Hampshire was called 'the County of Southampton' until 1959.

Portsmouth emerged as a prominent community in the 12th century, around the church of Thomas à Becket. Its first notable charter was extracted from Richard the Lionheart, in 1194, and entitled it to an annual fair and a market on Thursdays. It was an important concession, but did not affect Southampton overmuch, because Richard had already, in 1189, granted the merchants freedom of tollage, there, for all fairs and markets. In 1199, Richard's brother and successor, John, granted Southampton a charter that made Portsmouth 'an adjunct', obliging all local traders to pay their taxes, port and customs duties through Southampton. There was, however, a *quid pro quo*: in 1212 John ordered the sheriff of Southampton to build 'enclosed' docks in Portsmouth, probably the first permanent ship-handling facilities in the harbour since the Romans abandoned Portchester Castle.

Portsmouth had to wait until 1572 for some sort of autonomy, when it was granted its own customs house, which, to much *chagrin*, lost Southampton revenue and trade. However, such is the English love of anachronism and anomaly, it was not until the Municipal Reform Act of 1835 that Portsmouth Harbour ceased to be part of the port of Southampton – though, in the interim, nobody in Southampton appears to have been pompous enough to chuck their weight around with the Royal Navy on the basis of some, by then, ancient piece of parchment.

Traditionally, Southampton has had more problems with Winchester than it ever did with Portsmouth, and its merchants lavished a great deal of money in the right places to guarantee their rights against outside interference. In 1447, these rights were enshrined in a charter that made Southampton a county in its own right: 'the County of the Town of Southampton'.

Which presents us with a curiosity because, while the rest of Hampshire remained in 'the County of Southampton', Southampton itself became, and remains, a separate entity. So, in terms of full-time professional football (since Aldershot's demise as a League club, and Bournemouth having been shifted into Dorset in 1974), Pompey fans can sing *One team in Hampshire* without fear of informed contradiction.

This said, one can hardly claim that Southampton – like the Isle of Wight (like Bournemouth, part of Hampshire until 1974) – is a distinct geographical entity, so this book sticks to the media convention of including it in Hampshire, if only for the sake of simplicity.

Southampton went into decline in the Tudor period while, from the 17th century, Portsmouth emerged as one of the country's most important military ports. In *A Tour Through the Whole Island of Great Britain*, in the early 18th century, Daniel Defoe described it as 'the largest fortification, beyond comparison, that we have in England' and rhapsodised at some length on its prosperity and on most other aspects of life, warfare and mercantile activity there.

Conversely, Southampton was 'a truly ancient town, for 'tis in a manner dying with age; the decay of the trade is the real decay of the town; and all the business of moment that is transacted there, is the trade between us and the islands of Jersey and Guernsey, with a little of the wine trade, and much smuggling.'

As it happened, Southampton scuffed along as a respectable spa resort, but the local topography was against it becoming a Brighton or a Southsea. First, there was nothing that could remotely be described as a beach. Secondly, it sits at the head of Southampton Water, the most capacious natural harbour in England. With every major port in Britain, not least Portsmouth, choked with the traffic of the British Empire, it was realised that Southampton would be less than two hours from London by that marvellous new invention: the steam locomotive.

Men of business began a dialogue, cheques were signed, loans were raised, acts of Parliament passed and, by 1830, new docks were being built on the confluence of the rivers Test and Itchen and railway tracks were being laid between the harbour-side and London.

The railway was to become a major point of contention between Southampton's business community and Portsmouth's politicians. The London & Southampton Railway proposed to build a branch line between Eastleigh (on the London–Southampton line) and Portsmouth, but Portsmouth's Corporation objected: they wanted a direct line to London or nothing.

Short term, they got nothing and a curious situation arose: anyone in Portsmouth wishing to visit the capital was compelled to make his or her way by ferry to Gosport and from there catch the train to Eastleigh, where they would have to change for London: 'in the meantime,' according to the historian, A. Temple Patterson, 'quite a bit of trade moved to other ports – like Southampton – with railways.'

That being true, it cannot be claimed that Southampton's re-emergence as a major port affected Portsmouth that adversely. It was, after all, the home of the Fleet, and Southampton was most definitely concerned with passengers and cargo. It might better be argued that they were complementary: Portsmouth being busy with keeping the seven seas safe for British commerce; and Southampton… with British commerce.

Even in more recent times, with the decline of Britain as a military and economic power, there are not many conflicts of interest as far as the ports are concerned. And, notwithstanding the occasional spats over who should host which prestigious ocean yacht race and the recent relocation of Vosper Thornycroft from Woolston, both cities have their own singular preoccupations. It is certainly difficult to envisage any advantage that might be visited on one should the earth (or sea) open up and swallow the other. Although, it's worth adding that there are those in Hampshire who regard both Southampton and Portsmouth as unpleasant urban intrusions on their green and pleasant land.

As to the rivalry between the two football clubs, we – possibly – stand on the brink of a new era, one in which the rivalry could, at long last, be carried out at the highest level for the foreseeable future.

Which will bring us full circle, because, with the creation of Portsmouth FC and their instant success against the Saints, at the fag end of the 19th century, the Solent quickly became regarded as an area as passionate about its football as anywhere else in the kingdom.

That would appear to be an improbable notion for the national media to hold on to at present, but there is no real reason that reputation cannot be regained – in the nicest possible way.

Fingers crossed!

Dave Juson, October 2004

Part I

Derby Days

Dave Juson

... being a match-by-match account
of the first 209 meetings
between Saints and Pompey
1899-2004

Chapter 1
A Friendly Beginning

It all began – everything has to begin somewhere – at 5.15 pm on 7 September 1899, when His Worship the Mayor of Portsmouth, Alderman T. Scott Foster, kicked off from the centre-spot of what the *Southern Daily Mail* was calling the 'Goldsmith-ground' and which was 'situated "in the country",' the *Southampton Times and Hampshire Express* explained to its readers, 'some three-quarters of a mile beyond Fratton Station.'

Portsmouth's *Evening News* commemorated the occasion with attention-grabbing headlines:

PORTSMOUTH AT HOME
MATCH AGAINST SOUTHAMPTON

Then the reporter led off with a prophetic observation:

> The first of what, it is hoped, will be a long series of historic football battles took place on Wednesday at Fratton Park, as the new ground in Goldsmith-avenue has been named. There has always been a deal of rivalry between the two towns, but Southampton long since took the initiative in securing the services of a professional team.

This was not Portsmouth FC's first game, nor was it the first match at Fratton Park. 'Fully 5,000 spectators', according to the *Evening News*, had turned up to watch 'the first public trial match of the Portsmouth professional team', on the evening of Saturday 28 August, and the following Saturday the players had travelled to Chatham and won their first competitive game, a Southern League fixture, 1-0 – 'a mild sensation,' the *Football Mail* felt, against a side that had finished fourth in that League the previous season.

But Southampton, the Southern League champions, were in a different class from Chatham altogether. And, in sharp contrast to Portsmouth, they had been around forever. On the formation of the Southern League, in 1894, St Mary's, as they were then called, slipped in to its nine-team First Division by the intercession of the Fates. Having had their initial application rejected, they were invited to take the place of the 2nd Scots Guards, who had been posted abroad before the competition had got underway. Back then, Portsmouth did not really have a side with the potential to compete in Division II.

This is not to say there had never been any football rivalry between the two great ports: various clubs had emerged over the previous 15 years and contested honours for their respective communities.

The Good Old Days

No sooner had the South Hampshire & Dorset Football Association been founded in 1884 than it had organised Senior and Junior Cup competitions. Yet not one club east of Southampton Water – where rugby pre-dominated, much as the dinosaurs had several millennia before – entered for either trophy that first season.

The major driving force behind the new association was a Lancastrian, William Pickford, a journalist on the *Bournemouth Guardian*.

In his 1937 Golden Jubilee history of Hampshire football, Pickford recalls that two Portsmouth clubs – Portsmouth Association FC and Portsmouth Sunflowers FC – and two Southampton teams, Woolston Works and Geneva Cross (of the Royal Victoria Military Hospital at Netley), joined what had quickly evolved into the Hampshire & Dorset FA.

Although neither of the last two sides was based within the County Borough of Southampton itself, the Works, who were ostensibly made up of employees of the Oswald, Mordaunt & Co. shipyard, soon took up residence at the Antelope Cricket Ground in the town.

On the other side of Spit Head, Canon Norman Pares (winner of an FA Cup winners medal with the Old Etonians in 1879) appears to have been among the leading pioneers of the 'dribbling game', setting up Portsmouth Sunflowers – seemingly to give his three brothers and old chums from Eton and Cambridge University games when they happened to be in the district – and featuring prominently for the Portsmouth

Association club. His brothers also played for this side at times, as did A.C. Smith, the first Hampshire based footballer to earn international celebrity – although we shall see that it was not his skill as a sportsman that would bring him renown.

While most Hampshire and Dorset clubs were forced to select predominantly from callow locals, Woolston Works recruited their labour force from the shipyards of the nation. The banks of the Tyne, Wear and, most especially, the Clyde proved a fecund source of tradesmen who could play a standard of football previously unknown along the South Coast.

So it was that, on 14 October 1886, Sunflowers travelled to Woolston Park – why the game was not played at the Antelope we do not know – to dispute a place in the Second Round of the Hants & Dorset Senior Cup. The *Southampton Times* reported 'an unexpectedly easy' home win: 6–1 to be exact.

The Works went on to win the Senior Cup and to reach the final of a new competition, the Portsmouth & District Cup. It had been organised by Portsmouth Association who would themselves defend their town's honour against what Pickford would describe as 'this galaxy of Scotsmen'; though it might be added that one of their most accomplished players was Private J. Howarth, stationed at Netley Hospital, but formerly an FA Cup-winner with the Blackburn Rovers side of 1885.

Played on the Men's Recreation Ground (the non-officers part of the United Services Ground) the match was 'witnessed by about 800 people,' according to the *Southampton Times* – the first example we can find of the local press giving an actual attendance figure for a football match; an indication, perhaps, that it was an extraordinarily large assembly?

Looking back on that game, 52 years later, Pickford recalled that Portsmouth's 'prospects of beating Woolston were not considered worth betting marbles upon. So that we outsiders, who had felt the iron of the Woolston hammer, had no manner of doubt as to the result. All the more amazing, that Portsmouth win of 1–0.' Vexed and possibly dismayed, the Works protested the result on the basis that the game was played between rugby goals – but to no avail.

One of the heroes, on the day, was the aforesaid A.C. Smith, playing in the Portsmouth goal under the alias of Dr. Doyle – or, rather, Dr Doyle was for once playing under his real name. In a 1924 memoir, Arthur Conan Doyle, having long forsaken his Southsea medical practice – and, indeed, Southsea – and being apparently unaware of subsequent footballing developments on Portsea Island, proudly, but mistakenly, claimed he had played for the 'famous Portsmouth club', which undoubtedly got a few unintended laughs in Hampshire. But he never mentioned playing under a *nom de guerre*, nor has any explanation emerged as to why he did so. It is a mystery that we need a Sherlock Holmes to unravel.

In April 1887, the Hants & Dorset FA dissolved into two separate associations and the new Hampshire FA immediately took steps to organise Senior and Junior Cup competitions.

To nobody's surprise, Woolston Works carried off the Senior Cup that first season. To everybody's surprise – even their own, according to Pickford – the Junior Cup was won by an unsung club by the name of St Mary's, a side which played most of its home games on Southampton Common.

The Young Men of St Mary's

This club had been formed in 1885, by members of the St Mary's Church of England Young Men's Association, whose origins and early career we need not labour, given the detailed accounts in two recent Hagiology publications, but it is worth observing (for those not minded to pursue the Saints' rich and exciting history) that, by May 1888, when that first trophy was lifted by skipper, Charles Bromley, they had severed their connections with St Mary's Church and were already known as 'The Saints'.

From then on, they could not stop winning cup-ties. They went five seasons without being beaten in any official competition. They were even undefeated during their first tilt at the FA Cup in 1891: having beaten Reading 7-0 they were – harshly – expelled from the tournament for fielding ineligible players.

By the beginning of the 1892–93 season, St Mary's had won the Hants FA Junior Cup outright after three consecutive championships and were looking to do the same in the Senior Cup, which they would collect two years running. They would also begin to recruit professional players.

In the meantime, Woolston Works had gone into a decline, and rapid demise, after Oswald Mordaunt & Co.

The Antelope Ground,
which the Saints took over from the Works.

Freemantle, winners not only of the Hants Senior
Cup but of the Portsmouth & District Cup.

got into financial difficulties late in 1888 and the Saints, in short time, took over not only their place in the hearts of Southampton's sporting public, but their residence at the Antelope Cricket Ground. They could not, alas, keep winning cups for eternity and, when the inevitable happened, it happened with a vengeance.

At the Antelope Ground, St Mary's kept up a busy schedule of friendly fixtures with increasingly powerful opponents. Regimental sides from Aldershot, Portsmouth and London, as well as club sides from the capital, tended to supply the most belligerent opposition. St Mary's invariably won, until the 1892–93 season, when Maidenhead knocked them out of the FA Cup in the Second Qualifying Round and they were defeated in the Final of the Hants Senior Cup by local rivals Freemantle.

The Magpies, as Freemantle were known, also won the Portsmouth & District Cup that season, for the second time in succession, and won it outright the following year, beating St Mary's in the Final. The result was probably more galling for the Saints than for any of the competing Portsmouth teams or their supporters (the game pulled a big crowd), but it still meant that the Royal Navy town had yet to produce a side capable of matching Southampton's elite.

As it transpired, Saints put all local rivalries, and the frustrations they exacted, behind them in 1894, by the simple expedient of entering a higher sphere: the newly-established Southern League. Over the next three years, a steady stream of professionals would arrive, particularly from Stoke, among them trainer Bill Dawson.

During that summer of 1894, as the Southampton public eagerly anticipated the undoubted thrill of visits from such legendary footballing protagonists as Millwall Athletic, Luton Town, Clapton and Swindon Town, a momentous decision was made in Portsmouth to amalgamate two of the district's strongest clubs – 15th Company Royal Artillery, of Fort Fareham; and Gosport Depot Royal Artillery – to form Royal Artillery (Portsmouth) FC.

There was no question, at this point, of creating a side that might seriously dispute honours with St Mary's or, rather, Southampton St. Mary's, as they were now to be known – because there was no question that it would be anything other than an amateur outfit. But there was plenty of glory to be achieved in the amateur game.

The Royal Artillery
The story of Portsmouth's new club has been well documented, quite recently, by Kevin Smith, but it would be as well to venture a brief summary of their fabulous – if perfunctory and, ultimately, tragic – career, as their impact on the Portsmouth public was significant.

They won the Army Cup in 1895 and 1897, the Hants Senior Cup in 1896 (comfortably defeating Southampton St Mary's Reserves 3–1 in the Final) and the Portsmouth Senior Cup in 1897; but it was in the FA Amateur Cup that they made their national reputation. And, it should be noted here, back in the 1890s – in fact, into the 1950s – a good run in the Amateur Cup would make a club a national reputation.

The Royal Artillery reached the Final in 1896. Having lost 1-0 to Bishop Auckland at Filbert Street, they protested the result on the basis that the referee had cut the first half five minutes short, but the FA, whose judgments were consistently and irrevocably premissed on the incontrovertible certainty that their officials were infallible, was less than sympathetic.

Having won the Hampshire League in 1896-97, the Gunners were admitted into the Southern League Division II, joining such colossi as Warmley, Uxbridge, St Albans, Maidenhead and Old St Stephen's. It will be noticed, by more knowledgeable readers, that none of these sides exactly set the world alight in subsequent decades – although it should be appreciated that Wycombe Wanderers were numbered among this august confederacy.

Whatever, for an aspiring club, albeit an amateur one, with its players likely to be spirited away at the whim of a bureaucrat at the War Office, it was a big enough challenge for the time being. And they rose to it magnificently, winning 19 of their 22 games to top the division and then securing promotion by winning a series of 'test matches' against the bottom two teams of Division I.

This most spectacular rise to prominence went largely unheralded in Southampton. Having won the First Division undefeated in 1897, the Saints celebrated changing their name to Southampton for the 1897–98 campaign by sweeping to the semi-finals of the FA Cup, eliminating three Football League clubs on the way, before losing to eventual winners Nottingham Forest in a replay at Crystal Palace. The defeat, attributed to one of the more controversial refereeing performances in the tournament's history, saw the Saints concede two late goals in the teeth of a blizzard; but John Lewis, the referee in question, was regarded by the FA as more infallible than most match officials and Southampton's protests were futile.

The Cup run, and the brouhaha excited by its climax, catapulted the Saints to national prominence. And if they were being regarded as a 'first-class' club, the League they

competed in must, logically, be a force to be reckoned with as well.

Thus it was that the Southern League came to be regarded less as another regional competition than as a potential rival to the Football League itself. And let's be clear about this: apart from Woolwich Arsenal, who had been elected into that League's expanding Second Division in 1893, and Luton Town, who had defected from the Southern League in 1897, this 'Northern League' was not a great deal less parochial than its Southern counterpart.

IRATE TUTOR FROM THE NORTH:- Young men, I would have you remember that when I teach you anything for several years in succession I expect you to have learnt it. Away with thee, and let me see thy faces no more this season.
"Even so be it," said the downcast Saint to the cocky little 'Spur, as they dolefully wended their way, to await the time when Portsmouth should arise to vindicate the honour of the South.

Play Up Pompey, Goodbye Gunners

Even before the RA began their first season with the South's elite, moves were afoot to bring 'first-class' professional football to Portsmouth.

On 6 May 1898, the Southampton FC board noted a letter from 'J.E. Pink Solicitor of Portsmouth, asking if we would allow the directors of the new football club to inspect our new ground' – then emerging in a dell between Hill Lane and Bedford Place and due to open come September – and recorded that the Club Secretary, Mr Arnfield, had duly 'given them permission and had taken them over the ground for which they offered their best thanks.'

Some eight days later, the *Echo* divulged that 'Portsmouth Football and Athletic Company' were advertising 8,000 shares at £1 each:

They contemplate the formation of a football team, and with the proximity of the famous Southampton team and the formation of a team at Brighton, they believe a healthy rivalry would spring up, which would increase the popularity and income of the company.

For the 1898-99 season, though, the football hopes of Portsmouth rested with the Royal Artillery. If the town's footer lovers had any thoughts that the RA were going to match the Saints' performances in the Southern League, they were not loudly articulated. It must be stressed that, while the Gunners were a team of soldiers, who almost certainly led relatively privileged lives compared with most of their comrades in arms, the club was still obliged to select its players from a very small pool — more of a puddle, really. The Saints, like their protagonists, Bristol City, Millwall, Reading, Tottenham Hotspur *et al*, were at liberty to skim the cream (and, if it comes to that, scrape up the dregs) of the English and Scottish leagues — and go into considerable debt to do it.

All of which helped Saints and Spurs to reach the quarter-finals of the FA Cup that season. When each was swept out, however, by Football League opponents (Derby County and Stoke, respectively), the *Football Mail*'s cartoonist audaciously suggested (*opposite page*) that not only did they have much to learn from that 'Northern League' but that 'the honour of the South' could be in the hands of the new club emerging in Portsmouth.

The Royal Artillery struggled rather in Division I, but their progress in the Army Cup and the FA Amateur Cup was consolation of a sort — or it might have been had their dreams in the latter competition not gone up in smoke.

The *Portsmouth Times*, reporting the 3–1 Third Round victory over Harwich & Parkeston on 4 March, declared that, 'if the cup doesn't come to Portsmouth, it will be almost a

modern miracle.' The 'modern miracle' came about when their defeated opponents successfully protested to the FA that the Gunners were, in reality, a professional football club.

There was no secret in the fact that the RA team had spent a week at the White Lion Hotel, Aldeburgh, on the Suffolk coast. They trained and relaxed, played billiards and enjoyed, it was never denied, the odd cigar and the occasional glass of wine.

In fact, when called to account for their luxurious lifestyle, they admitted every charge but pleaded to the Amateur Cup Committee that, if they had transgressed any rule, it was in ignorance.

And much good it did them: the FA re-designated the players as professionals — and expelled them from the Cup. The *Football Mail* noted, with no little irony, that,

after all, the RA will be able to claim to have started professionalism in Portsmouth!

It may not be to their liking, but the Amateur Cup Committee have spoken, and their wisdom is, of course, beyond question.

MAXIM FOR AMATEURS

The Royal Artillery have been removed from the Amateur Cup Competition for going into training.
Moral: Don't train the Maxim gun whilst sitting on the cartridges and smoking cigars, or the result will be a burst up.

For the man from the *Mail*, it made a mockery of prevailing notions of 'respectability':

'Good old amateurism!' What a mockery the whole question is!
'Old Boys'* are permitted to enjoy themselves at other folks' expense for several months at a stretch, but the unlucky Tommies must be confined to barracks! 'Tis very funny.

Even had the Gunners survived their inquisition, even had they gone on to win the Cup, it's doubtful they would have survived as Portsmouth's favourites. The new company had already secured the services of Spurs' manager, Frank Brettell; a new football ground, conveniently located near Fratton Station, was under construction; and likely players were being identified.

So, even if the RA had retained their place in the Southern League's First Division, they would have had little chance of competing with what were being referred to as 'the Portsmouth professionals' – unless the new organisation was a complete debacle.

As it was, the Gunners, forced to play reserves to retain their amateur status, were bottom of the division, which the Saints won for the third year in succession. So, with Portsmouth being accepted straight into Division I, the RA decided, after losing a play-off with Cowes for their top-flight place, to retire from the League altogether. And their most outstanding player would defect to Fratton Park.

The question was: *could Portsmouth support a professional football club?*

There are two ways at looking at this: the positive and the negative. The positive was that there was no 'pyramid' in place to slow rapid progress to national prominence. The Southern League may not have had the quality in depth to match the Football League, but a position near the top of it would see them recognised as a 'first-class' club. And, that being so, if and when a 'national league' – a regular topic of press speculation – were to come about, they would be well placed to be selected for its premier division.

The negative was that, while professional league football had been established for 11 years, it was becoming self-evident that, although a lot of money could be generated through the gates of the successful big city clubs, healthy profits – as the ubiquitous and voluble critics of professional football were constantly pointing out – were elusive.

The Saints had become nationally renowned but consistently lurched from financial crisis to financial crisis; and Brighton United, formed in time for inclusion in the previous Southern League season, were on the brink of economic collapse. Like Portsmouth, and Bristol City back in 1897, Brighton had been accepted straight into the First Division but, unlike them, would not survive their second season.

Then again, the Saints not only continued to survive but to flourish, in the estimation of everyone – except that of their bank manager – and Portsmouth, with a population of 189,907 (according to the 1901 census), was a much larger town than Southampton, with a count of 105,500.

Portsmouth's new board had every reason to be confident. In acquiring Brettell from Tottenham Hotspur – who brought with him the experienced coach, William Brierly, trainer of the England side for four years – they had secured plenty of professional experience.

Frank Brettell had not only transformed Spurs from relative obscurity to Southern League championship contenders, but had been involved with the rise to prominence of both Everton and Liverpool. The only black mark against him (which appears to have gone unmentioned in the Hampshire press) was that he was less than successful in his stint at Bolton Wanderers – which had ended soon after their 4-0 FA Cup defeat by Southampton in 1898.

That the Saints should be invited to open Fratton Park was not to be wondered at.

Short of enticing Aston Villa, the most successful team of the era, or FA Cup-holders Sheffield United, to the big event, Portsmouth would have been pushed to obtain a more attractive fixture.

All that remained was to see whether the new club could really put up a respectable performance against the Champions of the South.

---

* By which he meant teams of former public schoolboys, the elite of whom were the Corinthians, a side that toured extensively and in considerable style.

A Friendly Beginning

Portsmouth 2 Southampton 0

Reilly	Marshall	Robinson	McLeod
H. Turner	Cunliffe	Meehan	A. Turner
Wilkie	A. Brown	Durber	Farrell
Cleghorn	J. Brown	Meston	Wood
Stringfellow	Clarke	Chadwick	Milward
Blyth		Petrie	

Fratton Park

Referee: not known   **Attendance:** not known

Portsmouth took the field first, wearing pink shirts with maroon trimmings – they had already been dubbed the 'Shrimps'. The *Evening News* reported: 'The Southampton players, made their appearance in their red and white shirts punctually at 5.15, and a minute or two later the Mayor, who was accompanied by Mr. John Brickwood, Major A.H. Bone, and Mr. F.E. Bretell (Manager), kicked off, Portsmouth having a slight breeze in their favour and defending the Milton end of the ground.'

It appears, by all accounts, to have been an entertaining spectacle. Dan Cunliffe beat Robinson, 'with a clinking shot', after 10 minutes. Thus making history by becoming the first player to score in a Saints-Pompey derby. His goal was 'greeted with terrific applause.'

In the second half, 'amid the greatest of enthusiasm, Clarke sent in a particularly fine shot, which easily found the net.' Which concluded the scoring.

The *Evening News* reported that a Southampton player had congratulated the Portsmouth manager on having 'got together a very fine lot' – a sentiment

Dan Cunliffe, scorer of the first goal in a Saints-Pompey derby

which the man from the *News* felt it 'safe to say, can be endorsed by every spectator who witnessed the excellent display.' The *Football Mail* joined in the euphoria:

FINE WIN OVER SOUTHAMPTON
'Twas a famous victory! Southampton people can say what they like, but there can be no getting away from the fact that Portsmouth whacked the Saints… And what is more, the new club thoroughly deserved their victory. Although the game was only a friendly, such keen rivalry as must always exist between two neighbouring clubs of about the same strength invested the match with the greatest possible intent, and there could not have been more enthusiasm or excitement on the ground had an [FA] Cup tie been in progress.

The *Southern Daily Echo* was disinclined, however, to rush to judgment on the strength of a friendly:

Although Portsmouth won on their merits the result must not be taken as a criterion of the relative strength of the two teams.
    Wait till they meet in a League match! Then there will be fireworks.

Running tally: Shrimps   1   Saints   0   Drawn   0

READ ON: For details of Pickford's Hants FA Jubilee book; Conan Doyle's *Memories and Adventures*; the two books – *Match of the Millennium* and *Full-Time at the Dell* – that have recently charted the Saints' origins; and Kevin Smith's history of the Royal Artillery, see 'Sources'.

If anybody thought to take a photograph of the two teams - or, indeed, either team - at the first meeting of the two clubs, we have yet to trace it. Meanwhile, the photographs below include 21 players from that first game.

With their customary collection of silverware before them and backed by the silk banner that honoured their third successive Southern League Championship in 1899, the Saints squad of 14 includes the 11 who went to open Fratton Park:
Back row: W. Dawson (trainer), Meston, Haynes, Chadwick, Robinson, Greenlees, Meehan, Durber, Mr E.C. Jarvis (director).
Front row: Turner, McLeod, Yates, Farrell, Wood, Petrie, Milward.

The Pompey side for their first game at Chatham (of which Smith was replaced by J. Brown for the derby four days later):

Back row: Turner, Reilly, Wilkie.
Middle row: Marshall, Blyth, Stringfellow, Cleghorn, Clarke.
Front row: Cunliffe, A. Brown, Smith.

A Friendly Beginning

Chapter 2
1899-1900: Into League Action

Their 2-0 win at Fratton Park was unquestionably propitious as far as Portsmouth were concerned, but the directors, supporters and players would probably have swapped it for a handsome haul of points from their next six league games, before they took on the Saints again.

They pretty much achieved that, with seven points from their Southern League fixtures and two from matches in the Southern District Combination - a new nine-team league affording mid-week fixtures against such crowd-pullers as Millwall, Tottenham Hotspur and Bristol City - clubs that they would meet, anyhow, in the Southern League. But there would be the added bonus of Woolwich Arsenal of the Football League, Division II.

In other words, the two sides - and their fans - could look forward, this season, to four league fixtures - starting at Fratton Park on 18 October 1899, under the auspices of the new Combination.

Wednesday 18 October 1899   **Southern District Combination**

Portsmouth   5   Southampton   1

Reilly	Marshall	Robinson	A. Turner
H. Turner	Cunliffe	Haynes	Yates
Wilkie	A. Brown	Durber	Farrell
Blyth	W. Smith	Greenlees	Wood
Stringfellow	Clarke	Chadwick	Milward
E. Turner		Petrie	

Referee: Mr Beardsley

Fratton Park
Attendance: 7,000

This first league encounter was greeted, as Portsmouth's *Evening News* put it, with 'unexampled enthusiasm': spectators arrived early, 'in cabs, breaks, and carts, as well as on foot, in [such] prodigious numbers [that] the stands were quickly packed to excess and money had to be refused, while the banks around the ground were thronged when the teams took the field.'

The *Southern Daily Echo* reckoned the crowd at 10,000, but the *Evening News* put it at 'nearly 7,000'. Even this more modest attendance would have been remarkable enough for a mid-week afternoon - they couldn't all be shop assistants with a free half-day - and for what was a game in a distinctly minor competition.

Saints won the toss and Pompey kicked off into the sun. The opening stages saw both defences kept active, Robinson, for Saints, being the busier goalkeeper.

Portsmouth opened the scoring when Marshall combined with Cunliffe 'in a clever run' and put over 'a lovely centre' to Smith, who 'banged the ball into the net.' Smith also collided with Robinson, who would play no further part in the game. Milward took over in goal and was beaten almost from the re-start, by Cunliffe.

Soon after, Haynes went into the forward line, 'leaving Durber by himself at the back.'

This interesting tactical ploy was usually referred to as 'the one back game', basically an off-side trap - it should be remembered that the off-side law then dictated three defenders between the first opponent and the goal, rather than two.

Having relieved Milward in the second half, Haynes was responsible for clearing a couple of corners in quick succession, while Reilly saved attempted strikes from Yates and Wood, but it was Pompey who got the next goal, through Brown.

Despite the three-goal, and one-man, difference between the teams, 'the game was full of excitement now, and the ball travelled from end to end in an extraordinary manner.' After Pompey had had a goal disallowed, 'Southampton again bucked up, and their forward play was characterised by dash and cleverness,' duly rewarded, with a quarter-of-an-hour to go, when Wood beat Reilly, 'close up'.

Portsmouth were not finished. Cunliffe capitalised on a 'bad mistake' by Haynes to make it 4-1, yet still 'the homesters… kept attacking in persistent fashion [and] Smith notched the fifth goal amid tremendous cheering.'

Come Saturday, Half-Time, the resident Portsmouth partisan in the *Football Echo*, used his 'Portsmouth Patter' column to remind his Southampton readers of

> that cold chill of dismay they felt on reading the fatal final figures - 5-1 for the Portsmouth lads.
> I think we can afford to rub it in by pretty loud cock-a-doodle-doing, for there is no doubt that the better team won.

His *Echo* colleague, writing under the name of Vectis - which may lead those acquainted with local terminology to infer that he came from the Isle of Wight - and in an idiosyncratic style that has been left untouched by editorial hand, seemed rather less inclined to be generous in defeat:

But listen to my tale of woe,
Pompey five, Saints one.
A great day for Pompey,
And the 'Chimes' were heard
With sickening frequency.
Pompey got 'swelled head,'
And there was a hot town that night.
All interest knocked out of the game
After accident to Robinson,
And it is very open to question
Whether Pompey would have won
But for the accident.
Saints' team was disorganised,
And no wonder they lost.
…
And with full team out,
And a good referee,
Who won't have unnecessary roughness,
Saints would win every time.
If Pompey can beat them
Under fair and square conditions,
We will acknowledge defeat,
And say, 'Well done Pompey.'
But it has not been yet.
Wednesday's game no criterion,
So we must 'bide a wee.'
Pompey pets not pretty footballers,
But rely on brute strength,
And go in for bashing.
They will do that once too often
One of these days.

Running tally:	Pompey	2	Saints	0	Drawn	0

The Teams

It will not, of course, be practicable to introduce each and every participant in the 200-odd games reported in this book. But it seems appropriate to take stock, here, of the squads that the two sides had assembled for their first season of League derbies.

The Saints

Vectis's evaluation was not exaggerated: he may have overdone the excuses, but there was no doubting Southampton's first-class credentials.

Jack Robinson, in goal, was a regular choice for England. Peter Meehan and Peter Durber, the full-backs, both came to Southampton with established reputations. Meehan, already capped for Scotland, had played for Hibernian, Sunderland, Celtic and Everton, while Durber had been procured during the close season from Stoke.

Sammy Meston had joined the Saints from Stoke, during the notorious raid on Potteries clubs in 1896, which became known as the 'Stoke Invasion'. Arthur Chadwick, at centre-half, was a future England international, while Rob Petrie, who completed the half-back line, had come south from Sheffield Wednesday, sporting the reputation of being willing to tackle an express train, 'if called upon'.

Jack Robinson

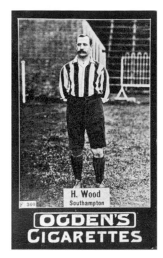

OGDEN'S CIGARETTES

H. Wood
Southampton

The left wing was an England international pairing of Alf Milward, who had made his name with Everton, and Harry Wood, formerly of Wolverhampton Wanderers and one of those rare individuals who enjoyed the billing of 'living legend'. In the centre was the tricky and temperamental Joe Farrell, now in his second sojourn at the club, having initially arrived in the Stoke Invasion. Inside-right Yates had arrived from Sheffield United. In fact, his right-wing partner, Arthur Turner, signed that summer from Camberley St Michael, was the only Saint with no standing at all. He would be capped by England the following season.

Of course, a squad as impressive as this was an expensive undertaking. Harry Wood was on £5 a week, while Jack Robinson commanded £5.10s. The directors were gambling on a good Cup run and improved League gates to stave off bankruptcy. The Board must have thanked the heavens to have a club with Portsmouth's potential to attract big crowds materialising on their very doorstep.

Pompey

The recruitment policy was a little more conservative at Fratton Park. Portsmouth went on record as saying that no player would receive over £4 a week, but Frank Brettell appeared confident he could build an effective team without recruiting stars. As the season kicked off, the *Football Mail* pointed out that,

> if names counted for everything, Portsmouth would be written down as below first-class form.
>
> There can be no getting away from this fact... The directors and Mr Brettell... did not follow the example of many of their rivals and secure men who had made themselves a reputation of several seasons' standing. Experience has shown that the old players, as a rule, are not to be relied upon so firmly as promising youngsters who have still to gain the premier honours of the football field. Several instances could be quoted of mistakes having been made in this direction... and the directors are certainly to be congratulated upon refusing to be tempted to invest more or

less bulky sums in attracting what are generally known to footballers as 'stars'.

> However, they very wisely introduced a few players of experience into the team, the idea, of course, being to give the younger men some confidence in themselves, as well as to furnish the necessary cool-headedness in times of difficulty or impending defeat.
>
> Taken all round, though, Portsmouth will be represented by a set of clever youthful performers, willing and anxious to do their utmost for the club, and before the season is much older we shall be able to form an opinion as to their merits and capabilities. At present one has only other people's ideas as to what each man is worth in a playing sense, and unfortunately 'paper form' is not always to be trusted.

The article goes on to profile a baker's dozen of imports from the north. Tom Wilkie, Tom Cleghorn, Dan Cunliffe and A.G. Marshall had all been on Liverpool's books, while Edward Turner, Harold Stringfellow and Nobby Clarke had all played for Everton. Preston North End were credited with supplying Sandy Brown and Robert Blyth. John Brown had arrived from Sunderland, George

Harold Stringfellow

Hewitt from Luton, George Barnes from Bolton Wanderers and Billy Smith from Wolverhampton Wanderers (whose brother, Steve, would arrive from Aston Villa at the end of the following season, whereupon the two of them would feature together in many a derby fixture). With the exception of Blyth, the grandfather of the intake at 27 years of age, they might all have been described as promising rather than established.

As to players already familiar to the Portsmuthians, Turner, Reilly and Halliday were considered 'too well-known to "Mail" readers to require the slightest introduction.' That was especially true of Matt Reilly, who had been the custodian for the Royal Artillery throughout their short, but glorious, career and had even found time, between Gunners' fixtures, to make a couple of Southern League appearances for Saints during the 1895-96 season. In short, he was firmly established as a 'hero' around the Solent. It had been a smart move by the Portsmouth

Gunner Reilly

executive to induce Gunner Reilly to sign-on after completing his army service: not only was he an outstanding performer, but his presence in the team would surely be enough to allay any lingering doubts among all but the most bloody-minded of the RA's devotees as to their switching allegiance to the new club.

In fact, it was obvious from the earliest days that the Shrimps were going to be at least as popular in Portsmouth as the Saints were in Southampton - as long as they could maintain some sort of form. And proof that they had absorbed most, if not all, of the Gunners' supporters became evident as the RA 'war cry', the 'Pompey Chimes', was soon heard reverberating around Fratton Park.

The first opportunity the Southampton public had to experience this masterpiece rendered by its new choir was 2 April, when Portsmouth FC paid their first visit to the town, for the return Southern District Combination fixture, not that either team was intensely engaged in the competition by this time.

They were, however, running neck-and-neck for the runner's-up place in the Southern League - and each, Pompey especially, had an outside chance of overhauling Spurs for the championship - while the Saints were preparing themselves for the FA Cup Final.

Pompey had enjoyed a bit of a Cup run themselves, winning through five qualifying rounds for the reward of a home tie against First Division Blackburn Rovers. After drawing both at home and away, Portsmouth lost the second replay 5-0. There were mitigating circumstances. Before the kick-off, the indomitable Reilly received a telegram from the Irish FA, informing him that he had been selected to play against England and, legend insists, played in a state of shock.

The Saints, exempted from the qualifying rounds since 1898, had eliminated three Football League opponents and Millwall (who had humiliated League champions-elect, Aston Villa, in the quarter-final), to reach the Final, where their opponents would be Bury of the Football League's First Division.

Southampton were hot favourites - in London and the South at least. Before playing in their first FA Cup Final, however, Saints would have to face Pompey three times in the space of 15 days.

Monday 2 April 1900   **Southern District Combination**

Southampton   1   Portsmouth   0

Robinson	A. Turner	Reilly	Marshall
Meehan	Yates	E. Turner	Cunliffe
Durber	Farrell	Wilkie	J. Brown
Meston	McLeod	Blyth	Smith
Haynes	Milward	Hunter	Clarke
Greenlees		Cleghorn	

Referee: Mr. Stark

The Dell
Attendance: 1,000

This fixture had been postponed so that 'the redoubtable English Cup Finalists,' as the *Evening News* put it, could concentrate on 'training for their Cup struggles.' But now Portsmouth were making their first visit to The Dell for a meeting of 'considerable interest... keen rivalry naturally exists between them, and, moreover, the Saints had two previous defeats to wipe off the slate. Yet the turn-out was poor: barely 1,000 people.'

There was no score in the first half when 'neither attack appeared' to the *Echo* 'to have any sting to it.' The Pompey forwards at least had an excuse, the *News* felt, in 'the narrow ground, which did not at all suit their long passing game.'

The second half appears to have been more stimulating, the only goal coming after half-an-hour, when 'Milward got through with a swift, low shot.'

Come his next *Echo* column, Vectis was exultant:

Monday's match with Pompey
As fairly evenly contested,
And Saints' win
Was thoroughly deserved.
Pompey didn't like the licking,
As it spoil their sequence
Of successive wins.
Neither did they like the gate,
Which was a paltry £30 odd,
Especially as the receipts at Pompey were £225.
That was earlier in the season,
When the competition was not a farce
It has since degenerated into.
It must not be forgotten, too,
That Pompey have Saints
To thank for drawing that gate.
So it cuts both ways.

The Saints then contrived to lose a couple of Southern League games. Their 2-0 defeat away to title-contenders Tottenham on Good Friday not only killed off any hope they might have had of retaining the championship, but seriously dented Pompey's chances of taking it at the first attempt - even in the unlikely event of their taking maximum points from their two out-standing Easter games with the Saints.

Alf Milward, scorer of
the game's only goal.

Running tally: Pompey **2** Saints **1** Drawn **0**

Saturday 14 April 1900 Southern League

Southampton   0   Portsmouth   2

Robinson	Turner	Reilly	Marshall
Meehan	Yates	Wilkie	Cunliffe
Durber	Farrell	Turner	A. Brown
Meston	Wood	Blyth	Smith
Chadwick	Milward.	Stringfellow	Clarke
Petrie		Cleghorn	

The Dell

Referee: Mr J. Stark   **Attendance:** 'barely 3,000'

Seven days before the Cup Final, Pompey returned to The Dell for what the *Echo* considered to be a meeting of 'more than ordinary importance, even apart from the rivalry which exists between the oldest and the youngest professional organisations in Hampshire' - the 'fight' to come second to Spurs in the Southern League.

This view of the game's importance was not shared by the Southampton public. Perhaps they had become so used to winning the thing as to be unmoved by the prospect of the runners-up spot. Or maybe they were more excited by the idea of being part of the huge reception for Boer War hero, Sir George White, who was docking at Southampton that afternoon. For whatever reason, the home supporters were heavily outnumbered by Pompey fans, evidently more moved by the thought of pipping the Saints for second place.

When the game got underway, Pompey looked the more likely to open the scoring, but needed a couple of 'Herculian' saves by Reilly to 'avert disaster'. Continuing in this hyperbolic vein, the *Evening News* described how 'still greater excitement followed':

> HA! HA! MR. ROBINSON... Pompey's front rank went down with a combined rush, and Brown tempted Robinson out to deal with an awkward drive. The international only partially cleared when Brown, who was lying at full length on the ground, twisted his leg round and steered the ball into the net amid deafening cheers and the singing of the 'Pompey chimes.'

It was Dan Cunliffe - who would plague the Saints, on and off, for the next six seasons - who settled it early in the second half, as 'getting possession on the half way line, [he] sprinted right through and scored a magnificent goal.'

Running tally: Pompey **3** Saints **1** Drawn **0**

Portsmouth 2 Southampton 0

Reilly	Marshall	Robinson	Turner
E. Turner	Cunliffe	Meston	Yates
Wilkie	A. Brown	Durber	Farrell
Blyth	W. Smith	Greenlees	Wood
Stringfellow	Clarke	Chadwick	Milward
Cleghorn		Petrie	

Referee: Not known

Fratton Park
Attendance: 10,000

An Easter Monday crowd of 10,000, more or less, witnessed 'a complete triumph for Portsmouth,' said the *Portsmouth Times*.

Two first-half goals - a Brown header and a Smith shot that gave Robinson 'no earthly chance' - sealed the 'triumph'. In the second half, 'Portsmouth did a lot of pressing, but they went in more for the fancy work, and were obviously contented with their lead.' Saints' form was, as on the Saturday, 'poor in the extreme, and there was really no comparison between the two teams... Unless there is a tremendous improvement [in the Final,] I'm afraid the Cup is a gift for Bury.'

Running tally: **Pompey** 4   **Saints** 1   **Drawn** 0

Jack Farrell (*below*) and Roddy McLeod, competitors for the centre-forward spot in the Cup Final. Farrell got the nod.

Final Word

The *Morning Leader* published an interview with Frank Brettell that was both a verdict and a prediction: his side had been 'wonderfully confident of beating Southampton both home and away, and [he] unhesitatingly gave his opinion that Bury would win the Cup by a comfortable margin. He thinks Southampton are stale.'

How right he was. The Saints, riven with internal recriminations about who should play at centre-forward - Jack Farrell or Roddy McLeod? - and at loggerheads with the directors regarding their failure to secure contracts for the following season, found themselves 3-0 down before they started playing and, even when they did begin to string a few passes together, were outplayed.

The final score was 4-0 to Bury. To say the supporters felt let down would be an under-statement.

Portsmouth finished the season in second place, just three points behind the champions, 'Spurs, and the Saints a further six points behind. Both clubs finished the season in debt. It was tough at the top.

Chapter 3
1900-04: Champions of the South

If anyone were inclined to identify the Golden Age of the Portsmouth-Southampton rivalry, then 1899 to 1907 would surely have to be it. It was an era when the two sides not only ran neck-and-neck for honours, but were regarded as among the country's elite. William McGregor, the 'father' of the Football League, said of his brainchild, in 1906, that 'while it does not include Southampton, Portsmouth and Tottenham Hotspur, it cannot be said to be truly representative.'

Tottenham? Why Tottenham? Well, having won the Southern League in 1900, they would become, the next season, the first club from that League to win the FA Cup, an achievement sandwiched by Saints' two losing Finals. They would never win that League again, though. Indeed, in the four seasons from 1900-04, the subject of this chapter, the Championship would never leave the South Coast, being won once by Pompey and three times by the Saints.

No wonder, then, that *derby days* at Fratton Park and The Dell soon assumed a festival atmosphere that few other fixtures in the Southern League appeared able to emulate – as captured by this *Football Echo* match report of 2 November 1901:

> Immediately the gates were opened at two o'clock there was a rush of people, and right up to the time of the kick off, and after, there was an extensive flow of spectators through every gate and turnstile. The Portsmouth contingent, numbering nearly 3,000, were early arrivals. The favours of both teams were freely displayed, and the utmost enthusiasm prevailed among the rival sections.

Inside the ground, the scene

> was very animated, the terraces and stands being absolutely packed. The dense mass of humanity formed a deep black circle with the red uniforms of some Engineers and Infantrymen peeping out here and there. The attendance was by some thousands far in advance of any gate this season.

One does get the impression that Pompey's travelling supporters were more conspicuous in Southampton than those of the Saints in Portsmouth during this period – and until well into the 1920s, in fact – but it could be that the newspaper reports gave a false impression, the *Southern Daily Echo* tending, as a rule, to be more interested in the behaviour of visiting supporters than the *Evening News*.

Quite naturally – this was, most definitely, the age of the train – rail was the usual method of transit, but – unsurprisingly perhaps, given the maritime proclivities of both populations – pleasure steamers are frequently recorded as ferrying supporters from harbour to harbour, as well as the legions from the Isle of Wight.

1900-1901

Smarting from their Cup Final humiliation, the Saints had a thorough clear-out at the end of the season, the most significant departures being those of Roddy McLeod and Frank Farrell, after the controversy about who should spearhead the attack against Bury. The arrivals included Arthur Chadwick, Edgar Chadwick (not related) and Wilf Toman.

Pompey's transfer dealings would prove more historically significant. Scottish international centre-forward Sandy Brown left for Tottenham, while Frank Bedingfield arrived from Queen's Park Rangers.

It is worth noting that the Southern League did not hold with transfer fees and its clubs, unlike those of the Football League, were not empowered to hold a player's registration against his will: technically, he was free to leave at the end of the season. *Ipso facto*, clubs were under no obligation to retain players, either – it's often difficult to know if they were pushed or jumped. Nor did the two Leagues recognise each other's contracts, so a disgruntled northern player was free, during the close season, to take himself south; and *vice versa*.

Portsmouth 0   Southampton 0

Reilly	Marshall	Robinson	A. Turner
E. Turner	Lewis	Blackburn	Chadwick
Wilkie	Joyce	Molyneux	Toman
Blyth	Smith	Meston	Wood
Stringfellow	Clarke	French	Milward
Cleghorn		Sharpe	

Fratton Park

Referee: Captain Simpson   **Attendance:** 'between 10,000 and 12,000'

'Though Southampton are under a cloud, and the Portsmouth star is shining conspicuously in the footballing firmament,' the *Football Echo* report began, this sixth meeting of the teams 'was not generally regarded as being by any means a certainty for the representative of the Naval town.' Which is somewhat hard on the Saints, who had played only two games, both away, losing one and winning one. Then again, Pompey were top of the league, with three straight wins.

It was a big event, the crowd including, for a change, 'a fairly numerous contingent from Southampton,' who appear to have had good value for money: while it was 'difficult', the *Football Echo* remarked, 'to become wildly enthusiastic over a goalless draw,' there was 'no mistaking the satisfaction felt in Southampton… over Saints' ability to hold their own on Fratton Park.' The Shrimp, the *Echo's* Portsmouth correspondent, saw it differently: while hoping not to be 'considered partisan', he nevertheless ventured that Pompey 'should have won' what 'an esteemed northern contemporary' had described as a 'truly great game':

> I have seen, mark you, many more scientific games of football at Fratton Park, but for a clinking ding-dong, robust game I must award Saturday's match the proverbial biscuit.

Running tally:	**Pompey**	4	**Saints**	1	**Drawn**	1

Southampton 0   Portsmouth 4

Moger	Yates	Reilly	Marshall
Sharp	Wood	Struthers	Joyce
Molyneux	Toman	Wilkie	Bedingfield
Meston	Chadwick	Hunter	Smith
French	Milward	Stringfellow	Clarke
Blackburn		Digweed	

The Dell

Referee: not known   **Attendance:** 'did not reach four figures'

'For the first time this century the Southampton team met Portsmouth, at the Archer's Ground.' That opening to the *Echo's* match report was a somewhat portentous introduction to the two sides' first meeting in the Western League.

This was a modest competition in which they were playing Bristol Rovers and Swindon Town, in place of Woolwich Arsenal and Chatham, while otherwise still facing the previous season's adversaries from the Southern District Combination.

The *Echo's* overture at least demonstrated, though, that the Victorians could count to 100, so that the 20th century began in 1901: none of that nonsense that overtook the world in 1999, when the next century – a millennium even – would be deemed to begin in 2000. The 'Archer's Ground' was, of course, the ground that the *Football Mail* preferred to call 'the Dell': it was just that nobody connected with Southampton Football Club appeared at all anxious to give it a definite – or, for that matter, definitive – name.*

Its attendance, on this occasion, was 'a very scanty one… the weather no doubt accounting for this.' Although the Saints went close when 'Reilly only just saved' from Yates, Bedingfield 'placed Pompey one up' at the interval.

In the second half, Joyce popped in two and Bedingfield added his second.

In the *Football Echo*, Recorder ascribed Southampton's 'heavy defeat' in a fast and even encounter 'to bad shooting, and nothing else. Their marksmanship was really painful to witness… Portsmouth thoroughly deserved to win.' The *Football Mail* drew two 'important' lessons from the match:

that interest in the Western League is in a woeful state of stagnation at Southampton, and that Pompey's improved form is no flash in the pan. There is always a certain amount of interest attaching to the encounters between these neighbouring clubs, and therefore on such occasions one naturally expects a satisfactory gate, but what can be said of the mere handful of spectators who assembled at the Dell on Wednesday? The weather clerk was certainly not in his happiest mood, and that doubtless had its effect upon the attendance, but that only two or three hundred spectators put in an appearance was ample testimony to the diminished interest in footer in Southampton.

Running tally:	Pompey	5	Saints	1	Drawn	1

Wednesday 20 March 1901   **Western League**

Portsmouth   2   Southampton   1

Rcilly	Marshall	Robinson	Yates
Struthers	Joyce	Blackburn	Wood
Wilkie	Bedingfield	Molyneux	Toman
Hunter	Lewis	Meston	E. Chadwick
Stringfellow	Clarke	Killean	Milward
Digweed		Paddington	

Referee: Mr F. Crabtree

Fratton Park
Attendance: 2,000

If the 'weather clerk' had failed the fans at The Dell, it was worse for the return a fortnight later: 'rain fell heavily all afternoon and a perfect gale prevailed,' the *Football Mail* recorded. 'The pitch soon became greasy and everything tended to prevent the players doing themselves credit.'

Yet, 'in spite of these drawbacks, the spectators had excellent value for money, and I doubt many of the two thousand onlookers went away dissatisfied—not even Southamptonians.'

Six players were 'crocked' during the game – the injuries appear to have been a greater feature than the goals – and each side finished with 10 men. Lewis and Bedingfield put Pompey two-up in the first half, with Wood pulling a goal back just before the interval. The second half was scoreless, the *Echo* feeling that Toman had missed an easy chance 'to make matters equal.'

Recorder made clear his priorities: he did 'not propose to enter into the details of the game played under the most miserable conditions imaginable, but rather to take the opportunity of discussing whether it is advisable for the Southampton Club to continue their connection next season with a League that brings them neither money nor glory.'

Running tally:	Pompey	6	Saints	1	Drawn	1

* We have not thought it necessary to trace when it officially became 'The Dell', with a capital 'T' but, except when quoting journalists who failed to adapt (or when using 'Dell' adjectivally, e.g, 'the Dell crowd'), we have used that capital throughout.

Southampton   2   Portsmouth   0

Robinson	Yates	Reilly	Marshall
A. Chadwick	Wood	Struthers	Lewis
Molyneux	Toman	Wilkie	Joyce
Sharp	E. Chadwick	Hunter	Smith
Meston	Milward	Stringfellow	Clarke
Lee		Cleghorn	

The Dell

Referee: Mr M. J. Stark   **Attendance:** 'Considering the state of the weather - fairly good'

Their Western League encounters dispensed with, the two sides now met on Easter Saturday, 'in battle array,' as the *Echo* put it, in a Southern League match 'fraught with much importance': with three games left to play, Southampton led the table and Portsmouth, with a game in hand, were still in the running.

Rain had 'made the turf exceedingly treacherous' but, although 'the conditions were against good

Arthur Chadwick (*above*) and Edgar Chadwick, whose passes led to Milward's goals.

football,... those who wended their way to the scene of the contest confidently anticipated a keen if not scientific match.' Since the two sides last met in this League, Pompey had 'fared badly, especially in their away engagements.' They had recently recovered their 'best form', though, while Saints' Good Friday defeat at Tottenham had left them 'all the more eager to defeat their neighbours, and so prevent the championship slipping from their grasp.'

With the advantage of having 'nearly a full team' against a side 'several men short', the Saints opened the scoring in the 10th minute. Receiving 'a lovely pass' from Arthur Chadwick, Milward was 'crowding on all sail' when he was fouled.

From Bert Lee's 'beautifully' placed free-kick, Milward, 'rushing up, piloted the ball into the net.'

Late in the second half, after 'a plentiful crop of free kicks, mostly against the visitors,' Milward scored again, from Edgar Chadwick's pass. Pompey finished the game on the offensive and 'Saints had as much as they could do to keep their citadel intact.'

The Shrimp grudgingly concluded that it 'was almost time that the Southamptonians had a look in' as he felt that 'the long succession of victories by Pompey was getting monotonous.'

Running tally: **Pompey**   6   **Saints**   2   **Drawn**   1

Final Word

Their second-ever win against Portsmouth practically secured the championship for the Saints. Pompey finished third, but their consolation was a second consecutive Western League championship. The Saints were seventh.

Whatever, the Saints' thunder was stolen by fifth-placed Spurs, who won the FA Cup Final. The heroes of their Cup run were ex-Saint George Clawley, in goal, and ex-Pompey centre-forward Sandy Brown, whose 15 goals remain a record for an FA Cup campaign.

If Spurs' Cup victory had undoubtedly dented the prestige of the Football League, it had also confounded the rankings in the south: on previous Cup form, Southampton and Millwall had looked the most likely sides to upset the northern applecart.

Meanwhile, as a reaction to the national concern over the outrageous pay demands from footballers and their agents, the FA decided, in its infinite wisdom, to introduce the 'maximum wage' – starting, from that summer, at £4 per week.

This was in fact a more than respectable income and there can't have been many players earning an awful lot more – although it was claimed that many of those who were thereupon left the game.

As we saw earlier, the Portsmouth directors had a policy of paying no more than this anyway. Conversely, you may have spotted that Southampton had a few players who would have to take a pay-cut (notably Harry Wood and Jack Robinson), but they had actually supported the new legislation. We need not dwell on how far the new rules, policed by the spirit of 'hear no evil, see no evil,' would be manipulated.

As far as Southern League clubs were concerned, it would make it more difficult to persuade disgruntled players to break their contracts with Football League clubs but, given the parsimony of many of them, the traffic south continued.

Of all the summer comings and goings at the two clubs, the most notable was the departure, for Plymouth Argyle, of Frank Brettell.

The fans were not to be told why. A 'detailed explanation' would serve 'no good purpose', according to *Football Chat*: 'let it suffice that the directors could not agree with him on certain rather important matters, and a mutual arrangement was arrived at by which he consented to resign.'

Robert Blyth, Pompey's popular captain, was appointed 'team manager,' to take care of the team, while the Board handled all financial matters. His new charges would include Arthur Chadwick, in a move from The Dell; Dan Cunliffe, returning from a season in the Football League with Second Division New Brighton Tower; and Steve Smith, coming from Aston Villa, as previously noted, to form a wing with his brother Billy.

Southampton also bought from Villa – centre-forward Albert Brown – but needed, with debts of £1,500, further to trim their playing staff, most notably in letting Chadwick go to their neighbours. They could afford to hang on to their star amateur, C.B. Fry, who had joined them the previous season but had yet to appear in a derby game. A gentleman amateur in the classic mould, Fry was one of the great sporting idols of the day. If more celebrated as a cricketer and athlete than as a footballer, his acquisition was a sensation, nonetheless.

Wednesday 4 September 1901   **Western League**

Portsmouth 1   Southampton 0

Reilly	Marshall	Robinson	A. Turner
H. Turner	Cunliffe	Henderson	McDonald
Wilkie	Bedingfield	Molyneux	Brown
Blyth	W. Smith	Meston	E. Chadwick
Chadwick	S. Smith	Lee	J. Turner
Cleghorn		Bowman	

Referee: Mr F. Crabtree

Fratton Park
Attendance: 7,000

The *Evening News* viewed this latest meeting as a show-down between the holders of the Western League shield and the champions of the Southern League: 'the two teams have fought several hard battles and up to the end

of last season "Pompey" came out with decidedly the better average, and in addition could boast that they have never yet been beaten in a League engagement at Fratton Park.' The *News* reported 'considerable interest... in the renewal of hostilities' and, as if hitting upon the cause of disappointing gates hitherto, noted that the kick-off had been 'fixed at 5.30 to give the working class an opportunity of being present'– although the pleasingly large attendance may have owed something also to the 'beautifully fine' weather.

After an 'exceptionally fast' first half, the second was 'fast and vigorous… although there was no intentional fouling.' The only goal, of a game in which the Pompey half-backs and the two goalkeepers 'caught the eye', came nine minutes from the end, when 'clever dribbling by the home left wing gave Cunliffe a splendid opening, and making no mistake "Danny" let drive, the ball entering the net in an oblique direction well out of Robinson's reach.'

The *Echo*'s 'Cherry Blossom' columnist was generously disposed towards the 'hot side' that Portsmouth had assembled: 'the forward line is a distinct improvement on that of last season, while the defence is as strong as ever.'

Running tally:	Pompey	7	Saints	2	Drawn	1

Wednesday 11 September 1901

Western League

Southampton   1   Portsmouth   3

Robinson	Harrison	Reilly	S. Smith
Henderson	McDonald	H. Turner	W. Smith
Molyneux	Small	Wilkie	Bedingfield
Meston	E. Chadwick	Blyth	Cunliffe
Lee	J. Turner	Stringfellow	Marshall
Bowman		A. Chadwick	

The Dell

Referee: not known

Attendance: not known

When Portsmouth came to The Dell a week later, Southampton were without Wood, Brown and Arthur Turner. Small, described as a 'Freemantle player', was tried at centre-forward.

Edgar Chadwick opened the scoring early in the second half, when he 'completely baffled the Portsmouth defence with a tricky run, and screwed the ball against the inside of the upright.' Goalkeeper Reilly cleared, but the referee gave the goal. Saints appear then to have dominated, but

the change that came over the game in the concluding fifteen minutes was as sudden as it was astounding. The Portsmouth forwards discovered a flaw in the home defence, and were not slow to make use of it.

W. Henderson
Southampton

OGDEN'S CIGARETTES

'The foul play of Henderson' threatened 'the reputation of Hants.'

Cunliffe slipped between Henderson and Lee, to equalise with 'a beauty that gave Robinson no chance', and Billy Smith added a second. The light now became so 'wretched' that, with five minutes to go, when 'the players could hardly be distinguished, Marshall's form was seen dashing for the home goal, and a shout from spectators in the vicinity announced that Pompey had scored another goal.'

For the editor of the *Football Mail*,

the only unsatisfactory feature of the game was the foul play of Henderson and the retaliations of Arthur Chadwick … I should be extremely sorry to notice ill-feeling arise between the Portsmouth and Southampton clubs; they have the reputation of Hants to maintain and must always remain friends.

Running tally:	Pompey	8	Saints	2	Drawn	1

1900-04: Champions of the South

Portsmouth 2   Southampton 2

Reilly	Marshall	Robinson	J. Turner
Wilkie	Cunliffe	Fry	Wood
Burgess	Bedingfield	Molyneux	Brown
Blyth	W. Smith	Meston	E. Chadwick
A. Chadwick	S. Smith	Bowman	Harrison
Stringfellow		Lee	

Fratton Park

Referee: Mr M. Kingscott (Derby)   **Attendance:** 'over 10,000'

This match was, for the *Football Echo*, 'the tit-bit' of the day's Southern League programme: 'not only in Hampshire, but throughout the whole of the South the greatest interest was manifested in this fixture, which possessed all the elements of attractiveness, the teams being neighbours, keen rivals, and… generally regarded as candidates for premier position in the League.'

Candidates, maybe – although for the moment Saints were lying sixth and Pompey fourth. Harrison gave the visitors the lead after only three minutes but Marshall equalised just before half-time, 'driving the ball home through a perfect sea of legs.'

Pompey went ahead 10 minutes after the resumption, when Robinson attempted to fist out a shot from Cunliffe, but the ball was 'charged into the net by Bedingfield and Billy Smith, much to the delight of the crowd, who made the air deafening with their cheers.'

The near-irresistible Bedingfield was credited with the goal but, despite continuing to dominate, Pompey were denied the win when Blyth handled and Brown scored from the penalty.

'ANOTHER SPLENDID GAME,' trumpeted the *Football Mail* and, if the Saints

were fortunate in escaping defeat, … they defended so pluckily, and with such grim earnestness, that they deserved their good fortune. Few teams in the country could have safely withstood the prolonged pressure which was brought to bear upon Robinson's charge during the first half. Time after time the Pompey forwards swept clean up to the goalmouth, only to be either forced back by Fry or Molyneux, or else to have their shots cleverly negotiated by the incomparable 'J.W.' Saturday will go down in history as Robinson's game.

Well, it took some time, but it has now.

Running tally: **Pompey**   8   **Saints**   2   **Drawn**   2

Southampton 3   Portsmouth 4

Robinson	A.Turner	Darling	Marshall
Fry	Wood	Burgess	Cunliffe
Molyneux	Wilson	Wilkie	Bedingfield
Meston	E. Chadwick	Stringfellow	W. Smith
Bowman	J. Turner	A. Chadwick	S. Smith
Lee		Blyth	

The Dell

Referee: Mr A.G. Hines (Nottingham)   **Attendance:** 12,000

It was only just November but this was to be the season's fourth and last League meeting between the two 'candidates' for the Southern League title. The Saints had

still played only six games in this competition and were lying fifth, two points and two places behind Pompey, though with two games in hand. This was sufficiently important to the fans, though, for The Shrimp to note, in that evening's *Football Echo*, that

> all through the week nothing – or practically nothing – has been talked of in Pompey.
>
> Business men have forgathered to discuss the chances of the teams, working men have been so much put off their usual balance that they have been able to think of naught else but the grate fite.

Hence 'the dense mass of humanity' that descended upon The Dell, as noted in the introduction to this chapter. All in all, the occasion merited a lengthy outline, in the *Echo*, of the fixture's history, how it was marked by a 'keen rivalry' and yet there were 'happy relations' between the two clubs and, indeed, their supporters.

This might be interpreted as an anxiety to stress the exemplary over the negative but – the odd exchange of the studs between players apart – there was no reason to doubt that

> the best of feeling exists between the teams, and only a few weeks ago, when they happened to be travelling in the same train, at the parting of the ways there were numerous exchanges of 'good luck'… In these days when players are only too ready to fly at each other's throats on the most flimsy pretext it is very gratifying to hear of a case of friendliness and good feeling between rivals, and especially neighbours.

Before it could be acknowledged that there was actually a game taking place, there was room for the usual preliminaries – the weather ('brilliantly fine and crisp'); the pitch ('in beautiful condition'); and the crowd ('animated', as usual) – and for some sensational team-news: Reilly was injured and was replaced by debutant Darling, 'practically an untried man.'

Pompey went ahead on eight minutes, Bedingfield scoring after a 'great burst' by Cunliffe.

Steve Smith added a second when 'Fry lunged at the ball and missed.'

Saints now put Darling to the test, although it needed a penalty by Edgar Chadwick to beat him. After Joe Turner had equalized in the second half, however, 'amid scenes of indescribable enthusiasm, hats, sticks and umbrellas being frantically waved,' they threatened to take the lead.

But, 'inexperienced as the custodian was, he showed superb coolness' and it was Pompey who scored next, from 'a clinking shot' by Bedingfield.

The Saints made it 3-3 when Edgar Chadwick 'beat Darling all ends up.' There followed 'a ding-dong struggle', as 'the ball travelled from goal to goal with amazing rapidity.' With a 'thick haze' now enveloping the ground, Cunliffe restored Portsmouth's lead, whereupon 'the home forwards made great efforts to equalise,' but the visitors held firm for 'a meritorious win.'

What's more, it took them to the top of the table and The Shrimp was unable to contain himself:

> What do you think of us now?
> Oh, yeas, thank you, we are very well satisfied.
> In fact to tell the truth, the whole truth, and nothing but the truth, we got more than we expected.
> …
> But what do you think ye of Saturday's struggle, ye Southamptonians?
> Wasn't it grand?
> From a spectator's point of view it was an ideal match.
> Fancy you know, two-one, two-all, three-two, three-all, four-three.
> What could be better or more exciting.
> There was not a dull moment
> And above all the football was distinctly Class (with a capital C, if you please).
> And the Saints and Pompey can play good football without there being anything in the slightest possible degree shady.
> Which makes it all the better for all concerned.

Running tally:	Pompey	9	Saints	2	Drawn	2

Final Word

Portsmouth proceeded to win the Southern League – by five points from Tottenham Hotspur – and the Western League, too. The best the Saints could manage was to reach the FA Cup Final again. They lost 2-1, after a replay to Sheffield United, in what the *Times* described as 'one of the best finals seen for some years.'

The editor of the *Football Mail* was impressed, all-round: 'after three years' experience of first-class football,' he reflected in his final editorial of the season, 'Portsmouth is in possession of a team capable of holding their own with the strongest in the land.'

And the achievements of the two sides were good for the county: 'interest in sport has fairly been aroused in Hampshire by [their] splendid performances' and it would be the *Mail*'s 'pleasing duty to foster that spirit to the upmost limits.'

1902-1903

A revolution took place in the game at the beginning of the season: new, innovatory pitch markings were introduced - markings which, with only the slightest of tinkering, remain with us today. The man responsible for the design was our old chum, William Pickford.

The Saints, despite their best efforts, lost a number of their Cup squad, although C.B. Fry remained. Pompey had signed the England half-back, Bert Houlker, from Blackburn Rovers but the most significant arrival

at Fratton Park was Sandy Brown, back from Spurs with a Cup-winners' medal in his baggage.

He had the unenviable task of replacing Bedingfield, who had contracted consumption half way through the previous season and would never play football again.

Bert Houlker was swapping his Blackburn strip for Pompey's.

Monday 1 September 1902   **Western League**

Southampton   3   Portsmouth   1

Robinson	Evans	Reilly	Marshall
Robertson	Wood	Turner	Cunliffe
Molyneux	Fraser	Wilkie	Brown
Fitchett	Barlow	Blyth	W. Smith
Bowman	Turner	Stringfellow	S. Smith
Lee		Houlker	

The Dell

Referee: Mr F.W. Beardsley   **Attendance:** 'Quite knight (*sic*) thousand spectators were present.'

The season opened, once again, with the Saints and Pompey in Western League action, this time at The Dell. The home side, as vanquished Southern League champions, had much to prove against the reigning champions of both the Southern and Western Leagues.

Echoist was, to say the least, chuffed with the way Saints 'got off the mark in excellent style' and 'won on their merit.' The three new forwards – Fraser, Barlow, and Evans – each scored, while two other newcomers, Fitchett and Robertson, 'played splendidly'. But 'Portsmouth did not seem as good as last year. Their forwards were scarcely so dashing and not nearly so accurate in their passing, while the backs were erratic.'

But the *Football Mail*'s 'Short and Sweet' columnist had reservations – not least about the Saints' methods:

Southampton got 'some of their own back' on Monday.
It was a hard game – just a wee bit too rough.
The Saints generally manage to sign on two or three 'vigorous' players.
Robertson and Fitchett started the rough play on Monday.
Fraser can also 'do a little bit' in the same line.
But Master Fitchett caught a Tartar when he ran up against Houlker,
'Kelly' [Houlker] is an awkward customer when he has been roused.

So their next meeting 'must have a firmer referee.'

Running tally: **Pompey**   9   **Saints**   3   **Drawn**   2

Portsmouth 4 Southampton 1

Reilly	Marshall	Robinson	Evans
Burgess	Cunliffe	Robertson	Brown
Wilkie	Brown	Molyneux	Fraser
Blyth	W. Smith	Fitchett	Barlow
Stringfellow	S. Smith	Bowman	Turner
Houlker		Lee	

Fratton Park

Referee: Mr A.J. Barker (Hanley)   **Attendance:** 10,000

Nine days later came the 'return'. It may have been only the Western League, but this was, for the *Echo*, 'a meeting of giants of the football world.'

The Saints, having lost the toss, kicked off towards the 'Station'. That appears to have been almost the last positive move they made. Pompey were three-up inside 20 minutes against their 'disorganised' visitors.

At the start of the second half, Fraser and Brown switched positions, but it availed Southampton little. Portsmouth remained in the ascendant and when Steve Smith 'kicked judiciously to Brown,' the latter headed their fourth. Joe Turner scored a 'splendid' consolation goal.

The 'Short and Sweet' scribe was impressed by the 'high-class' football but, warming to his theme of the previous week, he thought it 'just as well' that we had a first League referee! At times players on both sides threatened to get out of hand.

It is to be hoped that Pompey v Saints matches are not going to be rough games.

Recorder, in the *Football Echo*, was more concerned with the timing of the fixture:

It may be advantageous to the directors of the rival clubs to play the matches off so early [in the season], but as far as the public are concerned it is a mistake, and it is not desirable, too, from the players' standpoint inasmuch as they have not settled down to their work, and, as a consequence, are not able to display their true form. From every point of view it is advisable that the games between the Saints and Pompey should be worthy of themselves.

Which was probably true, even if it hadn't occurred to him after the Saints' victory the week before.

Running tally:	Pompey	10	Saints	3	Drawn	2

Southampton 1 Portsmouth 1

Robinson	Evans	Reilly	Marshall
Robertson	Wood	Burgess	Cunliffe
Molyneux	Fraser	Wilkie	A. Brown
Fitchett	Barlow	Blyth	W. Smith
Bowman	J. Turner	Stringfellow	S. Smith
Lee		Houlker	

The Dell

Referee: Mr A. Millward   **Attendance:** 16,000

Most definitely the plum fixture of the day, in the south at least. With the weather 'simply delightful', the atmosphere 'charmingly cool' and there being 'practically no wind,' the *Football Mail* judged the conditions conducive to a brilliant game. During the morning excursionists flocked into the town from all parts of the county, the Portsmouth contingent, which numbered upwards of a thousand, being easily distinguishable by their salmon and maroon rosettes.

Inside the ground, the away fans had self-segregated, 'in and about the east stand as usual,' from where they 'sent up yells of defiance, accompanied by the "chimes," which, however, were not so prominent as customary.' These were matched by what had become known as the 'Southampton Whisper': a chant of 'Yi! Yi! Yi!'

The Boer War had ended in May but uniforms were still prominent on the terraces. Many a soldier would have come up from Portsmouth, then a very large garrison town, others from the Royal Victoria Hospital in Netley, where they were either based or convalescing. One way or another, there was 'a brave display of scarlet and khaki, which showed up conspicuously in the dark setting afforded by the dense mass of civilians.'

Sandy Brown scored 'a curiously got goal.'

All that – and a brass band too!

Evans opened the scoring for Southampton, 'amid tremendous outbursts of enthusiasm.' But Portsmouth were soon back on terms, through 'a curiously got goal' from Sandy Brown. Or so said the *Echo* and the *Mail*, respectively.

From that point on, it was, all agreed, 'a grand game' and – the dropped point aside – a red letter day for the Saints, who took £400, a record for a Southern League match. But Recorder questioned whether The Dell was really up to catering comfortably for that many spectators: he did not doubt that 25,000 'could easily be accommodated at the Dell were no heed to be paid to their view,' but questioned whether 20,000 could get in 'and nearly all have a glimpse of the playing area.'

Running tally:	Pompey	10	Saints	3	Drawn	3

Saturday 10 January 1903   **Southern League**

Portsmouth 0 Southampton 3

Reilly	Marshall		Robinson	Bell
H.Turner	Cunliffe		Robertson	Wood
Wilkie	A. Brown		Molyneux	Fraser
Stringfellow	W. Smith		Meston	Barlow
A. Chadwick	S. Smith		Bowman	J.Turner
Houlker			Lee	

Referee: Mr A.J. Barker (Hanley)

Fratton Park
Attendance: 20,000

This was much, much more than a derby game. With half the season gone, Saints led the table with Pompey, two points behind and a game in hand, in third place.

The magnitude of the fixture appears to have inspired a greater interest among the Saints' supporters: a 'very strong following', estimated at 1,200, tested the capacity and ingenuity of the Railway Company.

The ordinary train which left the Dock Station just after noon was filled while the excursion train was packed long before the time advertised for it to leave. Quite three hundred people were left behind, but the local officials of the Railway Company, with commendable foresight, had arranged a reserve train, and this was placed in service, and was soon comfortably filled… The clear, blue sky which

prevailed at Southampton was flicked with clouds, and the weather was dull though fine when Fratton was reached. With loud 'Yi Yi's' the Southampton supporters announced their arrival, and merged into the vast throng and headed their way towards the ground. All roads converging on Fratton Park were packed, and vehicles of all descriptions sped towards Fratton Park heavily laden with people. The scene on the ground was very animated, and there was plenty of shouting and counter shouts rending the air. Mingling with the music of the Portsmouth Town Band. Long before half past two … both stands were crowded, as also were the open spaces on the cheap sides, while a great crowd thronged the approaches to the members' stand, jostling and pushing each other in their endeavours to find a spot from whence a complete view of the play could be obtained.

The Saints opened the scoring, four minutes after the interval, when Robertson's clearance was 'secured' by Joe Turner who crossed 'judiciously to Bell, who took the ball on top of his cranium, and sent the leather into the corner of the net, amidst terrific applause from the Southampton supporters. It was really a first class effort.'

As Pompey pressed for the equaliser, 'the Saints backs now commenced to kick out..., a proceeding which naturally did not find favour with the majority of the spectators.' They came again, however, and 'the last few minutes were crammed with exciting incidents,' including further goals from Fraser and Wood.

Joe Turner, whose 'judicious' cross set up the first goal.

| Running tally: | Pompey | 10 | Saints | 4 | Drawn | 3 |

Final Word

Within two weeks of this last derby of the season, Portsmouth would give a debut to new signing, C.B. Fry. Unable to dislodge newcomer Tom Robertson from the right-back spot at Southampton, Fry had fancied himself upfront. But a couple of games at centre-forward had raised questions about his ability to withstand the physical attention of Southern League centre-halves.

His stay at Fratton Park was spent entirely at right-back. Unfortunately, it lasted only three games. A bad tackle during Pompey's 5-0 trouncing by Everton, in the FA Cup First Round, brought a premature end to his competitive football career, although he still had many years ahead of him as a cricketer.

Southampton also went out of the Cup at the first hurdle - albeit after two replays with Notts County - so the two sides were able to concentrate on winning a League each.

The Saints took the Southern League championship again, for the fifth time in the competition's nine years, while Pompey won the Western League for the third consecutive season.

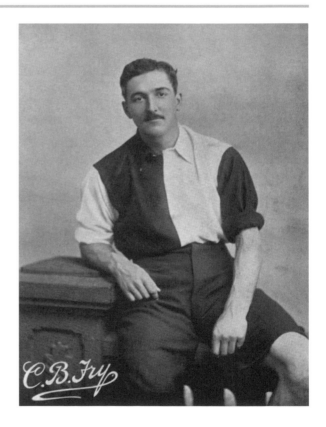

The Saints' summer signings included two recent Cup-winners: George Clawley, returning, with his 1901 medal, from Spurs – like Brown to Pompey the previous summer – and George Hedley, who had scored against them in the 1902 Final. And after just one season at Fratton Park, Bert Houlker transferred to The Dell.

The loss of their England half-back should not have been a problem for Portsmouth, who had arranged the signings of three Liverpool players. But Hell hath no fury like a Football League club scorned: Liverpool complained of poaching. The FA upheld the protest, fining Portsmouth £100, banning the three players from playing for them and suspending Bob Blyth and Harry Stringfellow, who had helped with the negotiations, for three months.

At stake were the different attitudes to transfers, as previously explained, of the Southern League and the Football League. The *Football Echo* reproduced an article on this matter by Alfred Gibson, one of the most esteemed of Edwardian sports' journalists, who considered that

the attitude of the Northern body may probably be described as resentful... One rejoices at the assertion of the dignity of the Football Association, while to some extent sympathising with the Portsmouth Club, who have been made scapegoats of a very common offence. That poaching has been existent for years is well known to those behind the scenes, and it is perhaps significant that the Football Association should have waited for a Southern club.

Wednesday 2 September 1903   **Western League**

Portsmouth   1   Southampton   2

Reilly	Marshall	Clawley	Harrison
Hogg	Cunliffe	Robertson	Wood
Wilkie	Brown	Molyneux	Hedley
Buick	Wheldon	Lee	Fraser
Chadwick	S. Smith	Bowman	Turner
Anderson		Houlker	

Referee: Mr A.J. Barker (Hanley)

Fratton Park
Attendance: 11,000

Amazingly, on two counts – it was a Western League fixture and it was midweek – over 11,000 people turned up to watch this game, 'including a large proportion of Southampton supporters, who made the journey by rail and steamer.'

Then again, it was the opening match of the season and it was the champions of the Southern League against the champions of the Western League.

Pompey began 'in splendid style', but it was the Saints who scored first, on 23 minutes, when Fraser 'deftly sent the ball into the net.' Pompey soon replied, though, when 'Robertson had the misfortune to slip in kicking'

and Wheldon scored. Pompey continued to press but the visitors again scored against the run of play. Harrison 'gave Wilkie the go-by' and squared to Fraser, who scored.

A 'ding-dong battle' ensued, according to the *Echo*, 'in which the brilliance of the Southampton defence was strikingly demonstrated.' They held out on a 'very slippery' surface, brought about by 'a drenching downpour' in the first half – so much so that their 'magnificent work... earned unstinted approbation on all sides' and Traveller of the *Football Mail* imagined that 'few will begrudge them their success.'

Running tally: **Pompey**   **10**   **Saints**   **5**   **Drawn**   **3**

Southampton   5   Portsmouth   2

Clawley	Evans	Reilly	Marshall
Meston	Wood	Hogg	Cunliffe
Molyneux	Harrison	Young	Brown
Lee	Fraser	Buick	Wheldon
Bowman	Turner	Chadwick	S. Smith
Spence		W. Smith	

The Dell

Referee: Mr A.J. Barker (Hanley)   **Attendance:** 'between 5,000 and 6,000'

In 'brilliant weather', Southampton 'started with tremendous dash', but Portsmouth took an early lead from Tom Brown's 'rasping drive'.

Fred Harrison soon equalised when he beat two men and 'completed an exceedingly fine effort by pulverising Reilly, amid tremendous cheering.'

The visitors regained the lead after 17 minutes: neither the *Echo* nor the *News* could identify the scorer, but the goal was eventually credited to Wheldon.

Having levelled again through Harrison, the Saints then took the initiative against a side reduced to 10 men when Buick left the field with a thigh-strain and the irrepressible Harrison added another three goals.

Five-goal Harrison

Running tally:	**Pompey**	**10**	**Saints**	**6**	**Drawn**	**3**

Portsmouth   4   Southampton   5

Harris	Marshall	Clawley	Evans
Hogg	Cunliffe	Meston	Hedley
Young	Rule	Molyneux	Harrison
W. Smith	Wheldon	Lee	Fraser
Buick	S. Smith	Bowman	Turner
Stringfellow		Houlker	

Fratton Park

Referee: Mr A.J. Barker (Hanley)   **Attendance:** 6,000

As if four League games between Pompey and the Saints were not enough, the powers-that-be came up with another way of getting the two clubs, and their adherents, together: the Southern Charity Cup.

The competition had actually begun the previous season, when the Saints went out to West Ham in the First Round and Pompey won it.

The weather was 'fine' and the crowd, hazarded at 6,000, was bolstered by 300 excursionists delivered at Fratton Station by Thomas Cook, from Southampton's Dock Station and all points east.

Pompey went into a two-goal lead. Sammy Meston 'miskicked badly' and apparently diverted a Wheldon shot past Clawley. Rule notched the second with 'a swift shot' following a cross from Billy Smith. Then Fraser and Harrison 'dribbled clean through the Pompey rearguard. The centre-forward [Harrison] was entrusted with the shot, and with a terrific drive he beat Harris all ends up.'

Pompey restored their two-goal advantage when 'Cunliffe and Rule pierced the visitors' defence, and while the Saints were clamouring for the offside the latter went in and scored.' The score at half-time was 4–3 to the home side, Marshall having netted for Pompey and Evans for the Saints – though in which order is hard to make out. Whatever, the second half was all Saints as,

somewhat inevitably, Harrison and then Bowman scored without reply.

The *Echo* felt that Portsmouth had been 'fairly beaten in the last ten minutes' when they 'were smitten hip and thigh, and it was only the steadiness of their backs that saved them.'

The Saints lost the semi-final against Millwall, 3-1.

| Running tally: | Pompey | 10 | Saints | 7 | Drawn | 3 |

Saturday 28 November 1903   **Southern League**

Portsmouth   0   Southampton   1

Reilly	Marshall	Clawley	Evans
Hogg	Cunliffe	Robertson	Hedley
Wilkie	Wheldon	Molyneux	Harrison
Stringfellow	W. Smith	Lee	Fraser
Buick	S. Smith	Bowman	J. Turner
Blyth		Houlker	

Fratton Park

Referee: Mr J.H. Strawson (Lincoln)   **Attendance:** 15,000

The excursion train that left the Docks Station at 12.45 p.m 'picked up a large quota from Northam, St Denys, and Woolston,' the *Football Echo* reported, for a journey on which the Southampton Town Band 'dispensed inspiring music.' If the idea of sharing a railway carriage with a brass band is not one to be contemplated lightly – although it may have been less daunting than overhearing a Walkman at full volume – the pre-match selections of the visiting band 'were keenly enjoyed' by the crowd of 15,000, the *Football Mail* claimed

The visitors duly took the lead in the 26th minute. A corner-kick from Dick Evans 'came out to Hedley, who drove it into the net.' And that was the end of the scoring, but far from the end of the entertainment – towards the end of the first half, *'a spectator used bad language to Houlker, which the referee heard, and stopped the game while he admonished the offender'* (emphasis added).

Southampton played 'a safe game' in the second half to secure the win that firmly established them at the top of the Southern League that evening – five points ahead of third-placed Pompey, who did, however, have four games in hand.

While welcoming the Saints' '"getting their own back" with Portsmouth this season,' the *Football Echo*'s Recorder noted that, in terms of matches won, they were still lagging behind Pompey, whose

> meteoric rise… was marked by a succession of victories over Southampton, victories that were astonishing both as regards to the frequency with which they occurred, and also the extent of their scoring. Those achievements naturally gave greater satisfaction to Portsmouth than any others, for loud rivalry creates a strong feeling.

George Hedley, scorer of the only goal.

| Running tally: | Pompey | 10 | Saints | 8 | Drawn | 3 |

Southampton 2 Portsmouth 0

Clawley	H. Turner	Reilly	Murray
Robertson	Hedley	Hogg	Cunliffe
Molyneux	Harrison	Young	Burnett
Lee	Wood	Stringfellow	Wheldon
Bowman	Mouncher	Buick	S. Smith
Spence		W. Smith	

Referee: Mr J. Lewis (Blackburn)

The Dell
Attendance: 15,000

The *Football Echo* was taken by the 'singular coincidence' that

> the two leading teams in the First Division of the League[Sheffield Wednesday and Manchester City], and the two top-sawyers in the Southern League, met to-day to clear the atmosphere regarding their respective championships. In the case of the Southern tit-bits the contestants were near neighbours as well as rivals, a fact that tended to considerably increase the interest which the general public took in the fixture.

The *Football Mail* was more parochial about the Championship 'struggle' between 'Hampshire's two crack clubs,' in which 'the whole of the South was interested':

> Victory meant much to either club; and to Portsmouth especially. Another defeat from the Saints would deprive them of their sole remaining chance of gaining premier honours, and no one realised the necessity of averting another overflow at the hands of the Dell brigade more than the Pompey players themselves.

As things stood, the Saints had 41 points from 28 games, while Pompey, with three games in hand, had 36.

The scale of Pompey's task, on the day, was emphasised by the quality of players excluded from the Saints' line-up: Fraser, Joe Turner, 'Kelly' Houlker, Sammy Meston and Dick Evans were all fit and being kept out by young pretenders, the most remarkable being the two Freds – Harrison, in his second season, and Mouncher, enjoying his first. Both of them were local discoveries. 'It is doubtful,' the *Football Mail* reflected, 'that the Portsmouth directorate would have refused

Billy Smith was frequently penalised for foul throws

to avail themselves of the services of the majority of the men discarded by the Saints this afternoon in favour of local lads!'

Adding a further *frisson* to the titanic struggle was the appointment of John Lewis as referee. The *Mail* noted that he 'had a special cheer on emerging from the dressing room.' That does not tell us whether the cheers were forgiving or ironic – or perhaps confined to Pompey supporters. John Lewis, it will be remembered, refereed the controversial FA Cup semi-final replay between the Saints and Nottingham Forest in 1898.

Lewis's notoriety was not confined, though, to that semi-final: he courted universal controversy and Pompey were early victims of his perverse decisiveness in this game. Having frequently penalised Billy Smith for foul throws, he awarded the Saints an 11th-minute free-kick. The mayhem created when Lee 'dropped' the kick into the goalmouth was described by the *Echo*:

> Reilly caught, and in dodging Hedley encountered Harrison. The custodian dropped the ball, which Harrison pushed with his foot over the line. Reilly, however, scrambled for it, and was instantly charged by three or four Saints. Mr. Lewis stopped the incident by pointing to the centre amid a tremendous outburst of cheering.

The *Football Mail* told a slightly different story, while not disputing that the Saints' second goal was 'well worked for and thoroughly deserved on the run of play.' Having 'dribbled away in the centre' with Hedley, Harrison 'raced' Reilly 'for possession. The centre forward "got there" first, and tipped the leather into the net.'

There was no further score and Bristol Rovers, having drawn 3–3 at Millwall, leap-frogged over Pompey into second place.

Surprisingly, perhaps, none of the Portsmouth newspapers appeared over-anxious to dwell on the Saints' 'doubtful' first strike. On the contrary, *Football Mail*'s 'Short And Sweet' columnist was disarming:

> Done again! Really it's too bad of the Saints
> Pompey can't do themselves justice against Southampton these days.
> They have gone down to the Saints in their last six successive matches.
>
> At one time it used to be the other way about.
> Perhaps it will be Portsmouth's turn again next season—who knows?
> Grumbling won't mend matters—nor will slagging the directors!

The *Hampshire Independent*'s football commentator could not help himself:

'The fight is o'wer, the battle won,' and the great game at the Dell, which was supposed to settle the question of the championship of the Southern League, has resulted in the triumph of the Saints over Pompey for the fifth time this season. We didn't want to chuckle and crow, for there is no need for such a performance, but the pre-eminence of the Saints over their professional brethren to the east of the county stands self-confessed.

The next three games would be played over the Easter weekend, when Southampton and Portsmouth would each take three points out of six.

Having managed only one point from their games with West Ham and Fulham, Pompey excited the cartoonist (*below*) by beating Spurs on Easter Monday and temporarily leaving them 'behind'.

The Tottenham cockerel was always fair game and how could any cartoonist resist Millwall's lion even when he was not in the story? The Saint had no need to worry about the loss of Easter points: he could sedately leave the scene with the Southern League shield.

Running tally: **Pompey 10** **Saints 9** **Drawn 3**

THE RESULT OF THE HOLIDAYS

Now Easter holidays are o'er,
And Pompey sits perplexed.
Some teams have left him weak and sore,
Good points they have annexed.

Some comfort Pompey yet may find...
Perhaps you may have heard...
Since Monday's match has left behind
The Body of the Bird

Portsmouth 4 Southampton 2

Reilly	Marshall	Byrne	H. Turner
Hogg	Cunliffe	Robertson	Wood
Young	Platt	Meston	Small
Stringfellow	W. Smith	Bowman	Spence
Buick	Holden	Metcalf	J. Turner
Blyth		Houlker	

Referee: Sergt. H. Coleby, RA.

Fratton Park

Attendance: 3,000

The Saints descended on Fratton Park for the season's swan song, haloed, once again, as champions of the Southern League.

And all 'with the laudable object,' said the *Evening News*, 'of augmenting the funds of the Hampshire Cricket Club.'

After five meetings already this season, all won by Saints, the *News* thought the attendance 'disappointingly small', especially 'considering the object.'

Pompey led 3-0 at half-time from a Cunliffe hat-trick. Platt added a fourth, while Spence and Wood scored for the Saints.

Running tally:	Pompey	11	Saints	9	Drawn	3

Final Word

Considering the pre-season trauma, and the absence of both Blyth and Stringfellow for the first half of the season – depriving them of six prominent first team players, if you include the departure of Houlker – Pompey had risen magnificently to the challenge to finish in fourth place.

As for the Saints, their six Championships in 10 years would never be repeated in the history of the Southern League as a first-class competition.

Yet the more significant achievement, for the future of the southern game, was perhaps the promotion of Woolwich Arsenal, as runners-up, from the Second Division of the Football League.

It certainly evoked lengthy, and prescient, consideration by the editor of the *Football Echo*, who feared for the 'far-reaching effects' on London's Southern League clubs:

If clubs in the North and Midlands can command the support of twenty or thirty thousand enthusiasts weekly there is no reason why the 'Reds'... should not attract something like twice that number, and in the course of time become the wealthiest club in the kingdom...

The London Southern League clubs were almost sure to suffer as a result of the Arsenal's promotion. First League football, by reason of its novelty and superior class... is bound to attract many who have hitherto bestowed their patronage on the Hotspurs, Fulham, Millwall and West Ham. And what will be the result of that? That is not easy to foretell, but fired by their neighbour's success, it is not inconceivable that other metropolitan clubs will seek to tread the narrow and arduous way that leads to premier football.

Whereupon the Saints and Pompey would find them stranded in a footballing backwater – without a paddle.

READ ON: William McGregor's 1906 assessment of Saints and Pompey is from the Gibson and Pickford history of the game. C.B.Fry's ill-fated transfer to Portsmouth is discussed, in some detail, by his biographer, Iain Wilton. See 'Sources'

Chapter 4
1904-07: The End of an Age

Southampton had dominated the first 10 years of the Southern League's existence. They had never finished lower than third and, once having overtaken Millwall in 1897, they had only twice failed to win the championship – in each of which seasons they had reached the Cup Final. But Portsmouth had proved persistent contenders, won a championship themselves and had certainly kept Saints' feet on the ground – and those of their supporters, too.

In fact, Hampshire could fairly claim to have a stronger national reputation for football, at this time, than London: do not doubt the *Echo*'s proclamation of 10 September 1902 (as recorded in the previous chapter) that Pompey v Saints was 'a meeting of giants of the football world.'

Yet, for all their past achievements, Hampshire's finest needed a bigger stage than the Southern League –

especially with sides like Spurs dropping big hints that they would like to jump ship and Bristol City already in the Football League, so that the frequent speculations, in the local press, as to the possibility of a 'national league' were beginning to take on an edge of desperation.

Still, if they could, between them, continue to dominate Southern League football, the prospects remained bright. *If.*

1904-05

There had been two major changes at Fratton Park: Matt Reilly, having consolidated his status as Man-made-Myth, departed to Dundee and Bob Blyth stepped down from management, to be replaced by Richard Bonney who, in an age before directors could take money from their clubs, resigned from the Board to take on the job. As

Sergeant Bonney, he had led the Royal Artillery side, whose rise and demise was described in Chapter 1.

Pompey's most notable signing was centre-half Tommy Bowman, from the Saints – who replaced him with Herbert Dainty from Notts County.

Thursday 1 September 1904 **Western League**

Southampton   2   Portsmouth   2

Clawley	Webb	Thompson	Porteous
Meston	Hedley	Walker	Cunliffe
Molyneux	Harrison	Young	Axford
Lee	Fraser	Bowman	S. Smith
Dainty	Mouncher	Buick	W. Smith
Houlker		McDonald	

The Dell

Referee: Mr A. Farrant (Bristol)   **Attendance:** 6,000 (at the kick-off - but much larger later)

Dan Cunliffe – by now, surely, Clawley's particular *bête noire* – opened the scoring on 25 minutes, netting a rebound after Axford had struck the bar. Pompey continued to press and were 'destined to have their persistent attacks rewarded.' Steve Smith outpaced Meston 'and kicked the leather at a convenient shooting

height across the mouth of the net.' Cunliffe met it to score 'a fine goal'.

The Saints reduced the deficit with a Harrison penalty and, after the interval, took the game to Pompey. Webb completed a three-man move with a centre that 'gave Harrison a glorious opportunity, which he missed.

A scramble ensued, [from which Webb] once again found himself in possession. He lifted the leather back into goal and Harrison equalised by means of a header, amid great enthusiasm.'

Traveller rejoiced, in the *Football Mail*, that 'Portsmouth have at long last managed to get a side together capable of holding their own with Southampton. At any rate, the Saints were a lucky team to escape defeat.' He expected 'a better exhibition of football' in 'the return struggle' a week hence: 'the Dell enclosure is too small.' Which was neither original nor clever, but probably needed repeating.

Running tally:	Pompey	11	Saints	9	Drawn	4

Wednesday 7 September 1904   **Western League**

Portsmouth 0 Southampton 2

Harris	Porteous	Clawley	A. Turner
Campbell	Cunliffe	Meston	Hedley
Walker	Lee	Hoare	Harrison
Blyth	W. Smith	Lee	Fraser
Buick	S. Smith	Dainty	Mouncher
McDonald		Houlker	

Fratton Park

Referee: Mr A. Farrant (Bristol)   **Attendance:** 10,000

The Portsmouth public seemed to share Traveller's hopes for 'the return struggle': a large turn-out at the more capacious Fratton Park included 'a considerable proportion [of] sailors and soldiers of the King.'

Saints took an early two-goal lead. When the ball was headed out of the Portsmouth goalmouth, 'Lee caught the leather on his cranium and directed it into the corner of the net.' Then Harrison met Mouncher's centre 'on the crown of his head and steered it' past a 'sprawling' Harris.

Soon after this, Meston 'ricked his leg' in attempting to tackle Steve Smith. 'His absence made a tremendous difference, as... Portsmouth pressed severely.' Yet, although they 'were able to deliver a series of determined attacks upon the Southampton citadel, and yet notwithstanding numerous shots, many essayed from point blank range, they entirely failed to score.'

This left 'football enthusiasts at Portsmouth... awfully glum, and no wonder,' said the *Echo* reporter, who was inclined to set the members of the Saints' rearguard on a pedestal, and invite all and sundry to behold the most indomitable defenders ever seen, challenging the contradiction from anywhere, and in the most conspicuous position one would place Clawley. In Southampton we had four years of Robinson, generally regarded as one of the most brilliant custodians who ever guarded a goal, and Robinson was invariably at his best when playing at Fratton, but the very finest exhibition the ex-international gave on this ground did not surpass that of Clawley's. It was quite dazzling.

The dazzling George Clawley

Running tally:	Pompey	11	Saints	10	Drawn	4

Southampton   1   Portsmouth   0

Clawley	Webb	Harris	Porteous
Meston	Bluff	Bowman	Cunliffe
Molyneux	Hedley	Walker	W. Lee
A. Lee	Wood	Campbell	W. Smith
Dainty	Fraser	Buick	S. Smith
Houlker		McDonald	

The Dell

Referee: Mr J.W. Bailey (Leicester)   **Attendance:** 12,000

No matter that Southampton had had the better of this season's Western League encounters, the two sides were enjoying similar fortunes in the Southern League, where Pompey trailed the Saints by four points but had two games in hand.

Yet the visitors were 'great favourites' for this meeting, according to the *Football News*, a new 'paper that had appeared on the streets of Portsmouth as a rival to the *Football Mail* (although the two 'papers shared graphics and a number of by-lines). With visiting excursions, by rail and boat, being well-booked, 'special arrangements were made by the Saints' directors to accommodate what was anticipated to be an abnormal crowd, temporary terraces on the running track being requisitioned.'

When the game got underway in 'ideal weather', the defences tended to dominate, so that 'shots of a dangerous character were not too frequent.' Even so, 'it was a grand game, only one thing being absent – sensationalism.'

The Saints began to gain the upper hand and, when Fraser centred, Hedley,

finding himself unable to shoot, passed back to Dainty. The centre-half rushed to the ball like a locomotive, and catching it fair and square with the inside of his foot, drove it home like a flash. Harris had no chance with it, and the Saints' spectators went well nigh mad with delight.

His team-mates were fairly pleased, too: according to the *Football Echo*, they 'nearly wrung Dainty's hand off.' Thereafter, Saints 'swarmed' around Harris's goal, but Pompey might have snatched a point in the 77th minute when Cunliffe, of all prolific strikers, 'missed an open goal.'

In his 'Pompey Chimes' feature that was common to both the old, and the new, Portsmouth 'papers, Sentinel was lyrical about the two teams who were now, for the first time, equal in respect of matches won:

> It is not often we are privileged to witness such a magnificent struggle… Absolute unanimity seems to prevail as to the merits of the match, and there was no question that we saw twenty-two men battle, individually and collectively, for all they were worth. A magnificent spirit of friendly rivalry exists between Portsmouth and Southampton, and no two teams in the country fight more determinedly or employ cleaner and healthier methods.

George Harris had 'no chance' with Dainty's drive but then kept the Saints at bay as they 'swarmed' around his goal.

Running tally:	**Pompey**	11	**Saints**	11	**Drawn**	4

Portsmouth   1   Southampton   2

Harris	Kirby	Clawley	A. Turner
Walker	Cunliffe	Meston	Wood
Young	W. Lee	Molyneux	Harrison
Digweed	W. Smith	A. Lee	Hedley
T. Bowman	S. Smith	Dainty	Fraser
McDonald		Haxton	

Fratton Park

Referee: Mr J.W. Bailey (Leicester)   **Attendance:** 'between 10,000 and 12,000'

With a quarter of the Southern League season yet to play, the Saints travelled to Fratton for another clash of 'special importance', the *Football Mail* reckoned: if they were to catch 'the Westerners' – Bristol Rovers – who were topping the table, 'their chances of retaining the championship practically hinged on… victory.' The prospect attracted visiting supporters in numbers that 'exceeded the most sanguine expectations'.

With six minutes gone, Harrison released Turner, who 'planted the leather well in the goal mouth, Fraser, timing splendidly, caught the ball on his cranium, and sent it past Harris.'

From this point on, the rain, and a consequently slippery ball, became an increasingly crucial factor – so much so that the *Mail* recorded 'two glaring miskicks by Harry Wood.' The idea that 'the Wolf' might miskick was not one that could easily be conceived of.

After the interval, 'Portsmouth made their re-appearance with dry jerseys, but

OGDEN'S CIGARETTES.

SOUTHAMPTON.

Bert Lee
'burst through
in splendid style'

it was still raining hard, and many of the spectators from uncovered parts of the ground had taken their departure.' Those home fans who remained were able to 'forget… their discomfiture,' however, when 'Lee burst through in splendid style' to equalise.

Pompey were no sooner on terms than an injury to Young reduced them to 10 men. They thereupon opted for 'the one-back game', as previously noted a high-risk offside tactic – especially with opposing forwards as fast as Harrison and as astute as Wood. It was Wood who duly sent Turner through to centre for 'Harrison coming up like an express' to score the winning goal.

Sentinel of the *Football Mail* surmised that 'not even their own supporters will deny [Saints] were somewhat flattered by the result.' That's as maybe, but it had put them ahead of Pompey, in terms of games won, for the first time in the history of this rivalry.

Running tally:	Saints	12	Pompey	11	Drawn	4

Final Word

A disappointing season for both clubs. Southampton could not catch Bristol Rovers and finished third, albeit seven points clear of eighth-placed Portsmouth.

The editor of the *Mail* thought it 'no wonder that the Portsmouth Club supporters are beginning to give Fratton Park a miss. Under the circumstances they have shown remarkable forbearance throughout a season of inexplicable inconsistency.'

Needless to say, there was no dancing in the streets along the Solent, either.

Harry Wood had retired, never to be adequately replaced. But he found immediately employment – as the trainer at Portsmouth, where he was joined by George Molyneux (*right*), the England international full-back who had won three Southern League Championship medals at The Dell.

There were major changes, too, to the fabric of Fratton Park. The terracing was extended to further sections of the ground and a new pavilion, with dressing rooms, was built, topped by a clock tower, financed by the brewer, Sir John Brickwood, the club's chairman.

The structure of southern football was considerably disturbed by the creation, at the impressive Stamford Bridge stadium of a new club, Chelsea. They duly approached the Southern League, with regard to

possible membership. Their overtures met with vehement opposition from Fulham and Tottenham Hotspur and, according to Chelsea's jubilee history, 'Southampton alone intimated that they would vote in favour.'

Perhaps the fact that their landlord, George Thomas, was now a Chelsea director influenced their vote, but it was all academic: Chelsea had applied to the Football League, where they were welcomed with open arms.

Another London club, Clapton Orient, were also admitted. This was catastrophic: with Woolwich Arsenal in the First Division and with Chelsea and Orient now joining Bristol City in Division II, the Football League had established a seriously firm foothold in Southern professional football.

Wednesday 6 September 1905   **Western League**

Portsmouth   0   Southampton   2

Cook	Warrington	Burrows	Tomlinson
Walker	Hunter	Clarke	Bluff
Molyneux	W. Lee	Warner	Harrison
Digweed	W. Smith	A. Lee	Harris
Bowman	Holden	Edmonds	Mouncher
McDonald		Houlker	

Fratton Park

Referee: Mr E. Case (West Kirby, Cheshire)   **Attendance:** 12,000

Portsmouth-born goalkeeper Tom Burrows, who had joined the Saints from St Mary's Swifts and had made one appearance at the end of the previous season, came in for the injured Clawley.

The Saints took the lead when Tomlinson crossed, at the second attempt, 'with lightning speed.' Harrison met it with his 'cranium' to score.

Harrison got his, and Saints', second goal seven minutes from the end when, in fading light, he received the ball at half-way and, 'feinting to pass, dashed right through the backs, … and, amid the applause of the spectators, who thoroughly appreciated the effort, dribbled the ball past Cook, and had only to steer the ball into the unguarded net.'

Running tally:	**Saints**	13	**Pompey**	11	**Drawn**	4

Southampton 5 Portsmouth 2

Burrows	Tomlinson	Harris	Warrington
Clarke	Soye	Walker	Cunliffe
Hartshorne	Harrison	Molyneux	W. Lee
A. Lee	Brown	Bowman	Hunter
Metcalf	Mouncher	Buick	Kirby
Meston		Digweed	

The Dell

Referee: Mr F. Townsend (Leamington)　　**Attendance:** between 6,000

After seven minutes, 'Harrison dashed through the visitors' rearguard, and when Buick and Molyneux cornered him, he stopped and changed his stride, and sent a swift cross shot which beat Harris all the way.' Midway through the half, Harrison put Tomlinson in and, when the ball came back off the crossbar, scored himself. The Saints added two more before the interval, through Tomlinson and Brown.

Pompey struck back after half-time, through a Walker penalty, after Hartshorne had 'handled in the fatal area' and Lee added a second for them.

But when 'the sphere was worked out to the right,' as the *Echo* put it, Tomlinson crossed for Brown to complete the scoring.

All in all, Sentinel reasoned, it was a triumph of 'straightforward go-ahead methods' over 'dilly-dallying'.

Running tally:	Saints	14	Pompey	11	Drawn	4

Portsmouth 1 Southampton 0

Harris	Warrington	Burrows	Tomlinson
Molyneux	Cunliffe	Clarke	Soye
Walker	W. Lee	Hartshorne	Harrison
McDonald	W. Smith	Hogg	Brown
Buick	S. Smith	A. Lee	Mouncher
Bowman		Meston	

Fratton Park

Referee: Mr Sutcliffe (Burnley)　　**Attendance:** 4,000

Evidently, it was felt by people of influence that the Hampshire public could not get enough of games between Portsmouth and Southampton Football Clubs. Among them were William Pickford and Sir Merton Russell Cotes JP, of Bournemouth.

The latter presented a 100-guinea trophy to the Hampshire FA, to be competed for annually between Saints and Pompey, the gate money to go the Hants FA Benevolent Fund, to support local players incapacitated by sporting injuries. Oddly, the competition would become known as the 'Pickford Cup'. Seemingly agreeing

that this additional game was needed, the *Echo* blamed the 'miserable weather' for the attendance falling below the 10,000 that might have been expected 'in fine weather'. McDonald scored the only goal of the game from Warrington's corner.

And that was that. But, maintaining the hyperbolic coverage of this superfluous meeting, the *Football Mail* recorded that Mr. F.J. Wall, Secretary of the Football Association, presented the cup and medals 'amid scenes of great enthusiasm.' All of which acted as a Muse to the *Football Mail*'s Pompeian:

CUP AND BALL

'I'll win the Cup,' said Pompey,
 'I'll win the medals too!'
The Saint replied. They're going –
 But not I think to you!'
Although 'twas far from fine;
This was their Wednesday outing,
 And charity their line.

The toss found Buick winner
 (He should have been in bed),
 'I'd rather lose a dinner
Than miss this treat,' he said.
Then Warrington he placed it
 (The ball I mean of course),
And brave McDonald faced it –
 'Goal!' shouted all, quite hoarse.

And that was all the scoring,
Though Saints and Pompey tried.
The rain kept on a-pouring,
 And many shots went wide.
So Pompey won the medals too.
Let's hope he keeps it up sirs –
Then won't we shout, Hooroo!

William Pickford, Hon. Secretary of the Hampshire FA,
after whom the Association's Benevolent Cup
became informally known.

Running tally:	Saints	14	Pompey	12	Drawn	4

Monday 13 November 1905   **Southern Charity Cup**

Southampton 4 Portsmouth 2

Burrows	Tomlinson	Harris	Warrington
Clarke	Jefferis	Stewart	Salter
Hartshorne	Soye	Molyneux	Kirby
A. Lee	Harris	Digweed	W. Smith
Hogg	Mouncher	Buick	S. Smith
Meston		McDonald	

The Dell

Referee: Mr A.F. Sutcliffe   **Attendance:** not known

If this charity Cup-tie received less media attention than the one a fortnight before – even the attendance being unworthy of the usual guesstimate – it got off, nevertheless, to 'a sensational start,' when Soye put Saints one-up in the first minute.

He added a second after 17 minutes, from 'as neat an effort as one could wish to see.' Pompey came back through Steve Smith in the first half and Kirby, from a penalty, in the second. But Meston restored Saints'

lead and a late goal from Harris 'concluded the chapter of goals.'

While Echoist was pleased to have seen 'the Salmonbacks well whacked', the 'World Of Sport' columnist in the *Evening News* coined a reaction to losing cup-ties that would become immortalised: the defeat need 'not occasion much heartburning, for Pompey can ill afford to run risks in such tournaments. They will need to give all their attention to their League games.'

Running tally:	Saints	15	Pompey	12	Drawn	4

Portsmouth   1   Southampton   0

Harris	Kirby	Burrows	Tomlinson
Walker	Cunliffe	Clarke	Soye
Molyneux	W. Lee	Hartshorne	Hedley
Bowman	W. Smith	A. Lee	Brown
Buick	S. Smith	Hogg	Mouncher
McDonald		Meston	

Fratton Park

Referee: Mr W. Chadwick (Blackburn)   **Attendance:** 'quite 14,000'

The two teams had already 'been in conflict' four times this season, yet the *Football Echo* felt that, familiarity notwithstanding, 'present engagements have lost little, if any of their attraction.' Despite the 'dull and threatening' weather, a good turn-out agreed with this assessment.

And 'tremendous enthusiasm greeted' the only goal of the game from Lee, 'the Salmon Backs' supporters almost yelling themselves hoarse.' Sentinel had not 'seen a better or more exciting' match between the two clubs and thought it 'a very long time since the Fratton Park spectators have evinced so much enthusiasm.'

His colleague, The Celt, the resident Saints' adherent at the *Football Mail*, likewise thought it 'a rattling game, better than which no one could desire to witness.' He reckoned, nevertheless, that, 'on the whole, the visitors had the better of the argument, and had they potted better … there might have been a different story at breathing time.'

Running tally:	Saints	15	Pompey	13	Drawn	4

Southampton   5   Portsmouth   1

Stead	Tomlinson	G. Harris	Kirby
Warner	Harrison	Walker	Cunliffe
Hartshorne	Hedley	Molyneux	Hunter
Hogg	Brown	Bowman	W.Smith
Houlker	Mouncher	Buick	S. Smith
Lee		McDonald	

The Dell

Referee: not known   **Attendance:** 14,000

While the *Football Echo*'s columnists were not to know how rare a treat an FA Cup-tie between the two teams would become, the occasion was surely more to shout about than the Benevolent Cup-tie of the autumn, so some kind of welcome for this first FA Cup meeting might have been expected from them.

Far from it! The Shrimp thought it 'a regular staggerer' and 'rough luck for both clubs,' while Recorder had hoped – like 'everyone in South Hants' – that they would be kept apart and 'go hand in hand,' all the way to the Crystal Palace.

The fans took a different view and the *Mail* reported an 'unprecedented' demand for tickets for the stands (tickets for the Dell *terraces* being more than 40 years away). Locals without such tickets were advised by the *Echo*'s Recorder to get there early, as 20 excursions were scheduled to arrive 'from all over Hampshire, and even Berkshire,' while the Portsmouth 'Dockyard Committee' (an autonomous grouping of Pompey supporters) had organised 3,000 rail tickets and Mr Wilkins of the Isle of Wight Steam Packet Company – 'an enthusiast' of undisclosed loyalties – had arranged 'three special boats'.

Based on the season's five previous meetings between the sides, Recorder predicted a win for the Saints, but Sentinel disagreed: were Pompey to 'play their best game, they should just about be good enough to win.'

The First Round of the FA Cup was not the only big event scheduled for 13 January 1906: the Conservative Government had called a General Election. It would prove to be a momentous election – a Liberal landslide, hailed by Lloyd George as 'a quiet, but certain, revolution' – but the voters of Southampton and Portsmouth would have to wait to play their part in it.

Showing an estimable sense of priorities, the powers-that-be in the two towns decided to defer the vote until after the weekend. Recorder wondered why: 'even if both take place on the same day… there will be ample time to attend the match and then vote.' Careless of the possibility that the returning officers, candidates and those charged with supervising the polling stations might want to see the game?

The day of the game 'broke grey, chilly, and wet' but

The voters of Southampton and Portsmouth were denied an opportunity to participate in Lloyd George's landslide victory pending Saints' landslide win against Pompey.

shortly after ten o'clock, just as the first of a score of excursionists was due, the conditions improved, and eventually the sun came out … The Portsmouth supporters shouted their well-known 'Hallo! Hallo!' as they marched towards the ground, and evoked a response from other trippers who favoured the Saints. The Dell was thrown open at one o'clock, and from that moment until the time of kick-off there was a continuous and ever-widening stream of humanity flowing through the gates.

But not as wide as had been predicted: the attendance was given as 14,000. That was probably all The Dell could accommodate, though, with anything like comfort – comfort being relative to the norms of the era – and the scratching of noses by spectators packed on the terracing was probably out of the question.

There were absentees from both teams. George Clawley and Tom Burrows were injured, which meant an FA Cup debut for third-choice goalkeeper, Bill Stead –

like Burrows a Portsmuthian – while John 'Sailor' Hunter stood in for Willie Lee, at centre-forward for Pompey.

It took only seven minutes for Fred Harrison to give the Saints the lead.

Usually a centre-forward, though occasionally a winger, Harrison had been swapped with inside-right George Hedley: a puzzling tactical shift, but it worked. 'So perfectly did Harrison and Tomlinson dovetail,' gushed the *Athletic News* correspondent, 'one would have thought their partnership had existed for years… as they employed original and ingenious moves and executed them without a hitch.'

Indeed, it was the Tomlinson-Harrison combination that set up the Saints' second goal, just before half-time, Brown heading past Harris 'from Tomlinson's perfect centre.' Pompey pulled one back when Cunliffe – who probably haunted the sleep of Southampton defenders, as much as Harrison did Pompey's – broke, eluded Houlker (no easy task) and set up Kirby for 'a lovely oblique shot' past Stead. This encouraged the visitors briefly to 'peg… away unpleasantly near the home goal,' until 'the Saints made a move over the neutral mark, Harrison in the van.' Drawing Molyneux out of position, he 'tipped on for Tomlinson' in a move which culminated in Hedley scoring, 'amid frantic cheering.' Brown added a fourth and Tomlinson made it five 'with a clinking drive.'

Recorder thought the result

one of the greatest surprises of the first round. Portsmouth were not merely beaten; they were utterly routed. The performance undoubtedly ranks amongst the best ever achieved by Saints, and will give the players increased confidence in the future.

The Shrimp had never seen Pompey 'play so wretchedly: their exhibition was a disgrace to any first-class club.'

The Saints made it to the quarter-final, where they went out 3-0 at Anfield.

Running tally:	Saints	16	Pompey	13	Drawn	4

Southampton 1 Portsmouth 2

Clawley	Tomlinson	Cook	Kirby
Warner	Jefferis	Molyneux	Hunter
Hartshorne	Harrison	Walker	W. Lee
Hogg	Brown	Digweed	Harris
A.Lee	Mouncher	Buick	S. Smith
Houlker		McDonald	

The Dell

Referee: Mr D. Hammond (Heywood)   **Attendance:** 7,000

The *Football Mail* was not too optimistic about Portsmouth's chances in the two sides' seventh and last meeting of the season, it being 'a recognised fact that this season Saints want a deal of "knocking" on their own compact little ground.'

By the end of the century, references to the Saints' 'compact little ground' would take the form of a compliment to their record there but, coming from the Portsmouth newspaper in 1906, the remark was perhaps somewhat patronising.

The *Football Echo* noted, as was now obligatory, that 'the public never seem to tire of encounters between these two sides' and, yet again, Saints needed a win to keep them in contention for the Southern League Championship.

They duly opened the scoring 'in a most remarkable manner.' Cook caught a shot from Hogg but then, 'to the amazement of everyone, he threw the ball into his own net, apparently under the impression he was flinging it outside the post,' the *Echo* concluded.

'The only excuse,' the *Mail* suggested, 'was that he apparently lost his head entirely.'

Ten minutes into the second half, Pompey capitalised on an error, almost as unlikely, from the Southampton defence. Houlker's miskick let in Willie Lee, who was brought down by his namesake, Bert, and Walker scored from the spot. With 15 minutes to go, Kirby (*left*) settled it 'with a magnificent shot.' The Saints were thereupon 'completely outplayed, Portsmouth continuing to show grand form in every department.'

Running tally:	**Saints**	16	**Pompey**	14	**Drawn**	4

Final Word

The Saints ended the season as runners-up and must have rued losing four Southern League points to a team they had taken apart so easily in the Cup; but, then again, they were five points behind the new champions, Fulham. Pompey were three points further adrift in third place, a position that Sentinel thought 'distinctly creditable' after a season that had not, 'for some reason or other, … engendered the same amount of enthusiasm as its predecessors.'

1906-07

Pompey made a few signings at the end of the 1905–06 season, the most notable being from Southampton: full-back Jack Warner; and Tomlinson, the winger who, in partnership with Harrison, had visited such misery on the Portsmouth defence in the Cup game at The Dell.

It was part of a clear-out for the Saints, whose finances were growing increasingly precarious, so that the emphasis remained on getting the wage bill as low as possible. And perhaps they hoped that Harrison would win them games nearly single-handed.

Southampton 2 Portsmouth 3

Clawley	Harrison	Phillip	Tomlinson
Clarke	Glen	Hisbent	Hunter
Eastham	Radford	Walker	Kirby
Robertson	Harris	Digweed	W. Smith
Bowden	Mouncher	Buick	Elston
Gray		McDonald	

The Dell

Referee: Mr F. Townsend

Attendance: 'not more than 3,000... at the start'

Neither side had started the season well. The Saints were without a win in the Southern League, although their misery had been relieved by a Western League win over Spurs, as depicted by the cartoonist below.

All of which perhaps explained the disappointing attendance. But it didn't take long for things to get interesting for those who had bothered to turn up. Within two minutes, Smith had put Portsmouth ahead and McDonald had soon made it two, the Saints being 'made to look very cheap indeed,' as the *Evening News* saw it, 'both in attack and defence.'

In the second half, Pompey scored a third and Saints got two back. While it was reported that Harrison scored the first of those come-back goals, the identity of the other two scorers somehow escaped the reporters. Kirby was eventually credited with the Portsmouth goal, but the mystery remains: who scored the Saints' second?

To be fair to both the local hacks, the game was probably completed in gathering gloom, they were telephoning their final reports on an extremely tight deadline and numbered shirts were more than 30 years away. The most likely scorer was Glen – but we stand to be corrected.

Both Echoist and Sentinel attributed Saints' comeback to switching Harrison from the wing to centre-forward: 'if Southampton are satisfied that they have a better leader of the attack they might hand him over to Portsmouth,' Sentinel suggested, 'just for old time's sake!'

Running tally:	**Saints**	16	**Pompey**	15	**Drawn**	4

PITY THE POOR FALLEN ONES!

The Two Poor Beggars: Won't you please help a poor fallen brother who's seen better days?
The Fulham Bishop: Er, I, ah, think I shall cross the road. I don't approve of begging.
Pompey: What a pity we can't help 'em without hurting ourselves!
The Spur: I believe the Saint's a fraud. He was knocking me and a friend about something 'orrible the other day!
(Luton were second in the table this time last year).

Portsmouth 3 Southampton 2

Cook	Tomlinson	Clawley	Everest
Thomson	Dalrymple	Clarke	Jefferis
Bowman	Kirby	Norbury	Harrison
Digweed	W. Smith	Hogg	Harris
Buick	Elston	Bowden	Mouncher
McDonald		Gray	

Fratton Park

Referee: not known

Attendance: 6,000

Both sides had players *hors de combat* for the return Western League fixture. The Saints gave a run-out to a reserve full-back, Victor Norbury, a professional cricketer for Hampshire.

Portsmouth were 3-0 up at half-time. Billy Smith gave them the lead after Bob Dalrymple, their new signing from Glasgow Rangers, had 'hit the cross-bar with a beautiful screw shot.' Dalrymple soon set up Kirby for Pompey's second and the two of them combined for Kirby to score again. Harrison got a couple back but, as the 'Pompey Chimes' columnist pointed out in the *Football Mail*, Portsmouth were now back on terms at 16 games-all. The Saints led on goals, though, by 64 to 62.

Statistics apart, however, he thought it 'noteworthy' that, 'no matter under what auspices the clubs meet, a keen, clean and well contested game is assured.'

Running tally:	Saints	16	Pompey	16	Drawn	4

1904-07: The End of an Age

Southampton 2 Portsmouth 0

Clawley	Jefferis	Phillip	Kirby
Clarke	Glen	Walker	Hunter
Glover	Harrison	Warner	Dalrymple
Hogg	Harris	Digweed	W. Smith
Bowden	Mouncher	Thomson	Elston
Gray		McDonald	

The Dell

Referee: Mr J.R. Mason

Attendance: 10,000

Third-placed Pompey were having a considerably better Southern League season than the Saints, who were sharing the bottom of the table with Luton Town, Northampton and Reading. Whatever, all the usual faces were there, including 'close on a thousand persons [aboard] the dockyard excursion from Portsmouth.'

The Saints took the lead on seven minutes, Harrison heading home a Mouncher corner. Mouncher (*left*) headed a second before half-time.

The 'On The Ball' columnist in the *Football Mail* blamed the absence of the injured Buick (*right*): it 'made all the difference in the world to the defence – and probably the result.'

Running tally:	Saints	17	Pompey	16	Drawn	4

Portsmouth 0 Southampton 2

Phillip	Tomlinson	Clawley	Jefferis
Warner	Dalrymple	Clarke	Glen
Walker	Kirby	Glover	Harrison
Digweed	Hunter	Hogg	Harris
Buick	Buckle	Bowden	Mouncher
McDonald		Gray	

Fratton Park

Referee: Mr J.T. Howcroft (Bolton)

Attendance: 3,800

While The Shrimp thought it would have been appropriate for the two clubs to field their Reserves for this charity fixture, his *Echo* colleague, Recorder, disagreed: 'as Southampton and Portsmouth institutions stand to benefit,' he very much hoped that 'both sides will put into the field adequate representatives of their full strength so that the fixture might attract a "gate" of substantial proportions.'

A less-than-substantial turn-out of 3,800 answered his call, to watch two sides 'practically at full strength.'

A Glen-Harrison-Jefferis move put in Mouncher for the opening goal and Harrison made it 2-0 near the end.

Running tally:	Saints	18	Pompey	16	Drawn	4

Portsmouth   1   Southampton   2

Phillip	Kirby	Clawley	Jefferis
Thomson	Dalrymple	Clarke	Glen
Walker	McKenzie	Glover	Harrison
Digweed	Hunter	Robertson	Harris
Buick	Elston	Bowden	McLean
McDonald		Gray	

Fratton Park

Referee: Mr W. Chadwick (Blackburn)   **Attendance:** 12,000

The two sides had gone out of the FA Cup in the Second Round, earlier in the month – Southampton to the eventual winners, Sheffield Wednesday. They had enjoyed contrasting fortunes, in two senses of the word, in the First Round, when Saints were drawn at home to Watford and Pompey to Manchester United, who boasted in their ranks one of the greatest, if not the greatest, footballer of the era: Billy Meredith (*below*).

In an act of stupendous folly, the Southampton board had reacted to this counter-attraction at Fratton Park by setting a 'one shilling gate', a move to which they were prone to resort for attractive games, and, as always, it provoked a howl of protests from their supporters. While 3,866 diehards had watched the Saints defeat Watford 3–1 at The Dell, 24,329 had turned up to see Meredith's southern debut and, by default, Manchester United, whom they would beat after a replay.

An injury to Jefferis had reduced the Saints to 10 men.

Their League fortunes had been similarly disparate. The Saints were in mid-table, yet looking uneasily over their shoulders at the relegation scrum, while Pompey, despite a recent run of erratic results, were still well placed in the championship race: second, a point behind Fulham with two games in hand.

In an 'extraordinary' early incident, Clawley was 'hurled to the ground. A terrific struggle ensued, legs and arms generally mixing up indiscriminately,' until the referee whistled for a foul on the goalkeeper.

The Saints opened the scoring, with Harrison nipping 'between Thomson and Walker, and outdistancing pursuit' before shooting past Phillip. They had by then lost the injured Jefferis, who had left the pitch for treatment. He returned after half-time, but only as 'a passenger' and eventually left the field for good.

The inevitable was not long in coming. After Clawley had again been 'bowled over as he fisted away,' Hunter equalised. Dalrymple then hit the bar but, with Saints' chances of surviving the closing minutes looking increasingly unlikely, Mouncher 'went right through on his own, and Thomson, seeing that a score was inevitable, tried to stop him.' Glen converted the penalty to earn the Saints an astounding victory – on the basis both of the season's form and of the share of the play.

This 'perverse' outcome upset Sentinel of the *Football Mail*: not only had it dented Pompey's championship hopes but it had cost them their unbeaten home record in the Southern League, which went back 12 months.

Running tally:	Saints	19	Pompey	16	Drawn	4

Monday 8 April 1907   **Hants Benevolent Cup**

Southampton   0   Portsmouth   1

Clawley	Putten	Phillip	Bainbridge
Eastham	Edwards	Thomson	Dalrymple
Glover	Jepp	Walker	Kirby
Robertson	Jefferis	Digweed	Smith
Thorpe	Radford	Buick	Buckle
Bowden		McDonald	

The Dell

Referee: Mr L. Bullimer (Northampton)   **Attendance:** 1,500

Despite the evidence of the previous season, the *Echo* still considered this a fixture worthy of 'numerous attendance' and attributed its non-realisation to the weather. Sentinel was more inclined to blame the weather for a 'somewhat poor display of football' but suggested that the poor crowd might be attributed to the Saints being 'fairly out of elbow with their supporters.' There were two first-half incidents of note: Buick was 'accidentally' kicked in the head by Jefferis and had to leave the field, 'bleeding profusely'; and Buckle scored for Portsmouth.

Buick – 'a marvel of pluck' in Echoist's book – returned to finish the game, 'although blood streamed from the gash in his head the whole time. One must admire his devotion to the side, but the wisdom of his action is very questionable.'

Running tally:	Saints	19	Pompey	17	Drawn	4

Final Word

Portsmouth finished runners-up to Fulham but Sentinel rated their season 'one of the most successful the Club has ever enjoyed.'

The fact that they had secured 'more points to their credit than they gained when they won the Championship, is in itself a complete vindication,' he reasoned, 'of the progressive policy which was determined upon' by the directors, following the club's lack of success in 1905–06.

Moreover, their 'gallant' win against Manchester United had impressed 'Northern critics – who are none too sympathetic in their dealings with the South as a rule – [yet who] were unanimous in admitting that the team was quite good enough to take its place and hold its own with the best organisations in the kingdom'

There was no consolation for Southampton who, for the first time in the history of the Southern League, had finished lower than third. And if that wasn't bad enough, the economies they had made proved fruitless, as attendances slumped.

There was bad news for both clubs to share, too: Fulham, as expected, defected to the Football League and the writing was now most definitely on the wall regarding the Southern League's status as a 'first-class' competition. Other clubs had also been making noises about jumping ship, notably Tottenham Hotspur and

Bristol Rovers – possibilities that had been the matter of much discussion in the football press.

'Is the Southern League doomed?' Posing that question and noting recent discussions on the 'fusion' of the two Leagues, The Shrimp was concerned to 'impress upon' his readers that 'the time is ripe for some definite effort to strengthen the position of Southern football.'

Suppose Spurs and other London clubs were to follow Fulham: 'would teams like Portsmouth and Southampton be able to continue [in] a comparatively second-rate competition?' He thought not.

And as if Fulham's departure wasn't bad enough, those upstarts Chelsea had been promoted to Division I.

THE PARTING OF THE WAYS.

Fulham : Well, ta, ta, you chaps ! I must be off. Got an important engagement elsewhere.
Pompey : Bloated aristocrat ! Think we ain't good enough for you, I s'pose. Guess you think you'll be travellin' first class next !

READ ON: The story of Chelsea's duplicitous applications to join two Leagues is told in Albert Sewell's jubilee history of the club. See 'Sources'.

Chapter 5
1907-14: Losing their Spurs

The Golden Age was over. For the next seven seasons, up to the outbreak of war, it would be very much a case of making do and hoping to hang on.

Both sides would finish, more often than not, in the bottom half of the Southern League and Pompey would even spend a season in its Second Division. Not that mediocrity mattered when it came to gaining membership of the Football League: Spurs would at last defect in 1908, after finishing seventh.

Meanwhile, talk of a National League would continue, but talk was all it was.

1907-08

In the summer's transfer activity, each club signed a player from the other, John Bainbridge moving to The Dell and Alex Glen to Fratton Park. And John Lewis, once of Pompey, joined Saints from Brighton.

Southern League fixtures would have a novel twist: the departing Fulham had been replaced by Bradford Park Avenue. Refused membership of the Football League, Bradford had been admitted straight into the First Division of the Southern League. This rather hinted at a certain desperation to compensate for Fulham's defection and, if it added a dash of the exotic to the competition's provincialism, Bradford's remoteness surely suggested that they would transfer to Division II of the Football League at the first opportunity.

Saturday 28 September 1907   **Southern League**

Portsmouth   3   Southampton   0

F. Cook	Bellamy	Lock	Bainbridge
Thomson	Wilson	Eastham	Jefferis
Walker	Kirby	Glover	F. Harrison
Digweed	W. Smith	Johnston	Costello
Beaumont	Williams	Thorpe	Hodgkinson
McDonald		Hadley	

                                                           Fratton Park

Referee: Mr Pickford (Bournemouth)   **Attendance:** 16,000

Neither Pompey nor the Saints had got off to a satisfactory start to the season. But the *Echo*'s Recorder had other things on his mind – like Brighton's 'rowdy' supporters and the prospect, in contrast, of another good-natured derby game:

> What I like about the Southampton-Portsmouth matches is that we get good football, and except on very rare occasions, an honest endeavour to play the game. In no part of the country is a local 'Derby' fought in a better spirit than it is in Hampshire, and if the Southampton and Portsmouth spectators act discreetly the contests between the teams will always be a pleasure to watch.

The *Evening News* was not over-confident regarding Pompey's chances, being especially concerned at their 'singular' misfortune 'in the matter of injuries to players' for games against Southampton: 'scarcely ever are they able to play a full team.'

The game was scoreless at half-time, but Pompey took the early initiative in the second, winning a corner after Lock had scrambled 'the leather outside the post.'

The kick 'was beautifully placed by Bellamy, and in the course of the scrimmage in the goalmouth, …it was impossible to say who scored, the players themselves being doubtful.'

Then, after more Pompey pressure, 'Williams raced down the touchline' and centred 'perfectly' for Kirby to head past Lock. And finally, with the visiting defenders 'clamouring for an offside, Bellamy sped away [and] centred. Lock jumped out and only partially cleared' – to Smith, who was 'lying handy' and scored. 'This cooked Southampton's goose.'

Recorder was inclined to blame the defeat on a first-half incident when Digweed allegedly put the ball out of play with his hand, with Bainbridge 'left with an easy shot'. But Mr. Pickford

'refused to listen' to the 'general appeal' for a penalty. After discussing the incident at some length, Recorder captured the innocence of the age: 'If there had been a single appeal he would have been quite right in ignoring it, but an appeal made simultaneously by several players is certainly prima facie evidence … and in the circumstances Mr. Pickford, I contend, should have consulted his linesmen.'

Bert Lock had a busy,
and miserable, afternoon.

Running tally:	Saints	19	Pompey	18	Drawn	4

Wednesday 4 December 1907 — **Western League**

Portsmouth 0 Southampton 2

Cameron	Birtles	Lock	Jefferis
Thomson	Knight	Robertson	Smith
Warner	Kirby	Glover	Jepp
Digweed	Glen	Johnston	Costello
Bowman	Dix	Thorpe	Hodgkinson
Beaumont		Hadley	

Fratton Park

Referee: Mr Howcroft (Bolton)   **Attendance:** 1,000

Fred Harrison was missing. Following a poor start to the season, the Southampton directors had received an offer they could not refuse (reputedly £1,800) for Harrison and Mouncher. The buyers were Fulham, the recent defectors to the Football League.

If those transfers rubbed in the way in which the South Coast neighbours were being gradually cast adrift, the *Echo* remained enthusiastic about the 'interesting football' Saints and Pompey had 'served up', even in the lesser Western League, a competition they were taking 'seriously'.

Indeed, they were vying for the leadership of their section.

The weather was so 'depressing' that the *News* thought it 'not surprising that the smallest attendance ever seen at a Southampton and Portsmouth match was present.' Despite having 'the climatic conditions against them,' the Saints were 'altogether the smarter team' in the first half and led at the interval, through a fifth-minute penalty by Glover. They continued to be 'the better combination' in the second half when Smith (*left*) made it 2-0, 'following a fine run by Jefferis.'

Running tally:	Saints	20	Pompey	18	Drawn	4

1907-14: Losing their Spurs

Southampton 0 Portsmouth 1

Lock	Jefferis	Cameron	Bellamy
Robertson	Smith	Thomson	Parton
Glover	Jacques	Warner	Kirby
Johnston	Costello	Digweed	Wilson
Thorpe	Hodgkinson	Buick	Dix
Hadley		Beaumont	

The Dell

Referee: Mr Howcroft (Bolton) **Attendance:** 1,500

Each side introduced a novice forward. Jacques, who had the thankless task of replacing Harrison in the centre of the Saints' attack, had made his debut the previous Saturday, while Pompey gave a trial to Parton of Oxford St Thomas.

Pompey got the only goal of the game when Kirby 'caught the home defence lying wide' and ran through to score. The general consensus, in the footballing press, was that Jacques, who missed 'two or three easy chances,' was certainly no Harrison. A cruel comparison, as Fred was in a class of his own, but Jacques never played for Southampton again. As for Parton, his one-match moment has been lost on Pompey's historians, to the extent that Portsmouth have been recorded as fielding only 10 men for this match. The result gave each side an identical record:

P 11   W 7   L 3   D 1   Pts 15

A superior goal average kept the Saints on top.

Running tally:	**Saints**	20	**Pompey**	19	**Drawn**	4

Southampton 1 Portsmouth 0

Lewis	Costello	Cameron	Bellamy
Eastham	Hadley	Thomson	Yates
Glover	Jefferis	Warner	Kirby
Johnston	G. Smith	Digweed	W. Smith
Thorpe	Hodgkinson	Buick	Dix
Bainbridge		McDonald	

The Dell

Referee: Mr W. Pickford (Bournemouth) **Attendance:** 'only a few thousand'

The Western League fixtures had been duly completed, with Southampton topping their section and Portsmouth second. But with just over half the season gone in the Southern League, the two sides were in mid-table.

If there was little at stake, then the *Echo* was not going to let it show: Saints and Pompey deserved a good crowd, because they 'invariably "play the game,"' and that is why the matches between them are so popular.' But a combination of fog, drizzle and bad light meant that 'the attendance was sensibly diminished.'

The only goal came in the first half, when Hodgkinson, who had been 'following a Macawber-like policy and standing in the middle of the field,' scored from Hadley's centre. Hadley limped off in the second half, reducing the home team to 10 men. Which appears to have been the second-most interesting incident of the game – at least until the ball burst.

Recorder credited Saints' win to a 'whole-hearted' defensive performance, while Sentinel attributed Pompey's defeat to the absence of the discovery of the season, L.A. Louch, an amateur centre-forward whose recent introduction to the side had transformed its Southern League goal-scoring: 'we found all the difference without him…, for the forwards lapsed completely into the old ineffective and spiritless style which characterised their efforts during the early months of the season.'

Running tally:	Saints	21	Pompey	19	Drawn	4

Final Word

And that was that for the season: only four derby games and all over by the end of January. The following Saturday, they each won their FA Cup Second Round tie. Pompey went out in the next round, but Saints again reached the semi-final.

Their 2-0 defeat by Wolverhampton was their first-ever by a Football League Second Division club. Wolves went on to win the Cup, so the Saints had gone out to the winners two seasons running. Yet their Cup record remained one to be proud of: this was their fourth semi-final in their 14 seasons in the Southern League – an achievement way superior to that of Portsmouth, who had yet to get beyond the Third Round.

But Pompey just had the edge in the League – ninth place, two points and two places ahead of their neighbours. Not a lot to shout about, but Sentinel was grateful for small mercies: 'seldom has a club starting off so badly made such a magnificent recovery.'

1908-09

The Southern League lost two more clubs to the Football League during the close season: Bradford Park Avenue and Tottenham Hotspur. In terms of form, neither was much of a loss: Park Avenue had finished 12th, two points behind the Saints, and Tottenham seventh, two places and one point ahead of Pompey. But the exodus of Spurs was, in terms of gates – especially those at The Dell, where they had been Boxing Day guests for the past nine seasons – near to devastating.

On the bright side, Queen's Park Rangers, the Champions, also attempted to join the Football League, failed to be elected and had to re-apply to join the Southern League.

The 20 clubs forming the First Division having already been settled for 1908–09, Rangers were re-admitted to a 21-club competition in which they would have to play all their games mid-week.

Saturday 26 September 1908   **Southern League**

Southampton   2   Portsmouth   0

Lock	Bainbridge	T. McDonald	Birtles
Eastham	Jefferis	Warner	Kirby
Robertson	Hughes	Clipstone	Louch
Johnston	Shearer	Digweed	McCafferty
Thorpe	Blake	Buick	Dix
Trueman		E. McDonald	

The Dell

Referee: Mr H. Smith (Boston)   **Attendance:** 16,000

The Saints went in to this match having scored 21 goals to achieve six wins in six Southern League matches. As the *Football Echo* pointed out, this was not merely 'an exceptionally fine record,' but 'the best in fact, in the country. Not even the famous Uniteds of Manchester and Newcastle could equal it, although each of them, like Saints, had won all their matches to date.'

With Pompey having won only one of their six matches, the Saints were 'prime favourites' to make it seven out of seven. The *Echo* vouched for 'every coign of vantage being utilised' long before the kick-off.

Its 'SAINTS SIMPLY IRRESISTIBLE' headline appears to have been a fair assessment, even if Bert Lock had plenty of opportunities to shine.

They opened the scoring when 'Blake tricked Digweed, and drawing the leather to his

left foot, sent across a perfect centre, which Bainbridge rushed into the net amidst tremendous enthusiasm.' As half-time approached, the Saints were 'overplaying the visitors to such an extent' that a second goal 'seemed inevitable'. It eventually came from 'a brilliant single-handed effort by Hughes.'

The *Football Mail* acknowledged that 'the Saints well deserved their victory… and the Portsmouth spectators took it like good sportsmen.'

Arthur Hughes, scorer of a 'brilliant single-handed' goal.

Running tally:	Saints	22	Pompey	19	Drawn	4

Wednesday 30 September 1908   **Western League**

Portsmouth   4   Southampton   2

T. McDonald	Birtles	Lock	Smith
Warner	Kirby	Eastham	McPherson
Clipstone	Reid	Glover	Hughes
Bowman	McCafferty	Trueman	Shearer
Buick	Williams	Thorpe	Hodgkinson
E. McDonald		Robertson	

Fratton Park

Referee: Mr E. Ashworth (London)   **Attendance:** 'close on 16,000'

Four days later, Pompey had their retribution when they inflicted on the Saints their first defeat of the season, albeit in the Western League.

Sentinel found the two games 'so utterly dissimilar' as to defy explanation.

In the opening half-hour, Portsmouth's attack was 'so persistent and hot… that it was bound to succeed.' And succeed it did when Lock came out to block Kirby's shot but 'failed to hold the ball, which Reid sent into an untenanted goal.' The first half ended 1–0. The second half was 'more even'. But the home forwards 'were always more effective' than Southampton's and, when Lock was beaten by Williams's centre, 'Reid and Kirby rushed the ball into the net.'

McPherson pulled one back for the Saints, but Reid scored Pompey's third, 'following a brilliant bit of headwork by Kirby.' With five minutes left, the Saints

came again with 'a lovely goal' from Hughes, only for 'the home forwards to break away' and set up Williams for his side's fourth.

Perhaps Southampton were capable of concentrating on only one competition at a time? Recorder certainly seemed to think so: their 'brilliant record' in the Southern League had

> had the effect of knocking a lot of interest out of their career in the Western League. Public opinion regards it as injudicious to attempt to win both competitions, believing that such an effort would involve too great a strain on the players. Very little surprise or disappointment was therefore caused by [this] defeat at Fratton Park.

He was, however, concerned that, in these two matches, 'elements of an undesirable character were introduced. It is difficult to state which side first offended …but the policy of retaliation was freely practised by both sides.'

Running tally:	Saints	22	Pompey	20	Drawn	4

Wednesday 28 October 1908

Western League

Southampton 4 Portsmouth 1

Burrows   Bainbridge
W.G Smith   Jefferis
Glover   McGhee
Trueman   Jordan
Thorpe   Hodgkinson
Jepp

Cameron   Kirby
Smith   Knight
Warner   Reid
Bowman   McCafferty
Buick   Long
Churchill

The Dell

Referee: Mr J. Howcroft (Bolton)

Attendance: 10,000

'Under the impression that the kick-off was fixed for half-past three,' Portsmouth turned up too late for the scheduled 3 o'clock start. It was 3.20 pm before they were on the field, 'facing a bright sun' but otherwise not warmed-up. Not surprisingly, they were soon on the back foot, as Bainbridge 'swung in some fine centres,' from one of which Jordan headed 'a neat goal.'

Bainbridge continued to be at the heart of the action, along with McGhee, a part-timer billed as a 'young schoolmaster'. It was from Bainbridge's centre that 'Jordan converted in brilliant style.' Then, just before the interval, McGhee 'slipped past Warner and scored with a capital shot.'

McGhee made it 4-0 after 55 minutes, when he 'neatly robbed Buick' and ran on to score 'a fine goal'. He was 'now worrying Buick considerably' but the next time he dispossessed him, his shot was cleared by Cameron.

Soon after that, the referee felt moved to stop the game and remonstrate with supporters. The *Football Echo* explained that they had been 'urging Bainbridge to "get his own back".' It is not clear for what, unless it be 'a regrettable incident' in the first half when Cameron had 'kicked at' Jefferis.

McGhee retired from the fray with 15 minutes to go, after receiving a kick. Trueman followed him – too late for Pompey to exploit a two-man advantage, although Reid did pull one back. Crippling kicks notwithstanding, it had been another 'good tempered contest,' but Recorder was concerned that the referee had been obliged to scold spectators:

Their influence in the course of a game is enormous, and if people would only depreciate any tendency to foul play, instead of encouraging it, we should soon find a great improvement in the tone of the game.

Running tally:	Saints	23	Pompey	20	Drawn	4

Saturday 30 January 1909

Southern League

Portsmouth 3 Southampton 0

McDonald   Kirby
Warner   McCafferty
Clipstone   Reid
Digweed   McMahon
Beaumont   Dix
Yates

Lock   Blake
Eastham   Jefferis
Foster   Costello
Johnston   Jordan
Jepp   Hodgkinson
Bamford

Fratton Park

Referee: Mr J.W. Heath (Burslem)

Attendance: 'a capital assemblage'

The Saints came into this return Southern League game, having taken only two points from their last five matches, reeling from a record home defeat – 6-0 to Swindon –

and amid rumours, as aired by the *Football Echo*, that there had been a 'free fight' in their dressing room after that debacle, in which a director had been struck.

Even so, they were still second in the table, four points ahead of sixth-placed Pompey, who had been picking up form. Injuries obliged the visitors to field four reserves but, 'with football enthusiasm rampant in Portsmouth, … there was a capital assemblage of spectators.'

Pompey opened the scoring 10 minutes before the interval. 'Dix made a splendid sprint down the wing' and when he centred, 'Reid was on the premises, and easily scored.' Shortly after, 'Lock suddenly staggered between the posts, and had to be supported,' seemingly from a head injury, and 'it took several minutes to bring him round.' Helped from the field at the interval, he was 'still dizzy' when the game restarted. He was immediately beaten when 'the home forwards went down the field at a gallop' and McCafferty scored from Dix's 'beautiful centre'. Reid added Pompey's third.

Recorder was philosophical about the defeat of Saints' depleted team by 'a side flushed with success' – although he had hoped that Pompey might 'take things quietly in view of [the following Saturday's] cup tie, and might be busted.'

Portsmouth would lose that tie, after a replay, to Sheffield Wednesday. Saints had gone out in the previous round to Bristol City, who would lose to Manchester United in the Final. For three consecutive seasons, then, the Saints had lost to eventual finalists.

| Running tally: | Saints | 23 | Pompey | 21 | Drawn | 4 |

Monday 22 February 1909   **Southern Charity Cup Final (held over from 1908)**

Southampton 1   Portsmouth 0

Lock	Smith	Cameron	Birtles
Eastham	Shearer	Thomson	Kirby
Glover	Ward	Warner	McCafferty
Johnston	Jordan	Digweed	Yates
Jepp	Hodgkinson	Beaumont	Dix
Bamford		McDonald	

The Dell

Referee: Mr H. Smith   **Attendance:** not known

So why was the final of a three-round competition being played 10 months after the semi-finals? Blame Millwall. Having reached the Final, the Saints had awaited the winners of the semi-final between Pompey and Millwall, who contrived to draw three times in April but could not agree a date for the third replay. Millwall being considered the more awkward customers, Portsmouth were awarded the place in the Final – eventually.

The only goal came in the 55th minute, Ward 'tipping the ball into the net' from Jordan's cross. Thereafter, the play became 'still more lively, the young Southampton forwards, well supported by Johnston and Jepp, setting a hot pace' – although Lock twice needed to save 'in great style' from the troublesome McCafferty.

Lamenting the number of Pompey's missed scoring opportunities, Sentinel ventured that 'a draw would have been a fairer reflex [sic] of the play.' He could understand Saints' being 'elated at their success': until now, they had 'not won a trophy of any sort since Harry Wood played for them.'

True – but unkind.

Sam Jepp helped to 'set a hot pace.'

| Running tally: | Saints | 24 | Pompey | 21 | Drawn | 4 |

Wednesday 10 March 1909

Hants Benevolent Cup

Southampton 1   Portsmouth 1

Lock	Bainbridge	McDonald	Birtles
Eastham	Hughes	Thomson	Kirby
Glover	Foster	Warner	Reid
Campbell	Jordan	Digweed	McCafferty
Jepp	Ward	Buick	Dix
Smith		Yates	

Fratton Park

Referee: Mr A. Farrant (Bristol)   **Attendance:** 2,000

Tradition demanded that the weather be wretched for this fixture. The *Echo* reported 'a bitterly cold north-easterly gale, [which] was followed by heavy rain… Not more than 2,000 braved the elements.'

Towards the end of a first half in which both defences had been 'excellent, considering the conditions,' Reid scored for Portsmouth. After the break, as 'rain fell in torrents, … Portsmouth were almost continually attacking.' But the Saints rallied, for Foster to equalise from a sudden breakaway.

The captains refused to play extra-time, and the match was drawn.

Running tally:	Saints	24	Pompey	21	Drawn	5

Monday 15 March 1909

Southern Charity Cup, First Round

Southampton 1   Portsmouth 2

Lock	Bainbridge	McDonald	Kirby
Eastham	Hughes	Thomson	McCafferty
Smith	Foster	Clipstone	Reid
Campbell	Jordan	Banks	McMahon
Jepp	Hodgkinson	Buick	Dix
Bamford		Yates	

The Dell

Referee: Mr C.W. Gillett   **Attendance:** 1,500

No sooner had they had settled the 1908 Final of this competition than the two sides were contesting the 1909 First Round. Indeed, it would be their third meeting in a minor cup competition in the space of 22 days and their seventh derby game of the season, in all. The *Echo* felt that 'the cold, wet, windy weather' must be a 'principal cause' of the poor attendance, but might not a surfeit of minor cup-ties and an overall familiarity have had something to do with it?

Whatever, all the goals were scored in the first half. The Saints took the initiative within two minutes, after 'a delightful bit of work' begun by Foster and carried on by Bainbridge, whose apparent centre cannoned off the far post into the net. Pompey now did most of the attacking, but found Lock in particularly good form. In a 10-minute spell just before the interval, however, he was beaten twice: McMahon netted from a Dix pass; and then Reid 'broke through' to score at the second attempt.

Running tally:	Saints	24	Pompey	22	Drawn	5

Southampton   4   Portsmouth   3

Burrows	Bainbridge	T. McDonald	Dix
Eastham	Jefferis	Warner	Yates
Glover	Carter	Thomson	Kirby
Jepp	Jordan	E. McDonald	Knight
Thorpe	Hodgkinson	Buick	Birtles
Trueman		Beaumont	

The Dell

Referee: Mr C.W. Gillett   **Attendance:** 1,500

More bad news for the Hants FA Benevolent Fund: although the game kicked-off as late as 5.45, the crowd was disappointing.

But, then, it was the fourth minor cup-tie on the trot and their eighth encounter of the season.

It nevertheless produced 'a rattling display of football', according to Echoist, in that the Saints were coasting at 4-1 when 'Pompey came along with a rush

towards the close, Kirby doing the "hat trick".'

Jefferis and Jordan each scored for Southampton and there were two goals for recent arrival, Bob ('Toddler') Carter, whose principal claim to fame, in the football record books, would be for fathering Raich Carter.

Two-goal 'Toddler' Carter

Running tally:	**Saints**	25	**Pompey**	22	**Drawn**	5

Final Word

It was, if nothing else, an epic season for Saints-Pompey matches. Honours were fairly even in the league, each side winning a Southern League game and each a Western League match.

There was also a revival in Southern League form, the Saints squeezing Pompey out of third place by just two points. Yet Sentinel thought it a 'disappointing' season for Portsmouth, especially when compared with the 'consistent, whole-hearted' performance of the worthy champions, Northampton. Having finished bottom of the table just two years previously, Northampton's fortunes had been radically transformed by their giving a first managerial appointment, in 1907, to a young former player of theirs: one Herbert Chapman.

1909-10

Once more, the prospect of a merger of the Leagues had been discussed during the close season, but it was all talk.

The Southern League now had 22 clubs in its First Division, while the Western League was no more. Given that matches in this League had hardly been cash cows for the contenders, its abandonment appears to have been overdue.

The new season brought a remarkable – if not much remarked-upon – sartorial adjustment at Fratton Park, where white shirts and blue knickers replaced the pink and claret. No more would Pompey be hailed as 'the Shrimps.' – although it must be said that this cognomen appears to have been dead for some time.

Southampton 3 Portsmouth 2

Burrows	Davies	Cope	Worthington
Eastham	Carter	Smith	Guy
Glover	McGibbon	Clipstone	Haycock
Robertson	Brittleton	Beaumont	Hakin
Jepp	Jordan	Shufflebotham	McMahon
Bamford			Dix

The Dell

Referee: Mr Mr T. Armitt

Attendance: not known (*receipts £72.14s*)

With each side missing injured players, Saints made the initial breakthrough, when 'a neat combination took the home forwards through' and McGibbon centred for Brittleton to score.

Pompey were quickly on level terms, with Haycock converting a Dix centre after the home defence 'had stopped, concluding the ball had gone behind.'

In the second half, 'play fluctuated with exhilarating frequency.' Hakin scored a second for Pompey but the game was won

for Saints with two goals by Charlie McGibbon (*left*), a one-season wonder whose claim to fame, in the Saints' annals, tends – rather like Bob Carter's – to be as the father of a famous son.*

Although Sentinel 'would sooner any other team beat us than Southampton,' he was 'not at all sorry' to see Pompey spared further participation in this insignificant competition. Saints would follow them in the next round, by losing 1-0 at Brighton.

Running tally:	Saints	26	Pompey	22	Drawn	5

Saturday 6 November 1909

Southern League

Portsmouth 1 Southampton 1

Cope	Birtles	Burrows	Bainbridge
Warner	Kirby	Robertson	Jefferis
Clipstone	Bowman	Glover	McGibbon
Beaumont	McMahon	Johnston	Brittleton
Buick	Dix	Jepp	Blake
Yates		Trueman	

Fratton Park

Referee: Mr B.M. Neville (London)

Attendance: 15,000

The first League game of the season between the two sides was blessed with 'lovely weather' and attracted what the *Hampshire Independent* judged to be 'quite the biggest excursion party that has accompanied the Saints for several seasons.' Pompey opened the scoring through Kirby, when Burrows could only parry McMahon's shot to him. Saints came back 'brightly'. After 'splendidly outflanking Warner,' Blake finished the move by 'negotiating a very acute angle [to drive] the leather into… the net amidst a great demonstration of enthusiasm.' A very busy second half produced no further goals.

Running tally:	Saints	26	Pompey	22	Drawn	6

* The son in question is Doug McGibbon, whose record-breaking achievement for Saints against Chelsea in 1945 has been rehearsed in just about every history of the club. But, unlike his father, Doug would never appear in a Saints-Pompey derby.

Southampton 2 Portsmouth 3

Burrows	Bainbridge	Cope	Long
Robertson	Jefferis	Thomson	Kirby
Glover	McGibbon	Knight	Bowman
Johnston	Carter	Worthington	McMahon
Jepp	Jordan	Shufflebotham	Dix
Trueman		Yates	

The Dell

Referee: Mr W.E. Russell **Attendance:** 'a handful of people'

The weather gods continued to oppress the Hants Benevolent Cup. Sentinel did not think it 'possible to imagine more dismal, dreary conditions than those which prevailed' on this occasion.

In the 15th minute, Trueman's shot 'was travelling rather slowly towards goal, when McGibbon dashed in, to Cope's surprise, and netted.' Kirby promptly equalised with 'a low drive, which went between Burrow's legs into the net. No one was disposed to blame the custodian, however, considering the state of the ball.' Indeed, despite the conditions, 'the game was producing excellent football, both sets of forwards combining well, but encountering keen tackling.' Portsmouth went 2-1 up when Dix's centre was 'brilliantly headed through by Kirby.' The Saints should have equalised 'immediately', but Glover's penalty kick was 'shot straight at Cope, who saved. He fell in doing so, and lost possession, but as Glover rushed in, Cope struggled to the leather, and pushed it aside.' Pompey added a third when McMahon converted a 'clever "push through" pass by Bowman' and, right on the interval, McGibbon headed 'a remarkable goal.'

Which concluded the scoring in 'a really fine match' that left Sentinel lamenting that 'the laudable purpose of augmenting the fund organised to assist necessitous players in the county, was utterly ruined, the receipts totalling less than will be required to meet the expenses of the match. This is a great pity.'

Running tally:	Saints	26	Pompey	23	Drawn	6

Southampton 1 Portsmouth 2

Burrows	Carter	Cope	Long
Eastham	Jefferis	Warner	Kirby
Robertson	Glover	Thomson	Bowman
Johnston	Brittleton	Beaumont	Haycock
Jepp	Blake	Shufflebotham	Williams
Trueman		Yates	

The Dell

Referee: Mr H. Thompson (London) **Attendance:** 7,000

Pompey came to The Dell without a manager. Richard Bonney had resigned shortly before the game. Pompey took a third-minute lead when Kirby's 'fast shot' from 15 yards 'went straight at Burrows, who should have saved, but let the sphere out of his hands and through his legs. Kirby wore "the smile that won't come off" as he walked back to the centre.' The Saints were promptly back on terms through Brittleton. Thereafter, 'raids at the respective ends were attended with much excitement,' but it was Portsmouth who got the decider in the 22nd minute, when Haycock 'beat Burrows all ends up.'

Running tally:	Saints	26	Pompey	24	Drawn	6

Final Word

Neither side had impressed their respective local newspapers. Southampton's fifth, and Portsmouth's sixth, place in the League were not good enough and each had gone out of the Cup in the Second Round.

And now Portsmouth had joined Southampton in the race to bankruptcy – a fate avoided, short-term, by the reconstitution of the company and a new share issue.

The financial situation was so precarious that the Pompey directors would not be replacing Richard Bonney as manager immediately, pending which former captain and player/manager, Bob Blyth, who was now on the board, would oversee the signing of new players – an interesting development as he had been suspended the last time he had been involved in transfer dealings.

1910-11

There were changes in the working conditions of the nation's footballers. The Football League and the Southern League agreed a retain-and-transfer system that would put an end to a disgruntled player walking out of his club and, for no consideration, playing for the team of his choice in the other League. The *Football Mail* cartoonist wondered (*opposite page*) about the outcome of the new system that was far more in the spirit of the Football League's arrangements than those of the Southern League. That said, it removed one of the obstacles to creating a National League – although, given how much its position had weakened in recent years, the option of turning the Southern League into a regional Division II appeared increasingly unlikely.

Saturday 10 September 1910 Southern League

Southampton   3   Portsmouth   0

Burrows	Buckenham	Cope	Noble
Eastham	Jefferis	Thomson	McMahon
Glover	Prince	Warner	Kirby
Robertson	Dunne	Worthington	Turner
Jepp	Blake	Buick	Long
Trueman		Yates	

The Dell

Referee: Mr J.B. Schumacher (London)   **Attendance:** 10,000

Sentinel's *Football Mail* report, that Saturday evening, began with a variation on the usual theme:

> The progress of Pompey is followed with almost as much interest in the neighbouring town of Southampton as it is in Portsmouth, while locally we watch the doings of the Saints with as much keenness as they do in Southampton. It is not to be wondered at, therefore, that when the two Hampshire rivals meet there should be a kind of local Derby and unbounded enthusiasm. The matches between the clubs both at the Dell and at Fratton Park attract a following from practically every part of the county, including the Isle of Wight, and to-day was no exception to the rule. Special trains were run from all parts in connection with the battle royal, and Portsmouth had the support of a very large section of their regular spectators [sporting] a prolific display of Pompey favours.

Jefferis 'engineered [a] magnificent piece of play,' which culminated in Percy Prince (*right*) heading Saints in front on 15 minutes.

Pompey threatened to equalise, but the Saints went 2-0 up when some 'smart wing play' by Blake led to a 'fluky goal' by Dunne. Jefferis added a third in the second half.

Running tally:	**Saints**	27	**Pompey**	24	**Drawn**	6

UNDER NEW MANAGEMENT.

Mr. New Season: Well, off we go; I wonder how they'll all work together?

Wednesday 30 November 1910

Hants Benevolent Cup

Portsmouth 2 Southampton 1

Cope	Noble	A.Brown	Jefferis
Thomson	Kirby	Easton	Dunne
Warner	Hall	Glover	Kimpton
Yates	Turner	Beaumont	H. Brown
Worthington	Long	Robertson	Blake
Knight		Trueman	

Fratton Park

Referee: Mr R. Rooke

Attendance: 'between two and three hundred'

The weather curse of the Hants Benevolent Cup struck once again. 'The weather was so bad,' the *Echo* reported, 'that the question of postponing the [match] was seriously considered. On account of the inconvenience that would have been caused the clubs, however, it was decided to play the match in conditions that could not possibly have been worse.'

Yet the game turned out to be 'surprisingly good, being fast, even, and interesting.' Portsmouth took a two-goal lead through Long, with 'a magnificent...

cross shot' and Hall, with 'a low shot, which passed Brown's prone form.'

The Saints struck back, just before half-time, through 'a clever individual effort' by Brown, who squeezed the ball 'between the post and Cope – a task which seemed almost impossible to accomplish.'

At half-time, the players swapped ends immediately and the game restarted without a break, whereupon they 'again contested every inch of the ground very strenuously, but there was no further scoring.'

Sentinel was concerned that the weather-reduced attendance had 'once again… left the charity out of pocket.' He thought it 'a mistake to play the game' and unequivocally blamed Southampton FC for this:

Its one object was to assist charity, and so far as I can see, there was absolutely no reason why it could not have been postponed until a subsequent date. Portsmouth made a suggestion, I believe, to that effect, but although the offer was made to bear half the expenses Southampton had been put to, those in charge of the visiting team would not acquiesce. So a deserving charity suffers.

This censure was probably deserved, even though the Saints were suffering the perennial financial crisis. It's difficult to see how insisting the game was played in front of a few individuals cowering in the stands – while hazarding the health and safety of their players, into the bargain – benefited anyone.

It was, one suspects, with some relish, that Sentinel paid off with an acid reminder:

Portsmouth have now won the Cup four times and Saints once.

Running tally:	Saints	27	Pompey	25	Drawn	6

Saturday 7 January 1911   **Southern League**

Portsmouth 0 Southampton 1

Cope	Noble	A. Brown	Smith
Thomson	Reeves	Eastham	Dunne
Warner	Kirby	Glover	Kimpton
Yates	Turner	Johnston	H. Brown
Worthington	Long	Monk	Blake
Knight		Trueman	

Fratton Park

Referee: Mr L.G. Swain (Northampton)   **Attendance:** 10,000

Both Portsmouth and Southampton were having grim seasons. Saints had been bottom of the division in October but had pulled themselves to mid-table over the next two months, while Pompey had slumped to what the *Football Mail* called 'a very serious position in the table.'

The only goal came after a sustained home attack in the second half, which ended with 'a fine shot' from Dunne. The defeat left Pompey four points and four places off the bottom and 'the seriousness of the set-back [could] not be overestimated,' Sentinel felt:

In fact our present position conjures up very unpleasant visions of the possibility of the Second Division, and… that is much too bad to contemplate. The Portsmouth Club, ever since its inception … has ever been regarded as one of the first-class professional organisations in the country, and [relegation] would be absolutely fatal. The Portsmouth sport-loving public have always shown themselves ready to support a first-class team, but I doubt very much if the Second Division of the Southern League would prove an attraction to them or pay its way. The class is not good enough for a town where we already have such keen local Service and civilian football.

Running tally:	Saints	28	Pompey	25	Drawn	6

Final Word

Portsmouth went down. There can be no doubting that 1910-11 was the most calamitous season in Pompey's short history. If not being in the top five had hitherto been considered a disaster, then the trauma of relegation defied adequate assessment.

With the Saints missing relegation by only a point, there was little cause for celebration in either town. Nor did the Cup bring any consolation: each side went out in the First Round.

1911-12

Each club had a new manager. Bill Dawson, the trainer who had been running the Southampton team, retired and the duties of the Secretary, Mr Arnfield, would henceforth be confined to financial matters – which cleared the way for George Swift to be appointed Secretary-Manager. He was not impressed with what he found and £820 was immediately invested in 11 new players.

The Portsmouth directors finally announced their delayed appointment: Robert Brown, plucked from back-room duties at Sheffield Wednesday. Even before the 1910-

11 season had ended in relegation, rumours as to whether the club would survive to play in Division II of the Southern League were circulating, as was speculation that a new syndicate would take over the club.

But, new manager apart, it was more or less the same club, with the same directors, that took on the responsibility of hastening Pompey back into the elite.

Bill Dawson, retiring after 16 seasons at the club.

Monday 18 September 1911   **Jack Eastham Benefit**

Southampton 2   Portsmouth 1

Knight	Wilcox	Sanderson	Turner
Eastham	Kimpton	Warner	Stringfellow
Robertson	Hamilton	Croft	Probert
Lee	H. Brown	Wardrope	Hunt
Denby	Handley	Hogg	Duncan
McAlpine		Reid	

The Dell

Referee: Mr G.H. Muir   **Attendance:** not known

With no league games to look forward to, the clubs could always contrive another fund-raising fixture of some kind and the *Portsmouth Times* could conduct the traditional inquest into a poor turnout for a worthy cause, hoping that Jack Eastham's employers had given him 'an adequate guarantee' against an inadequate gate.

Not that his club thought the occasion worthy of their first eleven: they 'put an experimental sort of team into the field, and did well to run the Saints to a goal.' In a

game that 'produced some pretty football, and was always interesting to watch,' Hamilton's penalty gave Saints the lead, following 'a mild sort of foul' by Wardrope on Handley.

McKenzie was allowed to substitute for the injured Wardrope in the second half, a 'circumstance which emphasises the friendly nature of the game.' Probert equalized for Pompey, but McAlpine struck back for the Saints. And that was that.

William Probert equalised for Pompey.

Running tally:	Saints	29	Pompey	25	Drawn	6

Wednesday 27 September 1911   **Friendly**

Portsmouth   1   Southampton   1

Sanderson	Jones	Knight	Sheeran
Cross	Hunt	McLean	H. Brown
Warner	Cullen	Ireland	Hamilton
Reid	Stringfellow	Lee	Gibson
Wardrope	Dowling	Curry	Handley
Menzies		McAlpine	

Fratton Park

Referee: not known   **Attendance:** 'very meagre'

In the short break between these 'friendly' meetings, the *Echo*'s Reviewer suggested that, even if Eastham's testimonial had brought a top Football League club, rather than Portsmouth, to The Dell, that game would not have attracted a 'much larger' attendance: 'friendly matches, no matter whom the contestants may be, have little "drawing" capacity.' Following this poorly-supported 'return friendly' at Fratton Park, the *Portsmouth Times* was similarly concerned that 'football crowds nowadays will not patronise games in which there is nothing at stake.' Furthermore, Southampton, having managed two draws from four Southern League games, were not much of an attraction.

Having had the better of a scoreless first half, the Saints went ahead in the second, through Brown. After Curry had gone off injured, Cullen equalised.

Running tally:	Saints	29	Pompey	25	Drawn	7

Wednesday 25 October 1911   **Hants Benevolent Cup**

Southampton   5   Portsmouth   1

Knight	Wilcox	Sanderson	Dowling
Grayer	Brown	Warner	Stringfellow
Robertson	Slade	Croft	Louch
Kimpton	Hamilton	Menzies	Cullen
Denby	Handley	Wardrope	Duncan
McAlpine		Reid	

The Dell

Referee: Mr G.J. Ross   **Attendance:** 2,000

After a couple of shadow-boxing friendlies, it was back to the real competition of the Hants Benevolent Cup. Southampton took it seriously enough and went ahead, after 25 minutes, through Slade. Brown made it 2-0 at half-time and Wilcox added a third early in the second half. But it was Pompey's Dowling, 'starting from just over the halfway line,' to run through and beat the advancing Knight, who was 'credited with the best goal of the lot'.

A 'collision' with Knight forced Duncan to leave the field and, although 10-man Portsmouth 'played up well,' Hamilton scored twice more for the Saints. The *Portsmouth Times* was obliged to 'admit that Portsmouth were outplayed throughout, and the score by no means exaggerated the superiority of the victors.' Sentinel was more begrudging in the *Football Mail*: he thought Saints 'lucky' to have won by such a margin; and it was, after all, only the second time they had won this affair in six years.

Running tally:	Saints	30	Pompey	25	Drawn	7

Portsmouth 2 Southampton 0

Sanderson	Pearce	W. Knight	Kimpton
Warner	Stringfellow	Eastham	Brown
A.Knight	Taylor	Ireland	Hamilton
Menzies	Rollinson	Denby	Gibson
Wardrope	Jones	Lee	Handley
Reid		McAlpine	

Fratton Park

Referee: Mr J. Baldock

Attendance: 3,741

It was FA Cup Third Round day. But Saints and Pompey had both gone out in the First Round to Southern League's Coventry City and Bristol Rovers, respectively – the first time Southampton had ever lost in this competition to a side from this League.

So what better than a derby game at Fratton Park? The attendance confirmed what should have been obvious from the season's previous friendlies: the Hampshire public was not excited by these non-competitive matches; and nor, for that matter, was the Hampshire press.

Whatever, Portsmouth lost the toss, and defended the Milton Road goal. Knight was the busier goalkeeper but 'continued to distinguish himself by effecting some smart saves,' until Rollinson's 'clever effort' beat him just before the interval. Although Saints attacked 'in dashing style' early in the second half, Pompey came again and Taylor made it 2-0.

Running tally:	**Saints**	**30**	**Pompey**	**26**	**Drawn**	**7**

Final Word

Pompey did not sweep all opposition away in Division II, but they finished as runners-up, on goal average, to Merthyr Town, and that was good enough to get them back 'among the premier clubs of the South.'

Much of the credit meted out by the *Football Mail* went to manager Robert Brown. The season also turned out to be 'satisfactory' financially, the Portsmouth-supporting public being enthusiastic enough to turn up in respectable numbers no matter how obscure the opposition.

But George Swift's excursions into the transfer market had seen Saints descend deeper than ever into the economic mire. They just managed, by three points, to avoid swapping places with Pompey.

1912-13

Not surprisingly, Southampton brought in another new manager, Jimmy McIntyre, who was compelled to work on a very tight budget.

The major change at Fratton Park was the playing colours. White shirts and blue shorts gave way to blue shirts and white knickers.

As if having their Southern League meetings restored was not enough and as if they had missed their Western League fixtures, Saints and Pompey joined a new league, the Southern Alliance, along with seven other Southern League clubs, including Cardiff City and Croydon Common of Division II.

Jimmy McIntyre came to manage on a very tight budget.

Southampton 2 Portsmouth 3

Knight	Blake	Sanderson	Wright
Coates	F. Taylor	Warner	Stringfellow
Ireland	Kimpton	A. Knight	J. Taylor
Denby	Prince	Menzies	Rollinson
Tyson	Andrews	Martin	Jones
McAlpine		Reid	

The Dell

Referee: Mr A.E. Farrant (Bristol)

Attendance: 10,000

The big news of the day was two-fold: Southampton had recruited C.F. Tyson, a one-cap amateur centre-half; and Bert Lee, their skipper and regular centre-half, had declined to play at full-back.

Each side had made only a 'moderate start' to the League programme but the *Echo* respected the visitors' claims to be their hosts' equals in attack and to have 'superiority in defence… local opinion avers that there is not a better pair of backs in the Southern League than Warner and A. E. Knight,' the former a Southampton 'reject'; the latter an international and Olympic medallist.

The renewal of Southern League hostilities had the Dell turnstiles 'clicking merrily' as the Pompey contingent arrived in their customary numbers, though mostly wearing new favours of royal blue and white, 'which blended much better than the old combination.'

The Saints were 2-0 up by half-time, through an Andrews penalty and Denby, even though they had never looked particularly comfortable. In the second half, 'Pompey swarmed round the Saints' goal' until Wright scored 'grandly' from Jones's 'beautiful centre', whereupon 'a terrific cheer from Pompey's supporters rent the air, and the utmost enthusiasm prevailed.' Continuing to play 'with

GALLAHER'S CIGARETTES.

J. WARNER, PORTSMOUTH, 1909-10.

There was 'not a better pair of backs in the Southern League.'

A.E. Knight

desperate energy', the visitors soon equalised through Rollinson as the Southampton defenders 'stood looking at each other' and, in the last minute, Stringfellow scored Pompey's winner.

The 'grit and determination' that Portsmouth showed in their come-back pleased Sentinel:

> You can forgive many faults when you see a team trying as Pompey tried, in the face of big odds. I don't say that the actual football was of the same class as we used to witness in matches between the old rivals in days gone by, but on the other hand no twenty-two players wearing the Portsmouth and Saints colours ever fought more strenuously or whole-heartedly for the points. And, after all, give me a team of triers in preference to one which can play when the fit takes it – and we have had some of this in days of yore!

Echoist took defeat badly: he considered it a 'most severe blow' in that 'it involved the loss of prestige as well as of League points, and may lead to [a] loss of public support.' He went on to upbraid a visiting player – he thought it was Jones – for what he obviously considered an unseemly exhibition of triumphalism following the winning goal. He had 'turned a succession of somersaults all the way from the goal area to the centre of the field.'

Where would it all end?

Running tally:	Saints	30	Pompey	27	Drawn	7

Wednesday 16 October 1912   **Hants Benevolent Cup**

Portsmouth   2   Southampton   0

Bradley	Wright	W. Knight	Kimpton
Murray	Dowling	Dobson	Taylor
A. Knight	Martin	Ireland	Turnbull
Menzies	Rollinson	Denby	Prince
Hamilton	Jones	McAlpine	Andrews
Reid		Salway	

Fratton Park

Referee: not known   **Attendance:** 2,000

The curse of the weather struck this fixture once again, but it could have been worse: 2,000 people had turned up before 'a drizzling rain commenced'; and the fog held off until the game was underway. In fact, the takings were £96, the largest-ever for this fixture.

The match gave the Saints an opportunity to give new centre-forward Turnbull, from Coventry City, a run-out and to impress the critics in Portsmouth and in Southampton. Pompey dominated the first half and Martin gave them a 1-0 interval lead. In the second half, the Saints for a time had more of the play but Pompey made it 2-0 when Knight scored after his namesake had parried his penalty.

Running tally:	Saints	30	Pompey	28	Drawn	7

Wednesday 6 November 1912   **Southern Alliance League**

Southampton   0   Portsmouth   3

Kitchen	Small	Sanderson	Wright
Lee	Taylor	Warner	Stringfellow
Coates	Turnbull	Dexter	Martin
Toomer	Brown	Menzies	Rollinson
Prince	Andrews	Hamilton	Jones
Salway		Reid	

The Dell

Referee: Mr R. Keay   **Attendance:** 'about two thousand strong'

It seemed that fans and players alike were treating the new League seriously. A turn-out of 2,000 or so was 'fairly large', the *Echo* felt, for a mid-week match and 'the earnestness of the contestants was speedily demonstrated'.

With both teams putting 'a lot of energy into their work, … each goal was menaced.' But Portsmouth were 2-0 up at half-time, through Fred Rollinson and George Martin and, not long into

the second half, Martin completed the scoring.

Pompey had now beaten the Saints three times already this season and the home side were, Sentinel felt, in 'a precarious position… their style of play was in marked contradiction to the bright and crisp football of Portsmouth.'

Two-goal George Martin

Running tally:	Saints	30	Pompey	29	Drawn	7

Wednesday 20 November 1912   **Southern Alliance League**

Portsmouth 2 Southampton 0

Bradley	Mouncher	Kitchen	Kimpton
Warner	Stringfellow	Lee	Turnbull
Knight	Martin	Ireland	Oatley
Menzies	Gibson	Denby	Andrews
Hamilton	Duncan	Salway	Blake
Reid		McAlpine	

Fratton Park

Referee: Mr R. Keay   **Attendance:** 'not much more than 2,000'

If the *Echo* had considered 2,000 a 'fairly large' attendance for the first Southern Alliance derby a fortnight earlier, it appeared to be disappointed that 'not much more than 2,000 spectators' turned out for the 'return' fixture.

Yet, given the dubious quality of this new competition, the miserable weather – 'a very powerful wind' was blowing 'a cold rain' – and the less than scintillating form of the two sides (Southampton had lost 8-0 at Crystal Palace four days before) the attendance might surely be regarded as respectable.

The Saints gave Oatley, of Cowes, a chance to show his mettle at centre-forward, while Pompey fielded a right-winger by the name of Mouncher (who, interestingly, hailed from Southampton, although it went unstated as to whether he was related to ex-Saint Fred Mouncher). Neither trialist went on to fame.

Denby spent most of the game as a passenger, 'consequent upon a kick he had received' during a goalless first half.

The gale Saints had faced in that half then dropped. But Echoist was not making excuses for the way in which Pompey had the better of the second half, scoring twice without reply, through Adam Gibson and Frank Stringfellow: Portsmouth had 'once more proved their superiority over the Saints.'

Running tally:	Saints	30	Pompey	30	Drawn	7

Saturday 25 January 1913   **Southern League**

Portsmouth 2 Southampton 0

Sanderson	Wright	Kitchen	Blackmore
Warner	Stringfellow	Coates	Dawe
Knight	Mounteney	Ireland	Prince
Arnold	Rollinson	Denby	Salway
Hamilton	Martin	Lee	Blake
Reid		McAlpine	

Fratton Park

Referee: Mr F. Curtiss   **Attendance:** 14,000

No matter that it was still only January, the *Football Echo* was billing this 'final' derby of the season as a shoot-out between neighbours in the 'danger zone' of the Southern League's Division I.

With Saints lying 16th, a point ahead of Pompey in 18th place, this qualified as 'an event of more than average interest.' Portsmouth had already beaten Southampton four times this season and 'the general feeling at the great naval arsenal' was that they would make it five wins and overtake their visitors.

The *Echo* awarded 'three-fourths' of the first-half play to the home side, but an 'excellent' Saints defence held firm until the hour-mark, whereupon Pompey were awarded a penalty, when Denby was adjudged to have 'pushed Rollinson as the latter was dribbling up to goal.'

Not only was Echoist disturbed by this decision – 'the whole incident was clearly observed from the press-box and Denby's tackle seemed to be perfectly legitimate.' – but he took informal soundings and reported, a week later, that, although a friend of his, 'who may be regarded as quite impartial, differs, nevertheless, I still adhere to my opinion.'

Frank Stringfellow
'cooked Southampton's goose.'

As it turned out Kitchen 'saved brilliantly', but the referee ordered the spot-kick to be retaken and Warner scored with his second attempt.

Pompey sealed the victory in the 80th minute when Stringfellow 'cooked Southampton's goose'.

| Running tally: | Pompey | 31 | Saints | 30 | Drawn | 7 |

Final Word

The result of the 68th meeting between the two sides restored Pompey's lead in respect of games won. It also meant that they overtook the Saints in the table and thereafter 'scarcely looked back', finishing the season in what The Shrimp acclaimed as 'quite a blaze of glory'. For all that, it took them no higher than 11th, but that was six places above Southampton.

Portsmouth's financial situation was looking up too, but Echoist was so despondent about the Saints' season as to conclude that 'new men are wanted in every section of the team except that of goalkeeper,' where the veteran Kitchen remained a 'first-class custodian ... who imparts confidence to every other member of the defence.'

1913-14

Wednesday 17 September 1913   **Southern Alliance League**

Portsmouth   3   Southampton   1

Sanderson	Hogg	Steventon	Binder
Warner,	Thompson	Brooks	Dominy
Knight	Powell	Ireland	Pothecary
Walls	James	Small	Smith
Harwood	Shaw.	Denby	Andrews
Abbott		Hadley	

Fratton Park

Referee: Mr Farrant didn't turn up; un-named linesman officiated   **Attendance:** 'only 3,000'

Although the attendance for the third Southern Alliance encounter between the two sides was up to 3,000, the *Echo* nevertheless wondered whether their meetings had 'lost their attractiveness, or whether the Portsmouth Club's followers have become indifferent to football.'

Pompey took a 2-0 lead through James and Hogg, but Saints pulled a goal back three minutes before half-time, when Andrews scored from the spot. In the second half, the inexperience of the stand-in referee – the linesman

who had taken over when Mr Farrant failed to arrive – began to tell. He lost control, as 'the game degenerated into a scramble,' with 'two or three players getting out of hand and indulging in retaliation, which should have been checked.'

Eventually, a penalty was awarded against Brooks for 'flooring' Thompson. Warner scored from the kick. Portsmouth soon had another penalty for a foul by Small. This decision generated 'quite a heated discussion among the players… and the Portsmouth linesman ran over to express his opinion.' James 'sent wide' from the spot.

Disappointed at the game's 'unpleasant' episodes, Echoist felt that, 'had the appointed referee turned up the match may have taken a much smoother course.'

Running tally:	Pompey	32	Saints	30	Drawn	7

Wednesday 24 September 1913   **Southern Alliance League**

Southampton   1   Portsmouth   0

Kitchen	Binder	Heath	Thompson
Brooks	Smith	Probert	Stringfellow
Ireland	Prince	Dexter	Cummings
Hadley	Andrews	Walls	Buddery
Denby	Blake	Harwood	Gibson
McAlpine		Arnold	

The Dell

Referee: Mr A.E. Farrant (Bristol)   **Attendance:** 'barely 3,000'

On a 'brilliant fine, though rather windy' late afternoon – the match was scheduled for 4.45 p.m, although it inexplicably kicked off 10 minutes early – an attendance of 'barely 3,000' was again deemed 'very poor'. But at least Mr Farrant managed to make it down from Bristol, this time, to referee.

The Saints were close to full strength (for what it was worth), Small and Lee being out, but Pompey were fielding only four acknowledged first team players, with five of the side making their first appearance of the season and four of those their debuts.

One of those newcomers was goalkeeper Heath who was 'completely beaten… after Smith had cleverly run through' the Pompey defence to set up Prince for the game's only goal.

Running tally:	Pompey	32	Saints	31	Drawn	7

Wednesday 8 October 1913   **Hants Benevolent Cup**

Southampton   0   Portsmouth   1

Kitchen	Kimpton	Sanderson	Upton
Brooks	Dominy	Johnson	Stringfellow
F. Smith	Prince	Knight	Thompson
Small	W. Smith	Arnold	James
Lee	Andrews	Walls	Shaw
McAlpine		Reid	

The Dell

Referee: Mr H.W. Hull   **Attendance:** 1,623

The *Echo* thought it 'really remarkable how persistently bad weather' plagued this fixture: on this occasion 'a terrific thunderstorm broke over Southampton, and ruined any chances of a big gate' – the more's the pity as, seemingly for the first time at The Dell, they were counting a derby crowd in, rather than guessing the gate.

The only goal came five minutes before the interval. The Portsmouth defence had been under prolonged siege but then, when Small and McAlpine 'sandwiched' Thompson, 'they both fell, and James, nipping in, scored with a splendid shot.'

Running tally:	Pompey	33	Saints	31	Drawn	7

Thursday 25 December 1913   **Southern League**

Portsmouth   2   Southampton   0

Portsmouth		Southampton	
Heath	Hogg	Steventon	Kimpton
Warner	Stringfellow	Smith	Dominy
Knight	Mounteney	Ireland	Prince
Walls	James	Hadley	Andrews
Harwood	Upton	Denby	Blake
Arnold		McAlpine	

Fratton Park

Referee: not known   **Attendance:** 16,000

A highlight, for London's *Sports Gazette*, of a 'colossal holiday football programme' was the well-attended Southern League double-header between Southampton and Portsmouth.

Although the visitors had 'much the better', the *Echo* felt, 'of the opening exchanges,' they found Heath in 'excellent form'. But the home side

> began to gain the upper hand, and a splendid movement initiated by Stringfellow led to Mounteney scoring from Upton's centre. After this Pompey never looked back.

The game had an 'extraordinary number [of] painful accidents.' After clashing heads with Upton, Denby was a passenger on the wing and the young Arthur Dominy had to deputise at half-back. The *Echo* pleaded this switch in mitigation for Saints' defeat.

That was perhaps unfair as Pompey had their share of casualties, including Mounteney who had gone off 'crocked' in the first half but had returned, although 'obviously in pain,' to score 'with a hard drive which almost broke the net.'

Running tally: Pompey   **34**   Saints   **31**   Drawn   **7**

Friday 26 December 1913   **Southern League**

Southampton   4   Portsmouth   3

Southampton		Portsmouth	
Steventon	Kimpton	Heath	Hogg
Smith	Dominy	Warner	Stringfellow
Ireland	Prince	Knight	Armstrong
Hadley	Andrews	Walls	James
Lee	Blake	Harwood	Upton
McAlpine		Arnold	

The Dell

Referee: Mr J. Talks (Lincoln)   **Attendance:** 19,291

There was, the *Sports Gazette* enthused, a 'magnificent attendance' for the Boxing Day 'return', with the East Stand closed half-an-hour before the kick-off and 'other parts of the ground being rapidly filled.'

That included the 'track stand', the temporary bleachers that were not infrequently erected in front of the stands, to increase capacity when a big gate was anticipated at The Dell.

In fact, the crowd was unprecedented for a League game, netting receipts of £781 and 'it may be taken as granted that there were on the ground quite 20,000,

when one includes the officials of both clubs, stewards, attendants, and people who gained admission other than by the gates.'

Which led, of course, to problems. As already noted, getting 20,000-odd people into the Dell was one thing – how many of them could actually see the pitch when they were there was another and the hunt was soon on for a vantage point, as 'scores of youths climbed on to the roof of the east stand, while a 'light corrugated iron roof' at the Milton Road end

1907-14: Losing their Spurs ──────────────────────── 73

'yet the proprietors of these same journals issue Sunday papers which contain two or more pages of football reports! Was ever inconsistency and hypocrisy so closely welded together?'

The *Southampton Times* accordingly supported, with a 'clear conscience' the appeal from the Southampton board 'to keep the old ship afloat in this time of stress and trouble.' With more than 20 players 'in military service' – albeit mainly as Reservists, who were available to play – and with so many Saints fans 'away serving their King and country, some at the Front, others on the sea, others again in India, and hundreds in Kitchener's Army,' the directors explained that they felt obliged to keep things going at home as usual. There are thousands in this town and port who, in various capacities, are doing the Empire's work; and the only entertainment the majority of them get is their Saturday's match at the Dell. It is the duty of the Club to provide entertainment, but it cannot do so without sufficient funds. If the normal conditions were prevailing there would be no need to appeal for additional support, but, owing to the war everything is abnormal, and there has been a tremendous slump in the gates. Notwithstanding the most rigid economy on the part of the directorate, and a monetary sacrifice, cheerfully borne, by the players, the financial position is steadily getting worse.'

Hence the call by the *Southampton Times* to 'make a special effort' to pack The Dell on Boxing Day.

---

25 December 1914   **Southern League**

Portsmouth   0   Southampton   1

Neil	Thompson	Wood	Curtin	
Potts	Stringfellow	Small	Dominy	
Probert	Budden	Ireland	Kimpton	
Walls	James	Hadley	Jones	
Harwood	Robertson	Denby	Andrews	
Abbott		McAlpine		

Fratton Park

Referee: not known   **Attendance:** 9.494

The four-figure attendance at Fratton Park may not appear much of a response to the exhortations of the Hampshire press, but Portsmouth would record only one higher gate all season – and, indeed, throughout the entire War.

When the Saints took the field, many of them were drinking hot *Bovril*. The explanation, as revealed by the *Echo*, was their late arrival, after their hired 'motor char-a-bank' had broken down on the hill out of Titchfield, at 10.25 – the kick-off being timed for 11.15. They had thereupon set off for Fareham by foot, in the hope of catching a train, and had completed that two-mile journey when their vehicle, repaired by the enterprising driver, caught up with them. He had them at the ground at 11.15. In short, it was all a bit of a rush.

A solitary, late goal settled a 'a fast and thrilling contest.'

A 50th-minute injury to Dominy had obliged Southampton to re-shuffle their forward-line and it was Andrews, finding himself at centre-forward, who met a 'splendid centre' from Curtin to secure a win that was more 'decisive' than the score-line suggests.

Len Andrews moved to centre-forward and scored the only goal.

Running tally:	**Pompey**	34	**Saints**	33	**Drawn**	7

Southampton 4 Portsmouth 3

Wood	Curtin	Neil	Thompson
Small	Dominy	Potts	Stringfellow
Ireland	Kimpton	Probert	Armstrong
Hadley	Jones	Walls	James
Denby	Andrews	Harwood	Robertson
McAlpine		Abbott	

The Dell

Referee: Mr C.C. Fallowfield (London)   **Attendance:** 7,086

The overtures of the Southampton board were of no avail, in so far as barely more than 7,000 – and this including 'a large contingent of Portsmouth supporters', the *Echo* reckoned – came to The Dell on Boxing Day. Not that the weather helped: 'rain ceased just before the game started.'

While the Saints' forward-line 'could not get going, … the opposing quintet were very fast and nippy.' And they soon produced 'a lovely goal' when Stringfellow headed in from Robertson's 'magnificent centre'.

As 'first one side and then the other attacked,' the Saints 'were not long in arrears. Denby lobbed the ball between the Pompey backs for Kimpton to essay a dash. The centre-forward snapped up the opening with avidity, and shot a magnificent goal just a fraction of a second before being bowled over.'

With the play continuing to be 'contested at a tremendous pace, despite the heavy treacherous ground,' there were three more goals before half-time.

Portsmouth regained the lead through Armstrong, who 'steered the leather into the net' to complete his 'clever dribble'. Andrews made it 2-2 but Pompey took the lead for a third time through Stringfellow..

And they continued to dominate the early stages of the second half. Yet the Saints equalised through Dominy and then Curtin put them ahead for the first time in the match. Shortly after that, James went off injured and with him went any chance of a Pompey come-back.

Argus seemed pleased, in the *Southampton Times*, that it should have been Southampton whose holiday 'double' had probably

put an end to Portsmouth's aspirations to carry off the League championship. It may seem hard that the hand that rings the death knell to their hopes was their old rival's, but on the run of the two holiday matches between the two Hampshire teams no one can complain that fortune unduly favoured the Saints. The great point that told was that they lasted better than their opponents.

Running tally:	Pompey	34	Saints	34	Drawn	7

Wednesday 28 April 1915

Portsmouth 2 Southampton 0

Neil	Stringfellow	Buddery	not available
Harwood	Abbot	James	
Tattum	Arnold	Metcalf	
Probert	Thompson	Potts	

(plus Hogg, Turner and/or Upton in some versions)

Fratton Park

Referee: Mr C.C. Fallowfield (London)   **Attendance:** 1,601

Cup football survived the War, albeit with the novelty of extra-time being played at the first time of asking in FA Cup-ties. Saints endured two such games before going

out in a Third Round replay at Hull, but Pompey made their usual early exit – at Bradford Park Avenue. Like the Leagues, the FA was pilloried for continuing to play during the War, even though it gave substantial sums to war charities. Similarly, the Hampshire FA decided to donate the proceeds of the Pompey-Saints Benevolent Cup match to Army hospitals in France.

This failed to swell the attendance beyond its customary size for this competition and the match seems even to have been shunned by the local press. Only the most cursory of reports of it, with no evidence of Saints' line-up or of Pompey's final selection, survive – a symptom, perhaps, of the perceived public disapproval of football still being played? Then again, the *Hampshire Independent* that week carried a handsome photograph of the Hursley Hunt meeting at Crabwood, readers supposedly having no problem with fit young men galloping across country on fit young horses.

Having shown 'some pretty football, and had much the better of the attacking,' Pompey deservedly led 2-0, through James and Buddery (*left*), at half-time.

They then monopolised the second half but goalkeeper Wood 'stood between them and a big score.'

| Running tally: | Pompey | 35 | Saints | 34 | Drawn | 7 |

Final Word

The season ended with the Saints in sixth place, a point ahead of Pompey; both clubs in financial difficulties; the debate on the ethics of continuing with professional football still raging; and Argus of the *Southampton Times* still railing against the cant of the game's detractors, who remained silent on the appropriateness of other sporting events during war-time.

1915-16

It came to pass that it became impractical, as much as inappropriate, to carry on professional football. As we have seen, the crowds were not there to support it and the rail system, most especially the South Western Railway, was too preoccupied to facilitate it.

So the first half of the season would consist of friendlies, with the two sides averaging one a month against each other. Then, in the New Year, they would join Swindon, Cardiff, Newport County and the two Bristol clubs in the new South Western Combination.

Saturday 11 September 1915   **Friendly**

Portsmouth 2 Southampton 2

Gray	Hogg	Wood	Wilcox
Potts	Turner	Durham	Dominy
Probert	Abbott	Slade	Wheeler
Booth	James	Lee	Andrews
Harwood	Dix	Campbell	Blake
Arnold		Salway	

Fratton Park

Referee: Mr J. Baldock   **Attendance:** 'between three and four thousand'

Dominy put Saints ahead after two minutes, from 'a pretty run by Blake' and Wheeler added a second, 'following a neat combined movement by the Saints' front rank.' James 'cleverly' pulled one back early in the second half and, 'as the game wore on, Portsmouth stayed the course better than their rivals. Several of the Southampton players tired perceptibly' but, although Lee put though his own goal, they hung on – 'a trifle lucky,' the *Echo* conceded, 'to come home with half the spoils.'

| Running tally: | Pompey | 35 | Saints | 34 | Drawn | 8 |

Saturday 2 October 1915

Southampton 1 Portsmouth 2

Wood	Blackmore	Gray	Armstrong
Durham	Dominy	Potts	Stringfellow
Slade	Wheeler	Probert	Whittaker
Small	Chambers	Abbott	James
Campbell	Blake	Harwood	Holmes
Kenny		Arnold	

The Dell

Referee: Mr H.W. Hull **Attendance:** not known

Faced with reporting yet another friendly, the *Echo* decided that it was time for yet another eulogy on the local rivalry: 'Southampton and Portsmouth are the oldest of friendly antagonists, and a meeting between the two sides never loses its attractiveness as a fixture, whether the game be a League contest or a "friendly".'

The match hardly lived up to that billing. In the first half, 'fouls were rather unpleasantly frequent, and some little temper was introduced into the game.' And all we know of the second half is that, according to the *Evening News*, 'Portsmouth twice found the net and Southampton also scored.'

Running tally:	**Pompey**	36	**Saints**	34	**Drawn**	8

Saturday 25 December 1915 Friendly

Portsmouth 1 Southampton 1

(probable)		(probable)	
Gray	Hogg	Gibbon	Wilcox
Potts	Stringfellow	Porter	Dominy
Probert	Turner	Slade	Wheeler
Abbott	James	Small	Page
Harwood	Marsh	Lee	Blake
Arnold		Passmore	

Fratton Park

Referee: not known **Attendance:** 2,000

With rain falling 'in torrents' for most of the match and much of the pitch under water, conditions 'could not well have been worse,' said the *Evening News*.

Even so, the home side was on 'excellent form, and controlled the elusive ball cleverly.' William James (*left*) and Stringfellow, who was 'in his element', each had 'atrociously bad luck' – so much so that Portsmouth, who 'deserved to win with a substantial margin,' were held to the one goal by Joe Turner (*right*).

Page replied late 'with the best shot for which Southampton forwards were responsible.'

Running tally:	**Pompey**	36	**Saints**	34	**Drawn**	9

Southampton   **2**   **Portsmouth**   **1**

Gibbon	Wilcox	Gray	Hogg
Lee	Dominy	Potts	Armstrong
Slade	Wheeler	Priestley	Turner
Kimpton	Andrews	Abbott	James
Small	Blake	Harwood	S. Smith
Passmore		Arnold	

The Dell

Referee: Mr R.C. Wilding   **Attendance:** 'quite a good one as things go nowadays'

The Saints' financial position was more than ever a matter of concern and, prior to the game, the clubs' directors once more appealed to the public for support. Alas, the weather - after heavy overnight rain, a 'strong wind blew across the ground' - was not exactly conducive to rallying around an economically beleaguered football club, although the *Echo* noted that the stands were 'well patronised'. James's 'low curling shot' on 25 minutes gave Pompey a 1-0 lead at half-time. The *Echo* could not find room for a report on the last 45 minutes, but the *Evening News* managed to squeeze in the essential details:

> Dominy equalised ten minutes after the restart, from which stage to the close the Saints had most of the game into which some temper was introduced, and three minutes from the close Dominy scored the winning goal amid great excitement.

Running tally:	**Pompey**	**36**	**Saints**	**35**	**Drawn**	**9**

Portsmouth   **2**   **Southampton**   **2**

Gray	Hogg	Wood	Wilcox
Potts	Stringfellow	Eglin	Kimpton
Probert	James (Turner)	Slade	Wheeler
Abbott	Flannigan	Ellerington	Andrews
Harwood	Armstrong	Campbell	Blake
Arnold		Passmore	

Fratton Park

Referee: Mr R. Pook   **Attendance:** not known

Friendly or not, 'the game opened at a fast pace,' according to the *Evening News*, 'and great keenness prevailed.' The Saints scored first through Andrews's 'really magnificent swinging shot.' from 25 yards. But 'this reverse spurred Portsmouth on' and James equalised with 'a clever effort'. In doing so, he collided with Wood and had to be carried off. The injury would ultimately lead to his substitution, though not before each side had again scored, through Hogg and Wheeler, respectively.

This was not, of course, the first substitution in this fixture – the Eastham Testimonial in 1911 had afforded such an indulgence – but it seems to be only the second in 81 derby games. As a further aside on the line-ups, note the presence, at right-half for Saints, of Ellerington. Like Charlie McGibbon and 'Tich' Carter before him (see the 1909-10 reports), the guest from Middlesbrough would become the lesser-known father of a celebrated son: Southampton stalwart, Bill Ellerington.

Although 'some clever football was seen' in the second half, there was no further score, thanks largely to Wood who 'played magnificently in the Southampton goal and absolutely saved his side.'

Running tally:	**Pompey**	**36**	**Saints**	**35**	**Drawn**	**10**

Southampton 4 Portsmouth 2

Wood	Wilcox	Middleton	Hogg
Bert Lee	Dominy	Potts	Stringfellow
Orbell	Wheeler	Priestley	James
Ellerington	Blake	Wilson	Flannigan
Campbell	Youtman	A. Lee	March
Tomkins		Arnold	

The Dell

Referee: Mr R. Pook   **Attendance:** 'small... at the start'

On another of those 'dull, drizzly and depressing' afternoons, the attendance was predictably 'small'. With Saints having 'rather the better of the matter up to the interval,' Dominy completed a first-half hat-trick.

Not that there was an interval worthy of the name. As the *Hampshire Independent* put it, 'the teams simply turned round and went at it again.' Pompey still failed 'to get into their stride, and were distinctly disappointing,' and conceded a fourth goal, through Blake, with a quarter-of-an-hour to go.

But then, 'with the Southampton defence taking matters rather easily,' Stringfellow pulled two goals back.

Running tally: **Pompey** 36   **Saints** 36   **Drawn** 10

Double-header bonanza

The next two games were played on same day, at the same time, for the same charity.

This odd scheduling was perhaps an attempt to maximise the proceeds – for the Hampshire FA's fund for wounded soldiers and sailors – without stretching the local train services any further. But that is only a guess. Whatever its motives, this enterprise was rewarded with 'glorious weather', quite out of keeping with this competition's traditions: 'if anything, it was,' in the view of the *Echo*, 'almost too warm for football.'

Southampton 2 Portsmouth 3

Webb	Jones	Middleton	Carnes
Ronna	Dominy	Probert	McBain
Frisby	Wheeler	Priestley	Salter
Ellerington	Denyer	Sanderson	Flannigan
Campbell	Blake	Lee	Dix
Milne		Arnold	

The Dell

Referee: Mr L.J. Duncan   **Attendance:** 'probably 3,000'

It took only 10 minutes for the Saints to be 2-1 up, goals by Arthur Dominy and Denyer sandwiching a header by Gunner McBain.

The *Echo* thought this 'pretty smart work', even if goals had 'been cheap at the Dell this season.' Flannigan made it 2-2 on 35 minutes, when his 'screw shot from near the corner flag ... hit the inside of the far upright and rebounded into the net. Nobody was more surprised than the goalkeeper, except, possibly, Flannigan himself.'

Although Flannigan went off injured in the second half, Pompey's 10 men won the Southampton portion of this double helping when McBain scored again.

Running tally: **Pompey** 37   **Saints** 36   **Drawn** 10

Saturday 8 April 1916   **Hants Benevolent Cup**

Portsmouth 7 Southampton 0

Gray	Hogg	Jobbins	Wilcox
Potts	Stringfellow	Hood	Quinn
Emerson	Richardson	Reed	Bradley
Abbott	James	Bone	Pearson
Harwood	Sparks	Wright	Lawson
Rymark		Thompson	

Referee: Mr J. Baldock

Fratton Park

Attendance: 2,000

The *Echo* may have found the game 'one sided' but it was nevertheless 'enjoyable'. In the first half, the *News* felt that 'the Southampton goal seemed to bear a charmed life,' holding out until James scored just before half-time.

After the break, the Saints 'were seldom out of their own half'. Having changed ends, they no longer had the charmed goal and Stringfellow (3), James, Richardson and Harwood all scored for Pompey.

Running tally:	Pompey	38	Saints	36	Drawn	10

Friday 21 April 1916   **South Western Combination (War League)**

Portsmouth 0 Southampton 2

Gray	Hogg	Webb	Willcox
Potts	Stringfellow	Bert Lee	Dominy
Probert	Abbott	Eglin	Wheeler
Harwood	James	Small	Milne
A. Lee	Flannigan	Ellerington	Blake
Arnold		Hadley	

Referee: Mr H. Thompson (West Norwood)

Fratton Park

Attendance: 6,000

The 'pleasant' April weather continued and there was an encouraging Good Friday turn-out of 6,000 for what the *News* considered 'a keen match between these old rivals.'

Pompey suffered an early disruption. Shirley Abbott, who had started at centre-forward, was injured – twice – and resumed on the wing. One of their military

Shirley Abbott, Pompey's centre-forward, who was twice injured and switched to the wing.

Bill Ellerington, who capped 'fine work' at centre-half for the Saints by scoring their second goal.

guests, billed in the manner of the time as 'Sergt Milne', gave the visitors a 1-0 lead at the break.

The only goal of the second half, in which Southampton proved themselves 'the better side', was scored by Bill Ellerington, who capped his 'fine work at centre-half [with] a long shot through a maze of players.'

Running tally:	Pompey	38	Saints	37	Drawn	10

1914-19: Goodbye to All That

Southampton   3   Portsmouth   0

Wood	Wilcox	Gray	Jones
Lee	Pearson	Potts	Stringfellow
Eglin	Wheeler	Priestley	Probert
Kimpton	Milne	Arnold	James
Ellerington	Blake	Wardle	Hogg
Tomkins		Ryman	

The Dell

Referee: Mr H. Thompson (London)   **Attendance:** 5,000

This would be the 10th and last meeting of the season, the *Echo* reflected, between the 'oldest and friendliest of rivals.' The 'chief honours' in the South West Combination were at stake: a draw or a win would assure Pompey of this championship, whereas a Saints win would give them a 'sporting chance' of it. The Bank Holiday weather had reverted to 'cold and dull, with a gusty wind'. After a 'dour' and goalless first half, Sergeant Milne was the star of the second. First, he 'dribbled through all opposition' to set up Wheeler, 'who headed the ball into the net amid a great roar of cheering.' Pearson made it 2-0, whereupon the Saints 'took charge of the game, and just before the end Milne headed a glorious goal.'

Running tally:	Pompey	38	Saints	38	Drawn	10

Final Word

Their Easter Monday win left Saints in second place, a point behind Pompey, each of them having a game left to play. A 7-0 trouncing of Bristol Rovers at The Dell was not enough to overhaul Pompey, who clinched the title by beating Swindon 6–1 at Fratton Park.

1916-17

It was all change for the 1916-1917 season, as Pompey and the Saints were allowed to enter the London Combination, a 14-team league that managed to provide 40 matches. The two sides would play each other four times, while each would have two to four fixtures with other clubs. How it was decided who played whom how many times must remain a matter of surmise, but it was most certainly a vast improvement on the previous season's arrangements.

Portsmouth   0   Southampton   1

Middleton	Abbott	Wood	Donaldson
Potts	Turner	Henry	Dominy
Probert	Seaman	Ireland	Quinn
Sanderson	McBain	Ellerington	Milne
Howard	Carr	Campbell	Blake
Gray		Tomkins	

Fratton Park

Referee: Mr David (Swindon)   **Attendance:** 4,000

The *Hampshire Independent* attributed Southampton's 'rather lucky' win to 'the magnificent display afforded by Sapper A. Wood in goal.' And the only goal of the game, after 30 minutes, seems to have had a streak of good fortune about it: 'Blake made one of his dashes down the left wing, and, after a preliminary skirmish near the touch line, centred, and the ball skimmed under the crossbar, Middleton having no chance whatsoever.'

This 87th meeting between the two sides saw Saints move ahead again – for the first time since November 1912. But playing London teams was proving tough: with a quarter of the fixtures now completed, Portsmouth were bottom of the table, although Southampton were a respectable fourth.

Running tally:	Saints	39	Pompey	38	Drawn	10

Saturday 27 January 1917   London Combination

Southampton   1   Portsmouth   0

Jobbins	Hunter	Gray	Hogg
Giles	Pearson	Probert	Lee
Ireland	Wheeler	Priestley	Tilley
Ellerington	Milne	Potts	Turner
Campbell	Blake	Wardrope	Carr
Tomkins		McBain	

The Dell

Referee: Mr W.R. David (Swindon)   **Attendance:** 'a couple of thousand'

It was a sign of the times that the *Echo* found the 'names of the visitors… a little unfamiliar.' Stringfellow and James were notable absentees, 'doing their bit' for King and country. Pompey were further handicapped when Turner went off, after a kick on the leg, and Wardrope 'was kicked in the mouth.'

As 'a cold wind blew across the ground, … spectators… punctuated the play by the rattle of their feet on the boarding of the stands to keep up the circulation.' Although Turner returned in the second half, the only goal of the game fell to Saints after 62 minutes, when Wheeler scored from a corner-kick.

Running tally:	Saints	40	Pompey	38	Drawn	10

Saturday 3 March 1917   London Combination

Portsmouth   1   Southampton   0

Collins	Shaw	Johnson	Blackmore
Barton	Simpson	Henry	Pearson
Probert	Armstrong	Giles	Quinn
Mercer	Pagnum	Burt	Slade
Powell	Carr	Campbell	Blake
Killigan		Milne	

Fratton Park

Referee: Mr Barrett (Swindon)   **Attendance:** 3,000

The match reports in both the *Evening News* and the *Southern Daily Echo* were overshadowed by the disquieting news that the price of each 'paper was going to be doubled to 'a penny' – although there were then, of course, 240 pennies to the pound.

Their reporters respectively found this 'interesting' game to be 'closely contested', with two 'sound' defences keeping clean first-half sheets. The home defence succumbed in the second half, however, when Carr headed the only goal from Armstrong's cross.

Running tally:	Saints	40	Pompey	39	Drawn	10

Southampton 2 Portsmouth 1

Johnson	Pearson	Gray	Hogg
Giles	Dominy	Probert	Mounteney
Gowers	Wheeler	Priestley	Armstrong
Pearce	Moore	Baily	James
Ellerington	Blackmore	Pettifer	Carr
Tomkins		Turner	**The Dell**

Referee: Mr J.R. Barrett   **Attendance:** '1,000... when the start was made'

Their March reverse at Fratton Park had been Saints' fifth defeat on the trot. And this had proved to be the mid-point of a dreadful run of 10 defeats lasting into the Easter weekend, when they had halted the slide with a draw and a win. So a miserable turn-out on a 'dull and showery' afternoon was perhaps to be expected – although the home fans might have anticipated a few goals against a Pompey side that had let in 32 in their eight Combination matches since that March win over Saints.

Joe Armstrong,
whose 'fast oblique shot'
gave Pompey the lead.

But it was Pompey who took the lead on 17 minutes, through Armstrong's 'fast oblique shot on the carpet.' Dominy soon equalised with a penalty, however, after Mounteney had handled in the area. The Saints clinched it in the second half, but the scorer and the manner of his winning goal go unrecorded.

Running tally:	Saints	41	Pompey	39	Drawn	10

Final Word

After their 10-match slide, Saints finished ninth in the Combination, having used more than 60 players in the process, with Sergeant Milne, their guest from Clydebank, making more appearances than anybody. Pompey, who just managed to pull themselves off the foot of the table, were one of three sides that conceded more than 100 goals in a season of football that was entertaining, not to say relaxed, with so many of the players doing full-time jobs or stopping by on leave from the services.

Details of that excitement were often difficult to come by, however, in the increasingly perfunctory, and frequently truncated, reports: newsprint was being rationed; there was a good deal of news from the Western Front and elsewhere to accommodate; and there remained that vocal body of opinion that held football to be a somewhat frivolous activity to indulge in during a war. It was a matter of proportion.

All of which meant that Saints' failure to play one of their 40 fixtures went unexplained. We do know that the presence of two Hampshire teams in a London table added to travel problems on a railway network giving priority to military transportation. Teams would often turn up late and, with it being hard enough sometimes to raise a team for a home match, away games could be even more problematic.

The London Combination had had enough – not only of Saints and Pompey but of Hertfordshire outposts, Luton and Watford, too – and all four of them were booted out.

1917-18

Banished from London circles, Southampton and Portsmouth were again forced to arrange a regular programme of friendlies, quite a few of them with each other. From January, they also had a new competition – the South Hants War League – along with Cowes, Royal Flying Corps School, Royal Navy Torpedo Depot, Thornycrofts and Harland & Wolff. Those other five teams each had a fair sprinkling of former professionals and, like Pompey and the Saints, could call on guest players. In fact, the two shipyard sides, Harlands and Thornycrofts, could, as often as not, call on more Saints than the Saints could (*see photo opposite*).

Saturday 1 September 1917   **Friendly**

Southampton   3   Portsmouth   2

Cooper	Blackmore	Middleton	Brooks
McFadyen	Dominy	Probert	Sims
Giles	Slade	Rhodes	Croal
Rutherford	J.Moore	Arnold	W.Moore
Pearce	Blake	Green	Rothwell
Tomkins		Ryman	

The Dell

Referee: Mr E. Tolfree   **Attendance:** 3,000

Denied competitive football, some 3,000 spectators turned out to see Saints and Pompey open their season with a friendly.

With Gunner McFadyen, formerly of Preston North End and Everton, and Corporal Rutherford, 'late of Fulham', in their ranks, Saints went behind, early on, to 'a neat shot' by Croal. Blake equalised after 35 minutes, with 'a brilliant bit of individual work' and Moore made it 2-1 to the Saints at half-time.

Dominy increased their lead in the second half. Probert 'reduced the adverse margin', from the penalty spot, but the home side held on to win..

Running tally:	**Saints**	42	**Pompey**	39	**Drawn**	10

Saturday 8 September 1917   **Friendly**

Portsmouth   4   Southampton   4

Middleton	Spink	Hall	Rutherford
Dunbar	Hogg	Giles	Pearson
Probert	Quinn	Priestley	J. Moore
Harwood	W. Moore	Walker	Milne
Goodwin	Rothwell	Foster	Croal
Arnold		Tomkins	

Fratton Park

Referee: Sergeant-Major W. Hawkins RMA   **Attendance:** 'fairly good'

Three-up at half-time, thanks to Moore (2) and Hogg, Portsmouth made it 4-0 early in the second half, through Quinn, and the game seemed, to the *Echo*, to be 'as good as over.' Whereupon 'the Saints pulled themselves together.' Milne started it with a 20-yarder and then 'Moore put on a couple of goals in quick succession.' Pearson completed the come-back and 'a remarkable game' ended in a 4-4 draw.

Running tally:	**Saints**	42	**Pompey**	39	**Drawn**	11

1914-19: Goodbye to All That

The dependence of Harland & Wolff upon Southampton players (*see the introduction, opposite*) is illustrated by this 1918-19 line-up.

Those numbered are **1** A.Dominy, whose exploits in this and the next two chapters hardly require elucidation here; **2** Small and **3** McAlpine, pre-war signings, who would not play for the Saints after the War; **4** Slade, an ex-Saint, by now with Fulham but guesting for Southampton and the shipyard. **5** T.Dominy, Saints Reserve; and **6** Chalcraft, a former Reserve. Conversely, **7** Fenwick and **8** Andrews, who had come from the North East as boiler-makers, would sign for Southampton and play for them in 1919-20. Two others, **9** Bradley (Hull City) and **10** Gilboy (Crystal Palace), were guesting both for Harlands and Saints. Incidentally, **11** Burnham would sign for Pompey but make only one friendly appearance.

Saturday 3 November 1917   **Friendly**

Portsmouth   3   Southampton   0

Collins	Hogg	Cooper	Blackmore
Probert	Danagher	Lyons	Dominy
Priestley	Hughes	Amos	Lee
Arnold	Turner	Roots	Moore
Harwood	Ashton	McClure	Pearce
Ryman		Tomkins	

Fratton Park

Referee: R. Pook   **Attendance:** 'something like 1,200'

An attendance of 'something like 1,200' for the two sides' third friendly engagement of the season was 'gratifying' to the *Evening News*.

Although Cooper was the busier goalkeeper, the ball kept 'travelling from end to end' in a goalless first half, which ended with the home side 'pressing hotly'. They maintained the heat at the start of the second half and Hughes duly headed in Hogg's corner to give them the lead. Another goal looked likely 'when Amos appeared to handle within the forbidden area, and a penalty kick seemed certain, but Mr. Pook, after consulting his linesman, bounced the ball instead, much to the general disgust.'

That served only to delay Pompey's second. When Cooper held a shot from Hogg, Arnold 'charged both ball and goalkeeper into the net.' Turner wrapped it up.

Running tally:	Saints	42	Pompey	40	Drawn	11

Tuesday 25 December 1917　　　　　　　　　　　　　　**Friendly**

Portsmouth　　1　　Southampton　　1

not available

Gray　　　　Blackmore
Ottaway　　Sims
Piggin　　　Lee
Wright　　　Pearce
Campbell　　Rutherford
McAlpine

Fratton Park

Referee: not known　　　　　　　　　　**Attendance:** 3,000

Having reflected on the outcomes of three friendly engagements already this season, the *Echo* never got round to reporting this Christmas Day encounter. Nor did the *Evening News* – although it did reveal that Southampton Ladies beat Portsmouth Ladies 4-0 at The Dell that day. It was left to the *Hampshire Independent* to divulge that Matthews scored for Pompey in the first half and Rutherford for Saints in the second.

Running tally:　　**Saints**　42　　**Pompey**　40　　**Drawn**　12

Wednesday 26 December 1917　　　　　　　　　　　　**Friendly**

Southampton　　2　　Portsmouth　　3

Hadfield　　　Blackmore　　Collins　　　'Smith'
Ottaway　　　Dominy　　　Probert　　　Danagher
Piggin　　　　Simons　　　Priestley　　Turner
Lee　　　　　Milne　　　　Arnold　　　Whalley
Campbell　　Blake　　　　Hollingsworth　Cummins
McAlpine　　　　　　　　Green

The Dell

Referee: Mr Jerram　　　　　　　　**Attendance:** 'a big holiday crowd'

The fifth meeting of the season was not quite the reunion it might have been: 'service calls' obliged Portsmouth to 'make a number of last minute changes, and the side, particularly the front rank, presented a very unfamiliar appearance.'

In the early stages, Smith – described as 'a well-known old Saint, who was deputising for the visitors' [but who remains unidentified] – was prominent, but it was Southampton who took the lead, Arthur Dominy

'making no mistake' from the penalty spot.

Turner levelled 'with a great goal' but Simons restored Saints' lead shortly before the interval.

Pompey won the game, however, with second-half goals from Danagher and Whalley.

Arthur Dominy,
who made 'no mistake'
from the spot.

Running tally:　　**Saints**　42　　**Pompey**　41　　**Drawn**　12

Portsmouth   4   Southampton   2

Middleton	Hogg	Hadfield	Smethurst	
Barton	Danagher	Parker	Blackmore	
Priestley	Turner	Piggin	Durnford	
Arnold	McKay	Porter	Pepper	
Howard	Quinn	McClure	Worcester	
Ryman		Bradley		**Fratton Park**

Referee: Mr Draper   **Attendance:** 4,000

For their first meeting in their latest war-time league the players produced football 'of a high standard.'

Portsmouth opened the scoring after 20 minutes when goalkeeper Hadfield, running out to clear, miskicked and fell, presenting Turner 'with a soft goal'. Pepper equalised but Piggin obligingly restored Pompey's lead when attempting to pass back to the accident-prone Hadfield. In the second half, Turner made it 3-1 with 'another soft goal.' By which time, it was Pompey's turn to take a pratfall: Quinn, 'in trying to clear miskicked into his own goal.'

McKay finished off the scoring with a goal that appears to have had nothing of the farcical about it.

Running tally:	Saints	42	Pompey	42	Drawn	12

Southampton   0   Portsmouth   4

Johnson (Hadfield)	Smethurst	Collins	Hogg	
Parker	Blackmore	Barton	Wooley	
Piggin	Durnford	Priestley	Woolworth	
Wright	Milne	Arnold	McKay	
Roots	Pepper	Howard	Quinn	
Porter		Turner		**The Dell**

Referee: Mr Jerram   **Attendance:** not known

The showers did not deter a 'capital holiday crowd, almost reminiscent of the good old days,' but they made the surface 'greasy' and the football 'was scrappy and frankly disappointing.'

Pompey showed 'a good deal more cohesion' and it came as 'no particular surprise' to the *Echo* when Wooley put them ahead on 10 minutes. It looked like 'a soft goal, but it afterwards transpired that Johnson strained himself in a vain effort to reach the ball, a mishap which hampered his movements afterwards.'

Wooley scored again and completed his hat-trick with the home defence 'in a bad tangle', before Hogg made it 4-0 just before the interval. Hadfield, who had missed his train at Basingstoke, turned up at half-time and was allowed to replace the injured Johnson. He kept a clean sheet but the Saints never looked like bothering Collins at the other end. There was 'a good deal of unnecessary feeling [in] the closing stages of the game' and Portsmouth finished with 10 men after Arnold had been cautioned and Turner 'ordered off the field.'

This 97th meeting was not only the first in which we have any record of a player being sent off but also the first in which Saints appear to have used a substitute. It was a significant landmark of another kind, though: Pompey eased ahead again in the number of games won – never again to be caught by the Saints.

Running tally:	Pompey	43	Saints	42	Drawn	12

Saturday 20 April 1918 **Friendly**

Southampton 2 Portsmouth 3

Hadfield	Smethurst	Trapp	Hogg
Parker	Blackmore	Miller	Whalley
Scott	Bradley	Priestley	Woodford
Wright	Simmonds	Arnold	McKay
Dines	Pepper	Jewet	Gill
Prince		Hollingsworth	

The Dell

Referee: Mr H. Wheeler   **Attendance:** 'a fine holiday crowd'

Having completed their league fixtures the previous Saturday, Portsmouth came to The Dell as South Hants War League Champions and Southampton, having won only one of the season's seven encounters to date, 'had something to rub off the slate,' the *Echo* reasoned.

This they failed to do, despite the addition of 'amateur international' J. Dines and of W.R. Scott, recruited from the Cadet Tank Corps Battalion.

The game kicked off in 'drizzling rain' and, with 'either end being visited in turn, [it] was contested at a rare pace.'

Pompey struck first, after 20 minutes, with 'a capital goal' by Whalley. Woodford made it 2-0 early in the second half but Pepper and Bradley brought Saints level – only for Whalley to clinch it for the visitors just before the end.

Running tally:	Pompey	44	Saints	42	Drawn	12

Final Word

Pompey won the new War League in style, dropping only two points and conceding but five goals. The two shipyard teams came next, with Saints a humiliating fourth – 13 points off the lead. Being the fourth-best team in Southern Hampshire was bad enough: being the third-best side in Southampton must have been an even bigger blow. That's if this League mattered at all: there were no reports of dancing in the streets of Portsmouth.

1918-19

The War continued. War-time football continued. There being no alternative, the South Hants War League would also continue, but without the airmen and sailors: the remaining five teams would play each other four times.

There remained plenty of slack in the season for friendly fixtures and, while the War brought shortages in most spheres of British life, there would be another glut of Pompey-Saints derbies.

Saturday 7 September 1918 **Friendly**

Portsmouth 5 Southampton 2

Collins	Evans	Hadfield	Smethurst
Probert	Armstrong,	Parker	Wiseman
Priestley	Turner	Lomas	Moore
Morris	McKay	Rutherford	Maclean
Harwood	Gill	Jewett	Blackmore
Green		Roots	

Fratton Park

Referee: not known   **Attendance:** not known

Under a 'broiling' Fratton Park sun, the two sides opened their season with yet another friendly. The man from the *News*, so excited by the occasion that he described it as a League match, noted with approval that, despite the wartime comings and goings, nine of the Pompey line-up had played the previous season.

Not that this continuity immediately availed them: they were behind after 20 minutes when a 'big shot' from Smethurst deceived Collins. Turner equalised and then, 13 minutes into the second half, put Pompey ahead. Gill, Turner again and Evans added further goals, before Moore pulled one back for Southampton.

Running tally:	Pompey	45	Saints	42	Drawn	12

Saturday 14 September 1918   Friendly

Southampton   1   Portsmouth   1

Hadfield	Smethurst	Collins	Hogg
Parker	Blackmore	Probert	Evans
Milnes	Tempest	Priestley	Turner
Roots	J. Moore	Prince	McKay
Jewett	Asher	Cooper	Gill
Wright		Green	

The Dell

Referee: Mr E. Tolfree   **Attendance:** not known

For the 'return' friendly, the Saints had guests: Tempest of Stoke and Milnes of Sheffield United. The former scored after 10 minutes, 'with a capital shot,' but Turner equalised from long range. Southampton 'had more of the play in the second half' and Collins was 'kept busy', but there was no further score.

Running tally:	Pompey	45	Saints	42	Drawn	13

Wednesday 25 December 1918   South Hants War League

Portsmouth   5   Southampton   1

Trapp	Hogg	Webb	Blackmore
Probert	Stringfellow	Parker	Smethurst
Priestley	Turner	Wright	Lacey
Arnold	Quinn	Diaper	Simmonds
Harwood	McKay	Jewett	Youtman
Porter		Samson	

Fratton Park

Referee: Mr Draper   **Attendance:** 5,500

The War had ended six weeks before Christmas – on the 11th hour, of the 11th day, of the 11th month, to be precise – but the substitute programme of war-time football would have to run its course. Which meant that it was Christmas as usual on the Solent, with two games between Pompey and Saints, the first of them before a pleasingly large post-war crowd of 5,500 at Fratton Park.

Within half-a-minute, Quinn had given Portsmouth the lead. Stringfellow put them two-up at half-time and scored again after the break.

Jack Harwood (*left*) made it 4-0 when he tried 'a long pot shot, taken from quite 30 yards out. Greatly to everyone's astonishment, Webb failed to negotiate the shot, and the ball dropped prettily just beneath the crossbar.' Smethurst pulled a goal back for the Saints but Quinn completed the rout, 'with a "solo" effort that took him clean through the opposing halves and full backs.'

Feeling that the score-line 'rather flattered' the home side, the *Echo* offered the excuse that 'Parker was hurt early in the game, and was afterwards unable to do himself justice.'

Running tally:	Pompey	46	Saints	42	Drawn	13

Thursday 26 December 1918   **South Hants War League**

Southampton 3 Portsmouth 6

Webb	Blackmore	Trapp	Hogg
Parker	Smethurst	Probert	Stringfellow
Blight	Lacey	Priestley	Turner
Diaper	Dunford	Arnold	Quinn
Jewett	Youtman	Harwood	McKay
Stamp		Green	

The Dell

Referee: Mr R.C. Jerram   **Attendance:** 'reminiscent of pre-war days'

'It was', said the *Echo*, 'like old times to be at the Dell,' with the Saints entertaining Pompey 'in the presence of a holiday crowd reminiscent of pre-war days.' That the visitors had 'been singularly lucky in keeping their players together' was again remarked.

Even so, Lacey opened the scoring for the home side after three minutes and that was how it stayed until 10 minutes before the interval when there was a sudden flurry of goals: Turner equalised; Dunford made it 2-1;

and Stringfellow levelled again. Soon after the resumption, Lacey gave Southampton the lead for the third time, only for Quinn to equalise once more. Pompey 'were playing a great game, and it was no particular surprise' when Stringfellow made it 4-3 with 'the best goal of the afternoon,' after which 'Portsmouth were top dog, and always looked a winning side.' Stringfellow added a fifth and Priestley's penalty wrapped it up 'just on the stroke of time.'

Running tally:	Pompey	47	Saints	42	Drawn	13

Friday 18 April 1919   **South Hants War League**

Portsmouth 1 Southampton 1

Trapp	Hogg	Wood	Johnstone
Probert	Stringfellow	Parker	Pritchard
Priestley	James	Green	Rawlings
Hamilton	Armstrong	Roots	Goode
Harwood	Turner	Campbell	Foxall
McKay		Hackett	

Fratton Park

Referee: Mr E.A. Rogers   **Attendance:** 8,000

The 'glorious' Good Friday sunshine brought Portsmuthians out in their thousands, the *News* recorded, 'on to the beach or along the roads to the hills laden with provender.' Some of them made it to Fratton Park, where a crowd of 'fully 8,000' reminded the reporter of 'the

piping days of peacetime, Southern League football.'

Pompey fielded nearly 'a full side' while the Saints had assembled 'their best team of the season,' the *Football Mail* judged. It included Alec Campbell – returning from military service and some 'capital' guest performances military service and some 'capital' guest performances for West Ham in the London Combination.

Portsmouth scored first when, from a Saints attack, the ball bounced out, and the Pompey forwards raced to the other end. Stringfellow initiated the attack, and the ball came to Hogg, who was well placed and found the net with a shot, just out of Wood's reach.

The home side 'continued to have a good share of the play' in the first half but Southampton came back, in the second, to equalise through a 'fast shot' by Rawlings – a maiden derby goal for a young centre-forward destined to become Saints' highest-ever scorer, until overtaken by Terry Paine.

Running tally:	Pompey	47	Saints	42	Drawn	14

Monday 21 April 1919

South Hants War League

Southampton 9 Portsmouth 1

Wood	Johnstone		Timpson	Armstrong
Parker	Pritchard		Probert	Stringfellow
Titmuss	Rawlings		Wynne	Turner
Roots	Goode		Hamilton	James
Campbell	Foxall		Harwood	Brownlee
Hackett			McKay	

The Dell

Referee: not known

Attendance: 'a fine holiday crowd'

After a 6-0 romp against Brighton on Easter Saturday, Portsmouth arrived at The Dell on Monday, 'weakly represented', the *Echo* conceded. They were behind after four minutes to a goal by Foxall but Stringfellow soon levelled. Further goals by Rawlings (2) and Campbell gave Southampton a 4-1 lead at the interval.

Yet 'one sound judge of football, an official of another prominent team' told the *Football Mail*'s Linesman of his willingness, at that stage of the game, to 'gamble a shilling' on an away win. Saints added five more

without reply, however, Probert missing a penalty. Pritchard, Goode and Foxall each scored and Rawlings got two more, a hat-trick that would not count in his 'official' tally, as he went on to become the only Saint ever to achieve 10 Football League hat-tricks.

Linesman could not quite believe it – by his reckoning, Arthur Wood (*left*) had been the busier 'keeper – but agreed with his friend's description of the game as 'a series of accidents', mainly attributable to Timpson who, in his second and last game in Pompey's goal, had 'lost his nerve completely after [Saints'] silly fourth goal.'

Running tally:	Pompey	47	Saints	43	Drawn	14

Final Word

That remarkable result concluded Saints' season in the South Hants War League, in which they again finished fourth, behind Pompey and the two shipyard sides. The loss of three Easter points to Southampton meant that Portsmouth came second, by that margin, to Harland & Wolff (seen with the trophy on page 87).

The season's 'Battle Royal' – as the *Echo* headline put it – occurred when these top two sides met at The Dell, on 29 March, in the semi-final of a hastily-contrived tournament called the Hants FA Victory Cup. It deserves a mention here, if only for the benefit of those readers who may be wondering when we are going to get down to the nitty-gritty of the Southampton-Portsmouth rivalry, the real meat – not all this palaver about football, but when the two communities seriously locked horns in bitter physical conflict.

You will have noted, in the foregoing accounts of the first 20 seasons, an occasional reference to frayed tempers among the players and their 104 meetings, in that time, appear to have produced only one sending-off (of Pompey's Turner in April 1918).

But, apart from the incident at Fratton Park in November 1903, when the referee 'admonished' a spectator for using 'bad language' towards Kelly Houlker, and at The Dell in October 1908, when Mr Howcroft upbraided a section of Saints' adherents for encouraging John Bainbridge to 'get his own back', derby-day crowds do not appear to have caused any serious trouble – well, none that the local press deemed newsworthy anyway.

This is not because society was better disciplined back in the 'good old days' – riotous behaviour has never been that unusual in England; and football was never immune to it – but there does not appear to have been any tendency in Southampton or Portsmouth to turn a pleasant afternoon supporting local heroes into an unseemly brawl. Until, that is, Pompey came to The Dell for that 'Victory' Cup-tie in March.

There was 'a good deal of unnecessary temper,' the *Echo* felt, in a match that ended in a 4-1 win for Harland & Wolff. But the worst was yet to come: 'as the players left the field the public swarmed over the ground, and an attempt was made by a section of the spectators to mob the referee.'

Although Sergeant Godwin of Aldershot 'reached his dressing room in safety, … a regular free fight followed on the field between the partisans of the rival sides, and it was not until more than one combatant had been badly mauled that order was restored.'

While not disputing the fairness of the result, the *News* took issue with the referee for his

> big mistake in arguing with players when his decisions were questioned… Had be been firm, and not tried to justify his decisions by argument, the disgraceful scenes after the match would not have occurred. It was most regrettable that the spectators got out of hand, and the attitude of a large number of Servicemen was not at all justified.

This criticism both of the referee and of servicemen in the crowd – a subtle hint that the rioting may have been sparked off by conscripts finding an excuse to take a poke at an NCO? – was absent from the Southampton newspapers: the *Echo* felt that Sergeant Godwin had 'handled a difficult game… admirably.'

Whatever the truth of the matter, the episode appears to have been a three-day wonder and the comment by the *Southampton Times,* on the following Saturday – that this was 'the first time that anything of the kind has occurred at the Dell, and the breach of the ethics of good sportsmanship has caused much resentment' – appears to have been the last word on the matter.

And rightly so. With so many young men dead and buried across The Channel, there was surely something especially unseemly about a parochial fight over a Victory Cup-tie.

Football now had 20 years of peace-time conditions to which to look forward – years of initially similar, but then very different, experiences for Pompey and Saints.

READ ON: The *Times* protest against war-time football is cited by Frank Keating in his 90th-anniversary recollections. See 'Sources'

Chapter 7
1919-24: In a Different League

Football returned to normal for the 1919 season – well, almost normal. Saints and Pompey were still in the Southern League casting 'longing eyes', as the cartoonist saw it, on the Football League.

The latter had again rejected 'fusion' but had expanded from 40 to 44 clubs, adding two new clubs to each of its two divisions. A solution was, however, only a season away. The First Division of the Southern League would be absorbed into the Football League, albeit as a humble Third Division.

So Southampton and Portsmouth would at last have the chance to climb through the ranks.

Portsmouth have been casting longing eyes at the League in common with other Southern clubs, but the suggested fusion scheme did not find favour.

1919-20

One of the new clubs elected into the expanded Football League Division II was West Ham United, which caused a lot of indignation in Southern League circles.

Sadly, so diminished was the Southern League by this time that the controversy was totally eclipsed in the national press by the even greater indignation provoked by Arsenal – who had dropped Woolwich from their name and moved to Islington in 1913 – being 'elected' to Division I, leapfrogging higher-placed Wolverhampton and Burnley.

The Southern League retaliated against the League's adoption of West Ham by scrapping the maximum wage. But it was too little too late: none of its clubs was any longer in the position to poach top League players, as Pompey and Saints had done at the turn of the century.

Saturday 26 July 1919   **Friendly**

Portsmouth 5 Southampton 3

Floyd	Riddle	Wood	Tee
Probert	Stringfellow	Parker	Dominy
Stevens	Turner	Fenwick	Rawlings
Thompson	James	Kimpton	Hinton
Harwood	Brown	Bradburn	Raybould
McKinnon		Andrews	

Fratton Park

Referee: Mr F.A. Rogers   **Attendance:** between 3,000 and 4,000

With the resumption of Southern League activity still five weeks away, Pompey and Saints met in an abnormally early friendly, as part of the Peace celebrations. Portsmouth took the opportunity to blood a couple of captures from war-time League opponents – goalkeeper Floyd from Cowes and Riddle, a winger from Thornycrofts – neither of whom would make it into the League team.

Seldom loth to talk-up a friendly derby, the man from the *Echo* nevertheless found it 'surprising' that this game proved 'keen, fast and full of incident.' In a flurry of scoring towards half-time, Dominy gave Saints the lead, but two goals from Stringfellow sent Pompey in 2-1 up. Dominy levelled early in the second half, but Portsmouth were soon ahead again, when Turner converted a pass from Brown, 'the best winger on view.' The imperturbable Dominy completed his hat-trick. But Pompey were playing 'the more forceful football' and, as the Saints' full-backs, who had each 'been "in the wars," tired towards the end of the game,' heroics from Wood could not keep out the home side, who made it 5-3 through Turner and James.

Running tally:	Pompey	48	Saints	43	Drawn	14

Saturday 18 October 1919   **Southern League**

Portsmouth 5 Southampton 1

Smelt	Hogg	Wood	Barratt
Probert	Stringfellow	Parker	Dominy
Knight	Armstrong	Campbell	Rawlings
Thomson	Buddery	Kimpton	Moore
Harwood	James	Bradburn	Foxall
Turner		Hackett	

Fratton Park

Referee: not known   **Attendance:** 'nearly' 20,000

Despite 'the restrictions and difficulties' of early post-war transport, the largest crowd since 1914 came to Fratton Park.

The visitors may have been down in ninth place, but Portsmouth were lying second in the table. And their 'superiority… was abundantly demonstrated' in a game that was 'the tit-bit of Southern League football' for the *Evening News*.

Leading only by an Armstrong goal at half-time, Pompey added three more, through Hogg (2) and James, before Dominy succeeded with 'a first-timer' from Rawlings's 'nice' pass. Armstrong completed the rout, though, with a minute to go.

Recorder was able to get some 'inside dope' for his *Echo* readers when he accosted the Saints party at Fratton Station after the match.

They were returning by train after another hazardous outward journey by char-a-banc: their vehicle had been backed into by a farm-cart which 'nearly broke it in two.'

Concurring with the Southampton player who felt they had been 'beaten by a fine side,' Recorder expressed his own admiration for Portsmouth as 'an excellent combination of foot-

ballers [whose] standard of all-round play... would not have disgraced First Division League football.'

Bert Rawlings,
the record-breaking goalscorer
who, on this occasion, set up
the goal for his senior strike-partner.

Running tally:	Pompey	49	Saints	43	Drawn	14

By The Way

The two sides each went out of the Cup at the first hurdle, Pompey at Valley Parade and the Saints in an Upton Park replay, thus adding to the insult of West Ham's defection to the Football League. Andrews broke his leg in that game and, on the urging of Bert Lee, Southampton replaced him with Bert Shelley, a young player from Romsey of the Hampshire League. He would play in every game for the rest of the season and would eventually break the club's appearance record.

Saturday 28 February 1920   **Southern League**

Southampton 0   Portsmouth 0

Wilcox	Barratt	Robson	Hogg
Parker	Dominy	Probert	Stringfellow
W. Turner	Rawlings	Knight	Buddery
Shelley	Moore	Abbott	Armstrong
Bradburn	Foxall	Harwood	James
Hackett		J. Turner	

Referee: Mr W.E. Russell

The Dell
Attendance: 17,879

If the meeting of the two sides at Fratton Park had been 'the tit-bit' for the *News*, this game was for Recorder 'THE MATCH OF THE SEASON'.

Pompey were heading the table, with the Saints in 14th place, 16 points in arrears. Interest was 'tremendous', as manifested in letters 'from all over the country' requesting reserved seats. The Southampton directors were determined, however, to 'follow their usual policy... and would give the seats to the first-comers on the day of the match. This will give the thick-and-thin supporters of the club an equal opportunity with any other spectators of witnessing the match.'

With 'the certainty of a huge crowd' – and most probably with Pompey's game against Harland & Wolff at The Dell the previous March in mind – Recorder was moved to address the subject of 'Barracking':

Without going into the obvious arguments concerning sportsmanship, it is bad business to shower insulting epithets upon the referee if he gives decisions which do not appear to some of the spectators to be correct. If such conduct continues one result will be that ten thousand people who like football and wish to see it played will have their enjoyment completely spoiled, and there will be the possibility of the Southern League taking the extreme course of closing the ground. The old days, when the referee had to make his escape by a back exit if the home team lost, are gone, and, so we hoped, had the days of barracking, as far as Southampton is concerned.

The crowd was indeed 'huge', but the 'REMARKABLE SCENES' that made the headlines were good-humoured:

> Everywhere in the town before the match the blue and white colours of Pompey could be seen fluttering gaily. Long before the time of the match the gates at Archer's-road and Milton-road were packed with long queues of spectators eager to get into the ground. Half-an-hour before the kick off the stands were absolutely crowded, and the terraces seemed to be so full that it was perfectly certain that all the men who wanted to get into the ground would be unable to do so. Every point of vantage was seized and more than one adventurous sailor and civilian climbed to a perilous place on the hoardings surrounding the field. Considerable amusement was caused by many people trying to climb the tiled roof of the telegraph office at the Archer's-road end of the ground and slipping down the precipitous slope. Not only did the people crowd in all the available places on the terraces and stands, but they were packed along the touch-lines

They were even on the telegraph posts and in the branches of trees at the Archers Road end.

All things considered one might have forgiven the players for standing around and watching the spectators – not that it was, by any means, a poor game.

Southampton began on the offensive – 'the first half was entirely in their favour' – but the longer the match went, the more dominant Pompey became and the Saints were long 'fighting with their backs to the wall [but] continued to hold out gallantly.' So much so that Recorder considered the result 'a triumph for the forcefulness of the home team' and, rather than attribute it to any 'falling off in form' on the part of the league-leaders, he praised the way the under-dogs had risen 'splendidly to the occasion'.

So a gallantly-gained point for the Saints, which did not affect Pompey's championship aspirations overmuch. There was, though, a worrying aspect to this encounter as far as Southampton were concerned: the suitability of The Dell as a venue for top class football. Spectators had been shut out with fewer than 18,000 people inside. Linesman, of the *Football Mail*, was scathing about the stewarding: 'those inside did not pack properly and thus make room for quite a large number from Portsmouth who did not arrive before the gates were closed.'

Pompey were greeted at Fratton Station by their adherents serenading them with a variation on a familiar refrain:

> Tho' you didn't beat the Saints
> Never mind!
> Tho' you didn't beat the Saints
> Never mind!
> You are still up on the top
> And you'll beat the blinking lot
> Tho' you didn't beat the Saints
> Never mind!

Running tally:	Pompey	49	Saints	43	Drawn	15

Saturday 15 May 1920   **Hants Benevolent Cup**

Southampton 2 Portsmouth 0

Wood	Williams	O'Donnell	Hogg
Parker	Dominy	Potts	Stringfellow
Titmuss	Rawlings	Probert	Abbott
Shelley	Boyes	Thompson	Quinn
Campbell	Foxall	Harwood	Youtman (Frampton)
W. Turner		J. Turner	

Referee: Mr R.R. Crump

The Dell
Attendance: 8,000

The usual Pickford Cup scenario: each side augmented by the odd new face, Pompey's being the goalkeeper, O'Donnell. At least, he was a new face in the Portsmouth goalmouth, although he was well-known in both towns in his full-time occupation as the conductor of the Royal Marine Artillery Band, which made frequent concert appearances on Southampton's Royal Pier. He was at fault with the first of Saints' two second-half goals when he 'met the ball in his hands, but allowed it to go over his head into the net.'

Foxall made it 2-0 in the closing minutes. By then, injuries had reduced each side to 10 men – and it would have been nine in Pompey's case had Frampton not been allowed to replace Youtman.

Pompey had arrived as League champions, yet the *Echo* was in 'no doubt that the Saints were the better side on the day's play, although when Stringfellow and his men got going Pompey's forwards impressed greatly by the easy swing of their movements.' As for conductor O'Donnell, he would not be required to give up the swinging movements of his day-job: this would be his one and only performance in the Portsmouth goal.

| Running tally: | Pompey | 49 | Saints | 44 | Drawn | 15 |

Final Word

A grand season for Pompey, who won their second Southern League Championship. Yet it was third-placed Cardiff who leap-frogged them into the Football League Division II – at the expense of Grimsby.

1920-21

As it transpired, Grimsby were reprieved when it was decided that the remaining 21 clubs in the First Division of the Southern League should join them in a new Third Division of the Football League.

No matter that Grimsby's nearest opponents would be Norwich City, the Saints and Pompey were at last in a position to reach the pinnacle of professional football on merit – with no need of any London-style 'election'.

Saturday 11 September 1920   **Football League Division Three**

Southampton   2   Portsmouth   0

Allen	Barratt	Robson	Thompson
Parker	Williams	Probert	Stringfellow
Titmuss	Rawlings	Knight	Buddery
Shelley	Moore	Abbott	James
Bradburn	Foxall	Harwood	Beedie
W. Turner		J. Turner	

The Dell

Referee: not known   **Attendance:** 18,000

A record attendance was expected for this historic meeting and when the gates closed on another Dell crowd of 18,000, a quarter-of-an-hour before the kick-off, Linesman of the *Football Mail* again complained that 'several thousand more could have packed in.'

When the band stopped playing, the crowd kept going: 'the Pompey Chimes were sung by gaily bedecked supporters and a good natured banter was indulged in.'

The Saints took the lead, after 15 minutes, when Moore beat Robson from Foxall's corner. Not long after, the referee 'upset' the Portsmouth players when he 'overlooked the appeal for a foul against Rawlings, who knocked Knight over, and then awarded a penalty for what appeared to [Linesman] to be a clear case of accidental handling by Probert.' Parker converted and Saints led 2-0 at half-time. And that's how it stayed.

'While congratulating our sporty neighbours on the success of their enthusiastic and go-ahead team,' Linesman felt that Pompey had had 'wretched luck'. Indeed they had. Soon after the injured Harwood had become a passenger at outside-left, Beedie, who had moved inside, 'received a nasty knock,' leaving the visitors with 'a pair of crocks as a left wing pair, neither of whom who could raise a trot.'

| Running tally: | Pompey | 49 | Saints | 45 | Drawn | 15 |

Portsmouth 0 Southampton 1

Robson	Thompson	Allen	Barratt
Frampton	Stringfellow	Parker	Dominy
Probert	Reid	Titmuss	Rawlings
Knight	Buddery	Shelley	Moore
Abbott	James	Campbell	Foxall
J. Turner		W. Turner	

Fratton Park

Referee: Mr A.L. Grinstead

Attendance: 20,585

A week later, Linesman was observing the arrival, in Fratton, of the soccer-lovers of Southampton, 'by vehicles various – train, char-a-banc, motor-car, boat and "push-bike" – and by half past two the stands were full and the enclosures packed.'

Pompey kicked-off 'towards the Workhouse' and were soon appealing for a penalty. They had Linesman's support – 'Reid was brought down as he ran through' – but not the referee's. Linesman excelled himself with his detailed account of the game's only goal, after nearly half-an-hour. It followed 'thrilling work by Foxall', whose centre

led to a scrimmage, in the course of which Campbell tried a shot, which Robson dived for. The ball struck the upright, and glanced back high towards the centre of the goal, and Rawlings headed in to the vacant net while Robson was on the ground.

On reflection, Linesman thought the goal 'a bit lucky'. But he conceded that 'the honours went to the better all-round eleven, though there was nothing much to choose between the

teams, and the odd goal verdict just sums up the relative values.' It was sufficient to make the away fans 'delirious with delight' and to create another 'remarkable scene'.

With the Saints in second place – behind Crystal Palace on goal average – and Pompey eighth, the mood in Portsmouth was reflected in 'an appalling number of letters' to the *Football Mail*. Linesman explained why none of them would be published:

Fred Foxall,
whose 'thrilling work'
led to the game's only goal.

While offering my apologies to readers for refusing to find room for their epistles, I must explain that first of all pressure on our space makes it impossible to publish their opinions; and secondly, I cannot see that any good purpose would be served in giving scores of ideas as to how the directors should select their side or the amount of money that should be expended to persuade Chelsea to part with Cock, or Millwall to transfer Broad.'

Running tally: **Pompey**   49   **Saints**   46   **Drawn**   15

By The Way

For the second season running, Saints suffered the ignominy of going out of the Cup (this time in the Third Round) to former Southern League opponents who had been catapulted into the Football League Division II: Cardiff City. Pompey went out two rounds earlier at South Shields, a middling side from that division.

Portsmouth 1 Southampton 0

Robson	Beedie	Parker	Barratt
Probert	Stringfellow	W. Turner	Dominy
Abbott	Buddery	Titmuss	Rawlings
Brown	Watson	Shelley	Johnson
Martin	Philpin	Campbell	Boyes
J. Turner		Butt	

Referee: Mr E. A. Head (London)

Fratton Park
Attendance: 6,740

A record crowd for the competition included the crew of a Japanese battleship on a courtesy visit to Portsmouth. One can only wonder what they made of the spectacle – let alone the 'Pompey Chimes'.

Every bit as unusual was the Saints' selection of goalkeeper: right-back Tom Parker. Tommy Allen was not available and there was no other suitable replacement.

Parker conceded the only goal of the game, 15 minutes into the second half, when Buddery headed home a centre from the left wing.

Tom Parker,
an unlikely goalkeeper.

Running tally:	Pompey	50	Saints	46	Drawn	15

Final Word

Although they had begun the season as Southern League champions, Pompey were not among the Third Division pace-setters. The Saints were. And they were looking like promotion contenders until two 1-1 draws with Crystal Palace over Easter, followed by a poor run-in, left them in second place, five points behind Palace. The first champions of the Third Division took the only promotion slot available.

1921-22

The Football League was now extended to 88 teams, with the Third Division becoming the Third Division (South) and a Third Division (North) being introduced. So Saints and Pompey would together be playing in their fourth different league in the space of four seasons.

The *Football Echo* found cause for optimism in both towns. The Portsmouth directors had 'adopted a wise policy in parting with players who were responsible for a deal of trouble at the early part of last season, and for much grumbling later on,' while retaining those 'thought worthy of confidence.' Which meant that 'practically the same eleven that finished up last season so well can immediately be placed in the field.'

The Saints' 'high hopes' of promotion were justified, Recorder felt: 'it may be unwise to anticipate success in such an uncertain game as football,' but he believed there was 'a real foundation for light-hearted contemplation of coming events.'

Southampton 4 Portsmouth 0

Allen	Barratt	Robson	Bligh
Parker	Dominy	Probert	Watson
Titmuss	Horton	Jenkins	Cherrett
Shelley	Johnson	Brown	Hoten
Campbell	Foxall	Martland	Beedie
Butt		Robinson	

The Dell

Referee: Mr J.T. Howcroft (Bolton)   **Attendance:** 4,663

Mr Arnfield (*right*) had been at Southampton, initially as the part-time 'financial secretary', since 1893. It was he who proposed the motion that the club become a limited liability company and he had been the company secretary of Southampton Football & Athletic Company since its foundation in 1898. So this 'benefit' was well deserved.

Both sides were going well in the new Division III (S), the Saints having dropped only four points in their first nine games, while undefeated Pompey were a point behind them. But even the *Echo* admitted that this match, with each attack under-strength, was 'naturally much different in character from a League encounter.' Having 'had the better of the exchanges in the first half,' the Saints proved 'a yard or so faster' than Pompey after the break, when all four goals were scored.

Dominy walked the ball into the net for the first. Foxall supplied a 'brilliant' cross for Horton to head the second and then completed a solo run for the third. Horton 'scrambled' the final goal 'towards the close of the game, when darkness was rapidly causing the football to become haphazard.'

It seems that the only respect in which Pompey matched Saints on the day was in their dress.

Praising both teams for the 'very smart style in which they turned out,' *Echoist* observed that, while 'the Saints have a reputation as "the best dressed side",' Portsmouth had, on this occasion, 'shared the honours of personal appearance.'

Running tally:	Pompey	50	Saints	47	Drawn	15

Portsmouth 1 Southampton 0

Robson	Blyth	Swinnerton	Barratt
Cooper	Stringfellow	Turner	Brown
Abbott	Cherrett	Titmuss	Horton
Wilson	Hoten	Shelley	Johnson
Harwood	Westle	Bradburn	Foxall
Robinson		Butt	

Fratton Park

Referee: Captain A. Prince-Cox   **Attendance:** unknown

The Great War now well and truly over, the shipyards and docks of southern England were rapidly shedding labour and both Southampton and Portsmouth established Unemployment Relief Funds. Pompey's chairman, the

Rev. Bruce Cornford – a former member of the Saints when they were still St. Mary's* – proposed a friendly at Fratton Park to support Portsmouth's efforts and the Saints agreed to travel down at their own expense.

'It was most unfortunate that the rain poured down and blotted out all chances of a good "gate",' sighed Reviewer in the *Football Echo*, but the takings would be supplemented by 'the subscription cards throughout the town.' As the conditions worsened during the game, the players 'slipped about in a humorous manner,'

Rev. Bruce Cornford, who proposed this unemployment benefit

which helped, it seems, to make it 'a delightful game' for the *News*.

A 'very even' game was won when Cherrett 'sent the ball past Swinnerton at express speed.'

In the exchange of speeches afterwards, Mr Bulpitt, for the Southampton board, hoped their League meetings, come March, 'would provide good gates and good play,' with the Saints finishing top of the table and Pompey second. While the visiting players 'chorused "Hear, hear," … some of the Pompey players winked the other eye.'

Running tally:	Pompey	51	Saints	47	Drawn	15

Saturday 18 March 1922 **Football League Division Three (South)**

Portsmouth 0 Southampton 2

Robson	Kennedy	Allen	Brown
Probert	Edwards	Parker	Dominy
Abbott	Cherrett	Titmuss	Rawlings
Wilson	Hoten	Shelley	Johnson
Brown	Beedie	Campbell	Andrews
Martin		Getgood	

Referee: Mr J. Head (West Bromwich)

Fratton Park
Attendance: 26,382

Shirley Abbott leads the home side out to a 'reception fit for champions.'

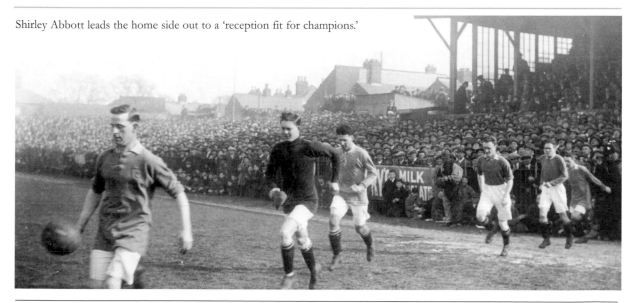

---

* There is a claim made for him that he played for the Saints. There is no record of this, but it could have been for the 2nd XI, or in one of those games that failed to make it into the local press – of which there were a fair few in the pre-Southern League days.

This game certainly produced the 'good gate' that Mr Bulpitt had wanted – a record for a League match at Fratton Park, no less – even if Plymouth Argyle were keeping the Saints and Pompey out of the top two spots he had been hoping for.

Here's how they stood:

	Played	Points
Plymouth Argyle	32	46
Southampton	**30**	**44**
Portsmouth	**32**	**43**

So, with 'the tremendous local rivalry between the two teams' here coupled with 'the keen struggle of the clubs to secure promotion,' the *Football Echo* justifiably described this as 'one of the most important matches of the season.' Having as ever gone out of the Cup sooner than Saints, Portsmouth had played two games more and 'most decidedly had to win' if they were to stay in touch.

While it was known that more than 1,000 away fans had arrived on excursion trains, the *Echo* thought it 'impossible to calculate how many made the journey… in motor cars, char-a-bancs, lorries, and bicycles.'

Having each come out to a 'reception fit for champions,' both sides played some 'fine football.' Kennedy hit the bar early on, but the Saints took the lead in the 17th minute, from 'a neat movement', started by Brown and completed by Rawlings: 'a fine goal'. Although Pompey then 'attacked hotly', Rawlings added a second after 65 minutes, while Fred Titmuss, 'his knickers torn…, was off the field changing' – after which the home side could make no headway against 'an irresistible defence'.

Running tally:	Pompey	51	Saints	48	Drawn	15

Saturday 25 March 1922   **Football League Division Three (South)**

Southampton   1   Portsmouth   1

Allen	Brown	Robson	Kennedy
Parker	Dominy	Probert	Mackie
Titmuss	Rawlings	Abbott	Cherrett
Shelley	Andrews	Wilson	Hoten
Getgood	Johnson	Brown	Beedie
Butt		Martin	

The Dell

Referee: Mr J. Head (West Bromwich)   **Attendance:** 17,000

The Saints took the lead after eight minutes when 'Johnson attempted to barge his way through.' Portsmouth defenders told the *Football Mail* that he had first 'knocked the ball down with his hand' and that his fall in the penalty area was caused by 'his own clumsiness'. The referee saw it differently, though, and Rawlings duly scored from the spot.

The lead lasted five minutes. Cherrett (*right*) equalised from a rebound after Martin's run and shot. Robson then sustained a dislocated finger and a head injury and was installed in the South Hants Hospital for two nights,

where he was visited, at every possible opportunity, by Arthur Dominy. By all accounts they built up a strong friendship. Abbott took over in goal, where his 'pluck was fully appreciated.'

It was an unsatisfactory result for both sides. Having lost their goalkeeper and played most of the game with 10 men, Pompey had achieved a plucky draw; but they needed more than a point. And if any Southampton fans could take satisfaction in their side's just about putting paid to Pompey's title aspirations, the fact remained that they had lost ground to Plymouth.

Running tally:	Pompey	51	Saints	48	Drawn	16

1919-24: In a Different League

Southampton 3   Portsmouth 1

Yeomans	Blyth	McPhail	Kennedy
Parker	Dominy	Probert	Mackie
Titmuss	Rawlings	Quinn	Strange
Shelley	Meston	Tumelty	Watson
Campbell	Clarke	Wilson	Gilchrist (Duncan)
Turner		Robinson	

The Dell

Referee: Mr J. Head (West Bromwich)   **Attendance:** not known

Reports of this game are not so much overshadowed by news of Saints' promotion, as swamped into oblivion, although Echoist found enough room in his column to relate that the receipts – £195 – were 'rather below the expected returns for such an attractive game' and to convey the basics: Southampton won 3-1, through goals by Dominy (2) and Rawlings. Which was more room than the Portsmouth press devoted to the game.

The *Echo* also produced line-ups – although the Portsmouth team (as faithfully reproduced here) is entirely different from that recorded in the club's history by Neasom and others.

Running tally:	Pompey	51	Saints	49	Drawn	16

Final Word

Grabbing a point at The Dell was not the most neighbourly of gestures on Pompey's part. Plymouth Argyle were pushing the Saints hard for the single promotion place and, when it came to the last Saturday of the season, they were two points ahead at the top.

The arithmetic was simple: if Argyle lost at Queen's Park Rangers and the Saints won at home to Newport County, then superior goal average would bring the Third Division (South) Championship to Southampton.

Two directors had been despatched to Loftus Road, to provide telephone bulletins, and many of the 9,000 crowd waited at The Dell, after a 5-0 win, to learn of QPR's 2-0 win – and of Saints' promotion thereby.

Pompey, meanwhile, were drawing at Reading, to finish third, eight points off the lead. When the Portsmouth players bought papers after the match and read of their neighbours' success, they 'gave a hearty cheer.' And a 'neighbourly and sporting telegram' was immediately despatched from the Portsmouth directors to The Dell:

HEARTY CONGRATULATIONS ON PROMOTION. YOUR GAIN IS OUR LOSS.

The man from the *Echo* doubted whether there had been, 'since the far-off day when the Southampton FC adopted professionalism,… a more epoch-making day in the history of the Club.' He envisaged that the 'spirit' of the reaction from Portsmouth

will further cement the splendid feeling which exists between the two Hampshire professional clubs, and the hope will generally be held that Pompey will quickly follow the Saints to the Second Division.

1922-23

They may have been 'neighbourly and sporting' at Fratton Park with regard to the Saints' elevation but, as the new season started, the *Football Echo*'s resident Pompey pundit was expressing concerns: for instance, would Pompey's home attendances suffer?

The gates at the pre-season practice matches were cause for optimism, he suggested: 'the directors, officials, shareholders and supporters have made up their minds to pull together in an attempt to join the Saints in the upper circle.'

Monday 4 December 1922   **James McIntyre Benefit Match**

Southampton   1   Portsmouth   3

Teams not known

The Dell

Referee: not known   **Attendance:** not known

James McIntyre had been the Saints' manager since 1912 – with a short break during the War – and had done a respectable job, even if his side was far from setting the Second Division alight.

Portsmouth turned up with eight reserves, according to the *Echo* (though which reserves remains a mystery, as not one report of this games carries line-ups), and were 'good value' for their 3-1 victory as, 'the more the Saints tried, the more Pompey piled on the pace.' Watson, Mackie and Strange got the visitors' goals, while Rawlings scored the solitary home goal.

This benefit match deserved more than this 'piffling display', the *Southampton Times* felt; and so did the spectators, who 'were positively disgusted with the don't care attitude of the players.'

Running tally:	Pompey	52	Saints	49	Drawn	16

By The Way

Pompey yet again went out of the Cup in the First Round – in a replay at Elland Road – but the Saints' best run since 1908 excited 'the fancy of Portsmouth football patrons.'

That's according to the *Football Echo*'s 'Pompey Chimes' column.

And that was after only one round – a round in which many a spectator had watched both Pompey and Saints, the *Echo* reckoned: when Saints were drawing at St James' Park on the Saturday, 'many spectators from Southampton and district' ventured to Fratton Park to watch the 0-0 draw with Leeds United while, come Wednesday, 'Pompey supporters went to see Newcastle whacked' in the replay at The Dell.

The Saints went on to lose a quarter-final second replay to West Ham.

So they missed appearing in the first Wembley Final but, with Portsmouth still having reached the Third Round only twice in their history, it was no wonder that the 'Cherry Blossom' columnist should feel the need to

draw attention to the great interest taken in the Portsmouth district in the Saints. We are all delighted at their great achievement.

Monday 16 April 1923   **Rowland Hospital Cup**

Portsmouth   1   Southampton   2

Newton	Meikle	Lock	Brown
Probert	Mackie	Tom R.Parker	Dominy
Quinn	Haines	Titmuss	Rawlings
Davies	Watson	Shelley	Johnson
Tom B.Parker	Beedie	Campbell	Andrews
Martin		Turner	

Fratton Park

Referee: F.C. Winton   **Attendance:** between 7,000 and 8,000

Their second meeting of the season 'was a really big test of strength between the two rival Hampshire clubs,' the *Echo* insisted.

True, this was just another friendly, but it was for a new trophy, exclusive to the two clubs: a 100-guinea cup presented by Mr. J.T. Rowland, to be played for, like the Pickford Cup, once a season to raise money – in this case for the hospitals of Portsmouth and Southampton.

The two clubs took it seriously enough to field their first teams and

> so intense was the struggle, and so keen [were] the twenty-two players concerned [that] every single second of a thrilling ninety minutes was fought with resolution… It could not have been a more stirring game had the two clubs been fighting at the top of the same League and this the deciding match.

The Saints took a two-goal half-time lead. Johnson headed in 'a wholly delightful centre' from Brown after 25 minutes and Rawlings almost immediately made it 2-0 from close range. The first goal was 'an illustration of the direct methods which Saints employed throughout,' in contrast to their opponents' inclination 'to hold the ball too long.'

That tendency notwithstanding, Pompey did score the goal of the game, when Martin swung a free-kick 'clean across the ground' to his outside-right. Meikle 'pulled his centre back too far' but the danger was not over:

> Watson tipped the ball back to Parker, the Portsmouth centre half-back, who was standing fully forty yards away from the goal. He took a first-time drive, and the ball flew, at a great pace, into the top right-hand corner of the net. Lock made a fine leap, and did just touch the ball with his fingers, but the strength of the kick carried the shot through.

| Running tally: | Pompey | 52 | Saints | 50 | Drawn | 16 |

Monday 23 April 1923   **Hants Benevolent Cup**

Southampton 2   Portsmouth 2

Lock	Brown	Newton	Meikle
Tom R. Parker	Dominy	Probert	Mackie
Titmuss	Rawlings	Quinn	Haines
Shelley	Johnson	Davies	Watson
Hough	Andrews	Tom B.Parker	Beedie
Turner		Martin	

The Dell

Referee: Captain A. Prince-Cox   **Attendance:** not known (*receipts £253. 2s .3d*)

Four days before the first FA Cup Final at Wembley and the massive demonstration of interest in top-class Cup football that it evoked, the Saints and Pompey met for another poorly-attended parochial tie.

It was Pompey's turn to take a two-goal lead. The first came after only three minutes, when Meikle's 'speed took him through', but it was Southampton's Parker who turned the winger's low centre into his own net.

Then, as the first half drew to a close, Pompey broke up a Saints' attack and Mackie 'threaded a path through' to score. Johnston pulled one back on 73 minutes, with

'a really fine goal from the edge of the penalty area' and then, with six minutes remaining, he supplied 'a fine cross-pass' for Dominy to equalise.

All of which meant that the season's three friendlies had produced a win each and a draw. And the Pickford Cup could spend six months in each boardroom, starting at The Dell, as Dominy won the toss. The losers, not for the first time, were the charity. Both financially and as a spectacle, the game had been an anti-climax, the *Evening News* concluded, to the charity match at Fratton Park the previous week.

| Running tally: | Pompey | 52 | Saints | 50 | Drawn | 17 |

After Arthur Dominy had won the toss for Southampton to have initial possession of the Pickford Cup,
the players were able to pose with both charity trophies.
Back row (left to right, players only): Shelley, Parker, Allen, Titmuss, Hough, Turner.
Front row: Brown, Dominy, Rawlings, Keeping, Andrews.

Final Word

Pompey's promotion ambitions were pretty much thwarted by October, during which Plymouth Argyle did the 'double' over them. Plymouth were again beaten into second place in Division III (South), this time by Bristol City. The side that had once been Saints' principal Southern League rivals – without ever winning that championship – before decamping to the Football League in 1901, had been relegated from, and replaced by Saints in, Division II, but had now won their way back at the first attempt. For their part, the Saints had a worrying start to Second Division life, failing to score in their first five games, from which they gained one point. They eventually pulled themselves together and ended the season in 11th place, with the remarkable statistics:

P42 W14 D14 L14 F40 A40 Pts 42.

1923-24

It was just as well for Pompey that Plymouth remained in their division, where they had become a kind of derby-substitute for their departed neighbours. As Portsmouth opened the new season at Home Park, the Pompey Chimes columnist in the *Football Echo* captured the significance of the occasion: since they had 'parted League company with our Saintly neighbours', Pompey's 'games of the season' had become those against Argyle.

> Not only has a keen sense of inter-port rivalry existed, and caused intense excitement among bluejackets ashore and afloat, but although unsuccessful, the two clubs have always been somewhere near the front of the race for the championship.

For the record, Pompey opened up with a 2-1 win. And they duly completed the double over Argyle a week later, to establish a four-point margin over their 'inter-port rivals'.

That would be the very margin by which they would pip them for the Championship come May.

In the meantime, the derby games between Southampton and Portsmouth would again consist, as in the previous season, of a pre-Christmas benefit match and the two end-of-season parochial cup matches – with a couple of Old Saints v Old Pompey games thrown in (but not included in our accounts).

Wednesday 14 November 1923

Bert Lee Benefit

Southampton 0 Portsmouth 2

Allen	Henderson	Kane	Kennedy
Parker	Dominy	Probert	Shankly
Hooper	Bruton	Davison	Haines
Shelley	Salter	Moore	Watson
Bradford	McDonald	Newman	Gilchrist
Turner		McNab	

The Dell

Referee: Mr V.G. Primmer **Attendance:** 'not more than 3,000'

A member of Saints' 1902 Cup Final side, Bert Lee had had a benefit in 1906. He had now earned a second as trainer, but bringing the Division III(S) leaders to The Dell proved not to be a great attraction, even though it was 'a glorious afternoon in the climatic sense'

Billy 'Farmer's Boy' Haines — nick-named for his Warminster Common roots — scored both of the goals.

Having finished off 'some good combined work by the Pompey front line' in the first half, he got 'right through on his own' in the second.

If Haines was individually the match-winner, the result reflected, for Linesman of the *Football Mail*, the superiority of a visiting *team*, dominated by reserves but in whose team-work 'there was always more method.'

Running tally: **Pompey** 53 **Saints** 50 **Drawn** 17

By The Way

Pompey's Cup run lasted the traditional 90 minutes, Newcastle winning 4–2 at Fratton Park, while the Saints saw off Chelsea and Blackpool before losing 2-0, in an away replay, to Liverpool, the League Champions.

Monday 5 May 1924

Rowland Hospital Cup

Southampton 2 Portsmouth 3

Allen	Henderson	Kane	Meikle
Parker	Dominy	Davison	Mackie
Titmuss	Rawlings	McColgan	Haines
Shelley	Price	Davies	Dearn
Campbell	Meston	Foxall	Beedie
Harkus		Martin	

The Dell

Referee: Captain A.J. Prince-Cox **Attendance:** not known

Pompey had warmed up for their two annual charity matches with the Saints by winning Division III (South). Their league season had finished on the Saturday with a 2-0 win at Gillingham, but they had clinched the championship three days earlier on what the *Football Echo*'s Pompey Chimes columnist described as 'a joy day at Portsmouth.' Their 4-1 win over Swindon Town had sent a crowd of 18,000 'wild with enthusiasm' and 'one of the loudest cheers' during the after-match speeches

'from the balcony of the club-house' had greeted the news that 'messages of congratulations had been received from the Southampton Club.'

All of which gave the *Echo* more reason than ever to build-up this charity match: having earned promotion, the visiting players were now 'anxious', readers were assured, 'to demonstrate that they are capable of beating a Second Division club.' True, the question of winning must be of less importance than raising money for charity but no matter how 'supporters view the games, it makes little difference to the players, for the inter-town rivalry always leads to keenness on the field.'

If the keenness of the contest is measured by its casualty-count, then this game was keen all right: the Saints ended the match with only nine men, having lost Meston to a 'sad accident' and Parker with a groin strain. Both went to hospital: the sponsorship of the game was proving appropriate.

Before that, Dearn and Haines, each set up by Meikle, had scored for Pompey, either side of a 'splendid' Rawlings goal for Saints. Once reduced to nine men, Southampton opted to play with one back and four forwards. They made a decent fist of it and, even after Haines had put Portsmouth 3-1 ahead, they pulled a goal back at the end, when Henderson 'dropped a corner kick beautifully' and Rawlings scored his second.

The players were presented with silver cigarette cases, instead of medals, by Sir Russell Bencraft, the grand panjandrum of Hampshire County Cricket Club and former president of St Mary's FC, in his capacity as a director of the *Southern Daily Echo*. The new champions of Division III (S) 'had won so many medals,' he 'humorously' remarked, 'that it was thought they would appreciate a change.'

| Running tally: | Pompey | 54 | Saints | 50 | Drawn | 17 |

Wednesday 7 May 1924   **Hants Benevolent Cup**

Portsmouth 2   Southampton 0

Kane	Meikle	Allen	Henderson
Davison	Mackie	Titmuss	Dominy
McColgan	Haines	Keeping	Rawlings
Davies	Dearn	Shelley	Price
Foxall	Beedie	Campbell	Clarke
Martin		Harkus	

Fratton Park

Referee: Mr F.C. Winton   **Attendance:** 7,496

Two days later, the champions received their neighbours – the first time two Second Division teams had ever met at Fratton Park. Pompey were 1-0 up inside three minutes, through 'a splendid cross drive' from Beedie.

They then did 'all the pressing,… playing exhibition football,' and Haines made it 2-0 on the hour. The scoring was over. And so, bar the dinner and all the speeches, was another season of derby friendlies.

| Running tally: | Pompey | 55 | Saints | 50 | Drawn | 17 |

Pompey were able to trump the Saints' trophy parade of the previous season by posing with both charity cups *and* the Third Division (S) shield.

The line-up (*left to right*) is: Mr J. McCartney (manager), Foxall, Kane, Davison, Probert, Parker, McColgan, Beedie, Davies, Mackie, Martin, Haines, Watson, Meikle, J. Warner (trainer).

Chapter 8
1924-27: Second Cousins

Once more, Pompey and Saints were in the same division and there was manifest optimism, in both ports, that the two clubs could soon be competing at the very highest level - just as they had at highest level of the Southern League. Given their pedigree and potential, what could possibly prevent it?

1924-25

It was 'no change' at The Dell, where the side had been good enough, the previous season, to be contenders in both League and Cup.

At Fratton Park, the news was of replacements. The Rev. Brucc Cornford resigned as chairman and director Bob Blyth, former player and player-manager, took over. And the *Echo* reported plans – to be implemented the following close season – to replace the 1,000-capacity South Stand with a 4,000-seater.

There were several reasons for improvements:

During the past season the Portsmouth club has lost much revenue because of the lack of sufficient stand accommodation, while the facilities for training the players have proved obsolete, and the visitors' dressing rooms far below the standard expected on the ground of a Second Division Club. As we have travelled around to visit pastures new the more we have blushed for the 'trimmings' at Fratton Park. Next year we shall be proud of the home of Pompey.

Saturday 27 September 1924   **Football League Division Two**

Southampton   0   Portsmouth   0

Allen	Henderson	Kane	Meikle
Parker	Dominy	Probert	Mackie
Titmuss	Rawlings	McColgan	Haines
Shelley	C. Price	Davies	Watson
Campbell	Carr	Foxall	Beedie
Harkus		Martin	

The Dell

Referee: Captain A.J. Prince-Cox   **Attendance:** 20,000

PORTSMOUTH STILL UNBEATEN
Capital Exhibition At The Dell

SAINTS PUT UP THE BETTER GAME
BUT FAIL TO SCORE

'History was made,' the *Football Echo* report began, as 'Southampton and Portsmouth met in a Second Division match for the first time.'

As the above headline trumpeted, Pompey came into the game unbeaten, while the Saints had lost four of their seven matches. So the Division II new boys were very much the 'form' team – except that 'form and the Hampshire "battle"… are two things,' the *Echo* suggested, 'which don't mix' – the moreso since the home line-up was, for the first time this season, 'the recognised first team of last season.'

There was a 'big following' from Portsmouth, many of them arriving in town early, 'where the Royal Blue colours were flying over the heads of motor-coach parties.' Some of the more 'determined' spectators were queuing 'fully five hours' before the kick-off and, when the gates opened at 1.30, the ground filled so quickly that they were closed half-an-hour later. The mood in the waiting crowd was one of 'suppressed excitement' until the arrival of the two teams caused 'a complete transformation':

> Wild cheers were raised and the din of bells and rattles created pandemonium. The Portsmouth supporters sang the 'Pompey Chimes,' but as the Saints followed closely on the heels of Martin and his men, the Yi! Yi! Yi's! drowned the chimes. Then the band played 'Auld Lang Syne.'

After that build-up, the game was perhaps destined to be something of an anti-climax – although there were no complaints about the 'capital exhibition' of football in a match dominated by two strong defences.

Opinion as to who should have won varied according to the loyalties of the reporters but it seems to be agreed that the two sides were well-matched.

Running tally:	Pompey	55	Saints	50	Drawn	18

Saturday 29 November 1924   **Football League Division Two**

Portsmouth   1   Southampton   1

Kane	Meikle	Allen	Henderson
Clifford	Mackie	Parker	Dominy
McColgan	Haines	Hough	Rawlings
Davies	Watson	Shelley	C. Price
H. Foxall	Beedie	Campbell	Carr
Martin		Harkus	

Fratton Park

Referee: Captain A.J. Prince-Cox   **Attendance:** 25,000

Since their historic meeting at The Dell, Pompey had lost a couple of games but were still faring better than the Saints, who had won only once in the meantime.

Even so, the visitors received, by the *Echo*'s reckoning, 'the bigger cheer from the crowd, whilst the band played "Auld Lang Syne",' and then proceeded to hold their own in a 'ding-dong struggle'.

Indeed, they even took the lead in the 79th minute, through 'a great right foot shot low at the post' from Dominy, only to be pegged back, four minutes from time, by Haines's 'splendid' effort.

A 'keen game' climaxed, for Linesman, in 'a highly dramatic finish'.

He reflected that 'the exchanges again demonstrated that the Saints are capable of rising to the important occasion in these exciting "local Derbies," no matter how badly they have previously performed against other clubs.'

Willie 'Farmer's Boy' Haines, whose 'splendid' late effort earned Pompey a draw.

Running tally:	Pompey	55	Saints	50	Drawn	19

By The Way

Having confounded the form-book in their derby games, the Saints yet again did so in the Cup, this time seeing off Liverpool on their way to their first semi-final since 1908. They bowed out 2-0 to Sheffield United, with Tom Parker having what modern football analysts term a 'nightmare', as he scored an own goal and then missed a penalty. Pompey reached the Second Round for the first time since 1912, but went out, after two replays, to Blackburn Rovers.

Portsmouth   2   Southampton   0

Kane	Meikle	Yeomans	Henderson
Clifford	Mackie	Hough	Dominy
McColgan	Haines	Titmuss	Bullock
Davies	Watson	Shelley	C. Price
H. Foxall	Dearn	Bradford	Carr
Martin		Harkus	

Fratton Park

Referee: Mr J.V. Pennington (Bournemouth)   **Attendance:** 7,590

The first of the two end-of-season charity encounters drew a more than respectable crowd to Fratton Park, among them a forceful presence from the crew of a visiting Italian warship.

Haines opened the scoring for Pompey, after three minutes, with 'a fine shot, taken without too clear a view of the goal.' Thereafter Pompey – 'much more eager than the Saints' – continued to dominate, with Haines and Mackie, who scored the second, being particularly troublesome. But then, when 'the game had been going quite nicely, … a "breeze" arose amongst one or two of the players. The play after this was inclined to be vigorous at times.' Quite how vigorous was not gone into – it was but noted that 'where the Saints and Pompey are concerned there is always plenty of "life" in the game.'

The players and the usual, extensive catalogue of VIPs were afterwards the guests of the mayor and corporation, for a 'do' at the Town Hall's banqueting chamber, where the players received, as the latest variation on medals, gold and diamond tiepins – the personal gifts of Mr J.T. Rowland himself, who had made a special trip to London to buy them.

Running tally:	**Pompey**	56	**Saints**	50	**Drawn**	19

Southampton   1   Portsmouth   1

Yeomans	Henderson	Kane	Meikle
Hough	Dominy	Clifford	Mackie
Titmuss	Bullock	Davison	'Smith'
Shelley	C. Price	Davies	Watson
Bradford	Carr	H. Foxall	Dearn
Harkus		Martin	

The Dell

Referee: Mr J.V. Pennington (Bournemouth)   **Attendance:** unknown

Pompey replaced Haines with the mysterious 'A. Smith' – described as 'a centre-forward from the Midlands' – and again took an early lead, when Martin's 'long drive' took 'an unexpected swerve' to confound Yeomans.

Dominy equalised when he 'beat both backs for pace' to score with 'a low shot'. The home team then dominated the rest of what was, for the *Echo*, a 'fast and exciting' game, but were thwarted by the 'brilliant' Kane. The usual cast of thousands – plus, unusually, 'ladies' – were then entertained at Price's Café where, during the welter of speeches, Saints' director Mr. W. Hammock suggested that a '"brotherhood" of the two clubs – a combination of the two elevens – play, say Sheffield or the City of London for charitable purposes.'

Running tally:	**Pompey**	56	**Saints**	50	**Drawn**	20

Final Word

Portsmouth's fourth place was more than creditable: although they finished nine points behind Manchester United, who took the second promotion place, they were four points ahead of seventh-placed Southampton.

But, then, that represented a recovery by Saints who had started so badly and whose manager, Jimmy McIntyre, had resigned in December, after which the Board, in conjunction with secretary George Goss, had run the side.

Perhaps the fans might take heart from another impressive Cup-run; or they might conclude that consistency was the problem.

1925-26

Pompey's season kicked off late, after the ceremonial opening of their new South Stand. Whereupon, they spoiled the party by losing 5-1 to Middlesbrough.

Perhaps the visitors had adapted faster to a major alteration in the rules of the game – aimed at encouraging attacking football – that had been introduced for this season: only two defenders, rather than three, would now be required in order to keep a forward onside.

Recorder reflected, in the *Football Echo*, that nobody could yet 'say how far-reaching' the effect of the new rule would be., although it was 'generally accepted' that the game will become one of even greater physical demand on the players... and probably many more goals will be scored. Some judges believe that football will lose in science what it may gain as a spectacle in other ways, and that a speedy man will gain greater prominence than a skilful player. That, in short, artistry will be swamped out of existence by kick and rush tactics.

He thought it 'most unlikely that the new rule will injure football to such an extent' and there could, of course, have been reasons other than especially poor adjustment why Saints and Pompey came into the first derby of the season, each with two defeats in two games.

Saturday 5 September 1925   **Football League Division Two**

Southampton   1   Portsmouth   3

Hill	Henderson	Kane	Meikle
Parker	Dominy	Clifford	Mackie
Titmuss	Rawlings	McColgan	Merrie
Shelley	Price	Davies	Watson
Campbell	Carr	Foxall	Beedie
Harkus		Martin	

Referee: Mr W. Musther

The Dell

Attendance: 'probably 18,000'

The third game of the season, then, for each side and one thing was certain: at least one of them would get their first point this afternoon

With the opening stages being played at a 'cracker' of a pace, it was anybody's game, until the luck began to go Pompey's way – and farcically so. On 27 minutes, Hill was shaping to save a 25-yard shot from Mackie when Parker – again! – 'suddenly shot out his leg to recover and touched the ball, but could not keep it out of the net.' Three minutes later Pompey went further ahead, from 'a brilliant movement', started by Merrie, which ended in Beedie heading in Meikle's 'splendid' centre: 'a worthy goal and cheered accordingly.'

Southampton were no less accident-prone in the second half, when Harkus's 'unexpected back-heel' missed Campbell and led to Merrie scoring the visitors' third. Price's late consolation goal for the Saints was scant reward 'for all the efforts they had made.'

Even the Portsmouth commentators regarded them as 'Dead out of Luck', the *Echo* reported.

Running tally:	**Pompey**	57	**Saints**	50	**Drawn**	20

Portsmouth   0   Southampton   3

Kane	Goodwin	Hill	Coundon
Clifford	Mackie	Hough	Bruton
Russell	Merrie	Keeping	Bullock
Davies	Williamson	Shelley	Meston
Foxhall	Toner	Bradford	Carr
Moffat		Woodhouse	

Fratton Park

Referee: not known   **Attendance:** 'between 6,000 and 7,000'

Jack Warner had been with Pompey since 1906, first as a player and then, from 1915, as the trainer. Born in Preston, he played for North End before spending the 1905–06 season at The Dell, failing to be retained because of a recurring knee injury, which turned out not to be anything like as serious as was suspected by the Southampton directors.

Whatever, this made Southampton appropriate opponents for Warner's testimonial and gave the *Echo* cartoonist an excuse to celebrate the neighbourliness of it all. So it was a pity – indeed, a matter of 'keen disappointment', according to the *Evening News* – that, with a long injury list and with this being the first of five games they would play in the space of 13 days, the Saints' line-up was predominantly a reserve one.

Yet it was they who scored first, against the run of play, through Bullock's 'glorious shot' in the 36th minute.

Pompey ran the game for the rest of the half, but the Saints dominated the second, as they 'swung the ball about, making one pass do the work of half-a-dozen by the home team.'

Bullock scored a second – a goal that 'would probably have been ruled offside before the law was altered' – and completed his hat-trick 'in the failing light.'

Running tally:	**Pompey**	**57**	**Saints**	**51**	**Drawn**	**20**

By The Way

After such a dismal start, the Southampton board had brought in the Reading boss, Arthur Chadwick, formerly of Saints, England and, of course, Pompey, in October.

Again drawn against Liverpool in the Cup, the Saints would go out at the first hurdle, in a replay at Anfield, three days before their 'return' League match at Fratton Park. Portsmouth would survive five days longer, before losing a second replay to Derby County.

At least Pompey had got beyond the First Round for a change – though only by virtue of the competition having been re-structured, the First and Second Division clubs now being exempt until the Third Round.

Portsmouth   1   Southampton   2

McPhail	Meikle	Hill	Coundon
McColgan	Mackie	Parker	Dominy
Martin	Haines	Keeping	Rawlings
Dearn	Watson	Harkus	Matthews
Foxhall	Beedie	Bradford	Carr
Moffat		Woodhouse	

Fratton Park

Referee: Mr W. Musther (London)

Attendance: 12,000

The home players could surely have done with a rest before their second replay against Derby two days later. With six inches of snow on the pitch on the morning of the game, they may have expected a break but, in 'a smart piece of work' applauded by the *Football Echo,*

> the club officials got busy early, and with 100 men they cleared the surface of the pitch, sweeping it beyond the touch lines. The ground was marked out in blue, for the ground was still white, except for a few patches where the grass showed through. Some of the merry stalwarts in the crowd amused themselves by snow-balling the band, and one of the shots hit the big drum.

A jolly good show, then, but hardly 'smart' – especially since the weather kept the attendance down to 12,000 and 'the uncovered portions of the ground were very sparsely peopled.'

Portsmouth were the first to threaten. But it quickly became evident that the surface was not ideal, when 'several players skidded without being able to reach' a Southampton cross, while 'turning at speed was next to impossible.'

Even so, after Matthews had put Saints ahead in the fifth minute, Haines performed 'a pretty turn', on 20 minutes, to equalise. The decider, 15 minutes after the restart, was another reward for nimble footwork that defied the conditions, as Rawlings 'slipped both McColgan and McPhail in his stride' to score into an open goal. Any chance Pompey had of getting on equal terms disappeared when Haines had to retire from the game, injured.

Recorder was pleased with a result that he thought

> all the more memorable because it was Saints' first away win this season. On the other hand, Portsmouth would have been beaten on their own ground only twice previously since they joined the Second Division. … Coming as it does when Southampton were passing through an anxious period, the victory should have a big effect on the Saints' subsequent progress. Perhaps, at last, the luck has changed.

McPhail (*top*) and McColgan were left stranded by Rawlings, as he scored the winning goal.

Running tally:	Pompey	57	Saints	52	Drawn	20

Southampton 2   Portsmouth 4

Thitchener	Smith	McPhail	Goodwin
Hough	Harris	Clifford	Mackie
Keeping	Rawlings	McColgan	Havelock
Harkus	Bullock	Davies	Watson
Shelley	Cribb	Foxall	Cook
Woodhouse		Moffat	

The Dell

Referee: not known   **Attendance:** not known (*receipts £105*)

The *Echo* had a new explanation for the traditional poor turn-out for this competition: 'the shadow which has arisen over the industrial life of the country': it was the first day of the 'General Strike'.

The *Evening News*, reduced to a single broadsheet by the national dispute, regretted that, 'for the first time in its existence,' it had been 'prevented … from publishing its usual full supply of news.' Which meant there was little room for a match report, let alone for speculating on whether the Southampton defenders had come out in sympathy.

Pompey took an early lead when, as in their September visit to The Dell, Harkus quite unexpectedly passed back – this time to his goalkeeper, who stopped the ball but found that he was standing over the line. When McColgan used his hands to intercept a centre, Keeping equalised from the spot. But then Thitchener had further alignment problems, when he appeared to 'to pull the ball down' from Foxall's header, 'but into the net.' A McColgan penalty made it 3–1 at half-time.

In the second half, Mackie added a fourth, before Bullock pulled one back for Saints. But the visitors were 'the better team', despite their new right-wing pair being 'obviously "green"', and [unable to] play at the pace set by the other players.'

The big after-game function was held, on this occasion, at the swish *South Western Hotel*, where the esteemed Sir Russell Bencraft, conscious of the 'very grave crisis in which the country stood to-day,' assured the gathering that 'he knew no people who would stand more steady for their country than the sportsmen.'

If there was any sympathy for the strikers it went unrecorded, as Mr Rowland duly presented the players and trainers with 'gold sleeve-links'.

Running tally:	Pompey	58	Saints	52	Drawn	20

Portsmouth 5   Southampton 1

McPhail	Goodwin	Allen	Henderson
Clifford	Mackie	Adams	Harris
McColgan	Haines	Keeping	Rawlings
Davies	Haywood	Shelley	Bullock
Bennett	Cook	Hough	Cribb
Moffat		Harkus	

Fratton Park

Referee: not known   **Attendance:** 'about 3000'

The General Strike was in its third day, but life went on – though you couldn't read much about it in a *News* still restricted to a single page. The Southampton defenders again appeared to have withdrawn their labour.

Pompey, showing 'superiority in attack', scored 'a neat goal' after five minutes, when Goodwin 'anticipated a centre from Cook, and positioned himself to flash the ball past Allen from short range.' Six minutes later, Haines 'beat three defenders in a race for the ball, and although he fumbled his shot, caused the ball to roll into the net just inside the post.'

And he scored again, following 'brainy play by Mackie,' to make it 3-0 at half-time

Apparently 'content with their lead, Portsmouth tried to weave patterns in the second half,' but Haines was still able to complete his hat-trick before Rawlings pulled a goal back for the Saints from Cribb's centre. Haywood rounded off Pompey's 'nap-hand'.

Running tally:	Pompey	59	Saints	52	Drawn	20

Final Word

A less than satisfactory season ended with Pompey in 11th place and the Saints six points behind, in 14th. Commentators in both the *Football Mail* and the *Football Echo* were inclined to blame the slow starts of their respective clubs on the new offside law, although this does not explain why these two sides should have found adjustment to the change especially difficult.

1926-27

Confidence was manifest – according to Commentator, a new *Echo* by-line – at both Fratton Park and The Dell.

While hoping Saints might 'do better this season,' Mr Chadwick was too 'cool-headed' to make rash predictions. Yet having made that point, Commentator was considerably less restrained in expressing the hope that the new season might 'hold as many triumphs for the old club to add to traditions which are as firm-founded and as high as any possessed by any other club in the country.'

Aspirations were even higher at Portsmouth, where there existed

something more than hope, but even such sane football officials as Mr. Robert Blyth (chairman), and Mr. John McCartney (secretary-manager) are really optimistic about Pompey's chances. Mr. Blyth told me the other day that he was really confident that this was going to be Pompey's big season, and I know him well enough… to appreciate he has a sound reason before he makes a statement of this sort.

Saturday 28 August 1926

Football League Division Two

Portsmouth 3 Southampton 1

McPhail	Goodwin	Allen	Henderson
Clifford	Mackie	Keeping	Taylor
McColgan	Haines	Hough	Rawlings
Davies	McKenzie	Harkus	Rowley
Foxall	Cook	Bradford	Murphy
Moffat		Woodhouse	

Fratton Park

Referee: Mr H.E. Bray (London)

Attendance: 28,200

Continuing in its pre-season vein, the *Echo* again remarked upon Portsmouth's belief that they had 'a championship team'; and they 'hoped to start off on the road to the First Division with a slashing win over the Saints.' A record crowd of 28,000 had come to see them try.

When they took the lead on 21 minutes, however, it was against the run of play. Haines ran clear to beat the advancing Allen, whereupon 'the Saints appealed for offside without shaking the referee's decision.'

Taylor equalised five minutes before the break, after 'some persistent play on the left wing.'

Both sides started strongly in the second half, but the defences dominated. It was proving 'a ding-dong struggle', but Pompey edged ahead again on 64 minutes. A 'curling centre' from Goodwin 'slipped into the net under the bar when Allen tried to punch clear, and Haines was on the premises. Probably it was when trying to keep one eye on the ball that Allen was beaten.'

Tommy Allen,
for whom little went right.

With 15 minutes remaining, 'a bout of passing' between Mackie, Haines and Davies culminated in McKenzies's 'slashing cross-drive into the net' for 'the best goal of the match so far.' And it remained the afternoon's best goal, neither side managing another despite 'close shaves' at both ends.

| Running tally: | Pompey | 60 | Saints | 52 | Drawn | 20 |

Saturday 15 January 1927

Football League Division Two

Southampton 0   Portsmouth 2

Allen	Henderson	McPhail	Goodwin
Hough	Rowley	Clifford	Woodhouse
Keeping	Rawlings	McColgan	Haines
Shelley	Taylor	Davies	Watson
Harkus	Murphy	Foxall	Cook
Woodhouse		Moffat	

The Dell

Referee: Mr H.E. Bray (London)   **Attendance:** 19,058

These are 'stirring times', wrote Commentator, in his preview of this game: the match was 'replete with interest' not only for 'the spirit of the rivalry between the two clubs,' but because each had 'bright promotion chances', with Pompey currently a point ahead of Saints.

Whereupon he offered an analysis of 'how close the battles between the rivals have been in the past.' Drawing not upon the full complement of 132 games reported above – but on the 41 games in the Southern League or Football League, in which 106 goals had been shared – he presented the tally:

Saints: 19 wins	Pompey: 14 wins	Draws: 8
Saints: 54 goals	Pompey: 52 goals	

There was a new pre-match attraction: community singing. The 'Silent Navy' having stayed behind in Portsmouth, the *Football Echo* judged, the noisy contingent who came to The Dell helped to make the singing 'a distinct success, [as] the huge crowd joined in lustily to the promptings of the band of H.M. Grenadier Guards and the energetic white-figured conductor.'

While the Saints were 'smarter on the ball' early on, they were not smart enough for long enough and it was Pompey who took the lead, after 23 minutes, through Haines. The only other goal of the game came in the 80th minute. While a 'winded' Harkus was off, receiving treatment, Haines went through, was tripped, got up and scored from the spot.

The *Echo* felt that 'there was little between the teams; in fact so little that a draw might easily have been the outcome,' but if anything might be 'seized upon to explain Portsmouth's victory, it was perhaps the smoother working of their forward line.'

That said, they had now gone three points ahead of Saints and this result would surely 'give them a big lift towards promotion.' Indeed, it would.

| Running tally: | Pompey | 61 | Saints | 52 | Drawn | 20 |

A mid-season view of promotion prospects...

The Saint (surveying the Pompey Sailor): "What a hope that fellow has! I'll cut him out yet."

By The Way

Three days before they came to The Dell to complete that crucial League 'double' over the Saints, Pompey had won a Third Round with Bristol Rovers to reach the Fourth Round for the first time ever. That was partly a product, of course, of the re-numbering introduced the previous season but then, true to form, they would go out in the next round at Reading, anyhow.

That would leave them free to concentrate on winning promotion, while Saints were busy reaching their third quarter-final in five seasons and their second semi-final in three. This time, their Division I victims included Champions-elect, Newcastle United.

The appellation 'Lucky Arsenal' might have been coined at the Stamford Bridge semi-final (but it wasn't), as even the London press thought the Saints were 'robbed'. There was certainly one 'palpable' penalty ignored by the indulgent referee – and a Southampton director claimed that his side should have had three.

They lost 2–1.

Monday 9 May 1927   **Hants Benevolent Cup**

Southampton   4   Portsmouth   1

Thompson	Henderson	McPhail	Forward
Adams	Rowley	Clifford	Mackie
Hough	Rawlings	Smith	Haines
Shelley	Lohse	Davies	Watson
Harkus	Murphy	Havelock	Cook
Woodhouse		Moffat	

The Dell

Referee: Captain W.J. Parker   **Attendance:** 'about 3,000'

Pompey arrived at the Dell having been a First Division club for two days.

In their honour, and in particular in honour of Willie 'Farmer's Boy' Haines, their top scorer, the band played

The Farmer's Boy, a popular song of some vintage. The crowd, maintaining this neighbourly gesture, 'heartily cheered the Pompey players when they entered the field.'

The home players, however, appeared more inclined to make a point than bend the knee. In the 13th minute, Rawlings went up with McPhail to meet a centre and 'so bothered the goalkeeper that Rowley was able to nip in and shoot at an angle into the net.'

The Saints scored twice more before the interval – through Rowley, again, in the 33rd minute and Rawlings in the 44th – each from a Murphy cross. In the second half, Haines passed up a couple of scoring opportunities, but when Thompson conceded a corner from one of his best shots, it led to a goalmouth scramble, during which 'the referee gave a penalty-kick, though why nobody knew.' Haines didn't miss this time, but then Rawlings promptly restored Saints' three-goal lead.

The players received silver cigarette cases and William Pickford congratulated Pompey on their promotion:

Five years ago Southampton showed Portsmouth the way from the Third Division; now Pompey had led the way to the First Division, where he hoped the Saints would soon join them, and that Bournemouth and Boscombe would follow the 'upward' trend.

Dick Rowley, scorer of Saints' first two goals.

Running tally:	Pompey	61	Saints	53	Drawn	20

Wednesday 11 May 1927   **Rowland Hospital Cup**

Portsmouth   5   Southampton   1

McPhail	Goodwin	Thompson	Henderson
Clifford	Mackie	Keeping	Rowley
E. Smith	Haines	Hough	Rawlings
Davies	Watson	Shelley	Lohse
Foxall	Cook	Harkus	Murphy
Moffat		Woodhouse	

Fratton Park

Referee: Mr R.J. Welch (Ryde)   **Attendance:** 7,000

Fratton Park, naturally enough, was in celebration mood. Prior to the kick-off, Jack Warner was presented with a pair of silver vases from his players, 'as an appreciation of his advice and keen assistance in helping them to promotion.'

He was then presented with the grand spectacle of his charges playing the Saints off the park. It took only nine minutes for Haines to 'nod' the first goal. Then, after a brief flurry of fouling, the game settled down and, with a minute of the first half remaining, Cook scored Pompey's second.

Although Rowley and Lohse each tested McPhail at the start of the second half, Portsmouth's front men were being 'much better backed up by the half-backs' than were the visiting forwards and Mackie 'banged' in a third goal. Lohse pulled one back but, as Pompey 'renewed their efforts' towards the end, Goodwin's 'clever overhead kick' and a second goal for Haines settled it at 5-1.

After the game, the players received 'gold collar pins' from the ever-generous Mr Rowland.

Presenting the trophy, Councillor Frank J. Privett, the Mayor of Portsmouth, provoked 'a mighty roar of cheering' from the Fratton Park crowd when he 'expressed the hope of the citizens of Portsmouth that the Saints would join Pompey in the First Division of the League at the end of the season.'

Running tally:	Pompey	62	Saints	53	Drawn	20

Final Word

The best that can be said for Saints' season is that it was profitable – thanks to the Cup run – but their League form might politely be described as disappointing.

On the last day of the season, Pompey had been second, eight points behind champions Middlesbrough, edging Manchester City into third place on goal average. They had to win, and win handsomely over Preston North End, to guarantee promotion.

They kicked off 15 minutes after the Manchester City match with Bradford City. Pompey were 4-1 up when the news reached Fratton Park that Bradford, already doomed to Division III (North), had been beaten 8-0. Hasty calculations were done on the back of fag packets – the pocket calculators of the day – and came up with the result that Pompey required one more goal to secure promotion. Willie Haines obliged and Pompey were up – by 0.00501 of a goal.

Promotion had been a most appropriate way to mark Portsmouth's elevation to city status, as was the introduction of a new by-line, 'Citizen', in the *Football Mail*. And Citizen it was who reminded readers of Bob Blyth's confident observation on the club's prospects at the beginning of the season: 'I think we have the best team we have had since the first three or four seasons of the Club, and I think with ordinary luck, and barring accidents, they will be in the fighting line.'

Which was not only prophetic but, given Pompey's now exalted position, gives a hint of just how highly-rated they were – along with the Saints, of course – a little over a quarter-of-a-century previously.

Regrettably for Southampton, it would be 33 years before they contested another seriously competitive game with their neighbours.

READ ON: Photographic evidence of Tom Parker's 'nightmare' semi-final of 1925 and several examples of the media's reaction to the penalty Southampton were denied in the semi-final of 1927 are to be found in *Match of the Millennium*. See 'Sources'.

Chapter 9
1927-39: On a Different Planet

There is no gainsaying Pompey's achievement, no matter how thin the margin of their placing over Manchester City – nor even the fact that City would have gone up if the present system of goal difference had been in place. Portsmouth had made it to Division I and, what's more, they were the first Division III club (North or South) to do so – a record than can never be taken away from them.

An ungenerous Saints historian – if, indeed, there is such a creature – might be inclined to argue that, on the strength of their League record between 1927 and 1939, Portsmouth were not the force in football that Southampton had been between 1898 and, say, 1908. But during their reign as Southern League top-dogs, the Saints had not been called upon to prove themselves week-in, week-out, against the leading dozen or so sides in the country. It was consistently contended, in our first four chapters, that the top three or four clubs in the Southern League, during the first decade of the 20th century, were strong enough to hold their own in the Football League Division I. It was by no means suggested, though, that the likes of Tottenham, Millwall, Portsmouth and Southampton would have been challenging the likes of Aston Villa, Sunderland, Newcastle United and Liverpool for the top honours. That said, each and everyone of them would have beaten Arsenal nine times out of 10.

After an insecure start to their top-flight career, Pompey settled down, finishing as high as third in 1931, but it was in the Cup that they were to cement themselves a reputation as one of the country's leading clubs.

Southampton, meanwhile, would be spending big money – on a new West Stand, very much along the lines of the new South Stand at Fratton Park. This was hardly surprising, as both were designed by Archibald Leitch, who was responsible for most of the major football ground re-developments between 1905 and the 1930s - from Ibrox to Stamford Bridge. The Dell's new edifice was officially opened before a match against Leeds United on 7 January 1928.

The problem was that the club had to sell players to pay for it. They rarely looked capable of promotion, never mind challenging Portsmouth's South Coast supremacy – although they did manage the odd, exceptional moment of point-scoring in the annual charity games between the two clubs. Highly exceptional.

1927-28

Monday 7 May 1928   Hants Benevolent/Hospital Cups

Portsmouth   6   Southampton   1

McPhail	Forward	Thompson	Prince
Clifford	Irvine	Bradford	Taylor
McColgan	Weddle	Keeping	'Newman'
Nichol	Watson	Shelley	Petrie
McIlwaine	Cook	Harkus	Luckett
Moffat		Woodhouse	

Fratton Park

Referee: Mr W.E. Stone (Worthing)   **Attendance:** 'just over 3,000'

Reasons to be cheerful on both sides of Spit Head: Pompey had managed to avoid relegation, by one point, from Division I, while the Saints conspired to avoid the drop to Division III (South) by two points.

The Saints' attack was led by a trialist, using the alias of 'Newman'. Although the first half appeared 'very even' to the *Echo*, 'better finishing' enabled Portsmouth to lead 3-0 – through Weddle's 'neat header' in the first minute; Irvine 'on the volley' from Cook's corner; and 'a good shot' from Watson – at the interval.

In the second half, Weddle completed his hat-trick, before Petrie pulled a goal back, but a fourth for Weddle wrapped it up at 5-1.

All in all, a convincing victory, emphasising the difference in class between the relegation zones of the First and Second Divisions.

Running tally:	Pompey	63	Saints	53	Drawn	20

By The Way

There was no return game at The Dell, for the Hospital Cup, this year. As the *Evening News* drily put it, 'Southampton could not find it convenient to field a team.' Instead, the Portsmouth-based winners of the Army Cup and the Navy Cup – Royal Army Ordnance Corps, Hilsea; and HMS Excellent, respectively – competed for the trophy at Fratton Park. The soldiers prevailed, 3-0 in a replay.

1928-29

Monday 6 May 1929   Rowland Hospital Cup

Portsmouth 1   Southampton 2

Gilfillan	Forward	White	Jepson	
Mackie	J. Smith	Hough	Harkus	
W. Smith	Weddle	Bradford	Rowley	
Nichols	Watson	Adams	Coates	
McIlwaine	Cook	Stoddart	Cribb	
Thackeray		Woodhouse		

Fratton Park

Referee: Mr W.B. Stone (Weymouth)   **Attendance:** not known

The Southampton party could not but be impressed by the changes to Fratton Park, most especially the new terracing at the Milton Road end, which had increased the capacity to 40,000. It was not as if there were many spectators on it to block the visitors' view of this expansion, this despite the fact that the home side had played in their first FA Cup Final only 10 days before.

Pompey had lost at Wembley to two Bolton goals in the last 13 minutes, having clung on with their left-back, Tommy Bell, injured in the first half and again in the second, limping out the game on the wing. Whatever, silverware would elude Pompey altogether this season.

Dick Rowley put the Saints ahead when Bert Jepson's centre was so deflected by Pompey's Alex Mackie as to give him 'an easy position' from which to score. Jepson (*left*) made it 2-0 with a 'hard shot'.

Portsmouth's goal came from the head of Jackie Smith, though Echoist agreed with those Southampton players who claimed the ball hadn't crossed the line.

The Cup was presented by the Mayor of Portsmouth (Cllr J.E. Smith) and the players received gold cuff-links from Sir John Rowland, the benefactor having now been knighted.

Running tally:	Pompey	63	Saints	54	Drawn	20

Wednesday 8 May 1929

Hants Benevolent Cup

Southampton 3 Portsmouth 2

White	Jepson	McPhail	Forward
Hough	Harkus	W. Smith	Watson
Bradford	Rowley	Mackie	Weddle
Adams	Coates	Moffat	Easson
Stoddart	Arnold	McIlwaine	Cook
Woodhouse		Thackeray	

The Dell

Referee: Mr W.B. Stone (Weymouth)

Attendance: 2,154

Two days later, it was the turn of the Portsmouth contingent to take a look at a noteworthy structural alteration to The Dell. On the evening of 4 May, almost immediately after the last home game of the season – a 3-0 victory over Swansea – the East Stand had burst into flames (*see above*) and was now a charred ruin.

This event was, naturally enough, front-page news in Monday's *Echo*, yet the fact that this match was played out in front of fire-gutted wreck went unmentioned in the match reports.

What was mentioned, with approval, was that the ball was put in a bucket of water before the kick-off: this would avoid a repeat of Monday's game at Portsmouth, which had been 'marred by the light ball in a high wind.' Although this was 'not done in a league match, … in the "good old days" it was not unknown to put the ball in a bucket of water when the ground was hard, and the ball light. Players can control it better, and the game is improved.'

The oddity of this apparently thoughtful reflection is that it makes no mention of a most recent recourse to this practice: no matter that it would not be done in a league match, the ball had been dipped in a bucket before Pompey's defeat at Wembley, according to the *Bolton Evening News*, 'to prevent it being too lively.'

Ironically, after Easson's fifth-minute goal, most of the game was played in a rainstorm which sent the crowd into the shelter of the West Stand. Saints equalised through a Bradford penalty and the drenched players turned straight round at half-time. Rowley made it 2-1 and then put Coates clear for a third. Easson scored his second in the last minute, running on with the home players appealing for offside.

The presentation of the Cup – plus cigarette cases for the players 'in recognition of their services in making the game possible' – took place indoors: the players were 'soaked to the skin, and it was inadvisable to expose them to the chill' before they had showered and changed.

Running tally:	Pompey	63	Saints	55	Drawn	20

1929-30

Monday 5 May 1930   **Hants Benevolent Cup**

Portsmouth 0   Southampton 0

Gilfillan	Ross	White	'A. Newman'
Mackie	J. Smith	Bradford	Fraser
Clifford	Weddle	Hough	Groves
Nichol	Easson	Shelley	Coates
Kearney	Cook	Stoddart	Arnold
Thackeray		Woodhouse	

Fratton Park

Referee: Mr Gibbs (Reading)   **Attendance:** 4,240

The Southampton team-sheet again included 'A. Newman', described as 'a player from the North of England,' who was being given a trial. The Saints turned up minus four first-team regulars, including Jerry Mackie and Willie 'Farmer's Boy' Haines.

Mackie and Haines featured in the previous chapter as the spearheads of Pompey's attack in their 1924 and 1927 promotion campaigns. Mackie had been brought to The Dell in March 1928, to replace Bill Rawlings after his transfer to Manchester United, and Haines followed at the end of the same season – if they had been good enough to get Portsmouth into the First Division, perhaps they could now do the same for Southampton?

Rain again had a part to play, as it 'made the turf somewhat slippery, and the players, studded for a hard ground, had some difficulty in maintaining a foothold.'

In the first half, the visitors 'had quite the better of the play,' the *Echo* felt – so much so that the home fans 'became rather ironical in their cheers.' But Pompey 'undoubtedly held the upper hand in the second half,' which was 'a triumph for the Saints' defence.'

Running tally: **Pompey** 63   **Saints** 55   **Drawn** 21

Wednesday 7 May 1930   **Rowland Hospital Cup**

Southampton 0   Portsmouth 2

White	Newman	Gilfillan	Ross
Hough	Jerry Mackie	John Mackie	Jackson
Bradford	Fraser	Hill	Methuen
Adams	Coates	Nichol	Woolston
Stoddart	Watson	Kearney	Lazenby
Woodhouse		Thackeray	

The Dell

Referee: Mr Gibbs (Reading)   **Attendance:** not known (*receipts £103*)

'A. Newman' made another appearance in the cherry stripes, the *Echo* having disclosed that his *nom de guerre* 'shrouded the identity of an outside-right who is at present attached to a First Division club.'

The *Evening News* admitted that Pompey were 'somewhat lucky' to win, through Methuen's two goals.

His first, on 49 minutes, excited the man from the *Echo*, as 'the ball struck the far post and cannoned into the net.' By the time he added a 'good' second, however, this reporter was showing more interest in how 'boisterous' the football had become.

Running tally: **Pompey** 64   **Saints** 55   **Drawn** 21

Monday 4 May 1931

Hants Benevolent Cup

'Hampshire County Team' 0   Portsmouth 4

Soffe Matson
Thomas Rawlings
Adams Haddleton
Butt Dominy
Harkus Coates
Warren

Gilfillan Forward
Mackie Ross
W. Smith Weddle
Nichol Easson
Allen Rutherford
Thackeray

The Dell

Referee: not known

Attendance: not known

VOL. XLII.—No. 13,144.   REGISTERED AT THE GENERAL POST OFFICE AS A NEWSPAPER.   SOUTHAMPTON, TUESDAY, MAY 5, 1931.   TELEPHONE No. 461 (5 Lines).   PRICE ONE PENNY.

SOUTHAMPTON UNABLE TO RAISE A TEAM.

SAINTS' TEAM SENSATION.

Fifteen Players Refuse Terms.

DISPUTE ABOUT WAGES.

Veterans Fill Ranks in Charity Match.

---

along with the game played at Fratton Park two days later – from inclusion in any chronicle of derbies between Southampton and Portsmouth. The visitors faithfully brought their first team – 10 of the side had played in the team that secured their fourth-place finish two days earlier – but the Saints fielded only one first-teamer, thanks to a boycott that the *Evening News* described as a 'DELL BOMBSHELL'.

The *Echo* account was initially matter-of-fact. For the first time in the history of the competition, Southampton had been 'unable to raise a team' to contest the Benevolent Cup:

> Fifteen of the Saints' players have refused the terms offered them to re-sign for the next season, and would not take part in the game. The Hampshire FA Secretary, Mr. G.J. Eden, raised a county team, assisted by some Saints' players who already re-signed, and the match was carried out.

This match made the front page of the *Echo* with the multi-layered heading shown here.

But it did so for reasons that should perhaps disqualify it –

But then, in keeping with the tone of the headlines, the reporter described this as 'the biggest sensation in the history of the Southampton Football Club' and named the 15 players involved.

Of the team assembled by Mr Eden, only Adams had been a first-team regular that season. Otherwise, the county was able to call upon some reserves and four ex-Saints – Butt, Dominy, Harkus and Rawlings – who were now playing in the Hampshire League.

Between this momentous introduction and the usual list of dignitaries involved in presenting the Cup, there was enough room left on the *Echo*'s front page to reveal that Weddle, Easson and Rutherford (2) had scored Portsmouth's four goals and to heap 'warm praise' upon those conscripts who had managed to make it 'very interesting for a long time, but fitness told before the end.'

Mr G.J. Eden,
Secretary of the Hampshire FA,
who called up 'veterans' to help
form a strike-breaking County side.

Running tally: Pompey **65** Saints **55** Drawn **21**

Portsmouth 2   Southampton 2

Gilfillan	Butcher	Soffe	Coates
Mackie	Ross	Thomas	Grover
Shackleton	Weddle	Adams	Haddleton
Nichol	Easson	Stoddart	Allen
Robson	Rutherford	Shelley	Crossley
Thackeray		Warren	

Fratton Park

Referee: Mr A.H. Kingscott (Long Eaton)   **Attendance:** 2,098

The Saints' turbulent end to the season continued to hog the *Echo*'s front page. It was all happening. George Kay – a member of the West Ham side that had ended Southampton's FA Cup chances in 1923 – had arrived from Luton to fill the managerial chair, recently vacated by Arthur Chadwick. Bert Shelley, who had not been involved in the headline-grabbing dispute, had recovered from injury to captain the side. And seven of the rebels had now signed their contracts.

None of them was in the side, however, at Fratton Park where three more Hampshire League players – Grover and Allen of Romsey and Crossley of Cowes – turned out for Southampton, or Hampshire, or whoever they were this time around. Pompey used the occasion to give trials to Robson, Shackleton and Butcher. Not that this experimental flavour impressed the public, of whom, the *Echo* observed, 'only a few' turned out. Indeed, it was felt that Mr Kingscott, who had recently refereed the Cup Final and had come, 'without fee,' to officiate, 'must have shared the disappointment of the home officials at the big slump in interest.'

Pompey were 'inclined', as the *News* saw it, 'to take things rather easily, which, after all, was perhaps, understandable.' Even so, 'there was far more genuine endeavour about the exchanges than is usually the case in these charity games, and the spectators were given full value for their money.' Allen opened the scoring for the Saints with a header, but Easson equalised and Weddle made it 2-1 at half-time by 'netting from a doubtful position.'

Having been on the defensive for much of the second half, Saints broke away for Haddleton to make it 2-2.

Running tally: **Pompey** 65   **Saints** 55   **Drawn** 22

1931-32

Before they got around to their usual end-of-season football fest for charity, the two clubs played a benefit game for the family of Pompey's centre-half, Bob Kearney (*right*), who had contracted pneumonia and died, aged 27, at the height of his career, leaving a widow and son.

It was decided to form a 'Combined Side' to play a London team. The combination lined up, on 16 April 1932 at Fratton Park, as:

Gilfillan, Alex Mackie (both Pompey), Keeping (Saints), Nichol (Pompey), McIlwaine (Saints), Thackeray, Forward (both Pompey), Jerry Mackie, Haines (both Saints), Easson, Cook (both Pompey). Sub used: Coates (Saints).

You will have noticed that ex-Pompey players dominated the Saints' representation, the idea being to pull in the crowd, obviously: Haines, Mackie and McIlwaine – especially 'Farmer's Boy' Haines – remained extremely popular among the Fratton Park faithful.

Whatever, it was an answer, of a kind, to the 1925 call (see page 113) of the Southampton director who had wanted the two South Coast clubs to play, as a 'brotherhood', against representative sides from London or wherever.

The London XI, drawn from six clubs, included Chelsea's Scottish star, Hughie Gallacher, and Arsenal's England winger (and future Spurs manager), Joe Hulme. The game ended 4–2 for the 'Hampshire side'. Easson opened the scoring and then Jacks of Chelsea 'scored two neat goals for the Londoners.' Early in the second half, 'a grand shot' from Haines, 'which "streaked" into the net,' brought the scores level. 'The crowd simply yelled "their heads off".' Easson then netted twice to complete his hat-trick and the scoring.

Monday 18 April 1932　　　　　　　　　　**Hants Combination Cup, semi-final**

Southampton　1　Portsmouth　0

Scriven	Matson	Gilfillan	Worrall
Adams	Brewis	Mackie	J. Smith
Sillett	Drake	W. Smith	Nicol
Woodhouse	Wilson	Nichol	Easson
Campbell	Arnold	Allen	Cook
Luckett		Thackeray	

Referee: not known

The Dell
Attendance: 2,337

From 1932, when Aldershot were elected into Division III (South), until 1974 – when boundary reforms took Bournemouth into Dorset – Hampshire had four League clubs. There would be just the two, of course, from 1992, when Aldershot ceased to be – 60 years after they first competed with Bournemouth & Boscombe Athletic, Portsmouth and Southampton for the Hampshire Combination Cup.

The pairing of the county's 'top two' did not galvanize the Southampton public, even though 10 of the Portsmouth side that had beaten FA Cup finalists, Newcastle United, 6-0 only two days before, would be on show. For their part, the Saints had to reshuffle, on account of injuries.

So Charlie Sillett (*above*), a former soldier who had come in at centre-forward that season, went to full-back where he would not only finish the season but play for most of the 1930s. He was another, like Ellerington and McGibbon, Seniors (see Chapters 5-6), whose son would become a famous Saint – Peter, subsequently of Chelsea and England – while his younger son, John, would go from Saints Reserves to Chelsea and later manage Hereford and Coventry successfully.

The highlight of the first half was a foul by Mackie on local favourite John Arnold, after which a section of the crowd became so 'noisy' that 'the referee posted a policeman at the spot.' The only goal of the game apart, the highlight of the second half, was Mackie being sent off, following an 'unfortunate incident.' So unfortunate that the *Echo* felt it indelicate to elaborate. Arnold had the last word. In the 67th minute, Gilfillan 'did well' to parry 'a terrific shot' from Matson, but the Saints' outside-left was on hand to force the ball over the line and secure a place in the Final at The Dell.

Southampton contrived to lose that game 3-2 to Boscombe, who had finished 15th in the Third Division (South).

| **Running tally:** | **Pompey** | 65 | **Saints** | 56 | **Drawn** | 22 |

Southampton 2   Portsmouth 2

Scriven	Neal	Gilfillan	Worrall
Adams	Brewis	Rochford	J. Smith
Sillett	Holt	W. Smith	Weddle
Belcher	Coates	Nichol	Easson
Bradford	Luckett	Allen	Cook
Woodhouse		Thackeray	

The Dell

Referee: Mr R. Rudd   **Attendance:** 612

Three weeks later, Pompey were back at The Dell for a more traditional fixture, in front of a traditionally small crowd – in fact, an even smaller one than was traditional.

With Drake, Arnold and Campbell all injured, the Saints were unable to field 'a fully representative team' and blooded amateurs, Belcher and Holt. Pompey, on the other hand, made only one change from the side that had completed their First Division fixtures two days earlier, giving a debut to 18 year-old Bill Rochford. While Belcher would not make the grade, Holt and Rochford would each go on to captain Southampton.

Although 'often beaten by the "skid" of the ball' on a 'very slippery' surface, the players 'showed some pretty football,' achieving 'good sweeping advances by long passing

Jimmy Easson scored Pompey's first and helped to make the second

besides chess-board manoeuvres.' Neal opened the scoring for Southampton, 'beating the defence for pace' and, as 'Gilfillan advanced and Rochford cut across, ... aiming accurately on the run.'

The Pompey equaliser came after 30 minutes, when Bradford half-blocked a shot from Jack Smith, 'the ball skidding off the side of his foot' to leave Easson a tap-in.

Holt beat Gilfillan with a 'low shot' to restore the Saints' lead, but Worrall levelled again, 'after a good passing movement between Easson and Weddle.'

Running tally:	Pompey	65	Saints	56	Drawn	23

Portsmouth 5   Southampton 1

Gilfillan	Worrall	Scriven	Neal
Mackie	J. Smith	Thomas	Brewis
W. Smith	Weddle	Sillett	Rawlings
Nichol	Easson	Belcher	Coates
Allen	Cook	Bradford	Luckett
Thackeray		Harkus	

Fratton Park

Referee: SQMS Gouge   **Attendance:** not known (*receipts £124 net*)

Pompey put out their first XI, Mackie returning in place of Rochford, while the Saints could be forgiven wondering what their best line-up might be, as Bill Adams was added to the casualty list. George Harkus and Bill Rawlings were again dragged out of retirement, as when they answered the call to the county's colours the previous season.

Given that Portsmouth had finished eighth in the First Division and Southampton 14th in the Second, it was perhaps inevitable that the difference in status would come to the fore after three games over such a short period – or maybe Pompey were just third-time lucky?

WILLS'S CIGARETTES

F. WORRALL (PORTSMOUTH)

Whatever, they won, despite the Saints taking the lead in the fourth minute, through a goal replete with nostalgia, as 'Rawlings set Luckett going in the style in which he used to send Foxall away on the left wing in the early seasons after the war.' When Luckett squared the ball, Neal arrived to score with a 'surprise' header. Harkus now began to feel a leg injury, and no doubt his age, while Belcher, the novice in the other wing-half berth, 'could not cope with the wiles of Easson and Cook.'

The equaliser came from Cook after 20 minutes and Weddle gave the home side the lead, three minutes later. Worrall and Easson (2) completed the scoring in the second half.

| Running tally: | Pompey | 66 | Saints | 56 | Drawn | 23 |

1932-33

Wednesday 5 October 1932   **Hants Combination Cup**

Portsmouth 6   Southampton 0

Gilfillan	Worrall	Scriven	Neal
Mackie	J. Smith	Bradford	Brewis
W. Smith	Nicol	Roberts	Drake
Nichol	McCarthy	Adams	Ruddy
Allen	Rutherford	Campbell	Arnold
Thackeray		Luckett	

Fratton Park

Referee: not known   **Attendance:** 3,997

Eight games into the season, seventh in Division I played eighth in Division II and, once again, the difference in class was evident.

Pompey's 'positional play and… more exact passing made them the more dangerous side. Their passes always found their man, and their plans seldom broke down by faulty play on their own part.'

Sep Rutherford, 'a very dangerous winger.'

Worrall (2) and McCarthy made it 3-0 at the interval.

Sep Rutherford, 'a very dangerous winger' who had made the third goal, continued to be prominent in the second half, in which Nicol scored twice and Worrall completed his hat-trick.

As Echoist put it, 'Portsmouth's superior team work told heavily.'

| Running tally: | Pompey | 67 | Saints | 56 | Drawn | 23 |

Portsmouth   5   Southampton   0

Gilfillan	Worrall	Foster	Holt
Mackie	J. Smith	Adams	Brewis
W. Smith	Weddle	Roberts	Drake
Nichol	Easson	Sillett	Ruddy
Allen	Rutherford	Bradford	Luckett
Thackeray		Woodhouse	

Referee: not known

Fratton Park
Attendance: 2,716

The fans were now being offered two Cups for the price of one: the Benevolent and Rowland charities would share the proceeds. The *Echo*'s belief that 'Southamptonians desirous of spending a few hours in an enjoyable manner will do well to make the trip to Fratton Park' was not, however, widely shared.

Soon after Worrall had given Pompey a 15th-minute lead, there was an 'incident'. Adams was clearing the ball when Weddle hooked his heels from behind. The full-back swung round but nothing came of it, save that the football was 'lively' for a while thereafter and Adams seemed inhibited, as if intent on avoiding a further clash. Worrall again and Weddle made it 3-0 at the interval.

Sillett added insult to injury by 'diverting the ball into his own goal when running into a cross shot by Worrall,' before Worrall – who else? – completed the massacre from Rutherford's centre, 'the Saints holding out for off-side.'

Running tally: **Pompey** 68   **Saints** 56   **Drawn** 23

1933-34

Portsmouth   1   Southampton   0

Gilfillan	Worrall	Scriven	Tully
Mackie	J. Smith	Adams	Brewis
W. Smith	Wallbanks	Roberts	Cole
A. Smith	Easson	Campbell	Ruddy
Nichol	Rutherford	Bradford	Neal
Thackeray		Luckett	

Referee: Corpl G.H. Allen

Fratton Park
Attendance: 2,215

With just over a third of the season gone, Pompey were seventh in the First Division, while the Saints were dragging along in 14th place in the Second – despite Ted Drake's 12 goals in 14 games, an explosive start to a scoring spree that would see him transferred to Arsenal come March.

The only goal of the game was scored by Wallbanks after 20 minutes. The light was so poor by half-time that it was decided to change ends without a pause. One cannot help thinking it must have been an eerie spectacle in the closing stages, as two sides competed in gathering darkness in the near-empty stadium.

Running tally: **Pompey** 69   **Saints** 56   **Drawn** 23

Southampton   1   Portsmouth   4

Scriven	Neal	Gilfillan	Worrall
Bradford	Brewis	Mackrell	J. Smith
Roberts	Sillett	W. Smith	Weddle
Woodhouse	Holt	Nichol	Bagley
Ward	Tully	Allen	Rutherford
Luckett		Thackeray	

The Dell

Referee: CSM W.B. Rainey (Aldershot)   **Attendance:** not known

It was again decided to combine the two annual charity matches – with the added attraction, for the home supporters, of bringing nine of Portsmouth's FA Cup Final side to The Dell.

Nine days before, Pompey had lost 2–1 at Wembley to Manchester City. It was a Final whose place in football folklore has nothing to do with the losers. The winning teenage goalkeeper, Frank Swift, famously fainted, at the end, as he reached into the net for his cap and gloves. And Stanley Rous, the referee, would be interviewed within days – by William Pickford, no less, and his committee – for the post of FA Secretary.

The visitors opened the scoring in this game, after 15 minutes, when Rutherford 'curled' a shot beyond Scriven's reach. The Saints equalised through Tully, within 'scarcely a minute.'

In the second half, the Saints had their moments, but Weddle converted a Rutherford cross – of which there were plenty in this encounter – and Jack Smith hit Pompey's third, with a 'glorious shot'. The *coup de grâce* was administered by Worrall, with a header.

Jack Smith hit Pompey's third, with a 'glorious shot'.

Running tally:	Pompey	70	Saints	56	Drawn	23

1934-35

Portsmouth   1   Southampton   0

(probable)		(probable)	
Gilfillan	Worrall	Light	Tully
Rochford	Bagley	Henderson	Pollard
Mackrell	Weddle	Roberts	Holt
Nichol	Easson	Woodhouse	Withers
Salmond	Rutherford	Bradford	Long
Thackeray		Luckett	

Fratton Park

Referee: Corpl G.H. Allen   **Attendance:** 2,215

Accepting that these end-of-season charity matches did 'not appeal very strongly to the public' and that playing for two Cups at once was a good move, Echoist felt that it was 'about time the Saints won one': they had gone six years without a win and could 'show only three draws in eight charity cup games.'

He was forced to confess that – even though Rutherford's only goal of the game 'was open to question,' for offside – Pompey deserved this sixth victory in the sequence.

But in a futuristic footnote, The Ranger commended Southampton's pioneering 'nursery' to their current betters: 'even if it cost £1,000 a year to run it would be a paying proposition if it produced one player a season.' He noted that the *actual* cost of a development that had enabled Saints to field five local lads – Light, Henderson, Withers, Holt and Long – in this game was £500 a year.

Running tally:	Pompey	71	Saints	56	Drawn	23

1935-36

Monday 27 April 1936   **Hants Benevolent Cup**

Southampton   1   Portsmouth   2

Scriven	Neal	Gilfillan	Worrall
Adams	Tully	Morgan	Grover
Sillett	Watson	Smith	Weddle
Henderson	Holt	Nichol	Bagley
McIlwaine	Fishlock	Salmond	Parker
King		Symon	

The Dell

Referee: CSM W.B. Rainey (Aldershot)   **Attendance:** 'only 1,000'

It was just as well that only the one Cup was being played for this season: the receipts were a miserly £54.

Watson headed the Saints into the lead but, on 27 minutes, Bagley headed an equaliser from Worrall's 'model centre'. Pompey got the winner two minutes into the second half. It was 'a curious affair', the *Echo* reckoned, when Adams turned a 'short centre' past his own goalkeeper.

Regretting that there would be 'very little for the Fund when the expenses are met,' Echoist felt that 'the question must soon arise as the whether this annual game is worth the trouble it entails!'

The answer to that question was simple: this would be the last *local* charity game of any kind – as opposed to the nationwide charity games they were to play in 1938 and 1939 – between the two clubs. Unless, of course, you regard player's testimonial matches as charities.

We hope we have reproduced this programme large enough for you to spot ex-Saint (and future Chairman), George Reader, running the line. His derby appearance as a referee is recorded in the first game of the next chapter.

Running tally:	Pompey	72	Saints	56	Drawn	23

Saturday 20 August 1938 | Football League Jubilee Match

Portsmouth 4 Southampton 2

Walker	Worrall	Warhurst	Bevis
Morgan	Groves	Williams	Parkin
Rochford	Beattie	Wilkinson (Chalk)	Tomlinson
Guthrie	Easson	King	Bates
Rowe	Parker	Affleck	Osman
Wharton		Hill	

Referee: Mr S.H. Moore (Lee-on-Solent)

Fratton Park

Attendance: 14,577

This game was about celebrating the *past*: all over the country, the Football League was commemorating its Golden Jubilee by promoting charity games between their member clubs.

Yet a glance at the line-ups provides an interesting glimpse into the *future* of Southampton's managerial/coaching staff.

Jimmy Easson would come to coach at The Dell (having first had that role at Portsmouth) and have a big influence on Ted Bates's managerial development. Bill Rochford and Sam Warhurst would apply unsuccessfully to manage the Saints in 1949 and Frank Hill would similarly miss out in 1952.

The Saints took a first-minute lead when Billy Bevis (*below*), a Pompey reject, 'tricked Rochford' and sent 'the ball over to the opposite side of the goal, ostensibly for a centre,' The Ranger insisted, 'but the ball passed over the players in front of the goal and entered the goal on the far side.' The game was 'tremendously fast and there was nothing of the friendly atmosphere about it.' Indeed, as Pompey fought back, some of the tackles on them 'were reminiscent of some of the old time duels between these two teams.' Beattie hit the equaliser, following a 'typical' Worrall centre.

Southampton were allowed a substitution at half-time, Chalk coming on for the injured Wilkinson. 'Before this youngster had a real chance to settle down,' however, Worrall, considered by the *Echo* to be 'one of the best right-wingers in the First Division,' had found ways and means to dance through' – so successfully that, in the space of six minutes, Groves, Easson and Worrall himself had added three more for Portsmouth. Tomlinson 'banged' one in for Saints and that was it.

Running tally:	Pompey	73	Saints	56	Drawn	23

Final Word

In the whole of the period 1927 to 1939, Southampton had won only one FA Cup-tie, while Portsmouth reached three Finals.

It was third time lucky for Pompey in 1939, when they trounced the favourites (in every sense) Wolverhampton Wanderers 4-1 in the Final at Wembley. Actually, luck didn't enter into it: Manager Jack Tinn ran a masterful Cup campaign, which climaxed with the inspired idea of bringing popular comedian Bud Flanagan into the dressing room before the game to relax the players.

Legend insists that the Portsmouth players had their confidence further boosted when autograph books were sent to them, *via* the Wolves changing room, for signing, and they noticed how shaky their opponents' writing was.

The cartoon below is not from a triumphalist Portsmouth 'paper, but from the *Football Echo*, and reflects just how popular Pompey's victory was in the rest of Hampshire, with the Saint, Bournemouth's Courtier and Aldershot's Soldier forming a guard of honour as Pompey escorts the Cup ashore, followed by Jack Tinn.

An idiosyncratic character, Tinn habitually wore spats – referred to as 'lucky spats' – which were a somewhat anachronistic addition to footwear even in the 1930s.

THE EVENT OF THE SEASON - POMPEY BRINGS A DISTINGUISHED VISITOR TO HAMPSHIRE

READ ON: The story of how Cup Final referee Rous promptly became the FA secretary is told in Bryon Butler's history of the Association. See 'Sources'.

Chapter 10
1939-46: A Longer Goodbye

As in 1938–39, the new season would kick-off with Football League Jubilee games, it being Portsmouth's turn to pop along the coast. In the past year, life had changed radically – Nazi Germany, which had regularly featured within the pages of the nation's newspapers for its intimidation of its neighbours and persecution of its own citizens, was becoming increasingly bellicose and was now a front-page fixture.

1939-40

It was no longer a matter of there being a threat of war, more of when there was going to be one. Two days before Whites played Stripes in The Dell's usual pre-season Practice Match on 12 August, there was a national black-out operation. And as the Football League season kicked off two weeks later – with Pompey at home to Blackburn Rovers and the Saints away to Newport County – the school holidays were ending early so that teachers and children would be ready for *their* practice session – of evacuation from the *Luftwaffe*'s flight-path.

Saturday 19 August 1939   **Football League Jubilee Match**

Southampton   0   Portsmouth   3

Warhurst	Bevis	Walker	Worrall
Perfect	Higham	Morgan	McAlinden
Emanuel	Tomlinson	Rochford	Anderson
Parkin	Bates	A. Smith	Barlow
Affleck	Perrett	Rowe	Parker
G. Smith		Wharton	

The Dell

Referee: Mr G. Reader (Southampton)   **Attendance:** 8,747

Portsmouth came to The Dell with not only 10 of their FA Cup-winning side – their captain, Jimmy Guthrie, had been sidelined by a car accident – but with the Cup itself.

They paraded the trophy around the ground before the game – a spectacular totem after a season in which they had finished only five points clear of relegation. But, then, Southampton had fared similarly in Division II and the gulf between the bottom of the First Division and the lower reaches of the Second was a wide one. Indeed, Pompey appeared superior even in the way they wore the latest innovation: numbers on their shirts. While he found their numbers 'prominent', Commentator complained that the Saints' black numbers on a striped background were not distinct enough.

And they were superior in the match, too. They won, as The Ranger of the *Evening News* saw it, 'without

Saints fans – so long without a Cup run – had a chance to touch the trophy when Pompey brought it to The Dell

effort', their 'sound' defence and their especially 'competent' goalkeeper being too good for the 'worthy' efforts of the home side..

Jock Anderson was the Pompey hero, with three goals 'as cool as an icebox' – not that many readers in pre-war Britain would ever have seen such a luxury item of domestic equipment. His first goal was 'calmly hooked into the roof of the net;' for the second, the net was 'three parts wide open'; and, finally, 'he just jumped up to head into the goal as Warhurst leaped to reach the ball sent over by Worrall.'

All in all, then, not a game to which Southampton contributed very much – unless you count the referee, George Reader. An ex-Saint, he had become a prominent referee and local head-teacher on his way to becoming a Southampton director.

Oddly, this was not a unique record: he shared these four credentials with George Muir, who refereed the derby game of 18 September 1911 – although Muir

never got to chair the Board and refereeing an Amateur Cup Final is perhaps not on a par with Reader's 1950 World Cup in Rio.

Jock Anderson,
Pompey's 'cool' hat-trick hero.

Running tally: **Pompey**   **74**   **Saints**   **56**   **Drawn**   **23**

By The Way

A week later, the League programme opened with 3-1 home wins for Portsmouth over Blackburn Rovers and Newport County over Southampton.

The season lasted all of three games. On Saturday 2 September, the day after the German army had marched into Poland, Pompey lost 2-1 at Bolton and Saints got their first win: 3-0 against Bury at The Dell. The United Kingdom declared war, the next day, and the assembly of crowds was forbidden, obliging all places of entertainment, even football grounds, to close immediately. On Thursday 6 September, the Football League cancelled the competition and advised clubs to pay their players off.

The expected air raids did not materialise – the *Luftwaffe* would be too busy in Poland for a while – and the closing order on places of entertainment was lifted on 9 September. But if the British people could now walk the blacked-out streets to the cinema, the football authorities would keep them in suspense a little longer – until 22 September when a momentous headline in the *Evening News* announced that there would soon be 'FOOTBALL AGAIN AT FRATTON PARK'.

Friendly and competitive matches would be permitted on Saturdays and public holidays, provided they did not interfere with the war effort. Attendances would be limited to 8,000 and there was another 'fly in the ointment,' Ranger pointed out, for clubs like Portsmouth, in so far as a 'maximum distance of travel, 50 miles' was proposed: 'if this becomes law, and it is rigidly applied, it will prevent the Cup holders from taking part in first-class football as long as the war lasts.'

So Pompey would not be able to play in London, where they were 'a popular draw', and would have to endure second-class football with the likes of the Saints.

Yet Southampton had even worse problems. They were unable to use The Dell at all. The RAF had requisitioned it and, as this was an official secret, they could not reveal why they were not playing matches in Southampton. Unable to be let in on the secret, the *Echo* was demanding an explanation: if Fratton Park, 'in the heart of one of the country's major Royal Navy ports,' was re-opening, then 'why should Southampton be the only place – or nearly only place – without some football for those who follow the game?'

Portsmouth   2   Southampton   3

Hull	Candy	Stansbridge	Veck
Morgan	Barlow	Holt	Bates
Duffield	Anderson	Noyce	Tomlinson
Bushby	Bagley	Webber	Bradley
Rowe	Parker	Carnaby	Perrett
A. Smith		G. Smith	

Fratton Park

Referee: not known   **Attendance:** 'not more than 3,000'

Who better to celebrate the return of football with than your nearest neighbours? Especially when your own ground was closed. The Saints became the first club to pitch up at Fratton Park after the declaration of war.

As with the Jubilee game, the match was won by a hat-trick. This one was from Tomlinson – and all inside the first 18 minutes. Barlow pulled one back with a penalty for a foul by Holt and Candy made it 3-2, two minutes before half-time. Which ended the scoring.

The 50-mile limit was soon lifted, so the four Hampshire clubs could play London opposition in a 10-team competition called League South B, which would start on 21 October.

Reg Tomlinson,
whose turn it was to score a hat-trick

Running tally:	**Pompey**	**74**	**Saints**	**57**	**Drawn**	**23**

Portsmouth   4   Southampton   1

Jackson	Bushby	Bernard	Bevis
Morgan	Barlow	Holt	Harris
Rochford	Anderson	Wilkinson	Briggs
Guthrie	Bagley	Dodgin	Bradley
Flewin	Parker	Webber	Perrett
A. Smith		G. Smith	

Fratton Park

Referee: not known   **Attendance:** 4,500

The Saints were able to compete in the War League, with the RAF allowing them to use The Dell again, but the first derby game in the competition was at Fratton Park.

Attendances were somewhat disappointing, the government's maximum of 8,000 proving unduly generous. As a Portsmouth director reasoned to the *Echo*, 'the men who were bob supporters* are now working on Saturday afternoon.' Neither was the football of pre-war quality, with so many players now in the services or in employment that took them out of the area or otherwise made them unavailable.

On the other hand, Jimmy Guthrie was back – for his first game since his accident. But this did not prevent Bill Bushby, signed as a replacement for Guthrie, from playing, too. In fact, Bushby would become almost a fixture in Pompey's war-time derby matches. He would also contrive to guest for Saints. Indeed, two other players in this game – John Harris, who had come from Wolverhampton to be Saints' principal guest during the early war-time seasons, and Portsmouth's Jock Anderson – would likewise turn out for both clubs during the War (a practice which is the subject of Chapter 15 below).

*In other words, they were paying, in today's currency, 5p for admission.

The 'score sheet told a false tale' for the *Echo*: 'the Saints had three-fifths of the play – but Portsmouth had four fifths of the goals.' That said, the *Echo* attributed their win to a 'sounder defence', faster closing-down and 'deadly shooting' – or, as the *Evening News* put it, 'superior finishing triumphed over undaunted persistency.' In the last analysis, the *Echo* concluded that 'the main reason' for the result was the difference between 'some cracking shots

from Barlow,' whose turn it was for a derby hat-trick, and 'some very poor shooting by the Saints.'

Bagley scored Pompey's other goal, while Bradley's penalty, after he had been fouled, was Southampton's solitary reply, three minutes from the end.

Bert Barlow,
the latest addition to the hat-trick pantheon.

Running tally:	Pompey	75	Saints	57	Drawn	23

Saturday 20 January 1940   **League South B**

Southampton 2 Portsmouth 0

Warhurst	Hassell	Walker	Bushby
Roles	Bates	Morgan	Barlow
Buckley	Briggs	Rochford	Anderson
Harris	Bradley	Guthrie	Bagley
Webber	Perrett	Allen	Parker
G. Smith		A. Smith	

The Dell

Referee: not known   **Attendance:** 2,499

Pompey had seven of their Cup-winning team on duty, as well as Jimmy Allen of their 1934 Cup Final side, who was now with Aston Villa. Allen would guest for both Portsmouth and Southampton during the War (again, see Chapter 15 below).

The *Echo* had not 'the slightest doubt' that 'the Saints deserved their victory, even though the two goals were "mistakes".' Both errors came in the first-half. Guthrie turned a 'cross-pass' into his own goal and Briggs capitalised on a back-pass from Allen.

Running tally:	Pompey	75	Saints	58	Drawn	23

Saturday 23 March 1940   **League South C**

Portsmouth 3 Southampton 1

Walker	Bagley	Warhurst	Hassell
Summerbee	Mason	Holt	Bates
Rochford	Saunders	Mordey	Smyth
Guthrie	Barlow	Harris	Bradley
Flewin	Parker	Webber	Sherbourne
Tann		Briggs	

Fratton Park

Referee: not known   **Attendance:** not known

Saints and Pompey had completed their 'B' League fixtures and were now playing in a 'C' League, otherwise consisting entirely of London clubs.

This game was interesting for the inclusion of more guests than usual. The Saints fielded Mordey of Charlton and Smyth of Aberdeen, but Tom Parker was finding it difficult to attract guests of sufficient quality. Chelsea had offered him Smalles and Tennant for this game but neither, said the *Echo*, was 'up to the necessary standard'.

For their part, Pompey played two more guests who would also appear for Saints: Preston's George Summerbee – another of those players who would become better-known for fathering a famous son (Mike) – and Charlton's Bert Tann. And their first two goals came from guest forwards: Brentford's Saunders in the 16th minute; and Jimmy Mason of Third Lanark (*right*), just after the restart.

Bates replied for Southampton 'with a grand long shot' but, with a minute to go, 'Barlow scored a smashing goal, volleying the ball into the net at such a pace that

one of the Saints' players commented "fourteen goalkeepers couldn't have stopped it".'

There was, for the *Echo*, 'nothing more interesting in the whole match' than the performances of Bert Barlow and John Harris:

They were the outstanding players on the field. Barlow, a tremendous worker, was always thrusting at the Saints' defence, but Harris was always with him. Indeed it was a duel that went on throughout the whole ninety minutes with unrelenting energy and skill by both men. It was worth going a long way simply to watch these two matching science, speed and stamina.

Running tally:	Pompey	76	Saints	58	Drawn	23

Wednesday 24 April 1940   **League South C**

Southampton 1   Portsmouth 0

Warhurst	Walsh	Walker	Bushby
Holt	Bates	Morgan	Barlow
Mordey	Briggs	Royston	Anderson
Harris	Bradley	Guthrie	Bagley
Allen	Osman	Flewin	Parker
Webber		Summerbee	

Referee: not known   **The Dell**

                                                                Attendance: not known

It seems not to be disputed that Bradley scored the only goal of the game, just before the interval from a penalty, and that Walsh of Derby County played on the Saints' right wing. Such were the vagaries, however, of guests coming and going – and of reporters' attempts to keep abreast – that one aspect of the *Echo*'s report is at odds with the line-ups shown above. Produced by historians of the respective clubs,* these have Allen playing, on this occasion, for the Saints. But the *Echo* had Allen in the Pompey side, where he was said to be prominent, along with Barlow, Anderson and Bagley. Then again, they would have us believe that Morgan was playing in goal.

Running tally:	Pompey	76	Saints	59	Drawn	23

Final Word

The season ended with honours even, each side beating the other twice. Southampton finished bottom of League South B and eighth in League South C.

Portsmouth were seventh in the former table and bottom of the latter.

*The line-ups are derived, like several for this chapter, from the *Pompey* history by Mike Neasom and others and from the researches of Gary Chalk for the yet-to-be-published 'prequel' to *In That Number*.

1940-41

Pompey and Saints spent this season in the Football League South – although that was something of a misnomer. It encompassed 34 clubs, from as far north as Stoke and Nottingham, but games were organised on a sub-regional basis, so that neither side ventured north of Watford.

Moreover, the number of fixtures against particular opponents varied: Watford played Saints six times but Pompey only three times. And while Pompey played five of the 10 London clubs in this League, Southampton faced London opposition only once, when they lost to

Crystal Palace, the eventual winners of this rather chaotic competition.

Southampton continued to have trouble recruiting, a problem compounded by having to play all their games away from 30 November. The Dell pitch had received a direct hit during a bombing raid, which caused Rollsbrook, the stream that ran underneath it, to flood the ground to a depth, it is said, of three feet. There being shortages of labour and materials, and more essential blitz damage in the town to repair, The Dell remained closed for the rest of the season.

Wednesday 25 December 1940   **Southern Regional League**

Portsmouth 1 Southampton 2

Littlewood	Emery	White	Hassell
Morgan	Taylor	Creecy	Fox
Rochford	Black	Cummins	Roper
Guthrie	Bagley	Salter	Stroud
Flewin	Parker	Harris	Laney
Summerbee		Barry	

Fratton Park

Referee: not known   **Attendance:** 1,992

Portsmouth's Christmas guests included Corporal Black of Third Lanark, 'who in normal soccer times,' the *Echo* claimed, 'would be recognized as the big-price Scottish star coveted by English clubs.' The Southampton side

had an average age of 19. With only John Harris born outside Hampshire, their 10 locals included Roper and Stroud, two youngsters with a future, but seven of them would never feature in 'official' football, post-war.

This 1940-41 line-up of Southampton's young hopefuls includes five of the 10 locals who turned out against Pompey on Christmas Day 1940: **1** Creecy, **2** Barry, **3** Stroud, **4** Salter, **5** Fox. Also present is **6** Roles who would play in the next derby fixture and make more war-time appearances than any other player for Saints.

One of those seven, Tom Hassell, opened the scoring for the Saints in the first half. Parker equalized in the second half and then Roper hit the winner. Pompey's 'advantage in experience' had been overcome by the young Saints' 'refreshing enthusiasm for the game.'

| Running tally: | Pompey | 76 | Saints | 60 | Drawn | 23 |

Saturday 8 February 1941   **Southern Regional League**

Portsmouth   5   Southampton   2

Flack	Emery	White	Hassell
Morgan	Emptage	Roles	Higham
Rochford	Wilkes	Angell	Southern
Guthrie	Barlow	Ellerington	Stroud
Flewin	Parker	Harris	Mee
Summerbee		Barry	

Referee: not known

Fratton Park

Attendance: 'over 2,000'

The teams wore black arm bands, in remembrance of Bob Blyth (*left*), who had died that week. Some of his deeds as Pompey's first skipper, and then as a long-serving director, were recorded in our early chapters.

Tom Parker had some more youngsters on show, including Bill Ellerington, on his way to becoming a fixture, and Albie Roles, who would make more war-time appearances (188) than anyone for the Saints. But they did have a new, experienced guest: Bertie Mee, from the School of Massage at Netley Hospital, where he was practising the physiotherapeutic skills he would later hone at Highbury.

Jack Tinn had managed to recruit some seriously useful guests – Flack of Fulham; Emptage of Manchester City; and Wilkes, a naval sub-lieutenant and West Brom amateur – for this game; and on this occasion experience would prevail over enthusiasm.

Wilkes netted in the first minute. Harris equalized for the Saints, shooting 'unerringly', said the *Echo*, 'with his left foot from a narrow angle.' Midway through the second half, Pompey hit two quick goals, Wilkes and Parker doing the business. Shortly after that, a Harris penalty made it 3-2. Then Higham left the field injured, to return as a 'passenger' on the right wing. The 10 young Saints now had 'no chance'. Wilkes completed his hat-trick and Guthrie converted a last-minute penalty.

Tom Parker's youngsters had been leaking goals – they had now conceded 28 in their last five League games – but Jack Tinn told them after the match that 'if you play like you did to-day you will beat Brentford.'

| Running tally: | Pompey | 77 | Saints | 60 | Drawn | 23 |

By The Way

The Portsmouth manager was referring to the first leg of a War Cup-tie due to be played the following Saturday. While Pompey were away to Chelsea, Southampton would be playing the 'home' leg of their tie with Brentford at Fratton Park.

Given that the bombing of Portsmouth had been every bit as heavy as that of Southampton, the survival, intact, of Fratton Park should perhaps be as celebrated as that of St Paul's Cathedral. But while their own ground awaited repair, the Saints could accept the invitation of the Portsmouth directors to 'make Fratton Park your real home' for the occasion. In that spirit, those Southampton supporters who went over to Fratton for the tie were joined, Echoist reported, by Pompey fans who 'adopted the Saints for the day.'

The result was a 2-2 draw but Brentford won the second leg 5-2. Pompey lost each of their legs to Chelsea, to go out on a 7-2 aggregate.

Portsmouth 6 Southampton 0

Winch	Emery	McSweeney	Hassell
Morgan	Black	Roles	Fox
Hooper	Ward	Lanham	Roper
Guthrie	Barlow	Creecy	Stroud
Flewin	Parker	Harris	Willis
Summerbee		Barry	

Fratton Park

Referee: not known   **Attendance:** 2,300

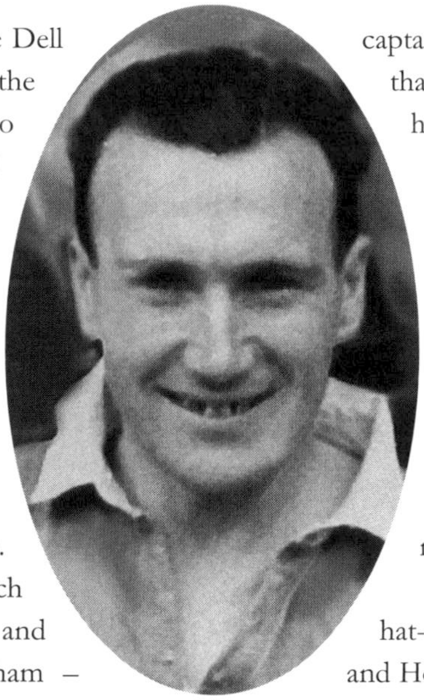

Just seven days before this fixture, The Dell was in the wars again. The centre of the West Stand went up in flames. Strange to relate, Southampton was not bombed that night. In fact, the RAF admitted responsibility: they were still using the West Stand for hush-hush business and something being stored there exploded; what, exactly, remains uninvestigated. As the Saints were unable to play at home anyway, this latest set-back was a minor disaster.

Each side had a newcomer or two. Pompey's included a player from each Sheffield club: Hooper of United; and Wednesday's Ward. And Harry Lanham – captain of the Southampton Schoolboys side that had reached the national finals in 1932 – had come home from Norwich City to become another 'war-time only' first-teamer.

It was a game of two halves. Saints were unlucky to be trailing 1-0 to Ward's goal, scored just before the interval – after Hassell had twice hit the crossbar and Roper had struck the goalpost: 'in each of these three instances,' the *Echo* claimed, 'the Pompey goalkeeper could not possibly have saved.'

In the second half, Ward completed his hat-trick, with Cliff Parker (*left*) getting two and Hooper the other.

Running tally:	Pompey	78	Saints	60	Drawn	23

Portsmouth 8 Southampton 1

Walker	Emery	McSweeney	Hooper
Morgan	Rowe	Roles	Hassell
Rochford	Moores	Lanham	Roper
Guthrie	Black	Creecy	Stroud
Flewin	Parker	Harris	Laney
Summerbee		Barry	

Fratton Park

Referee: not known   **Attendance:** not known

A late end to a long season. The Saints had beaten Bournemouth to reach this Final, while Portsmouth had seen off Aldershot at home: 10-5! True, the Shots had replied with a 9-2 defeat of Pompey, in the League, underlining the unpredictability of war-time football. Even so, a win against war-time Aldershot was not to be sniffed at. The military's Physical Training Instructors were being trained at 'the Home of the British Army' and, as a lot of footballers were being inducted as PTIs, Aldershot FC were in an enviable situation.

With Portsmouth being both a garrison town and a major naval base, Jack Tinn also had a supply-line of classy guest players, while Tom Parker was left to scour the army camps of Salisbury Plain or simply rely, as we have seen, on blooding local youngsters.

Moores, a Royal Marine appearing for the first time, top-scored with four in

Pompey's 8-1 win, a result that brought their aggregate in the last five games to F 28 A 19.

If that suggested a care-free attitude to war-time football, such an attitude was evident, to the *Echo*, in the response of the Southampton directors and players to their mauling by their neighbours: 'it was a cheery, sporting gathering' of what the Chairman, Mr Sarjantson (*left*), described as 'a club without a home.'

Running tally:	Pompey	79	Saints	60	Drawn	23

Final Word

In a season when some of the League South's 34 teams completed many more matches than others – the range was from 10 games to 36, with Saints and Pompey each playing 31 – placings were based on goal average.

Portsmouth's aggregate of 92:71 earned them a respectable ninth, while the peripatetic Southampton came 32nd, with their 53:111

1941-42

Having virtually avoided Southampton in 1940-41, the London clubs could now make the ostracism complete: there would be a London League in 1941-42 – and London War Cup games to go with it.

Portsmouth joined the 'rebellion', along with Aldershot, Reading and Brighton, leaving the Saints to scuff by in what was left of the League South. Reduced to 13 clubs, it retained the format of teams playing a varying number of games against a restricted range of fellow-members.

Southampton's 10 League matches included four against Bournemouth & Boscombe Athletic, another side thriving on military guests, but the match-of-the-season was the Christmas Day visit to The Dell of Bristol

City. Only two of their party arrived and the popular adage that fans should always take their boots was given substance when three spectators volunteered to be among City's nine *impromptu* guests.

Meanwhile, Portsmouth were lording it in the far superior metropolitan affair – played on a proper basis of home and away games against every other member – in which they finished runners-up to Arsenal, with only two defeats. They also reached the Final of the London War Cup, losing 2-0 to Brentford at Wembley. And they drew the Hants Combination Cup Final 4-4 with Aldershot, who had put out the Saints.

The net result of all of this was that were no derby matches this season.

1942-43

The London clubs returned to a reconstituted League South, denuded of Midlands sides.

Although it consisted of 18 clubs, each side would play only 28 games. At least one game against each other

member was guaranteed, however, and Saints even had the honour of playing the mighty Arsenal twice (and losing twice), as well as reviving the traditional Christmas exchanges with Pompey.

Portsmouth   2   Southampton   3

Walker	Wilson	Light	Barnes
Morgan	Griffiths	Tann	Stamps
Rochford	Davie	Roles	Whittingham
Guthrie	Martin	Rothery	Bates
Flewin	Parker	Harris	Buchanan
Bushby		Stroud	

Fratton Park

Referee: not known

Attendance: 'about 10,000'

A surprise result, even if the Saints' side had rather more experience than when the two sides last met. True, they fielded a new local, goalkeeper Walter Light, in his first game since signing professional.

But the 24 year-old Ted Bates (*right*), was playing in a forward-line that boasted four guests. Derby's Jack Stamps and Bradford City's Alf Whittingham would each score freely for them, the former briefly and the latter longer-term. Walley Barnes, an amateur on Pompey's books, would become a full-back and captain Wales, while Chelsea's Peter Buchanan had been capped by Scotland before the War. Buchanan was another wandering star who guested for both Saints and Pompey. So did Brighton's Jock Davie who was on this occasion playing for Portsmouth.

'There was much of a cup-tie atmosphere' in a surprisingly large crowd. There being no public

transport, it had not been 'generally expected', according to the *Evening News*, 'that the match would attract a very large gate.' If you were unable or unwilling to walk to Fratton Park, you would probably have needed to cycle: even if you were one of the few who owned a motor car, would you have had the petrol coupons?

The match got off to a 'sensational' start, Portsmouth getting a penalty within four minutes. But Griffiths shot high and 'all Light had to do was throw his hands up and turn the ball over the bar.'

Whittingham scored twice before half-time. Martin, of Clyde, pulled one back but Bates headed Saints' third. Griffiths completed the scoring. Some 'good crisp football' had given the visitors a 'thoroughly deserved' win, the *Echo* felt.

Running tally:	Pompey	79	Saints	61	Drawn	23

Southampton   0   Portsmouth   2

Light	Buchanan	Walker	Moores
Tann	Bates	Morgan	Griffiths
Roles	Whittingham	Rochford	Martin
Barnes	Stamps	Guthrie	Bushby
Harris	Laney	Flewin	Parker
Stroud		McKillop	

The Dell

Referee: Mr A.W. Wooldridge

Attendance: 17,000

It was a record war-time crowd at The Dell, there being 6,000 more in the ground than had turned up for the previous home game against Arsenal. Tom Finney had made his solitary guest appearance for the Saints in that match but the No.11 shirt now reverted (although not in the programme) to Les Laney, another often called-upon local lad who would never get his peace-time chance.

The *Echo* reporter found the occasion

> reminiscent of the old-time clashes between the two clubs [with] spectators thronging to the ground, and I saw several men – in festive mood – with coloured paper hats on their heads, and banging triangles. Then there was also a mouth organ group, and another party of spectators who lustily sang the 'Pompey Chimes' as Guthrie led his side on to the field, just before a policemen had 'directed' a soldier and a sailor, who were kicking something about on the pitch – probably a cap – back to their places in the crowd. Yes! The stage was set for a 'local Derby.'

Although the Saints started well, Pompey 'exacted full revenge', as the *Evening News* saw it. Martin headed their first – 'a very good goal' – on 26 minutes.

Then, in the first minute of the second half, Roles appeared to divert a cross into his own goal, although Moores 'made quite sure by urging the ball further into the goal.'

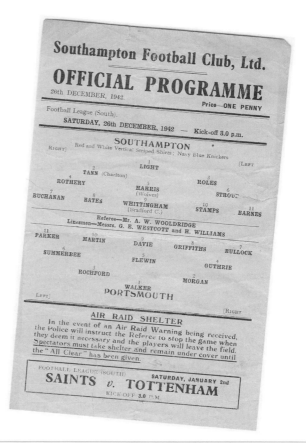

| Running tally: | Pompey | 80 | Saints | 61 | Drawn | 23 |

Saturday 24 April 1943   **Friendly**

Portsmouth   0   Southampton   0

Walker	Ridgeway	Jones	Roper
Morgan	Taylor	Tann	Bates
Rochford	Whitchurch	Roles	Whittingham
Guthrie	Barlow	Pond	Stamps
Steel	Setchell	Harris	Mitten
Bushby		Stroud	

Referee: not known

Fratton Park

Attendance: not known

Each side had completed its League and Cup fixtures on 10 April, so there was room for a friendly or two before the season was out. Pompey used the occasion to field four guests – including, from Newcastle, a 17 year-old Ernie Taylor, later of Blackpool and England fame.

Southampton's guests included Charlie Mitten (*right*) from Manchester United and Carlisle's Harold Pond, another of Chapter 15's played-for-both brigade. Commentator seemed to be more taken with the guest-

parade than the football, his account of which amounted to the Saints' having 'plenty of the play throughout the match, but [they] simply could not get the ball into the net, which is unusual for the Saints' forwards.' The

News recorded Pompey's 'big let off' in the eighth minute, when Harris fired a penalty-kick straight at Walker, and reflected that, while 'a goalless match is often a dull affair, … this could not be said of [this] match, and considering it was a "friendly" between two neighbouring rivals, it was an extraordinarily good game.'

Running tally:	Pompey	80	Saints	61	Drawn	24

Final Word

Arsenal were League South champions. Portsmouth came fourth, with Southampton two points behind them in fifth place. Not that those placings mattered much: at this time, European competition meant preparing for a heavily-armed invasion of the continent.

1943-44

In June, Tom Parker left the Saints. Although it would prove permanent, the move was originally 'for the duration of the war.' So, rather than find a temporary manager, the Chairman, Mr. John Sarjantson, resigned from the Board to become Secretary-Manager. Parker arranged for Barnes to go to Arsenal and the Board interrogated him as to his suspected part in the defection to Chelsea of Harris, Mitten and (briefly) Whittingham.

Jack Tinn continued to captain the good ship Fratton Park and, in the long run, experience would tell, although the Saints would have their moments.

Saturday 25 December 1943   **League South**

Southampton 6   Portsmouth 3

Jones	Roper	Walker	Parker
Drinkwater	Bates	Morgan	Bushby
Roles	Whittingham	Martin	Cook
Dodgin	Sheppard	Guthrie	Sears
Ramsey	Wardle	Flewin	Cumner
Stroud		Dickinson	

Referee: not known

The Dell
Attendance: 7,314

Christmas Day at The Dell produced 'a good deal of excitement – which made up for the lack of science in the play'.

Portsmouth appeared to the *Echo* 'to have departed quite a bit from their former characteristic First Division plan and purpose.' But, then, who needed science or purpose, when 'the swing of the game, the cropping up of surprises, and the final score left the crowd in very good humour'?

Pompey were 2-1 up at half-time. Parker gave them a 25th-minute lead and Arsenal's Cumner set up Cook of St Johnstone for a second on 40 minutes. Bill Dodgin, a 1939 signing who had not

played in a derby game since that first season at war, pulled one back a couple of minutes later and Whittingham, back from Chelsea, headed against the post.

Three penalty kicks were awarded in the first 18 minutes of the second half. Whittingham took the first one and scored when yet another penalty save by Harry Walker (*left*) came back to him. He took the next one, too, and made it a 'first-shot affair'. Sears of Grimsby was then fouled and Parker made it 3-3 from the spot.

After an interlude of 'equality', there were 'more surprises in store for the spectators – and the players,' as each of the Pompey full-backs conceded an own goal.

But the best was yet to come, as Bates forced his way through to hit a rising shot into the net.

A 'good holiday game', said the *Echo* – and quite an introduction to this derby fixture for two future England stars. Alf Ramsey, centre-half in an Army XI the Saints had beaten 10-3 in August, had duly joined Southampton, although he had signed amateur forms for Portsmouth in 1940.

And 18 year-old Jimmy Dickinson was making his away debut for Pompey.

Running tally:	Pompey	80	Saints	62	Drawn	24

Monday 27 December 1943 **League South**

Portsmouth 4 Southampton 2

Walker	Parker	Jones	Roper
Morgan	Bushby	Drinkwater	Bates
Martin	Cook	Roles	Whittingham
Guthrie	Sears	Dodgin	Sheppard
Flewin	Cumner	Ramsey	Wardle
Dickinson		Stroud	

Referee: not known **Fratton Park** **Attendance:** 13,000

Wingers Roper and Grimsby's Wardle were the main threat as an unchanged Southampton side started 'as though…determined to complete the "double".' But the visitors 'spoiled their chances of scoring,' the *Echo* felt, 'by persisting in slamming away instead of employing a little more ball control and steadiness.'

Pompey 'gradually took control' and, continuing to 'play… the more sedate football,' scored twice in the space of three minutes. Bushby headed the first after 25 minutes and then Storey beat Jones from close range. Four minutes later, Flewin tripped Bates and Whittingham converted the penalty to make it 2-1 at half-time.

Bushby scored again on the hour and Kerr added a fourth with 15 minutes remaining.

The Saints kept coming and 'a long cross lob' from Sheppard, a recently-signed amateur, deceived Walker.

Reg Flewin (*right*) conceded a penalty for Saints' second goal. Don Roper (*far right, top*) was Saints' 'main threat' and Bill Bushby (*far right, bottom*) scored both of their goals.

Running tally:	Pompey	81	Saints	62	Drawn	24

Saturday 8 April 1944   **Friendly**

Portsmouth   2   Southampton   1

Walker	Anderson	Jones	Roper
Morgan	Thomas	Coupland	Miles
Crossley	Storey	Roles	Hodges
Guthrie	Parker	Evans	Sheppard
Summerbee	Cumner	Ramsey	Grant
Harris		Dodgin	

Fratton Park

Referee: Mr A.E. Gernam (Aldershot)   **Attendance:** not known

Although each side had four League or Cup fixtures in April, they had a couple of free Saturdays in which to cram in a pair of friendlies.

Saints included Manchester City's Grant, who would join them post-war, while John Harris, their leading guest at the start of the War, was making one of his rare guest appearances for Pompey.

Barlow gave Pompey an early lead with 'a long drive'. But the visitors then 'crowded on considerable pressure' and 'excellent efforts' from Dodgin and Grant had to be turned round by Walker.

It remained 1-0 at half-time, after which Portsmouth 'became much more lively.' Even so, Saints equalised in the 68th minute, when Hodges won 'a race for the ball' with Walker and slotted into an empty net. Eight minutes from the end, though, Ward's 'surprise shot' decided it.

Although he scored, Hodges is not to be found in the 'official' records: he is another of those players who popped up for a friendly but never featured in a competitive match.

Bill Dodgin tested Walker with an 'excellent effort'.

Running tally:	Pompey	82	Saints	62	Drawn	24

Saturday 15 April 1944   **Friendly**

Southampton   3   Portsmouth   0

Jones	Roper	Walker	Parker
Shimwell	Bates	Mills	Buckingham
Roles	Whittingham	Stubbings	Sears
Corbett	Barnes	Guthrie	Barlow
Ramsey	Grant	Black	McArdle
Dodgin		Bushby	

The Dell

Referee: not known   **Attendance:** not known

The second meeting, a week later, was an altogether grander affair. Commentator went so far as to declare it 'one of the most enjoyable' matches he had 'seen at the Dell this season.' It may have been 'listed as a friendly, [but] it had all the "bite" of a competitive clash, and that is the reason why games between the Saints and Pompey are always "alive" from start to finish.'

In anticipation of a free Saturday, Arsenal's Walley Barnes had asked Jack Tinn for a game. Portsmouth didn't need him, but Southampton had a vacancy at

150   *1939-46: A Longer Goodbye*

"TURF" CIGARETTES

WALLEY BARNES
ARSENAL & WALES

50 FAMOUS FOOTBALLERS Nº 17

inside-left. So that's the position in which the versatile Barnes (*left*), just three weeks away from winning his first Welsh cap at right-back, came to guest.

He was, in fact, one of three future international right-backs in the Southampton line-up, along with Ramsey and Sheffield United's Eddie Shimwell.

Alf Whittingham headed the opening goal, just before half-time.

Some 'good play by Bates' set up Barnes for Southampton's second, mid-way through the second half, and Barnes completed the scoring, near the end, 'bursting through the defence and nearly bursting the net with his powerful shot.'

In his error-prone autobiography, Barnes claims that different newspapers credited him with anything from one to three goals, but he insists that he 'actually scored all three.'

Really?

| Running tally: | Pompey | 82 | Saints | 63 | Drawn | 24 |

Final Word

Spurs won the League South, followed by four other London clubs. Pompey finished sixth, the Saints 13th.

1944-45

Another League South season and all the usual suspects to be played, but in improving circumstances.

The British public were by now more than accustomed to coping with the travails of day-to-day life, not to mention the ubiquitous presence of American servicemen. In June, Portsmouth and Southampton had been major launch centres of the largest invasion in military history, as Allied troops poured across the Channel to Normandy, and both ports were working at full tilt to facilitate the offensive, which was now, very definitely, taking place on the Continent, rather than in the skies above the South Coast.

Optimism regarding the imminent conclusion and the eventual outcome of the War was high, football crowds were beginning to grow again and, if the quality of the matches might sometimes be doubtful, the competitive spirit and gusto with which they were played was seldom called into question – especially when Pompey and the Saints were brought together.

Saturday 30 September 1944   **League South**

Portsmouth 3   Southampton 1

Walker	Kerr	Warhurst	Roper
Morgan	Emptage	Egglestone	Bates
Rochford	Whitchurch	Roles	Whittingham
Guthrie	Wayman	Evans	Walker
Flewin	Parker	Dodgin	Roberts
McLeod		Stroud	

Referee: Mr H.F. Parvin (Brighton)

Fratton Park
Attendance: 13,695

Each side fielded guests who were new to the fixture. Pompey's included Charlie Wayman, a sailor from Newcastle United.

His 'grand piece of work' set up Whitchurch in the 18th minute, but a 'simple goal' from Whittingham made it 1-1 at the break. In the second half, the Saints 'went off with their usual rush, but when pushed back they had to take one of their worst hammerings they have had this season.' Yet 'although they were so completely swamped', ... Southampton refused to take the count' – even after Kerr had restored the home side's lead on 65 minutes. Wayman put an end to their hopes, though, with an 85th-minute goal.

The naval guest would make but seven appearances for Pompey, scoring six times.

He certainly impressed Bill Dodgin, who would tell the Newcastle *Evening Gazette*, three years later, that it was this performance that made him want Charlie Wayman in Southampton's attack.

| Running tally: | Pompey | 83 | Saints | 63 | Drawn | 24 |

Saturday 13 January 1945   **League South**

Southampton   2   Portsmouth   4

Warhurst	Roper	Walker	Harris
Moss	Bates	Morgan	Anderson
Roles	Whittingham	Rochford	Evans
Egglestone	Ramsey	Guthrie	Bushby
Dodgin	Hassell	Flewin	Jefferies
Stroud		Summerbee	

Referee: Mr C.E. Argent

The Dell
Attendance: 11,294

If The Ranger of the *Evening News* felt that 'all the old rivalry between these two clubs was brought to boiling point in this match,' it is not entirely clear how. That's because he was more intent on enthusing about an individual performance that had brought him to the point of overflowing.

Since the two sides met in September, Portsmouth had brought in a couple of local prospects. Fred Evans would manage only 11 post-war appearances for them, but Peter Harris would top 500. Not only would he score a hat-trick, and make the other goal, in this game, he would move The Ranger to champion his international

hopes. A fortnight earlier, Don Roper had turned in a performance against Arsenal that had seen him hailed as the successor to Stanley Matthews for England. But on their showings in this match, The Ranger reasoned, 'Roper would not have been given a second thought, so completely was he outshone by young Peter. The Saints' defence did not know what to "buy" for him. His speed and two way swerve had them beaten almost every time.'

In the Southampton programme, the following Saturday, The Saint had a slightly different take on the outside-right contest: while Roper had been 'well watched... and... starved by his colleagues,' Harris had been 'allowed far too much liberty' by Saints' 'left defence'. Even so, he considered Pompey's new winger 'a really promising youngster, and a delight to watch.'

Whatever, Harris and then Evans, from his centre, gave Pompey a 2-0 lead. Whittingham pulled one back midway through the first half, but Harris made it 3-1 before the break. In the second half, when Roper 'crossed the ball from almost on the line between the corner flag and the goalpost, the ball swerved across the face of the goal and entered the net.' Harris had the last word with 15 minutes left.

| Running tally: | Pompey | 84 | Saints | 63 | Drawn | 24 |

Portsmouth 7 Southampton 4

Walker	Harris	Stansbridge	Roper
Morgan	Thomas	Corbett	Bates
Crossley	Anderson	Roles	Mills
Guthrie	Storey	Evans	Dorsett
Summerbee	Parker	Ramsey	Hassell
Dickinson		Stroud	

Fratton Park

Referee: not known   **Attendance:** not known

Each forward line included two guests. Pompey had Thomas of Brentford and Gateshead's Storey, while Dorsett from Wolves and Chelsea's Mills were guesting for the Saints. Dickie Dorsett, who had scored his side's only goal against Portsmouth in the 1939 Final, must surely rank as the greatest catch here, but it was the 'thrustfulness and ball control' of Thomas (*right*) that made all the difference, for The Ranger, in this game. There were five goals in the first half, four of them in the opening 20 minutes.

Storey and Thomas put the home side two-up, Roper pulled one back, but Thomas and Harris made it 4-1 at the interval. After Saints had pressed, 'almost without a break,' for the first 25 minutes of the second half, Thomas popped in two more for Pompey: 6-1.

The visitors 'took up the running again' and, with 10 minutes left, Dorsett started 'another burst of goal-scoring.' Two from Hassell made it 6-4 but Parker completed this five-minute flurry of goals, wrapping it up at 7-4.

Running tally:	Pompey	85	Saints	63	Drawn	24

Final Word

Pompey had done splendidly against the Saints, winning all three games and hitting the net 14 times, a pretty convincing margin of superiority. Then again, the Saints had scored seven goals against their rivals – they had lacked nothing in front of goal, scoring 96 league goals in 30 games – and finished fifth in the League South, with Pompey seven places and 11 points behind.

No sooner had the competitive football season ended, than the war with Germany did too: peace was declared on 8 May. The fighting continued in the Far East, so the docks, in both Portsmouth and Southampton, were as preoccupied as ever with the war effort – but without the inconvenience of aerial attack.

1945-46

The Japanese (with the exception of a few soldiers without wireless sets on remote Pacific Islands) surrendered on 14 August.

The War was over but it was a little late for football to return to its pre-war format. So the War Leagues continued on a regional basis, although the League South now consisted of 22 clubs, each playing the rest twice on

the customary home-and-away basis, giving the Saints some juicy fixtures against such elite clubs as Aston Villa, Arsenal and Derby County – not to mention Portsmouth. Conversely, Pompey were forced to slum it with the likes of Newport County, Swansea Town, Plymouth Argyle and, of course, Southampton.

It was all a matter of perspective.

Portsmouth 3 Southampton 2

Walker	Harris	Cruickshank	Roper
Morgan	Haddington	Dodgin	Bates
Rochford	F. Evans	Roles	Brooks
Bell	Barlow	H. Evans	Bradley
Flewin	Parker	Ramsey	Hassell
Dickinson		Stroud	

Fratton Park

Referee: not known **Attendance:** 23,061

A pattern seemed to have emerged in these derby games: Pompey would take a lead, the Saints would battle back, give their rivals an anxious time and, eventually, not quite manage to get back on terms. This was one of those games that ran to the script, once Portsmouth had been helped by a couple of Ramsey errors, in the space of 10 minutes, to overcome what The Ranger considered a 'shaky start'.

Ramsey had begun the season at centre-forward but, despite scoring four goals in two games, had reverted to centre-half, with Brooks of Burnley guesting at No. 9. For the first Pompey goal, he 'seemed to be caught between two minds whether to head the ball or let it fall and get it away in the tackle.' As Evans feinted to the right and went to the left, Ramsey slipped and Evans ran clear to score. Harris made the most of Ramsey's second error to put his side two-up. Haddington added a third, five minutes before the interval.

Jack Bradley (*right*) scored twice, midway through the second half, 'and it was then that the real battle began.' In a 'quite hectic' final 15 minutes, each goal 'escaped by a coat of paint on more than one occasion' and, when the efforts were on target, both Walker and Cruickshank were at their 'best'.

Running tally: Pompey 86 Saints 63 Drawn 24

Southampton 3 Portsmouth 1

Warhurst	Roper	Walker	Harris
Stear	Bates	Morgan	Stott
Roles	Ramsey	Rochford	Evans
Evans	Bradley	Bell	Barlow
Dodgin	Hassell	Flewin	Froggatt
Stroud		Hopkins	

The Dell

Referee: Mr W.E. Player (Bournemouth) **Attendance:** 18,279

Alf Ramsey
was having another game at centre-forward.

Jimmy Dickinson
had gone to sea

Alf Ramsey was back at No.9 but Jimmy Dickinson had been sent to sea. Pompey still had six local players in the side, though.

They included two debutants, both too late to be accommodated by the progamme-printer (*overleaf*): John Hopkins, who would get just the four war-time outings; and Jack Froggatt, who would go on to play more than 300 times for the club.

Having come to Portsmouth as a teenager from his native Sheffield, Froggatt had signed amateur forms before joining the RAF, from overseas service with whom he had just returned.

The Ranger doubted 'if any Pompey supporter can remember the club turning out half a dozen locals in any one match before' – a reminder of the difference between Portsmouth and the nursery that had seen Southampton through the War.

Even so, in this last war-time meeting of the two sides, Pompey still fielded five players – Walker, Morgan, Rochford, Barlow and Flewin – who had played for them before the War, the first four of them being survivors, of

course, of their Cup-winning side. Saints had four such players in their line-up – 1937 debutants, Warhurst and Bates, and 1939 arrivals, Dodgin and Bradley .

Warhurst and Dodgin would each be praised, in the following Saturday's programme, for their performances in this game. Dodgin had been a model to follow, said The Saint, for 'playing the game with his head.'

Which may help to explain why, within a couple of months, he would be appointed player-coach and, by the end of the season, would be the manager.

In The Ranger's book, the Saints dominated the second half, 'slamming them in from all angles.' Walker was in heroic form, one 'marvellous save' being applauded by Roper, whom he had just foiled.

But he was still 'on one knee after saving a previous shot, when Bates 'snapped up a chance' in the 55th minute. Bradley added a second, three minutes later, and, on 73 minutes, Roper 'raced through' from halfway to make it 3-0.

Pompey's consolation came five minutes from the end, a debutant's goal for Froggatt.

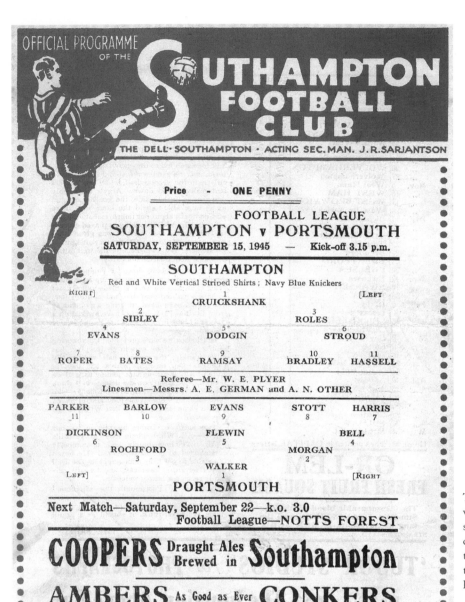

OFFICIAL PROGRAMME OF THE

SOUTHAMPTON FOOTBALL CLUB

THE DELL· SOUTHAMPTON · ACTING SEC. MAN. J. R. SARJANTSON

Price - ONE PENNY

FOOTBALL LEAGUE
SOUTHAMPTON v PORTSMOUTH
SATURDAY, SEPTEMBER 15, 1945 — Kick-off 3.15 p.m.

SOUTHAMPTON
Red and White Vertical Striped Shirts ; Navy Blue Knickers

[RIGHT]

1
CRUICKSHANK

[LEFT]

| 2 | | 3 |
| SIBLEY | | ROLES |

| 4 | 5 | 6 |
| EVANS | DODGIN | STROUD |

| 7 | 8 | 9 | 10 | 11 |
| ROPER | BATES | RAMSAY | BRADLEY | HASSELL |

Referee—Mr. W. E. PLYER
Linesmen—Messrs. A. E. GERMAN and A. N. OTHER

| PARKER | BARLOW | EVANS | STOTT | HARRIS |
| 11 | 10 | 9 | 8 | 7 |

| DICKINSON | FLEWIN | BELL |
| 6 | 5 | 4 |

| ROCHFORD | | MORGAN |
| 3 | | 2 |

WALKER
1

[LEFT]

[RIGHT]

PORTSMOUTH

Next Match—Saturday, September 22—k.o. 3.0
Football League—NOTTS FOREST

COOPERS Draught Ales Brewed in **Southampton**

AMBERS As Good as Ever **CONKERS**

The programme
was printed too
soon to include the Portsmouth
debutants and long before
the printers of
the Southampton programme
learned how to spell 'Ramsey'.

Running tally: Pompey 86   Saints 64   Drawn 24

Final Word

The final League South season was remarkable, especially for goals: Aston Villa, Derby County and West Bromwich Albion each exceeded a ton and the Saints hit 97 - one more than the champions, Birmingham. That said, they finished a lowly 16th, having conceded 105.

Which, amazingly, was not the worst defensive record in the League.

Pompey finished four places and nine points behind the Saints, but with a far saner goal aggregate: F 66 A 87.

READ ON: The summary (on page 148) of developments at The Dell in 1943-44 is derived from *Dell Diamond* (drawing upon the Board minutes) and Walley Barnes's autobiography, also used for the match report of 15 April 1944. See 'Sources'.

Chapter 11
1946-66: Ships in the Night

To say that League football resumed in August 1946 where it had left off is no exaggeration: the season's fixtures would show hardly a change from the programme that had been abandoned one week into the 1939–40 season.

After the seven-year hiatus, the public flocked to watch. By today's Premier League standards, the football dished up for them might appear to have lacked a certain edge of sophistication. It pitched 11 men against 11 – and sometimes 11 against 10, substitutions being regarded as unmanly and, literally, uncalled for. It was robust – shoulder charging, especially of goalkeepers, being *de rigueur* – tackling was routinely intimidatory; the teams invariably lined up with five forwards, two wing-halves, a stopper centre-half and two full-backs; and, we are led to believe, most goals emanated from fleet-footed wing play, climaxing in a conversion by a tricky inside-forward or a flying No.9.

"TURF" CIGARETTES
JIM DICKINSON PORTSMOUTH & ENGLAND
50 FAMOUS FOOTBALLERS Nº 42

That may be a caricature but the end product was indisputably exciting, unpredictable and highly entertaining. And crowd-pulling, too: attendance records established at The Dell and Fratton Park in the spring of 1949 would prove most durable, the former lasting 20 years, while a gate of 51,385 seems likely to remain a Fratton record for a while yet.

"TURF" CIGARETTES
JACK FROGGATT PORTSMOUTH & ENGLAND
50 FAMOUS FOOTBALLERS Nº 33

Not that the performances of Saints, in Division II, or Pompey, in Division I, made an immediate impression. For the 1947-48 season, Portsmouth had a new manager – Jack Tinn had been replaced by Chief Scout, Bob Jackson – while the highlights of Southampton's seasons would be Bill Dodgin's signing of Charlie Wayman, on the strength of his performance for Pompey against him in September 1944 (as recorded in the previous chapter), and a Cup-run that took them into the Sixth Round, way beyond

anything they had achieved for 21 years – a period in which their neighbours, FA Cup bystanders during their first 25 seasons, had reached three Finals and even won the thing.

The next season, 1948-49, would prove to be the indicative test of how the two sides had come through the War, not least in the nurturing of young, mostly local, talent. Southampton's youth development had attracted considerable positive comment during the War, but two of their successes, Roper and Stroud, had departed – upwardly and downwardly, respectively – while, of those who remained, two, Ramsey and Ellerington, would be competing for the No.2 shirt, not only for Saints but for England. This was the season, though, when it would all come together for Portsmouth who had brought three youngsters – Jimmy Dickinson, Peter Harris and Jack Froggatt – through towards the end of the War (as noted in the previous chapter) and who had found Royal Marine, Len Phillips, and sailor Jimmy Scoular serving on their doorstep, and playing locally, in 1945-46.

It gelled so well for Bob Jackson's side in that 1948-49 season that they won the League Championship – and then repeated the feat the following season, as Tinn's starlets began to be capped and to become cigarette-card heroes.

The side went unbeaten at home for a run of 32 First Division games, eventually succumbing to Blackpool in a game recalled in Chapter 16 below. That may seem a lot less to shout about than the 42-match unbeaten run, home or away, of Brian Clough's Nottingham Forest, let alone the achievements of the Arsenal side that overtook that record at the start of the 2004-05 season. But such statistical comparisons must not be allowed to blind us to the immensity of what Portsmouth achieved at a time when football, as a spectator sport, was at its peak in England and when England's reputation as a footballing nation was beyond repute. And they did it with a team that, unlike many of their rivals, began the 1948-49 season with no established stars. Theirs was a towering achievement.

Not that the success of a side, from a football outpost on the south coast, was acclaimed at the time. Take the reaction of Charles Buchan. In his 1949 introduction to the *News Chronicle Football Annual*, he grudgingly noted how Pompey's 'strong team-work, determination and craft' had won the Championship, but regretted that 'no team succeeded in capturing the limelight like Manchester United and Arsenal had done in previous years.' In the 1950 *Annual*, despite the near-record attendances across the Football League, he lamented that football had lost its '"old-time" spectacular brilliance' and that 'the supply of talented players is not equal to the demand.' And, by the way, Portsmouth retained their title, albeit only on goal average.

If such a curmudgeonly disposition had any adherents in Southampton, it was not manifested in the trainloads of spectators arriving at Fratton Station from Southampton, eager to watch the emerging Pompey side against some of the stars of the day (a phenomenon relived by some of those travellers in Chapter 16).

Not that the Saints were failing to make a mark themselves – or, rather, narrowly missing making a mark. As their neighbours stood astride English football, they just missed promotion three seasons running. In 1948, Wayman's 17 goals in 27 games were not enough as Southampton finished third in the Second Division, four points adrift of runners-up Newcastle United, the side that had let him go. The following season, Wayman had scored 32 times in 35 appearances when he was carried off, injured, at White Hart Lane. With only seven games remaining, they were eight points clear at the top of the table. Without a fit Wayman, they managed only four more points and Fulham and West Bromwich Albion overtook them – whereupon their manager moved to Fulham and Alf Ramsey to Tottenham.

Internal appointment, Sid Cann, initially failed to make an impression in 1949-50, but a late run took them level on points with runners-up Sheffield Wednesday and third-placed Sheffield United. Wednesday's goal average was superior to that of Saints by 0.065.

The great pity of all of this – for the purposes of this book, at least – is that, during these halcyon days for both clubs, they did not meet once, not even in the most inconsequential of friendlies.

1951 to 1960

During the 1950s, they would meet four times: the first three of these would involve experiments with floodlighting; the fourth would be a way of filling a blank Fifth Round Saturday.

They played their first post-war match in October 1951, with Pompey still a force in the First Division and the Saints in evident decline. The game was merely a friendly, the result carrying no great meaning. Yet in retrospect, it might now be regarded as significant, had it not been played between two South Coast clubs.

The point is that it was played under lights. It is seemingly no coincidence that the two League clubs pressing ahead, in 1950-51, with the installation of floodlights, were Southampton and Arsenal. Each had visited Brazil – in 1948 and 1949, respectively – where they had experienced floodlit football. Bill Dodgin had

the unique advantage of having been on both trips – first as Saints' manager and then as Arsenal's guest. When he took those and other benefits with him to Craven Cottage, he left behind players and coaches who had experienced the Brazilian way, not to mention Cllr Rex Stranger, the director who had master-minded the tour.

The new manager, Sid Cann, had not been in that party but he, too, was an enthusiast for floodlighting – as a way of facilitating evening training sessions. The potential for bringing in some extra cash was soon spotted, however, although there was free admission to a 30-minutes-each-way experiment against Bournemouth in October 1950.

Despite the fact that the spectacle was marred somewhat by fog and the lack of any goals, most of those who witnessed it were inclined to declare the experiment a success: the future of floodlit football in Southampton appeared to be assured, even if there were grave reservations elsewhere.

The first competitive match under lights at The Dell – and in the UK – was a Football Combination fixture between Saints and Spurs Reserves sides on 1 October 1951 and, again, observers from the football world (south of Watford at least) were impressed, despite the obvious shortcomings of the system.

Following the Tottenham game, however, a meeting of the Football Combination banned football under lights 'until the Football League recognises it.'

Yet the Spurs chairman, F. J. Bearman, who chaired that meeting, told the *Echo* that neither he nor his Board were against it: his club would be installing lights just as soon as they could.

And the Portsmouth directors were likewise keen, they said, to jump aboard the pioneers' wagon.

Monday 22 October 1951

Hampshire Combination Cup

Southampton 2 Portsmouth 2

Kiernan	Day	Butler	Ryder
Gregory	McGowan	Stephen	Reid
Sillett	Brown	Ferrier	Clarke
Horton	Dudley	Beale	Phillips
Wilkins	Edwards	Froggatt	Gaillard
Mallett		Wilson	

The Dell

Referee: Mr H.C. Dowell (Bournemouth)

Attendance: 22,697

The outsize crowd for this parochial Cup-tie could suggest a special interest in watching football under lights or in seeing the first derby for 12 years – or maybe a bit of both? Any spectators attracted by Commentator's hype that eight internationals were likely to be on view would have been disappointed: only three of them – Froggatt (England), Stephen (Scotland) and Kiernan (Ireland) – turned out on the night.

The occasion still merited, though, a boastful headline in the *Echo*:

SUCCESS OF POMPEY VISIT

That was mainly a reference to the floodlighting but also to the way in which the underdogs raised their game:

There is no doubt that football looks better under lights. Everybody was delighted with the game. It certainly was a very good exhibition of soccer, and the suggestion – it was not unkindly made – that Saints should play all their games under lights was a measure of the pleasure all experienced when watching the slick movements of the players, the swift combination, and the many goalmouth thrills.

The spectacle is about to begin for the large crowd.

An excerpt of how Orf saw the game for the *Echo*.

With Jimmy McGowan impressing and Jack Edwards having his 'best game this season,' Saints took the game to Pompey.

They went ahead when Edwards 'drifted' in from his wing to score the first floodlit goal by a Southampton player at The Dell. Beale equalized before half-time with 'a slashing cross-drive.' In the second half, Duggie Reid made it 2-1 with 'a great header' and Frank Dudley's 'splendid headed goal' completed the scoring. Dignitaries queued to tell the *Echo* that they were impressed with the lights and Bob Jackson confirmed Pompey's keenness to install them. Mr Eden suggested, on behalf of the Hampshire FA, that, as the game had been drawn, Portsmouth should take the Cup home with them and that Southampton visit Fratton Park to play a 'decider' once their floodlighting was up and glowing.

Running tally:	Pompey	86	Saints	64	Drawn	25

Monday 2 March 1953 **Friendly**

Portsmouth 1 Southampton 1

Uprichard	Harris	Christie	Day
Stephen	Phillips	Ellerington	Williams
Ferrier	Henderson	Sillett	McDonald
Scoular	Gordon	Elliott	Walker
Froggatt	Dale	Horton	Hoskins
Dickinson		Mallett	

Referee: Mr A. Bond (London)

Fratton Park
Attendance: 22,714

The Fratton Park lights were ready and Southampton had come to launch them in what the *Echo* described as 'the promised return fixture.' It would not be the 'decider' that Mr Eden had hoped for, but this was no ordinary friendly: more than 22,000 spectators were attracted by the novelty. They included travellers from the Isle of Wight, reassured by the news of an adjustment to the floodlit age: a special late boat would leave Portsmouth Harbour at 10.15 pm.

Each side had replaced their manager since their last meeting, Eddie Lever having taken over from Bob Jackson and George Roughton having been brought in at The Dell.

In an injury-wracked season – the latest casualty, Alec Simpson, had broken his leg two days before – Southampton managed to field eight of the players who had taken Blackpool to a Fifth Round replay in the FA Cup. An achievement that came close to depriving the nation of the legendary 'Matthews Final' masked, however, a dire season in the League. They were currently only one place clear of the relegation positions. Portsmouth, lying 13th in Division I, were in comparative clover.

The reporters were again more interested in the floodlighting than the football. It was not mounted on the elegant pylons that today dominate the skyline for train passengers gliding towards Fratton Station: the lights in the corners of the ground were augmented by further lighting on the roofs of the stands. Mr Vernon Stokes, the Portsmouth Chairman, went to great lengths, in the programme, to explain how the club's own tour of Brazil in 1951 had led the directors to crave lights 'in four clusters on towers erected at the four corners of the ground,' such as they had seen in São Paulo. Indeed, he seemed determined, despite earlier protestations, to make it clear that the Fratton Park system owed nothing to the pioneering efforts at The Dell.

Notwithstanding complaints that the corners were 'rather shadowy', Portsmouth appear to have succeeded in improving on Southampton's arrangements: although 'visibility at times was marred by fog, ... as seems characteristic of floodlit football, it was all very good entertainment.'

In 'a hard, good game,' the goals came from a Harry Ferrier penalty in the 35th minute and 'a well-taken shot' by Roy Williams, early in the second half.

At the post-match dinner, Mr Sarjantson, the Southampton Chairman, accepted an iced cake, in the form of a football pitch – a gesture of sympathy from his hosts, the *Echo* claimed, for his club's position. 'We are going to cut ourselves a slice of luck from this cake,' he said. 'I think this cake will just about do the trick.'

It didn't. Two months later, the Saints were demoted for the first time in their history.

The next time the two clubs met, Southampton would be back in Division III (South).

Running tally:	Pompey 86	Saints 64	Drawn 26

Monday 7 March 1955   Friendly

Southampton 1   Portsmouth 3

Kiernan	Foulkes	Dore	Newman
Ellerington	Mulgrew	Gunter	Gordon (Pickett)
Traynor	Day	Mansell	Henderson
McLaughlin	Walker	Cairney	Rafferty
Wilkins	Hoskins	Rutter	Rees
Simpson		Dickinson	

Referee: Mr A.W. Smith (Aldershot)

The Dell
Attendance: 5,259

With Portsmouth among the Championship contenders and the Saints challenging for promotion, Observer considered this 'an attractive floodlit match.'

The public was not to be fooled, though: after the excitement of innovation, the crowd for this friendly was of more traditional proportions.

Two players, in particular, caught the eye: one for his coolness, the other for his efforts to keep warm. The former was, inevitably, Jimmy Dickinson. The latter was Fred Kiernan, Saints' Irish international goalkeeper, who 'set a new fashion by wearing track-suit trousers over his shorts throughout the match,' a wise move on a 'snowy, cold evening,' especially in the first half, when the visiting forwards failed to 'keep him warm' (*see right*)

Indeed, Southampton 'looked the "class" side—until it came to shooting.' They went ahead eight minutes into the second half, Eric Day converting a penalty after John Hoskins had been fouled. The lead lasted 17 minutes, whereupon Portsmouth scored 'three excellent goals' in the space of six minutes. Two of them came from Ron Newman, the former Newport (Isle of Wight) player who had recently signed from Woking, each set up by the versatile Wilf Rees, occupying his fourth position of the season in Portsmouth's forward-line. He had been well held by Bill Ellerington, but he twice eluded him 'cleverly' to set up Newman, either side of a Rafferty header from Mansell's free-kick.

| Running tally: | Pompey | 87 | Saints | 64 | Drawn | 26 |

By The Way

While an attendance of 5,000-odd is an indicator of how floodlighting was now becoming taken for granted by the fans, the Football League continued to express doubts on what it considered a dangerous subject.

They finally relented the following season. On 22 February 1956, more than four years after The Dell had staged the first competitive match under lights, Fratton Park became the first stadium to host a floodlit Football League match, when Newcastle United visited – and slightly spoiled the historic moment by winning 2–0.

Southampton had meanwhile made a change that would prove historic for the club.

In October 1955, their Reserves coach, Ted Bates, had been appointed manager.

Saturday 16 February 1957   **Friendly**

Southampton 3   Portsmouth 1

Christie	Day	Uprichard	Stenhouse
Wilkins	Mulgrew	McGhee	Gordon
Traynor	Reeves	Wilson	Henderson
McLaughlin	Roper	Phillips	McClennan
Parker	Hoskins	Dickinson	Dale
Elliott		Pickett	

Referee: Mr J.W. Hunt (Emsworth)

The Dell
Attendance: not known

POMPEY at the DELL!

BOTH SAINTS AND POMPEY ARE SWEATING (HOT & COLD) ON A RETURN TO THE SECOND DIVISION

I CAN NOT TELL THEE A LIE— THE BALL IS THINE!

NAY! 'TIS THY BALL— I INSIST!

IT WAS A REAL OLD-FASHIONED CHUMMY AFFAIR —

Both sides were out of the FA Cup and had the Fifth Round Saturday free. So, with golf in La Manga not yet an option, what better than to meet at The Dell for what Orf labelled, in the *Echo*, 'a real old-fashioned chummy affair'?

Pompey were struggling in Division I, lying 21st, albeit with games in hand, while

Ted Bates had taken Saints into fourth place in Division III (South). The new manager had inherited a side in which his longstanding team-mate, Eric Day, was a free-scoring No.9.

But he had moved Day back to the wing and experimented with several centre-forwards.

These included Derek Reeves (*right*), who had been on Pompey's books before going into the Army. Reeves had been top-scoring at No.8 this season but now had another outing at No.9.

Although marked by Jimmy Dickinson – then having a brief spell at centre-half – Reeves 'was always threatening the defence with his quick thrusts and energetic work' and was overall 'without a doubt a success' – sufficiently for the *Echo* to wonder whether Portsmouth might regret having let him go. He set out his stall with two 'excellent' left-footed

goals. The first was a 'powerful drive, which by its pace and direction gave Norman Uprichard no chance.'

For the second, he took a 'skilful and intelligent pass' from Hoskins and 'the ball fairly rocketed into the net.'

The Saints' other goal was an 'excellent' effort by Day, running through the Portsmouth defence. Pompey finally got on the score-sheet late in the game with a McClennan tap-in.

This ebullient performance was something of a false dawn for Southampton, although the introduction, four weeks later, of 17 year-old Terry Paine would soon help Reeves to establish himself as an exceptional Third Division striker.

As for Pompey, this game perhaps underlined the obvious: the team needed re-building; and fast.

Running tally:	Pompey 87	Saints 65	Drawn 26

1960-61

Demotion is not the worst thing that can happen to a club – especially if it bounces straight back. Then again, many don't.

The Saints were a case in point. They were in no shape for an early return to the Second Division. Having traditionally struggled financially, the club had become reliant on cheques from directors and hand-outs from the Supporters Club to stave off insolvency. But, perhaps as much by luck as judgment, the ingredients for promotion would fall into place in the late 1950s.

These lucky breaks have been recorded in Ted Bates's biography and the details need not be rehearsed here. You could say they started with his appointment. Although members of his successful Reserves side had assumed their coach was on his way to the manager's job, there were those in the club who thought him no more capable of that transition than Sid Cann had been. If it took him a considerable commitment and long hours to

achieve what he did, Bates always talked of his good fortune as a manager. Take two examples. He was lucky – if not as spectacularly as Jack Tinn at the end of the War – to find so many good youngsters on his doorstep: the outstanding 1957 Youth side would yield Terry Paine, John Sydenham and Tony Godfrey.

And then the club's horse-racing connections would fortuitously bring to The Dell a young Londoner, Charlie Livesey, whose sale to Chelsea in 1959 enabled Bates to bring in three players – Huxford, Conner and O'Brien – who hardly missed a game between them, as his blend blasted their way to the Third Division championship in 1960, with a sensational FA Cup win at First Division Manchester City thrown in.

Which would mean a Second Division reunion, in 1960-61, with a Portsmouth side very much in decline. They had clung on to First Division status, by goal average, in 1957-58, whereupon they had parted company with Eddie Lever. He was replaced by Freddie Cox who had taken Bournemouth & Boscombe to the quarter-finals of the FA Cup. As Pompey historian, Colin Farmery, has put it, his 'apparent ability to turn sows' ears into silk purses on a shoestring seduced an increasingly cash-conscious board.'

The established Jimmy Gordon and the up-and-coming Derek Dougan and Ray Crawford were among the players sent on their way, as Cox 'set about trying to confirm his theory that lower division sweat could take

the place of First Division style. It was a policy doomed to failure.' That failure took the form of relegation to the Second Division in 1959.

The next season saw Jimmy Dickinson convert to left-back and Peter Harris retire with TB, as Pompey just escaped a second successive relegation that would have meant passing the promoted Saints on the way.

As it was, the two sides could meet in Second Division football – or, indeed, any competition that counted – for the first time since 1927.

Saturday 27 August 1960   **Football League Division Two**

Southampton   5   Portsmouth   1

Reynolds	Paine	Beattie	Fraser
Davies	O'Brien	Rutter	Saunders
Traynor	Reeves	Dickinson	Newman
Clifton	Mulgrew	Howells	Campbell
Page	Sydenham	Snowdon	Cutler
Huxford		Chapman	

The Dell

Referee: Mr C.H. Rogers (London)   **Attendance:** 28,845

How things had changed since Jimmy Dickinson – the sole survivor, following Peter Harris's retirement, of the Championship side – made his away debut at The Dell in 1943. Now 35 and the last vestige of a great side in free-fall, he was facing 11 Championship medallists – even if it was only Division III – in a team unchanged from walloping Bill Shankly's aspirant Liverpool in mid-week. Southampton fans had had to wait a long time for the

Football Echo headline that summed up their third game of the season:

AFTER 33 YEARS
SNAPPY SAINTS OUTCLASS POMPEY

The *Football Mail* did not demur: the 5-1 'thrashing' was 'a triumph for much superior play.'

Having 'opened up the Pompey defence,' Terry Paine scores the first goal.

With the atmosphere 'electric', the teams came out to 'thunderous applause'. Cliff Huxford opened the scoring with a 'brilliantly taken goal' on 25 minutes. Having 'got the better of Howells in a high-kicking duel in mid-field,' he ran on to 'crash' a 25-yarder past Beattie.

Saints scored a second in the 36th minute – a penalty from George O'Brien, after he had been fouled by Chapman – and added two more, in the space of four minutes, before the interval. The first of these came when Terry Paine 'opened up the Pompey defence' and fed Reeves, 'whose shot beat Beattie and struck the inside of the post with such power' that it spun back into the path of Paine, who was following up, to score.

Paine had hitherto been well held by Dickinson, but the home forwards were generally 'giving the Pompey defence a harrowing time.' Rutter was having problems with John Sydenham and when he fouled him just outside the penalty area, Traynor's free-kick was helped on by Reeves to Mulgrew, whose header eluded Beattie's outstretched arms.

This seemed to provoke a 'spot of bother between rival groups of supporters', of which Linesman had a good view: it occurred in front of the press box. He was also able to report a semblance of a recovery by Portsmouth, led by Newman who 'crashed' a 56th-minute goal, hit a post and twice tested Reynolds. But the Pompey defence continued to be kept busy and, in the 75th minute, 'paid the penalty for some slow thinking.'

When Sydenham crossed, O'Brien was given time to lay the ball off. Linesman says it went to Reeves; Observer claims it was Mulgrew; whoever it was had his shot indisputably deflected past Beattie by Dickinson.

So both sets of supporters now knew the answer to the question of who was 'top dog', as posed by Janus in the *Football Mail*: 'Southampton's quick, fine attack was just too much,' he concluded, 'for a crumbling Pompey defence, and after 30 years the Saints are cock-of-the-walk.' Yet it was 'in some ways… rather a hollow win,' Observer felt:

> Pompey, on the day's showing, did not look as good as half the sides Saints met in the Third Division last season… One of the Saints' forwards said afterwards he had rarely found it so easy to get round defenders as he did [in this game] because they were so slow in the tackle.

John Sydenham was causing problems for Rutter.

Running tally: **Pompey**   87   **Saints**   66   **Drawn**   26

Saturday 31 December 1960

Football League Division Two

Portsmouth 1 Southampton 1

Beattie	Priscott	Reynolds	Paine
Rutter	Chapman	Davies	O'Brien
Dickinson	White	Traynor	Reeves
Howells	Newman	Conner	Mulgrew
Gunter	Cutler	Page	Penk
Harris		Huxford	

Referee: Mr A.G. Sturgeon (London)

Fratton Park
Attendance: 31,059

AFTER INSPECTION, REFEREE STURGEON – WHO ONCE SENT TWO TEAMS OFF – MADE THE MISTAKE OF SENDING THE SAINTS AND POMPEY ON!

THEN WHEN THE GAME STARTED HE WAS BUSY TURNING DOWN SAINTS' PENALTY APPEALS

Believe me, I'd like to help you but I just can't find the spot!

AND SO THE GAME DEGENERATED INTO A NEW YEAR'S EVE FANCY DRESS – WITH TERRY PAINE DISGUISED AS A GOALKEEPER

WE WOULD LIKE TO DRAW TOM MULGREW BIGGER THAN ANYONE ELSE BECAUSE HE SAVED OUR SHIRTS AND FACES –

Ted Bates had stuck by his champions, although Harry Penk, the former Pompey winger, had been bought as cover while John Sydenham was doing his National Service and had just started his most substantial spell of the season.

This combination had been good enough to keep them in contention and, with just over half the season gone, they were four points off the lead.

Pompey's main goalscorer, Ron Saunders, was out injured while Ron Newman was making his last appearance before departing to Leyton Orient, one of the sides down near the bottom of the table with them.

The comparative performances of the two sides were reflected in their gates. Attendances at The Dell were now routinely exceeding those at Fratton Park – in part, perhaps, because Southamptonians were nowadays less inclined than they had been to pop down to Portsmouth when the Saints were away (in the manner described in Chapter 16), but mostly because Pompey supporters were becoming every bit as demoralised as their neighbours had been back in the early 1950s. Still, if there was one thing destined to boost the gates at Fratton Park it was the reborn rivalry with the Saints – not least because everyone with a red-and-white scarf wanted to be there: the *Football Echo* estimated that 10,000 of them made the trip along the A27, by one means or another, to be part of the ground's biggest gate for two years.

The various reports in the *Echo* and *Mail* used words like 'tense', 'exciting' and 'thriller' but they all agreed that the football was less than satisfactory, even if the mud, rather than the players, took the major share of the blame. Janus went so far as to reason that 'the match should not have been started under such appalling conditions, but both sides pulled out all the stops and gave the crowd great entertainment.'

Ron Reynolds left the field after 12 minutes with a burst blood vessel in his throat. Terry Paine took his jersey for the next 26 minutes, during which he was not tested once. Meanwhile, an element of needle crept into the proceedings. Linesman attributed this to a tackle by Huxford, but Observer blamed the Portsmouth players for 'too many fouls' – three of which merited penalties.

The Southampton defence, with Reynolds restored to it, was 'completely bamboozled' in the 75th minute. Pompey had a free-kick just outside the area, which Harris 'shaped' to take. But it was Chapman who drove 'the ball through them and past Reynolds, who seemed unsighted.'

1944-66: Ships in the Night

Five minutes from the end, Harris toppled Paine and the referee this time 'awarded a hotly-disputed penalty.' Beattie was so pleased at saving Page's spot-kick that he 'jumped for joy after clearing, and a small boy ran on the field to congratulate him.'

But the Saints came again and 'snatched an equaliser in the dying seconds.' After Paine and Reeves had each had a shot charged down in a

goalmouth scramble, Mulgrew took his chance.

It was not a particularly good result for either side. Southampton slipped a further point off the lead, while Portsmouth were now one of five clubs bracketed together, four points above the relegation spots.

Beattie goes face-down in the mud to deny O'Brien.

| Running tally: | Pompey | 87 | Saints | 66 | Drawn | 27 |

Final Word

In the remaining 18 games of the season, both sides dropped down the table – the Saints to eighth, Pompey to 21st and relegation.

The club historians, Holley and Chalk, blame Saints' decline on the heavier grounds that 'seemed to stifle [their] style of play.' According to Pompey historians Jeffs, Farmery and Owen, Freddie Cox attributed his team's slide to the 'lack of co-operation from senior players.' But the club's chroniclers tend to blame Cox.

He was relieved by coach Bill Thompson in February but the side ended March with only one win since before Christmas. By the time George Smith arrived as manager in April, relegation was a near inevitability.

It had been a steady, but then accelerating, drop from the heights of 1950. Yet Pompey had remained, for the football historian Geoffrey Green, one of the 'outstanding' clubs of the 1950s. He thought it

ironic that a decade begun with flying colours should end in relegation to the Second Division and, within two more seasons, even down to the Third. A club can never afford to live on past laurels; football is a hard task-master.

That judgment is perhaps a little harsh. Those laurels had been won by a young side, half of whom had been reared or stationed on the club's doorstep. Youth of that calibre is not a renewable resource.

1961-62

Saturday 12 August 1961   **Friendly**

Southampton   0   Portsmouth   2

Reynolds	Paine	Beattie	Priscott
Davies	O'Brien	Gunter	Gordon
Traynor	Reeves	Wilson	Saunders
Clifton	Mulgrew	Brown	Middleton
Page	Penk	Snowdon	Cutler
Huxford		Dickinson	

Referee: not known

The Dell
Attendance: 5,440

It was quite like old times – the first pre-season engagement between the two clubs since the Jubilee games before the War. And, for good measure, the Reserves were meeting at Fratton Park.

Not that Observer was as excited about the game as the *Echo* once tended to be by these derby friendlies: it proved to be 'very much a practice game [and] a bit dull. There is never quite the "edge" to these matches that there is to a game with points at stake, and though there was the usual local rivalry and keenness to win I felt both sides held back a little.'

He was not inclined to dwell on the details of Pompey's 'double' – their Reserves won 4-2 – being somewhat preoccupied with the Saints' need of 'fresh blood'. Ted Bates had come into this game still with only Penk added to his Championship side. But John Page would injure his back in training in the week before the League campaign started and never wear a first-team shirt again.

Tony Knapp would arrive for a record transfer fee and would seriously settle in – starting with two ever-present seasons.

Running tally:	Pompey 88	Saints 66	Drawn 27

1962-63

Inspired, no doubt, by their pre-season success at The Dell, George Smith's Pompey cruised back to Division II at the first attempt. They topped the Third Division, thanks mainly to some stunning away form that produced 12 wins.

There was, during the summer, a major transformation to the Portsmouth skyline, when four, 120ft-high floodlighting pylons appeared at Fratton Park.

The Dell – as we are on the subject – had not the space to accommodate such dramatic erections but, during the summer of 1960, catwalks had been constructed on the stand roofs, so that the lighting could now be mounted in clusters along their lengths, instead of being slung from under the eves as they had been hitherto.

The Saints finished the 1961–62 season in sixth place, their highest position in the Football League since 1950.

1944-66: Ships in the Night

Portsmouth 1 Southampton 1

Milkins	Barton	Reynolds	Paine
Gunter	Gordon	Davies	O'Brien
Wilson	Saunders	Williams	Kirby
Brown	McCann	Wimshurst	Burnside
Snowdon	Dodson	Knapp	Sydenham
Dickinson		Huxford	

Fratton Park

Referee: Mr R.E. Smith (Newport, Mon.)

Attendance: 32,407

Fratton Park's largest crowd since 1958 was bolstered, naturally enough, by a substantial body of Saints' adherents, most of whom appear to have crawled along the A27 in a traffic jam that backed-up from Southsea to Bursledon.

Pompey had got off to a fairish start to the season and, after a dozen games, were bubbling away in mid-table and well placed to get into the promotion frame. Encouraged by early season form, the Board allowed George Smith to splash out £6,000 on the Coventry inside-forward, Albert McCann.

The Saints had struggled from day one. They were six games into the season when they got their first win, against Charlton, boosting their points total to three. Ted Bates spent the eye-watering sum of £47,000 in just over a week, to bring George Kirby from Plymouth Argyle and David Burnside and Stuart Williams from West Bromwich Albion. Results improved, but not dramatically, and when Southampton turned out at Fratton Park, they were four points behind their hosts.

They were still four points adrift when they left. A 1-1 draw generated descriptions like 'dour struggle', 'spirited battle' and 'stern test for both teams.' In other words, another derby that was not a footballing classic.

While Reynolds was initially the busier 'keeper, Milkins was the first to be beaten, on 14 minutes, by a powerful shot from O'Brien. Unfortunately for the Saints, Kirby was in an offside position. Then, after Sydenham and McCann had each mishit shots and Paine had messed up a couple of opportunities, Pompey went ahead, on 33 minutes, through 'an absolutely brilliant shot from Barton.' O'Brien got the Saints on terms in the 56th minute, when he 'rose spectacularly to glide' a Paine corner past Milkins with his head.

Although Linesman felt 'the big crowd must have gone home thinking that a draw was a fair result,' Reynolds had needed to be 'on brilliant form', bringing off 'the save of the afternoon, diving backwards to turn Saunders's header for a corner.'

Opposite page: A friendly section of the largest crowd at Fratton Park since 1958.

Above: The despairing dive by Milkins cannot keep out O'Brien's 'spectacular' header.

Running tally:	Pompey	88	Saints	66	Drawn	28

By The Way

It was a winter of discontent, made glorious summer by an epic Saints' Cup run.

On 22 December, a 3-1 home win against Newcastle left Pompey in sixth place, just four points off the second promotion slot. The Saints had by now succeeded, with agonising sluggishness, in emerging from the relegation zone, but it still looked like a long winter ahead.

A very long one, as it turned out. Their fixture at Bury, that day, was one of 12 matches postponed, while another seven games were abandoned. And that was just the start of it – the start of the 'Big Freeze'. Although the two sides each managed to play on Boxing Day, their matches the following Saturday were postponed. And neither of them would complete another League game until 23 February – the Saturday before their scheduled 'return' fixture.

They would see a little FA Cup action, though. By dint of covering three-quarters of Fratton Park with 'dark brown peat,' Portsmouth played, and drew with, Scunthorpe in the Third Round on 26 January, three weeks after the scheduled date.

All Southampton had to show for January was a Cup win against York City – as awarded by the Pools Panel, sitting for the first time.

After nine postponements, Saints managed, come February, not only to meet, and beat, York but to see off Watford in Round 4.

The thaw was slower in the north, so when March and the derby game came round, Portsmouth were still waiting to replay at Scunthorpe, while Southampton as yet had no idea who their next opponents would be: Sheffield United, their eventual Fifth Round visitors, had yet to play their Third Round tie.

Saturday 2 March 1963   **Football League Division Two**

Southampton   4   Portsmouth   2

Reynolds	Paine	Armstrong	Barton
Williams	O'Brien	Gunter	Gordon
Traynor	Kirby	Wilson	Saunders
Wimshurst	Burnside	Harris	McCann
Knapp	Sydenham	Snowdon	Lill
Huxford		Dickinson	

Referee: Mr J.K. Taylor (Wolverhampton)

The Dell
Attendance: 25, 463

There was still enough frost for the Dell pitch to have been 'liberally sanded'.

But 'although still hard, [it] was in better condition than at any time since the freeze-up started.'

In otherwise 'ideal' conditions, 'with bright sunshine making it just right,' in Linesman's book, 'to watch a local derby of this nature,' the biggest Dell gate of the season, to date, included a large Pompey contingent, 'jamming the main roads towards the ground, and loud in their enthusiasm.'

The 'promotion "dark horses",' as the *Echo* saw them, Portsmouth had reinforced their squad during the Freeze: Micky Lill (from Plymouth Argyle) would be making his debut for them, while this would be a first away appearance for John Armstrong (from Nottingham Forest).

Lill was involved in the opening goal on 16 minutes, taking 'a good pass' from Saunders and crossing. The ball struck Traynor, 'as he was pressed near the goal-line,' and went past Reynolds. It got worse. Saints other full-back, Stuart Williams, was injured and helped off. Cliff Huxford took over at right-back, while O'Brien moved to left-half.

Yet the 10 men took the initiative. They equalised after 33 minutes when 'a beautifully-judged centre' from Sydenham 'was met by Burnside, who beat Armstrong in the air and glided the ball in with his head.' Six minutes later, Paine made it 2-1, 'with a real surprise goal.' Seemingly 'shaping to beat Wilson,' just inside the penalty area, 'he suddenly unleashed a shot which went straight through the left-back's legs [and] completely fooled Armstrong.'

Returning just before half-time, with four stitches in his right shin, Williams went on to the right wing. Not that he played the traditional 'passenger' role: 'he was standing in just the right spot to hit the ball back into the net after a shot from Paine had rebounded off the crossbar.' It was 3-1, against the odds, at half-time.

In the second-half, Pompey appeared to have got one back through Saunders, but there were those at the Milton Road end who would have sworn the shot had hit the side netting. Jack Taylor, the future World Cup Final referee, had his doubts too. Having consulted his linesman and awarded a goal-kick, he then held up play for 'repairs' to the net.

From then on, while Reynolds had a far from relaxing time, the Saints had the whip hand. With 11 minutes left, Burnside made it 4-1 from O'Brien's centre. But Saunders brought some respectability to the score-line, five minutes later, turning in another cross from Lill, and then, at the death, had a shot hit the underside of the bar.

George O'Brien (*bottom left*) was obliged to move to left-half, leaving the bulk of the goal-scoring to David Burnside.

Above: Burnside soars to beat Armstrong and 'glide the ball in with his head' for his first goal.

Below: He and O'Brien (*right*) are both grounded as they watch the ball cross the line for his second.

| Running tally: | Pompey | 88 | Saints | 67 | Drawn | 28 |

Final Word

Pompey's defeat at The Dell was the beginning of a nine-game run of League defeats, which saw them drop well out of the promotion race. They finished the season in 16th place.

The Saints continued to climb – to reach the giddy height of 11th. But that was all something of an irrelevance to the supporters, as they watched their side beat First Division Sheffield United and Nottingham Forest in successive rounds of the FA Cup, the latter by 5–0 in a second replay at White Hart Lane (where Pompey had eventually been eliminated in a Fourth Round second replay by Third Division Coventry). That earned Southampton their first semi-final appearance for 27 years – against Manchester United at Villa Park – and won them the *Giant Killers of the Year* award. But that was all they won: a fluky goal by Denis Law saw United through to Wembley, where they beat the favourites, Leicester City.

The signing of John McGuigan from Scunthorpe was hardly sufficient to justify Observer's contention that the Saints were entertaining 'higher hopes of success than they have had since they returned to the Second Division in 1960.' But their giant-killing Cup run must have given the side a certain degree of confidence.

Whatever, it was a rather more upbeat view than that of the Portsmouth manager. Having brought in John McClelland from Queen's Park Rangers and the Crystal Palace pair, Brian Lewis and Roy Lunniss, George Smith told the *Football Echo* that he expected to 'be a respectable Second Division side. About halfway I reckon. I know that's not being terribly ambitious, but it's honest. In the past, whatever league we've been in, we've hung on by our eyebrows. Halfway will be an improvement.'

A reasonable enough assessment, perhaps, but what a curiously blinkered historical perspective from which to make it!

On the opening day, each side flattered to deceive. Southampton beat Charlton Athletic 6-1 at The Dell, while Portsmouth, even more impressively, won 2-0 at Maine Road, against freshly-relegated Manchester City. Then, in the eight League games before they were due to meet each other, Pompey had three straight defeats and won only once, while Saints went six games without a win before winning twice coming into the game.

Saturday 28 September 1963   **Football League Division Two**

Portsmouth 2 Southampton 0

Armstrong	McClelland	Reynolds	Paine
Gunter	Gordon	Williams	O'Brien
Lunniss	Saunders	Traynor	Kirby
Campbell	McCann	White	McGuigan
Dickinson	Lill	Knapp	Sydenham
Lewis		Huxford	

Fratton Park

Referee: Mr N.C.H. Burtenshaw (Great Yarmouth)   **Attendance:** 29,459

So it was that the two sides came into this game two points part, although Saints' nine points were sufficient for 10th place in the table while Pompey lay 18th.

The familiar traffic jams on all routes from Southampton were a problem not only for the fans. Players' stories of their manager climbing out of the team coach to direct the traffic may be an exaggerated feature of the Ted Bates legend, but the *Football Echo* reliably informs us that this happened more than once on this particular occasion.

Despite this inconvenience, and the slender points difference, form appeared to favour the Saints: Pompey were yet to win at home. But it took only 11 minutes for that to change. As the *Football Mail* headline trumpeted,

**TWO-PUNCH START
SHATTERS SAINTS**

The Saints lost the toss and immediately lost possession from the kick-off. Whereupon,

> McClelland slipped a pass out to Lill, who took a moment or two to get it under full control before crossing to the far post where Saunders rose up to head the ball past Reynolds. It was a far from easy one for the centre-forward and he ended up falling among the photographers.

Despite Lill's deliberations, the goal was clocked at 25 seconds. Pompey maintained that early initiative and, although Paine and O'Brien threatened to breach the home defence, Reynolds's goal looked the more vulnerable. The referee needed to indulge in some finger-wagging – Gordon, Traynor and, inevitably, Kirby, each earned 'words' – before Lewis made it 2-0 on 11 minutes. Running on to a throw-in from McClelland, he beat his man and scored at the second attempt, as he fastened on to a rebound off Reynolds.

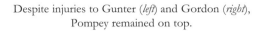
Despite injuries to Gunter (*left*) and Gordon (*right*),
Pompey remained on top.

Four minutes later, Reynolds's match – and, as it turned out, his career – was over. As recalled by his son, in Chapter 16 below, the Saints goalkeeper was led from the field, 'his shoulder obviously completely detached, to the extent that he appeared to be cradling the arm from falling off.' Huxford went in goal and hostilities were renewed.

In fact, the hostilities got more hostile, 'with fierce tackling on both sides,' and Mr Burtenshaw was obliged to remonstrate further with the offenders. These inevitably included Roy Lunniss and Terry Paine, whose clashes would become legendary. When Paine retaliated for a foul by his marker, Linesman thought it 'behaviour most unbefitting an England international.'

The match was temporarily reduced to 10-a-side when Gunter went off for treatment, but he returned to limp out the rest of the game on the left wing, Campbell taking over at the rear. In the second half, Gordon also showed signs of injury, but Portsmouth maintained their numerical advantage and, with Dickinson – recently

established at centre-half for the remainder of his career – 'well on top' of the rumbustious Kirby, they hung on to win a 'scrappy' game.

If Observer found it typical, in that regard, of this local derby, he regretted that that there was also 'a lot more vigour in the exchanges than was necessary.' Janus agreed: 'even with the tension of a local Derby, some of the football in the first half was little above the level of an undignified brawl.' The referee's handling of it all was deemed 'sensible', which is to say that he wagged his finger, had 'words' and even took a few names: you had to carry a loaded weapon onto the pitch, to be dismissed in those days.

George O'Brien at least brought a moment of light relief, and 'a huge roar of laughter,' to the proceedings when Lunniss brought him down just outside the penalty area. Linesman enjoyed the way 'he made a great play of crawling just over the penalty area line before looking up at the referee and inquiring as to whether it was a spot kick.' The much-put-upon Mr Burtenshaw was unmoved.

Running tally:	Pompey	89	Saints	67	Drawn	28

Saturday 8 February 1964   **Football League Division Two**

Southampton 2   Portsmouth 3

Godfrey	Paine	Armstrong	McClelland
Williams	Chivers	Wilson	Summersby
Traynor	Kirby	Lunniss	Saunders
Wimshurst	Burnside	Lewis	McCann
Knapp	Sydenham	Dickinson	Barton
Huxford		Campbell	

The Dell

Referee: Mr J. Finney (Hereford)   **Attendance:** 26,171

This was when the fervour of certain Portsmouth supporters first stepped over the line – at least as far as Southampton Football Club and the *Echo* were concerned. When staff came to open The Dell on

Saturday morning, they found 'Play Up Pompey' daubed on walls around the inside of the ground, the club flag lowered to half-mast, the goalposts painted blue and a score, 'in Pompey's favour, on the scoreboard.'

The authorities were not amused: 'all this meant a morning's work for four men and cost the club £20 to clear,' fulminated the *Football Echo*. The reaction elsewhere was amusement.

Those spectators who had battled their way through the by now traditional traffic jams to be there in good time had a pre-match treat: Tommy Traynor was presented with a watch by the Southampton chairman, George Reader, to mark his 500th appearance (friendlies included) in the first team. Saints' midweek visit to Swansea having been postponed, this was actually his 499th game but, rather than wait a week for the visit of Middlesbrough, the club decided to go ahead and exploit the derby match, when Jimmy Dickinson (now with over 700 games in Pompey blue to his credit) could literally be brought into the picture. The two sides had been following each other up and down the division all season. Southampton were currently lying sixth, with Portsmouth two points and three places behind them. But the 'underdogs' captured the *Football Mail*'s headline:

SAINTS ALIVE! IT'S A POMPEY 'DOUBLE'
Great victory at The Dell

A 'fiercely-contested, thrilling local derby' got off to a fast start and the teenage Martin Chivers, who was keeping out George O'Brien, beat two defenders and hit the post from 20 yards. But it was Pompey who 'combined better' in the opening exchanges and whose 'speed and quick tackling gave the talented Southampton attack no time to settle down.'

And their closing-down was rewarded in the 20th minute when McClelland 'nipped in to rob Traynor,' Saunders centred and McCann headed wide of Godfrey. Three minutes later, McClelland set up a second goal when he nodded Saunders in to score. Saints recovered well from the shock but were twice more denied by the woodwork, Kirby heading against the crossbar and Chivers again hitting the post.

Observer acknowledged that Pompey 'were playing with great dash' and their passing was 'a good deal' superior. But the reporting of the next goal, in the 36th minute, was decidedly partisan:

> Paine beat Dickinson in the middle of the field, pushed a long pass through for Chivers to run onto, and the young inside-right, taking his chance well, steered the ball wide of Armstrong into the net (Observer, *Football Echo*).

> It was rather a lucky goal. Paine got the ball on the rebound and it carried through to Chivers, whose shot trickled into the net just inside the post (Linesman, *Football Mail*).

If there was an exchange of views, or punches, in the press-box, it went unreported. Anyhow, Linesman graciously declared Portsmouth's third, in the 53rd minute, 'a shock goal', as Southampton 'had started to build up a series of dangerous looking attacks.'

The goal came from 'Pompey's danger weapon,' John McClelland, who sent in Ron Saunders and, when the ball was blocked, followed up to 'flash' it past Tony Godfrey.

Any hope Saints might have had of getting on terms took a blow in the 78th minute when a foul by Roy Lunniss (*right*) ended

the participation of Wimshurst – who will tell you that when the Pompey full-back despaired of catching Paine, he was resigned to being clobbered instead. On this occasion, Paine had been playing a bit deep for Lunniss to get him – too deep, in everybody's estimation, to be effective – but he popped up in the 88th minute to take a pass from Burnside and 'easily' beat Armstrong.

It was, however, a case of too little too late and nobody was about to dispute Pompey's superiority.

Although each side had done the double over the other more than once in their Southern League days, this was only the second double of their Football League encounters, Pompey having previously done it to Saints in 1927.

Reflecting that 'the keen rivalry between the two clubs is equalled by the partisanship of their followers,' Observer felt that this double would be 'a bitter pill' for the Southampton fans to swallow.

| Running tally: | Pompey | 90 | Saints | 67 | Drawn | 28 |

Final Word

The two sides spent the rest of the season swapping places in the upper reaches of mid-table. The Saints eased themselves two points clear on the final Saturday when they won and Pompey lost.

Two days later, they stretched the gap to four points – and four places – with a 6-1 win over Rotherham that took them to 100 goals and fifth.

1964-65

Saturday 12 September 1964

Football League Division Two

Portsmouth 0 Southampton 3

Milkins	McClelland	Hollowbread	Paine
Wilson	Gordon	Williams	O'Brien
Lunniss	Hiron	Hollywood	Chivers
Lewis	McCann	Wimshurst	Burnside
Dickinson	Dodson	Knapp	Sydenham
Harris		Huxford	

Fratton Park
Attendance: 25,024

Referee: Mr W.J. Gow (Birmingham)

Neither side had got off to a scintillating start to the season. Both were in the bottom six. After three games and three goals, Ron Saunders – Pompey's leading goalscorer for the previous six seasons – was transferred to Watford and his place given to summer signing, Ray Hiron, the former Fareham and Hants FA XI centre-forward. Hiron would prove himself a useful striker but, even with the benefit of hindsight, the decision to part with Saunders is a bemusing one.

These were, however, early days. The sun had its hat on and the crowd was in shirtsleeves. And there was no reason to believe that a 'fast and spirited' game was not a contest of equals – well, not until the18th minute when Wimshurst surged through and shot from the edge of

the area. Milkins could only push the ball into the path of Chivers who, with the departure of Kirby, was now in a twin spearhead with O'Brien.

The Saints' second goal came on the verge of half-time, from a corner needlessly conceded by Harry Harris. O'Brien (who rarely took corners) 'cracked' the ball quickly into the penalty area, where Paine (who rarely headed the ball) ran in to head well wide of Milkins.

In the second half, Pompey continued to press, but Saints went further ahead in the 55th minute when, from 'O'Brien's 'great pass', Sydenham 'cut inside and hammered a tremendous shot into the far corner of the net.' This was the cue, alas, for 'excited Saints fans' to come 'on to the pitch carrying banners.' Whereupon, 'a fight broke out' and the police had to remove the trespassers before the players could get on with it, the action remaining 'keen', the *Football Echo* reckoned, 'until the end, with Saints doing most of the pressing.'

Linesman was not a happy hack: only 'the calm and collected play of veteran campaigners Jimmy Dickinson and Alex Wilson' had preserved Portsmouth from 'even deeper waters'. The combination of Saunders's departure and this defeat by the Saints led to a good deal of vexation in Portsmouth. George Smith immediately brought in Ron Tindall, who had been given a free-transfer by Reading.

The supporters were far from mollified: 'how can the club hope to win promotion to Division One,' asked Half-Back in the *Football Echo*, 'by signing a player who is given away by a Third Division side?'

Running tally:	Pompey	90	Saints	68	Drawn	28

Saturday 16 January 1965   **Football League Division Two**

Southampton 2   Portsmouth 2

Hollowbread	Paine	Milkins	McClelland
Williams	O'Brien	Tindall	Lewis
Hollywood	Chivers	Lunniss	Hiron
Wimshurst	Melia	Gordon	Edwards
Knapp	Sydenham	Dickinson	McCann
Huxford		Harris	

Referee: Mr T.W. Dawes (Norwich)

The Dell
Attendance: 23,991

Another derby game at The Dell, another personal landmark for a player. Jimmy Dickinson was making his 750th appearance for Portsmouth. The crowd joined in the demonstration of admiration, as the players of both sides applauded him on to the pitch.

Yet with the Saints at the rear of the promotion pack and Pompey at the bottom of the division, the 39 year-old Dickinson badly needed a follow-up on the field to this most appropriate entrance, which had been accompanied by the band playing 'For He's a Jolly Good Fellow.' So 'the sweetest music of all to the craggy veteran,' Pat Collins suggested in the *People*, 'must have been when the final whistle signalled a shock point for Pompey' – while the Saints, who 'might have run up half-a-dozen goals in the first 30 minutes,' would 'be kicking themselves for dropping a point.'

Each side had a recent arrival at No.10. Dennis Edwards, who was making his debut for the visitors, had come from Charlton for £15,000 – half what Southampton had paid Wolves, just before Christmas, for Jimmy Melia.

It was Melia who opened the scoring in the 35th minute, when Portsmouth failed to clear a corner. But Lewis equalised with a similar goal, five minutes later.

That appeared to give Pompey a boost – Linesman felt they hade enjoyed 'amazing luck' to avoid 'crossing over four goals down' – and they started the second half looking more assured than they had in the first. Indeed, in the 57th minute, they went ahead when Milkins's 'long goal-kick' was played on by Lewis to Hiron, who 'flashed' the ball past Hollowbread.

Southampton, Linesman averred, 'looked rattled'. But they were soon back on terms, from a move started and finished by Melia on 64 minutes. 'Now battle was joined in earnest,' the *Sunday Telegraph* attested, as, 'amid mounting excitement, the Saints strove for the winner. But Dickinson and company did wonders in defence, while Milkins foiled O'Brien and Chivers with spectacular saves.'

O'Brien and Hiron each then missed a chance and Chivers had an effort disallowed. 'Nerve tingling stuff indeed' in a match that was not, Linesman felt, 'for the faint-hearted. In fact, it was the most closely contested local Derby... for years.'

Not to mention a triumph, on his special day, for Dickinson, whose 'coolness', allied to the saves of Milkins, had kept Pompey in the game.

1944-66: Ships in the Night

The two sides applaud Jimmy Dickinson onto the pitch before his 750th appearance for Pompey.

The visible Southampton faces are (*left to right*) Knapp, Hollowbread, Wimshurst, O'Brien, Melia, Sydenham and Hollywood.
The visible Portsmouth faces are those of Harris (*nearer camera*) and Milkins.

Running tally:	Pompey	90	Saints	68	Drawn	29

Final Word

The Saints finished fourth – back to their 1950 position. They had what it took going forward but, even if you score 83 goals, the second best tally in the Second Division, it's difficult to gain promotion when you concede 63.

Pompey survived – with a little help from their neighbours. They went into the last day of the season, level on points with Swindon, but with an inferior goal average. Swindon's 2-1 defeat that afternoon meant that they would be relegated, while Portsmouth would survive, if they could draw their evening match at Northampton. As the home side were already promoted, maybe they could achieve this. They did. So Jimmy Dickinson, whose 40th birthday and 764th League appearance it was, could retire with his side clinging on to Division II status and looking forward to at least one more season of derbies against the neighbours who were threatening to exit the division in the other direction.

A romantic finish for Dickinson, then, but truly the end of an era. While Southampton stood where they had been in 1950, how far adrift were Portsmouth from those halcyon days.

The major question begged in Portsmouth was: what would happen without Gentleman Jim? The chances of ever finding and nurturing any kind of replacement were effectively abandoned during the summer when it was announced that the club was scrapping its Reserves and Youth team set-ups and selling off their training ground at Tamworth Road. This exercise would leave them with 16 full-time players – once Ron Tindall had finished his summer cricketing obligations with Surrey.

The Saints were now getting bigger gates and being reckoned promotion contenders with a team that contained three locals – Paine, Sydenham and Chivers – each of whom had gained England honours at one level or another. Terry Paine had played in all four of England's close-season games and was clearly part of Alf Ramsey's World Cup plans.

On the open transfer market, these three forwards would each have fetched considerably more than the £20,000 the Portsmouth board expected to save, annually, by their economies.

This season would also witness a radical change in the rules that would transform football, irrevocably, and forever. Substitutions were to be allowed. Just one, and only for injury, which seems reasonable enough now, but there were those involved in the game who claimed it was 'not football' and insisted that players would feign injuries so that tactical changes could be made. Gosh!

Saturday 28 August 1965   **Football League Division Two**

Southampton   2   Portsmouth   2

Hollowbread	Paine	Armstrong	Lewis
Williams	O'Brien	Wilson	McCann
Hollywood	Chivers	Lunniss	Hiron
Walker	Melia	Gordon	Edwards
Knapp	Sydenham	Radcliffe (Barton)	McClelland
Huxford		Harris	

The Dell

Referee: Mr J. Lowry (Neath)   **Attendance:** 26,665

'Such friendship has existed for so long between Southampton and Portsmouth,' Rex Brian lamented in an unidentified national, that it seemed 'almost a shame that they should have to clash at all in the frenzy of modern League soccer.'

That said, he saw the encounter as a clash of styles, between the Saints' emphasis

> on soccer's arts and crafts – entertainment comes first and no one at The Dell must forget it – [and] the slightly more brash approach of Pompey… The flashing épée will be in the hands of Saints. The more unwieldy claymore will be brandished by Harry Harris… and his down-to-earth men.

Frank Leyland's verdict, in the *News of the World* – that 'Southampton had the class and Pompey the bustle' – would appear to vindicate Brian's assessment, but Leyland was, overall, appalled by a match that had 'excitement' but which 'was not one of which Second Division teams ought to have been proud. There was too much petty fouling and loss of temper. There were 44 free-kicks.'

Other reporters pretty much concurred and Observer was even more scathing about 'one of the worst games' he had seen in years: it was 'no credit to Second Division standards, or, for that matter, Third or Fourth.'

The Saints took the lead on 13 minutes when Cliff Huxford's free-kick into the goalmouth was deflected into the path of Jimmy Melia who knocked it home from the edge of the box, via the far post.

In the 28th minute, history was created when Portsmouth's young centre-half, Vince Radcliffe, broke his leg, in tackling Huxford. Tony Barton had the distinction of being the first substitute in a competitive fixture between the two clubs – or, indeed, any competitive match at The Dell.

Harry Harris (*right*) went to centre-half in the re-shuffle but that did not stop him 'steaming through', on the brink of half-time, to 'slam' a 30-yard equaliser.

Both sides were guilty of poor finishing in the second half. Martin Chivers was especially culpable, but was presented, in the 71st minute, with an opportunity to make amends: Armstrong came out to gather Sydenham's centre but dropped it and Chivers 'pounced' to restore his side's lead. It lasted all of three minutes – until Hiron's quick throw-in put in McCann to score with 'a tremendous shot'.

Running tally:	Pompey	90	Saints	68	Drawn	30

Saturday 5 February 1966   **Football League Division Two**

Portsmouth 2   Southampton 5

Armstrong	Lewis	Forsyth	Paine
Wilson	Portwood	Hare	Chivers
Tindall	Edwards	Williams	Dean
Gordon	McCann	Wimshurst	Melia
Haydock	McClelland	Knapp	Sydenham
Harris		Huxford	

Fratton Park

Referee: Mr E.D. Wallace (Swindon)   **Attendance:** 25,860

By the time the Saints arrived at Fratton Park in February, Ted Bates had used 20 players. It had all been so different at the beginning, the side that had drawn with Portsmouth in August being barely disturbed in a splendid six-game start. But that sixth game involved another career-terminating injury to a goalkeeper, when John Hollowbread left the pitch and Ken Wimshurst became the club's first substitute under the new dispensation.

And the casualty list kept growing. The line-up against Pompey included December signing, Campbell Forsyth, the Scottish international goalkeeper, and two of the youngsters who had come in: Norman Dean (*left*) and Tommy Hare. One of seven wearers of the No. 9 shirt so far this season, Dean had not exactly impressed anyone as an international prospect, but he did have a happy knack of scoring goals – five in his five League games to date.

Pompey's scope for changes was more limited, especially after their squad of 16 had been reduced to 15 by Radcliffe's broken leg, although a replacement centre-half – Frank Haydock from Charlton – had made his debut on the same day as Forsyth and become a regular.

They were doing quite nicely, sitting in mid-table and, while not exactly safe from relegation, were more comfortably placed than at the same stage the season before.

The Saints, for all their comings and goings, were threatening to do better than in the previous campaign, as they struggled with four other clubs to stay in the frame with leaders Manchester City.

Which is why Janus reflected, in his *News* preview, that this game meant more to the visitors than 'prestige and the championship of the South Coast': if their promotion 'dreams' were to 'remain alive', they badly needed to win. And win they did – though nothing like as emphatically as the score suggests.

They took the lead on 21 minutes when, as Janus saw it, 'Paine's corner carried well wide to Sydenham and when he cracked the ball hard back into the goalmouth it hit Dean's legs and rocketed into the corner of the net.' As Dean recalls, 'it was coming over like a bullet about waist-high; so I just stuck my leg out. I either had to stick my leg out or keep out of the way.'

Two minutes later, Chivers made it 2-0. As at The Dell, goalkeeper Armstrong 'came out and got hold of the ball, but dropped it,' giving Chivers a tap-in. The Saints now dominated for a while, but it was Pompey who scored next, just before half-time, when Lewis headed in McClelland's 'floated' cross.

The home side had the better of the early exchanges in the second half and equalised after 10 minutes. Paine, not noted for his tackling back, 'raced shoulder-to shoulder' with McCann, and just when he 'thought he had won the duel, McCann followed through to slam a great shot in off the under-side of the crossbar.' Southampton were now hanging on and, a minute later, 'luckily' scrambled the ball off their goal-line, following a drive from Edwards.

Indeed, when they regained the lead in the 70th minute, even Observer admitted it was against the run of play, as 'passes by Paine and Melia… left Dean with a simple scoring chance right in front of goal.' To say that Melia 'passed' is perhaps a euphemism: Linesman's suggestion that it was a 'miskick' seems not to be disputed.

Dean completed his hat-trick, six minutes later, when Sydenham made a long pass to Paine, who in turn put Dean through from the half-way line and, 'with Armstrong failing to come far enough out to intercept,' the novice centre-forward was able to bring his tally to eight in six games. The goalkeeper was again at fault in the 84th minute when he fluffed a pass-back from Haydock and let Chivers in once more.

Janus recalled a comment, from earlier in the week, that all Southampton needed to yet gain promotion was luck… Saints had luck, luck and still more luck. In fact, it was luck that gave them four of their goals.

Don Woodward was impressed, in the *Daily Express*, by the sheer 'variety of goals – fluked, blundered, and thundered.' As Melia told him, though, 'the score could have been 9-8, and I'm not saying in whose favour.' For his part, Woodward rejoiced that 'this WAS football – good, thumping local derby stuff, with enough bite to satisfy those who insist: "It's a man's game".'

Plum of the *Evening News* took defeat well.

Running tally:	Pompey	90	Saints	69	Drawn	30

He concluded that 'it would not be quite accurate to say Portsmouth deserved a share of the spoils. But they were desperately unlucky to lose so heavily. Still, one minute you're up, the next you're down. That's football.'

Indeed, but Pompey were not going down, while the Saints were still a long way from getting up: with a third of the season remaining, they were four points and three places removed from the second promotion slot.

Tuesday 10 May 1966

John Hollowbread Testimonial

Southampton 6 Portsmouth 1

Forsyth	Paine	Milkins (Armstrong)	McClelland
Webb	Chivers	Barton	Edwards
Williams	Dean	Wilson	Hiron
White(Wimshurst)	Melia	Gordon	McCann
Knapp	Sydenham(Chadwick)	Haydock	Kellard
Walker		Lewis	

Referee: Mr G. Martin (Whitchurch)

The Dell
Attendance: 10,757

The timing of this match, in recognition of the curtailed career of John Hollowbread, was remarkable.

Portsmouth had finished their season the Saturday before, in 12th place – not wonderful, but good enough to nurture some belief that the worst was over and that there was now something to build on. And the financial situation had improved, too.

But the Saints still had a game to play, the following week, away to the Champions, Manchester City. Only the previous evening, their fans had taken over East London to watch a 1-1 draw at Brisbane Road that all but secured promotion to Division I at last – just 39 years after Portsmouth made it.

Saints still needed to avoid losing by six goals at Maine Road, though, in order to be sure of promotion. Yet, despite his cautionary line when they opened the bubbly the night before – 'I'm drinking champagne, but I'm not celebrating' – Ted Bates started with 10 of the side who had played at Orient and who would be playing, unchanged, in Manchester.

Having had an easy ride from the Brisbane Road pitch the evening before, Martin Chivers was enjoying another one at Fratton Park.

A bold move – though maybe Pompey had undertaken to forgo derby traditions and to tackle gently, if at all?

If they had, then it was unfair of the *Echo* to rub it in:

> The Saints at half-power, and then at full power, pulsating with stylish confidence that reflected the club atmosphere of success... turned on a devastating performance in the final half-hour... to crush Portsmouth 6-1. Playing well within themselves at first and coasting, almost gently, to a 1-1 draw at half-time, Saints unleashed the full force of their scoring ability to crack in five goals in those last 30 minutes.

Dean, somewhat inevitably, opened the scoring in the 12th minute, from a move involving both of his wingers. But Hiron equalised seven minutes later, perhaps just as inevitably from a cross by McClelland, who had developed a habit of making goals against his neighbours.

Chivers started the second-half rampage with a penalty on the hour, after Tony Barton had fisted his shot over the bar.

He followed up, in the 71st minute, with 'a brilliantly taken goal from the edge of the penalty area from a Wimshurst through-pass.'

Whereupon the Saints hit three more – through Melia, Dean and even David Walker – in a four-minute spell that had their supporters 'dreaming of similar havoc among First Division defences next season.'

And if that seems premature, John Sydenham has explained that his manager's

David Walker,
a contributor to the 'havoc'.

caution was not generally shared around the town: 'everyone wanted to… celebrate, but you had this nagging thought… that, if you got beat 6-0, it would be all over.'

There were six more days to wait.

Running tally:	Pompey	90	Saints	70	Drawn	30

Final Word

Manchester City did not score six. In fact, nobody scored and the 0-0 draw meant that, by one whole point, Southampton had edged Coventry City into third place and were promoted as runners-up. Not the most comfortable of margins, but slightly more convincing than Pompey's elevation in 1927. Not that anyone was so impolite as to bring this up at the time.

If, conversely, there are Portsmouth fans who begrudge their neighbours the alleged 'luck' of taking three points from them, they should try talking to Bristol City fans of 50+ about the three indisputably fortunate points that Saints plundered from their side at Easter. So deeply was this injustice felt that City's matchday programme would be full of the need for revenge when Southampton went to Ashton Gate in the FA Cup – and lost – eight months later.

Give or take a few testimonials, Pompey would have to wait another eight years for an opportunity.

READ ON: Ted Bates's appointment and his lucky breaks are recounted in detail in *Dell Diamond,* along with Ken Wimshurst's recall of being the sacrificial lamb when Lunniss could not catch Paine and the various reactions to Saints' draw at Brisbane Road. Saints' 5-2 win at Fratton Park is recalled by Norman Dean in *Match of the Millennium.* Bristol City's grudge is recounted in detail in *In That Number.* The club histories referred to are Colin Farmery's *Portsmouth: Champions of England;* the Southampton *Complete Record* by Chalk and Holley; and the Portsmouth *Pictorial History* by Jeffs, Farmery and Owen. For details of these chronicles and of Geoffrey Green's *Soccer in the Fifties,* see 'Sources'.

Chapter 12
1966-96: In Reverse Order

So, it came to pass that the Saints were now the First Division club, with Pompey left stranded in Division II. This might be regarded as a reversal of the natural order of things but, as the previous chapter charted, it was now a long time since Portsmouth looked like going anywhere but down, while Southampton – who, until the mid-1920s, it might be argued, had looked the more likely side to reach Division I – had shaken off a 40-year torpor.

It's all a matter of where you stand – although, it should be added, the Saints' glory days in the Southern League had long been forgotten by the local, never mind the national, media by the time paradise, with its many mansions, was finally reached. Further, all things considered, there was absolutely no reason why both clubs should not both be in the top flight at the same time.

1966 to 1974

During these eight seasons, there would be but four South Coast derbies, first a friendly on another of those blank Fifth Round days and then a testimonial every two seasons or so.

Saturday 11 March 1967   **Friendly**

Portsmouth   2   Southampton   2

Armstrong	McCann	Gurr	Judd
Wilson	Hiron	Hollywood	Chivers
Pack	Pointer	Jones	Davies
Gordon	Kellard	Fisher	Melia
Tindall	Jennings	Webb	Thompson
Harris		Walker	

Referee: Mr R.F. Prichard (Salisbury)

Fratton Park
Attendance: 13,609

Pompey might have been entertaining the Saints in the FA Cup Fifth Round, instead of which their respective Fourth Round conquerors – Spurs, the eventual winners, and Bristol City, who had wrought the revenge referred to in the previous chapter – were meeting at White Hart Lane.

Yet this anti-climactic friendly attracted an unusually large crowd, including a healthy away contingent. The Southampton fans had not had a lot to cheer about in the top flight – apart from the relentless goal-scoring of Ron Davies, whose failure to find the net in the last three games was unprecedented – and

their side were lying 19th, thanks to Davies's goals being more than cancelled out by those conceded, including 25 in the last eight League games.

That woeful run had begun with a 5-1 defeat by Blackpool. Hughie Fisher (*left*), the winners' star that day, had just joined Saints and this game offered him and young Reserve, Mick Judd, an 'unofficial' debut.

It turned out to be a 'morale booster', Observer felt, for both teams – for, even if the defences 'were a bit suspect at times,' the goals they conceded were 'worthy ones'. The first, on 18 minutes, came from Judd's 'powerfully hit shot' from the edge of the area. Pompey struck back in the 51st and 57th minutes, through 'excellently taken drives' by Jennings and Harris, and Davies completed the scoring, six minutes later, 'with one of his well-known headers.'

And Fisher made his mark in an incident 'near the by-line, when he beat two opponents by some really dazzling footwork.'

It brought 'a big cheer from supporters on both sides.'

| Running tally: | Pompey | 90 | Saints | 70 | Drawn | 31 |

Monday 20 April 1970   **John Sydenham Testimonial**

Southampton   2   Portsmouth   4

Martin	Paine	Milkins	McCann
Kirkup	O'Brien	Hand	Munks (Pointer)
Fry	Channon	Ley	Hiron
Gabriel	Fisher (MacLeod)	Youldon	Bromley
Walker (Kemp)	Sydenham	Harris	Jennings
Saul		Storrie	

The Dell

Referee: Mr D. Nippard (Bournemouth)   **Attendance:** 10,145

The local reporters took distinctly different perspectives on this testimonial for John Sydenham. The *Echo* focused on the 'most unfriendly affair' that developed at the Milton Road end between the 'Saints skinheads' and the 'Portsmouth boot boys [who] had taken over one half of the terrace.'

But Mike Neasom, in the *News*, ignored the trouble on the terraces, reserving his contempt for the Southampton players: while the fans had been given 'a fair return for their cash' by the visitors,

> bored, slap-happy, Saints seriously short-changed them. Pompey were slick, imaginative and eager to do well in this friendly which, to them at least, carried local prestige. They deserved their convincing win. But while Pompey were doing their best to add the spark of life to the match, Saints, careless and listless, were doing their best to kill it off.

Jimmy Gabriel 'nodded' Saints' first goal.

The game had opened promisingly enough, with Milkins – who had already booked the Saints for his forthcoming testimonial – having to be at his best to save from Paine, Channon and Sydenham. But Pompey were first to score, on 22 minutes, through Bromley, only for Gabriel to equalise, a minute later, by 'nodding' home a Gerry O'Brien centre.

Whereupon, according to Neasom, 'promise of a lively battle quickly died.'

Jennings converted 'a low, fierce centre' from Hand in the 27th minute and two second-half goals by Hiron made it 4-1. With 12 minutes to go, Channon pulled one back, 'but by then the match had lost its meaning for the suffering fans.'

The *Echo* reported further skirmishes at Central Station, seven arrests and a train vandalised but, for Neasom, 'the losers were the public, football itself – and, above all, future beneficiaries.'

| Running tally: | Pompey | 91 | Saints | 70 | Drawn | 31 |

Portsmouth   0   Southampton   7

Milkins	Piper	Martin	Paine
Smith	Reynolds	McCartney	Channon
Collins	Hiron	Hollywood	Davies
Hind	Wilson	Steele	O'Neill
Youldon	Ley	McGrath	Talkes
Munks		Gabriel	

Referee: not known

Fratton Park
Attendance: 8,793

As the *Echo* headline-writer observed, this was a night of 'mixed fortunes' for John Milkins.

As John Hughes went on to explain, the Pompey goalkeeper 'collected £3,000 cash consolation for the public indignity of having seven goals drilled past him in his testimonial match.'

His humiliation began on 12 minutes when Brian O'Neil rounded off 'a brilliant headed one-two' with Jimmy Gabriel with 'a superbly volleyed goal to grace any soccer occasion.' And it got worse:

> Portsmouth were never in it after that. And the difference in class between these sides was embarrassing as Saints, playing with insolent ease, strolled to a 5-0 half-time lead.
>
> It just was not Pompey's night. With Saints having completed their seven-goals-in-65-minutes demolition job, Ray Hiron had a 'goal' disallowed for a foul on the goalkeeper by Richard Reynolds.

The 77th-minute goal that completed the scoring also came from O'Neil: 'a vicious 25-yarder which left Milkins groping.' In the meantime, even John McGrath had got on the score-sheet, while Ron Davies and Gabriel bagged two each.

It was as if Saints wanted to counter, two years on, the *News* verdict on the Sydenham testimonial. They had

demonstrated – and 'quite rightly', Reg Betts reasoned in the *News* – that 'there should be no sentiment in front of paying customers.'

John Milkins, to whom 'no sentiment' was shown.

Running tally:	**Pompey**	**91**	**Saints**	**71**	**Drawn**	**31**

By The Way

The Saints had now had six seasons in the First Division. They had yet to set it alight but a couple of seventh-place finishes, in 1969 and 1971, had got them into Europe – in the Fairs Cup and its UEFA successor.

At Fratton Park, meanwhile, nothing appeared to be going right. Ron Tindall had taken over team management in April 1970, but crowds had continued to dwindle and – whatever the directors' claims to the contrary – ambition amounted to finding the wherewithal to keep the club in existence and in Division II.

But they had reverted to some kind of youth policy. An attempt to use Waterlooville as a 'nursery club' had

fallen foul of the Southern League but, in 1972, Ray Pointer, having retired from playing that summer, was appointed to develop a youth team. Yet if they couldn't afford to be without a youth team, the stark reality was that Portsmouth couldn't afford to do very much at all. On 16 December 1972, Middlesbrough drew 0-0 at Fratton Park, in front of 4,688 spectators, leaving Pompey in 21st place in Division II.

There was a guest at that game, however, who was more inclined to see the positive aspects of the spectacle than the more obvious negative ones. Which is why the *News* was able to headline, on its front page 12 days later, a 'huge cash boost for Pompey.' Southampton businessman, John Deacon, had joined the Board and, although he 'declined to talk about the sums involved,' the *News* understood that 'his investment will enable the club to think big in the transfer market.'

And so they did – starting the very next day with the return of former-Fratton Park hero, Bobby Kellard, from Crystal Palace. But that was only the taster: three new players would arrive in time to line up as regulars in 1973-74: Welsh international full-back Phil Roberts; Arsenal's Scottish winger, Peter Marinello; and the centre-forward Matt Busby had described as the best in Europe, Ron Davies. If Davies had earned that honorific title in better days, he had become – and surely remains – a Southampton legend.

One way or another, Deacon was, as Colin Farmery has put it, 'buying, and buying big.' John Deacon was a Southampton City councillor who had been keen, as a Saints shareholder, to join the Board. So why had a businessman with money that he wanted to invest in the Saints been allowed, it might be asked, to go and throw it around at Fratton Park, instead? Was this not further evidence of the club's lack of ambition? When the rumour-mill grinds, it will generate counter-rumour – which included, in this case, suggestions that the directors at The Dell were less than enamoured of Deacon's style of accountancy.

Who better to ask about this than an accountant who had long served on the Southampton board, latterly as its Chairman? Guy Askham confirms that it was indeed a question of style, but only in the sense that Deacon's 'face didn't fit'. The likes of Sir George Meyrick, John Corbett and Col. Reddy were 'gentlemen farmers', old money as it were: 'John Deacon was an entrepreneur – they were not.'

The new money wooed John Mortimore to Fratton Park as manager, with his longstanding friend, Ron Tindall, becoming General Manager. Ted Bates's former Assistant Manager had discussed, with Southampton Chairman George Reader, the newly-advertised post of Team Manager Designate.

But the title didn't appeal and Deacon's style did. Lawrie McMenemy decided he could live with the title and arrived to await Bates's stepping upstairs.

The main picture shows Lawrie McMenemy (*left*) and Ted Bates. McMenemy had decided he could live with the title of 'Team Manager Designate', while waiting for Bates to move upstairs.

John Mortimore (*inset*), who disliked the implications of the title, fancied his chances with John Deacon.

Portsmouth   0   Southampton   0

Best	Marinello	Turner	Paine
Roberts (Lewis)	Kellard	McCarthy (Mills)	Channon
Wilson	Davies	Peach	Osgood
Piper	Mellows	Fisher (Gilchrist)	Chatterley
Went	Stewart	Earls (Waldron)	Stokes
Stephenson		Bennett	

Fratton Park

Referee: Mr D. Nippard (Bournemouth)   **Attendance:** 8,302

The line-ups speak for the activity of the new managers. John Mortimore had continued to spend the 'new money', splashing out £155,000 on Paul Went, while Lawrie McMenemy, having succeeded Ted Bates in November, had brought in Turner, Peach and Osgood.

These changes could not prevent Saints' slide down the table from fifth place in December. Indeed, many would say they were the cause. And the Saturday before this friendly, they had again become a Second Division club, a 3–0 victory at Goodison Park being insufficient to keep them up, as they became the first victims of the newly-introduced three-up, three-down system.

Norwich City and Manchester United went down with them. The nation (well, Fleet Street) mourned United's unlikely demise, but the prospect of home games against them must have cheered the Division II Chairmen and their bank managers. John Deacon must have thought he had won the pools: Manchester United and a big South Coast derby at Fratton Park.

The Saints approached the game cautiously, showing signs of nervousness in defence, while Channon and Osgood 'appeared to be tempered by a sensible reluctance to take any foolish daredevil risks which might have brought any serious injuries. Portsmouth, on the other hand, were an enterprising, aggressive outfit who worked non-stop in creating chances.'

But they could not score – not even Ron Davies, the most resolute player on the pitch in John Hughes's estimation, who 'showed tremendous determination to score against his old club,' but without luck. The best scoring effort of the night came from Lewis, who hit the bar from 30 yards, while, Davies apart, Marinello (twice) and Stewart both came close.

The Saints were hardly in it, though Bennett was commended for kicking off the line twice and Waldron, who came on as a sub in the second half, was 'impressive'.

Terry Paine had been left out at Everton to deprive him of another ever-present season. But it meant more than that: he had made the last of his 815 official appearances for Southampton – to which this trip to Fratton Park was a postscript.

Terry Paine, for whom this match was a postscript to his record 815 'official' appearances for the Saints.

Running tally:	Pompey	91	Saints	71	Drawn	32

Saturday 14 September 1974   Football League Division Two

Southampton   2   Portsmouth   1

Turner	Gilchrist (Stokes)	Best	Marinello
Mills	Channon	Roberts	Kellard
Peach	Osgood	Wilson	Davies
Fisher	O'Neil	Piper	Reynolds
Bennett	O'Brien	Went	Hand (Ellis)
Steele		Stephenson	

The Dell

Referee: Mr C. Thomas (Treorchy)   **Attendance:** 19,361

The world was not holding its breath. The Saints were 19th in the table and without a win in six games. Pompey, although they had won once, were a place below them.

Having piloted the Saints down into Division II, Lawrie McMenemy might have been regarded as the more precariously-placed manager but, as derby day approached, it was John Mortimore who was sacked, to popular consternation in Portsmouth. The protests were buried in a flurry of publicity from John Deacon, hinting that Bill Shankly, recently retired from Liverpool, and Denis Law were among those still in the frame, now that Sir Alf Ramsey had turned down the job, despite being 'flattered by the offer.' As it transpired, the appointee – on the very eve of the game – was indeed Scottish and once of Anfield: Ian St. John.

It turned out to be another sad day in the litany of deteriorating match-day experiences. A train was vandalised on the way to Southampton – not one light bulb survived – and the police arrested 250 passengers, most of them 'young people, including girls.' Meanwhile, shoppers were rushed in Above Bar and windows in the area, including some at the *Echo* offices, were smashed, proving that a few dozen yahoos can make life pretty awkward for people when they set their 'minds' to it.

The game was not a great spectacle either. Five players were booked and one was sent off. Brian Hayward reasoned, in the *Echo*, that, while 'not an ugly affair', the match had 'a generous helping of "professional niggling" and… a referee who always interprets the laws strictly.'

Bobby Kellard started it by conceding three free-kicks in the first three minutes, but Jim Steele was the first to be booked – for a foul on Nicky Piper 'that was neither vicious nor premeditated.' Kellard and David Peach were next into the referee's little black book. Mr Thomas was so 'concerned about what was happening off the ball,' that he visited the dressing rooms at half-time to lecture both teams: 'I am always sad when I have to book players,' but it was up to the referees, he told the *Echo*, 'to help stamp out what is wrong with the game.'

In between all the argy-bargy, the odd bit of football broke out, not least from Peter Osgood and Mike Channon. Osgood's 'accurate volley' from Channon's far-post cross opened the scoring in the 43rd minute. Pompey, 'who hardly launched a move of real penetration throughout the game,' equalised with a 58th-minute penalty. Paul Bennett had held down Ron Davies, who converted the spot-kick without a problem.

The Saints 'always appeared capable of scoring again,' though. Osgood missed narrowly, 'after a piece of super play by Channon,' who was then himself a fraction wide. In the 77th minute, they brought on Bobby Stokes. Portsmouth-born, the teenage Stokes had been part of the local football scene recalled by David Reynolds in Chapter 16. But with his home-town club having no Youth-team football to offer him, he had become an apprentice at The Dell. He might otherwise have been on the other side in this, his first derby game.

A minute later, Saints regained the lead. Channon and Brian O'Neil each touched on Gerry O'Brien's corner, so that the ball reached the far post where the waiting Osgood scored his second.

Which concluded the scoring, but not the incidents. Osgood was booked – which apparently provoked a 'youngster' to invade the pitch – and, in the 82nd minute,

Steele was booked again, this time for body-checking Piper. So he was sent off – an act of 'injustice' that evidently upset O'Neil, who was duly booked for fouling Piper, soon after.

Underlining that the relations between the clubs remained amicable – even if there was a distinct hostility between a teenage minority in the two conurbations – Ron Tindall told the press that he would support Steele if he were to appeal.

Meanwhile, on the hooligan front, the police spent Sunday visiting the homes of those taken into custody, before or after the game, and explained to the parents what their little darlings had been up to the previous day. The *Echo* approved: 'the small boys who went home boasting of rides in "meat wagons" on Saturday and telling of "pie and chips" served to them by police in cells or exercise yard, were not so happy when an inspector or sergeant arrived to speak to their parents.'

Running tally:	Pompey	91	Saints	72	Drawn	32

Thursday 26 December 1974   **Football League Division Two**

Portsmouth   1   Southampton   2

Best	Marinello	Turner	Stokes
Roberts	Foggo	Mills	Chatterley
Hand	Stewart (Bartlett)	Steele	Osgood (Holmes)
Piper	Wilson	Fisher	Peach
Went	Mellows	Bennett	O'Brien
Stephenson		Blyth	

Referee: Mr J.K. Taylor (Wolverhampton)

Fratton Park
Attendance: 19,534

Things were not going to plan. Of the three relegated clubs, Manchester United and Norwich City, United especially, were well in the running to bounce back to Division I. But although they had recovered from their abysmal start, the Saints were a single point above Pompey, with more chance of being downwardly, rather than upwardly, mobile.

The late news was that England regular Mike Channon would not be playing. Although Southampton got off to a flying start, Portsmouth had the two best chances early on. Went hit the post and, from the rebound, Stewart brought 'a brilliant save' from goalkeeper Turner.

The Saints made the breakthrough after 13 minutes. When his corner was partially cleared, David Peach 'swung the ball across to the far side of goal for Peter Osgood to soar and find the net with a 15-yard header which floated high over Best and then looped down into goal.' Then 'a lightning-quick raid down the left flank,' involving Gerry O'Brien and Bobby Stokes, ended in 'a picture goal' by Peach.

Southampton went into their shell a little after this but 'Pompey never seemed likely to close the gap.' When they

Paul Bennett feels he can tackle Andy Stewart with his eyes shut. Jim Steele looks suitably impressed.

did so through Norman Piper (*right*), in the 87th minute, it was too little too late. The Saints defenders 'clearly appeared', to Peter East of the *Echo*, 'to hesitate when the ball was played through to Piper and he was allowed to get clear on his own,' but that was 'the only smear', he felt, on a 'fine' defensive display.

Ian St John was not so impressed with the way his opponents had brought off their first-ever Football League double in this fixture: 'we were

by far the better side and we played all the football. The difference between the two sides was that they took their chances, and we didn't.'

He was bound to feel hard done-by: two points at this stage could open up quite a gap. The Division II table, the next morning, showed the Saints, with 21 points, in 15th place, eight points behind third-placed Norwich, while Pompey, with 18 points from two more games, were 19th, only two points ahead of the bottom two.

| Running tally: | Pompey | 91 | Saints | 73 | Drawn | 32 |

Tuesday 6 May 1975   **Ray Hiron Testimonial**

Portsmouth 2 Southampton 1

Figgins	Marinello	Turner (Middleton)	Crabbe
Roberts	Kane	Andruszewski	Channon (Waldron)
Wilson	Graham (Eames)	Peach	Stokes
Piper	Hiron	Holmes	Earles
Went	Mellows	Bennett	O'Brien
Cahill		Steele	

Fratton Park

Referee: Mr D. Nippard (Bournemouth)   **Attendance:** 5,374

Ray Hiron – hauled in from Hampshire League football, you may recall, to save Pompey in their darkest hour – had duly established himself as a hero at Fratton Park, where he was affectionately known as 'Twiggy'.

But the 'willowy' physique that had earned him that soubriquet had made him a target of derision at The Dell. If that was far from fair to such a proven goalscorer, it can hardly have accounted for the poor following from Southampton for his well-earned testimonial. At the end of a rather disheartening season, the supporters were entitled to feel that they had done enough supporting and to rest content with the 'double' recorded over Portsmouth.

And if the Fratton Park faithful might have been expected to give Hiron a salutational send-off in his last game

Ray Hiron

before a transfer to Reading, they too had had little to celebrate. The attendance may have been 'a bitter disappointment' to the *Echo* but it should not perhaps have surprised anyone.

He may have been financially rebuffed but 'the long, lean striker [was] hungry for goals in this his last game in Pompey colours,' Bob Brunskell recorded in the *Echo*. It took him only 35 seconds to open the scoring with a header and just a few more minutes to make it 2-0 when Peter Marinello's shot 'thudded back off the post.' Whereupon the visitors 'eased their way back into the game, dominated the second-half and deserved at least a draw.'

Mike Channon had a couple of chances – a delicate angled chip and a thunderous drive – before he gave way

1966-96: In Reverse Order

to Malcolm Waldron after half an hour. Peter Osgood and he had turned out, at Elland Road the night before, in Norman Hunter's testimonial and neither was fully fit. Osgood sat this one out, but Channon felt obliged to make a brief appearance. The Saints' second-half domination brought them just the one goal, a header by Bobby Stokes with three minutes remaining.

| Running tally: | Pompey | 92 | Saints | 73 | Drawn | 32 |

Final Word

The 1974-75 season was a bitter pill for Southampton and their supporters. They finished 13th, while both Norwich and Manchester United went straight back into the top flight – not even a double over Pompey could compensate for the failure of a side that, on paper at least, looked good enough to hold its own with all-comers. There was little to warm Portsmouth and their followers, either. They ended up in 17th place and, although the margin between them and the relegated clubs was wider than in the previous season, a lot of money had been invested in a side that was not producing anything like the expected results.

1975-76

Hope springs eternal at the beginning of every season and there was room for optimism at The Dell. Mike Channon was still there and so was Peter Osgood. But these were players of proven First Division quality, while what Lawrie McMenemy needed was a side that could claw its way back up to that division. He had been rebuilding to that end but the team had not been anything like good enough to achieve it last season. Yet the only close-season signing was Welsh international right-back Peter Rodrigues, a free transfer from Sheffield Wednesday, who had just dropped into Division III.

As for Pompey, the financial crisis continued. Staying up – and maybe a Cup run or two – was about the best that could be hoped for.

Saturday 27 September 1975   **Football League Division Two**

Southampton   4   Portsmouth   0

Middleton	Fisher	Lloyd	McGuinness (Marinello)
Rodrigues	Channon	Roberts	Reynolds
Peach	Osgood	Cahill	Graham
Holmes	McCalliog	Piper	Wilson
Bennett	Stokes	Went	Mellows
Blyth		Hand	

The Dell

Referee: Mr P. Reeves (Leicester)   **Attendance:** 17,310

It was the ninth game of the season. Pompey were 21st, with five points, and the Saints fifth, although that was almost entirely due to their having won all four of their home games.

Whatever, it didn't look good for the visitors and, as it turned out, this was a derby game that went to form. Portsmouth looked 'tidy and purposeful' early on. Piper went close and Reynolds hit the bar from 35 yards with a 'fierce wind-assisted shot.' Saints 'probed and tested the Pompey defence' for the rest of the half, but it was not until the 40th minute that they went ahead.

David Peach 'pumped his pass into the teeth of the gale,' the strength of which carried the ball over the defence into the path of Channon. His angled shot was blocked by Lloyd but he put away the rebound 'with deadly accuracy.'

'Portsmouth were beaten,' Brian Hayward figured, 'from that moment'. Peach opened the scoring in the second half, seemingly surprising the defence and fooling the goalkeeper by shooting from a 35-yard free-kick, the ball going in off Lloyd's near post as he 'scrambled along his line.' On 64 minutes, 'a remarkable goal' by Channon made it 3-0. This time, it was Peter Rodrigues who 'floated the ball forward on the wind' to him:

> There seemed not the slightest likelihood of a goal… to everyone except Channon. From a spot midway between the goal and corner flag, and as close as two yards to the by-line, England's premier forward hooked the ball way over the top of Lloyd into the far side of the net. The cynic will label it a fluke, but Channon has achieved the impossible before. He tried the only thing that was on and it came off in breathtaking fashion.

Channon had gone four games without a goal and been 'below his best' but, in the 80th minute, he completed his hat-trick when 'he climbed magnificently at the far post to meet Peach's corner… with a powerful header.'

For the triumphalist man from the *Echo*, the Saints had 'confirmed their position as the south coast's leading club, [as] Channon's fire power produced a salvo that was simply too great for Portsmouth's defences' –

though Hayward's credits also included the midfield support and 'the incisive raiding on the flanks' by the full-backs.

A 'bitterly disappointed' Portsmouth manager was having none of this: 'we played equally as well as our opponents,' Ian St John told the *Echo*, 'but just look at the way the chances went. We hit the bar and the ball came out, but when Peach hit a post it went in and Southampton got a goal.'

He predicted that 'one day it will be our shots that go in and someone else's which bounce out.' Perhaps that day would come soon. Perhaps Pompey would get the run of the ball and move out of their relegation slot?

What of the hooligans, you ask? There may have been no mention of them in the previous two games, but they now re-appeared in force: 'police and alsatians stood guard behind both goals, with the main force at the Archers Road end where the Portsmouth fans were segregated. They even fought among themselves before, with their team four-down, they made en masse for the exits.'

Mick Channon,
having been 'below his best,'
bounced back with a hat-trick.

Running tally:	Pompey	92	Saints	74	Drawn	32

Tuesday 6 April 1976   **Football League Division Two**

Portsmouth   0   Southampton   1

Figgins	King	Turner	Gilchrist
Lawler	Piper	Rodrigues	Channon
Ellis	Graham	Peach	Earles
Roberts	Kamara	Holmes	Williams
Cahill	Mellows	Blyth	Stokes
Viney		Bennett	

Fratton Park

Referee: Mr R. Capey (Crewe)   **Attendance:** 24,115

Mick Channon demonstrates how to 'crash home a brilliant goal' and hold the pose for the photographer.

The FA Cup had been providing a welcome distraction – at least in Southampton – from the less than satisfactory League form of the two sides. Pompey had flattered to deceive, winning a Third Round replay at First Division Birmingham, only to succumb to Second Division Charlton, in a home replay, in the next round.

But only three days before this re-scheduled League game, the Saints had booked their ticket to their first-ever Wembley Final. Three of the side that had beaten Crystal Palace in the semi-final on Saturday – Jim McCalliog, Peter Osgood and Jim Steele – had celebrated too earnestly. Following an evening of unauthorised socialising in a certain Southampton hostelry, they found themselves omitted from the party for Fratton Park. Paul Bennett, Pat Earles and Steve Williams were drafted in, the last two for their first team debuts.

Saints' inclusion of two untried Youth team players should have been good news for Pompey, who were anchored to the bottom of the division and desperate for points, but this did not stop Mike Neasom billing the game, in the *News*, as a 'glamour clash with FA Cup Finalists Southampton.' Peter East was more realistic, in the *Echo*, in his reference to a 're-vamped Saints' team' and surprised that the substitution of Earles for Osgood should have been lost on 'a large proportion of the crowd, [so] that they began hurling "Chelsea reject" abuse at young [Titchfield-born] Earles, who has played for no other club than Southampton.' Not to recognise a 5ft 7ins debutant is excusable, but for any serious football follower to mistake him for a 6ft 1 ins international star is baffling indeed.

As the re-organised visitors 'took time to settle,' they benefited, as East gently put it, from 'Portsmouth's customary poor finishing.' Mellows and King were 'off target and Piper and Kamara were harassed out of good positions by timely interceptions from David Peach and Paul Bennett.' Even so, goalkeeper Turner was kept busy and needed to save superbly from Piper to keep the game goalless at half-time.

The Saints midfield of Holmes, Gilchrist and Williams began to get more of a grip in the second half, demonstrating, to Peter East, 'that sheer hard work can carry a side through.' That hard work was rewarded, on 89 minutes and nine seconds, when Earles headed down a cross from Gilchrist, for Channon to 'crash… home a brilliant goal.'

Southampton had done the double over Portsmouth for the second consecutive season and, although the Saints again failed to gain promotion, Pompey were denied a chance of revenge the following season. As Mike Neasom lamented,

this was perhaps the cruellest cut of this season of cruel cuts for struggling Pompey. It was the cut that severed the last thread of their hold on Division II – yet typified completely so much which has haunted the club this season.

Relegation was now a certainty.

| Running tally: | Pompey | 92 | Saints | 75 | Drawn | 32 |

Final Word

Like Pompey in 1939, Saints beat the overwhelming favourites at Wembley.

And it cannot have been lost on fans on either side of Spit Head that Southampton's late winner against Manchester United was scored by Portsmouth-born Bobby Stokes (*right*).

The effect on the city of Southampton was every bit as memorable as Pompey's triumph – but there was no threat to Portsmouth's unique place in the record books: Saints would not hold the Cup for seven seasons.

Ironically, that is how long it would take Pompey to return to Division II. And by that time, the Saints would be long gone.

1976 to 1987

Pompey's fall from grace was completed in April 1978 when they dropped into Division IV. Perhaps the saddest aspect of the episode was that Jimmy Dickinson had been persuaded, the previous November, to step into the managerial breach in place of the 'suspended' Ian St John.

Dickinson took the job on out of loyalty and, with regard to keeping Pompey in the Third Division, was on a hiding to nothing. That the good ship HMS Portsmouth would sink into the Fourth Division was heartbreaking enough; that Gentleman Jim was at the helm when it happened defies metaphor.

That same month the Saints, as runners-up in Division II, returned to the First Division. It had taken four seasons, but they had done it. They had little problem resettling in the top flight and, in that first season back, reached their first League Cup final, losing 3-2 at Wembley to Nottingham Forest.

These 11 seasons would involve only three derby meetings, but they would include a passionate FA Cup-tie.

Friday 16 May 1980   **Duggie Reid Testimonial**

Portsmouth   2   Southampton   4

Mellor (Knight)	Gregory	Katalinic (Gennoe)	Rogers (Puckett)
James (Garner)	Laidlaw	Golac	Channon (Blochel)
Styles	Perrin	Richardson	Hebberd (Pratt)
Ellis	Bryant	Williams	Hayes (Moran)
Davey	Purdie (Rogers)	Waldron	
Brisley (Barnard)	Whitlock (Baker)	Holmes	

Referee: Mr A. Robinson (Waterlooville)

Fratton Park
Attendance: 11,233

The 200th derby between the two sides was a double celebration: a testimonial for Fratton Park groundsman Duggie Reid; and Pompey were on the up! They had squeezed back into Division III in the fourth and last promotion place, but up is up however you look at it.

Reid had been, of course, a leading light in Pompey's glory years – as relived in Chapter 11, just in case you need reminding. And he had been the joint-leading goalscorer, when Peter Harris and he each contributed 33 goals, across those two Championship-winning seasons.

The occasion clearly demanded opponents with a degree of kudos about them, preferably with a star striker. If hardly of Champion class, the Southampton side that had just finished eighth in Division I was not short of pedigree and had a goalscorer capable of attracting this *Echo* headline:

CLASSY SHOW BY CHANNON

Phil Rood followed that headline with a report that poignantly captured the contrast between the old and the new:

> Saints produced the First Division touches and Pompey provided the First Division nostalgia that added up to a bumper testimonial for Duggie Reid … More than 11,000 turned up to honour the Scot who had given 30 years service to Pompey as a player and groundsman. In return they were treated to a sample of the good old days … before getting a taste of today's reality.

In other words, a nostalgic parade, that included Harris, Froggatt, Phillips and Dickinson, was followed by a display of 'Saints' top flight class and sharpness.'

A Steve Williams header gave the visitors a seventh-minute lead and 'the bite of a South Coast derby had

everyone forgetting this was just a testimonial.' Steve Perrin nodded an equaliser, from Ian Purdie's cross, three minutes later, but when Mick Channon was brought down in the area by Steve Davey, Malcolm Waldron converted the 18th-minute spot-kick.

A quarter-of-an-hour later, Perrin got his, and Pompey's, second and, 'for a few minutes Pompey were fully in the fray until Channon made his class tell.'

He had just blazed over and was being 'taunted' by the home crowd but, a minute before half-time, he 'provided the perfect answer,' as he ran on to Nick Holmes's through-ball to score.

In a second half that 'had little chance of matching a thrilling first,' nothing much happened, 'apart from a fine save by Ivan Katalinic to deny Leigh Barnard,' until the last 10 minutes.

During this hectic finale, Channon completed the scoring from 25 yards and substitute Steve Moran 'twice hammered the ball against the woodwork with shots old "Thunderboots" Duggie Reid himself would have been proud of.'

Really? The Championship marksman would surely have expected *his* shots to go in.

Running tally:	Pompey	92	Saints	76	Drawn	32

Tuesday 22 December 1981   **Hampshire Professional Cup**

Portsmouth   2   Southampton   1

Knight (Gosney)	Hemmerman	Katalinic	Keegan
McLaughlin	Tait (Rafferty)	Golac (Watson)	Channon
Bryant	Barnard (Berry)	Holmes	Moran (Wallace)
Doyle	Cropley	Williams	Armstrong
Aizlewood	Crown	Nicholl	Ball
Rollings		Waldron	

Fratton Park

Referee: Mr D. Letts (Basingstoke)   **Attendance:** 6,649

Somewhere, deep in the deepest labyrinths beneath the headquarters of the Hampshire FA, it was decided to conjure into existence a 'new' competition: the Hampshire Professional Cup. Although, as it involved

Aldershot, Bournemouth, Portsmouth and Southampton, it bore a distinct resemblance to the Hampshire Combination Cup, played between the same four teams in the 1930s, as featured in Chapter 9.

The big difference from the 1930s was, of course, the relative status of the county's top two. The Saints were now a First Division side, packed with internationals many of them with experience in Europe, while Pompey were in Division III. The Cherries and the Shots were both in the Fourth Division so, all in all, Southampton, given the inclination, ought to stroll it. Whether anyone cared or not was another matter.

As it happened, both managers welcomed the game. Some appalling weather meant that neither side had played for a fortnight or more.

Portsmouth got off to a good start but Southampton's 'top flight class' told in the 41st minute when 'Mick Channon left the home defence standing' to score from David Armstrong's free-kick.

However, it was David Crown who took the plaudits, revelling, as Mike Neasom put it in the *News*, 'in the space allowed by a careless and undisciplined Ivan Golac.' The attacking tendency of the Yugoslav right-back, which led David Peach to dub him 'the best right-winger we had,' gave Crown the freedom, on the stroke of half-time, to level the scores.

In the 67th minute, he again exploited the space afforded him by the inattentive Golac, pulled Chris Nicholl out of position and sent in a low cross for Jess Hemmerman to slot home.

Lawrie McMenemy was gracious in defeat: 'the result wasn't important' and his side had had the 'competitive game with no injuries' that he had wanted – 'the only thing wounded was our pride.' He was also impressed by the crowd:

the atmosphere out there was good. I never cease to be impressed by what happens down here. There aren't many places where you would get 7,000 people on a night like this.

Ivan Golac, 'the best right-winger' Southampton had.

Indeed. As the *Echo* put it, 'the mammoth roar at the end… said it all.' Beating Southampton mattered to the home crowd 'so much more than a winter's night workout' for the players.

A point reflected in the Fratton Park attendance of under 4,000, come April, for the Final. Pompey beat Aldershot 1-0.

Running tally:	Pompey	93	Saints	76	Drawn	32

Saturday 28 January 1984   **FA Cup, Fourth Round**

Portsmouth   0   Southampton   1

Knight	Webb	Shilton	Holmes
McLaughlin	Dillon	Mills	Moran
Sullivan	Hateley	Dennis	Worthington
Doyle	Biley	Williams	Armstrong
Tait	Rogers	Agboola	Wallace
Aizlewood		Wright	

Referee: Mr L. Shapter (Torquay)

Fratton Park
Attendance: 36,000

It was billed as 'The Game of the Century' from the moment Southampton followed Portsmouth out of the FA's little black bag – in Hampshire at least. Well, it was 78 years since the two clubs had last met in this competition. And if the local footballing public was galvanised by the prospect, the local media were utterly infatuated. The *Echo* and the *News* competed with each other as to which of them could get more hysterical, while the local TV channels had what seemed to be almost daily bulletins on the teams.

Amidst the brouhaha, the Hampshire Constabulary girded their loins for a busy day.

As to the football, Pompey had good reason to fancy their chances. They were back in Division II and manager Bobby Campbell had assembled the nucleus of what was, potentially, a very good side, spearheaded by the clever (some would even assert crafty) Alan Biley and the impressive Mark Hateley, and steered by Steve Aizlewood, Kevin Dillon and Neil Webb. It was one of those teams that happens everywhere from time to time: one that, on its day, could beat anybody.

Meanwhile, the Saints were having their best season in their First Division history. Built on the foundations of a firm, fast-breaking defence, with outstanding players in all positions, notably Peter Shilton – arguably the world's greatest goalkeeper – Mark Wright in the centre of the defence, Steve Williams and David Armstrong in midfield and the quicksilver Danny Wallace and that elegant, if ageing, 'maverick', Frank Worthington, up front with an on-form Steve Moran.

If Pompey were going to win, even the most self-deluding Pompey supporters realised, their side would have to play, proverbially, out of their skins. That this was a possibility was not discounted in Southampton, where the mood might be described as apprehensive – the Saints had, after all, been eliminated from the Milk (League) Cup by Rotherham.

It was, undoubtedly, a classic Cup-tie, in that the tension generated – both with regard to the awesome atmosphere spawned by Fratton Park's largest crowd since November 1957 and by the sheer nature of the occasion itself – had a demonstrable effect on the quality of the football.

Initially, Pompey were the happier of the two sides, chasing everything that moved and thereby denying the Saints the space they rarely had difficulty finding in the First Division and restricting wing-backs Mick Mills and Mark Dennis to defensive duties.

Meanwhile, a shower of coins descended on, and back out of, the Milton End, where the Saints' supporters were billeted; bananas and racist vitriol were directed at Danny Wallace and Reuben Agboola; and more coins were directed towards the pitch. Both linesmen were struck.

The *Echo*'s Bob Brunskell dubbed it 'a tale of two strikers – one who returned home a hero, the other who will toss and turn through a few sleepless nights dwelling on what might have been.' Which was harsh on Alan Biley, who had two close-range chances of beating

Alan Biley,
condemned to sleepless nights,
after losing the 'tale of two strikers'

Shilton: one, with a first-half header – following a corner from John McLaughlin, touched on at the near post by Mick Tait – which was sent over the bar; the second in the 87th minute, when a cross from Alan Rogers found him 'unmarked on the six-yard line. Again, though, he raised his gun-sights too high and his shot flew over the bar.'

Bob Brunskell was sympathetic: 'I suspect the awesome sight of Peter Shilton, filling his goal like some super-protective giant, had an off-putting effect on Biley.'

Pompey might have had a penalty in the 19th minute, Agboola bringing Hateley down in the box. The referee, unlike the home partisans, was unimpressed. The Saints had their moments, too: Wallace attempted a spectacular overhead kick, which connected with a defender's face instead of the ball, and sparked stern admonishments from the home players; Alan Knight pulled off the best save of the game, from Mills; and Williams narrowly missed with a 25-yard drive.

But perhaps the most significant incident of the game, certainly the one identified by Bobby Campbell and the *News*, emanated from a throw-in conceded by Portsmouth on the hour. As Dennis shaped up to take it, he was felled by a coin flung out of the North terrace.

There was a fuss: Dennis had to be treated; the referee had words with the police; the police glared into the bank of spectators; and then the game carried on, the delay having lasted not much more than a minute.

A minute into injury time, 'a fine angled pass by Worthington put Armstrong clear on the right, in came the cross and Moran's left foot did the rest.' The acclaim, not to mention the relief, with which this goal was greeted at the Milton End might have been heard back in Southampton – if it hadn't been for the fact that the noise was almost sucked into the silence of the other three sides of the stadium.

The goal that settled the tie.

Steve Moran's
'left foot did the rest'
after a move involving
(*clockwise from the right*)
Frank Worthington and
David Armstrong,
in time added on
for the injury caused to
Mark Dennis
by a coin-thrower.

Aftermath

Phil Rood, summing up in the *Football Echo*, collated the respective views of the two managers. Lawrie McMenemy admitted that he

> would have settled for a draw… It could have gone either way and once they started slinging the long balls into the box it seemed that something must break…
> We were playing all the football but playing too deep…
> They were enthusiastic and very fit … but I've rarely seen a team so gutted as they were at the end. I can totally sympathise with Bobby Campbell because when the dust settles they will feel they at least earned a replay and no-one in our dressing room would argue with that.

He had enjoyed the 'cracking atmosphere' and made light of the crowd behaviour: 'we're in the Fifth Round, picked up £4.50 in loose change and two pounds of bananas.' But Portsmouth's manager was counting the cost of the coin-throwing incident:

> Their goal was a minute into injury time and the game eventually ran three minutes over the time but the trainers didn't go on, so that [stoppage] could be the only reason.

He otherwise lamented spurned goal-scoring opportunities and felt the fact that the away fans had been 'blowing for the final whistle five minutes before the end' told a story:

> if anyone is honest they would admit that we had the edge. Any neutral watching the game wouldn't have known which side was from the First and which was from the Second. It was a sickener to lose to that late goal.

Bobby Campbell was not the only one who thought the result was a 'sickener'.

That there was a potential for trouble was never doubted by anyone. The *News* catalogued how the hooligan element got off to an early start, when a Pompey fan, on his way to the game, was mugged for his ticket. He ended up in casualty rather than cheering his team on.

After the game the visiting supporters were kept in the ground for a protracted period before being escorted back to their transport by police. Even the most confrontational of them had cause to be appreciative, as frustrated Pompey 'fans' went on what the *News* called a '£20,000 Trail Of Damage.'

Sixteen plate glass windows were smashed, six police vehicles damaged, 18 people ended up in hospital, pubs were trashed, the Co-op building set on fire and 59 people arrested. And the question asked, among the bulk of the faithful, 'what has this got to do with football?' The answer being: 'nothing.' It had even less to do with Southampton – and, even if it did, what had those responsible proved by smashing up their own town and terrorising their fellow-citizens? A rhetorical question: one might as well ask what bus shelters have done to cause them offence.

And there is a moral here, because even the most biased Saints supporter at Fratton Park that afternoon would concede that Pompey deserved another crack at the Saints at The Dell. The less charitable (and there are plenty of them) would add that, because the coin that sent the game into added time had been chucked by a Portsmouth supporter, they had sown the seeds of their own destruction. That's not entirely logical – it isn't as if the game lasted any longer as a result – and it's a harsh judgment on the generality of Pompey fans: why should 30-odd thousand of them be condemned because a few, unrepresentative poltroons used a football match as a pretext for aimless violence?

As Superintendent Bob West put it, they were 'a small minority who were bent on causing disorder at all cost.' But, he told the *News*, the police had been 'generally well-pleased… The bulk of the fans, both from Southampton and Portsmouth, behaved admirably and acted with great cooperation.'

In short, that small minority had ruined the experience of an epic derby game that otherwise brought great credit to both clubs.

Whatever one's sympathies, it would be interesting to know how the coin-thrower has slept since that game.

Running tally:　　　**Pompey　93**　　　**Saints　77**　　　**Drawn　32**

Final Word

Southampton reached the semi-finals at Highbury. Their supporters discovered how Pompey fans must have felt when they went out to a goal scored by Everton's Adrian Heath in the dying minutes of extra-time. Some of them recovered from their numbness fast enough to confront the jubilant Everton fans, who had run onto the pitch at the final whistle, and were dispersed by mounted police.

There was some consolation in the League, where the Saints interrupted what had been long proclaimed in the press as a 'two-horse race' between Liverpool and Manchester United with a late surge that took them into second place – their highest-ever finish – two points behind Liverpool, but three ahead of United.

Portsmouth, both the city and the club, appeared demoralised by the derby defeat. The season ended in anti-climax as Pompey's form deteriorated and relegation became a distinct possibility. At the end of the season, Mark Hateley moved to AC Milan for a cool £1m plus.

1987-88

Portsmouth   2   Southampton   2

Knight	Fillery (Dillon)	Flowers	Townsend
Swain	Kennedy	Forrest	Cockerill
Hardyman	Baird	Statham	Clarke
Whitehead	Quinn (Sandford)	Case	Hobson
Mariner	Hilaire	Moore	G. Baker
Gilbert		Bond	

Referee: Mr R. Lewis (Great Bookham)

Fratton Park
Attendance: 20,161

Jimmy Case drives the ball at the referee, while Saints' Glenn Cockerill
and Pompey's Micky Quinn look on. The referee is Mr Lewis of
Great Bookham, a wonderful place-name for a match official - in the days
before the practice of revealing the referee's residence was abandoned.

Saints' Graham Baker (No.11) looks disgusted
and Paul Mariner (*right*) seems strangely
puzzled as Vince Hilaire congratulates
Clive Whitehead on scoring the second goal.

This game not only brought Pompey and Saints together again in the same division, after a break of 11 years, but this was their first meeting, after 88 years of derby games, at the top level.

The *Echo*'s Graham Hiley thought the game worthy of the occasion: it 'was everything a local derby should be – and more! It was fast and furious but fair and provided five-star entertainment.'

After a little probing by both sides, a good deal of competitiveness in the midfield and anxious moments in both penalty areas, Vince Hilaire opened the scoring with 'a marvellous piece of opportunism' in the 21st minute, as 'he cashed in on a mix-up between Tim Flowers and new-boy Derek Statham, squeezing between them to loft home a cheeky toe-poke.'

Saints levelled four minutes later when Cockerill made a 'powerful surging run from midfield' and slipped the ball to Clarke, who stroked it past Knight. The Saints took the lead three minutes into the second half. Clarke played a one-two with Hobson and was left with 'all the time and space he needed to pick his shot at the far post as Knight moved to cover the nearside.'

Just before the hour, Alan Ball made a 'cunning' reshuffle. Top goalscorer Micky Quinn was substituted by Lee Sanford. He slotted into the defence, which released Paul Mariner, the former England centre-forward who had been looking distinctly uncomfortable at centre-back, to play in his customary striker's roll.

Pompey, most especially Mariner, began to look significantly more at ease and Clive Whitehead, who had come on a free-transfer during the summer, 'hooked home' a knock-down by Ian Baird, 'as Saints lost concentration for a few precious seconds at the back.'

There were 16 minutes left but it appeared – perhaps it was fatigue? – that both sides had decided that a draw was a fair result.

Running tally:	Pompey	93	Saints	77	Drawn	33

Southampton 0   Portsmouth 2

Burridge	Townsend	Knight	Horne
S. Baker	Cockerill	Whitehead	Kennedy
Statham	Clarke	Hardyman	Quinn
Moore	G. Baker(Le Tissier)	Dillon	Connor
Bond	D. Wallace	Blake	Hilaire
Case (Rod Wallace)		Ball	

The Dell

Referee: Mr A. Gunn (Burgess Hill)   **Attendance:** 17,002

There are some days when you should just stay in bed, and the popular choice for an extended lie-in is Sunday. However, a number of factors being taken into consideration, predominantly Hampshire's hooligan element, it was decided to start the match at noon on Sunday. A number of lie-ins were disturbed in the quiet suburb of St Denys early on Sunday morning when, in what its perpetrators probably regarded as a manoeuvre worthy of Rommel at his most diabolical, a horde of Pompey's roughest and toughest disembarked from a train at St Denys station and marched chanting down Adelaide Road.

The plan had two crucial flaws. First, they had exited the station on the wrong side to take them directly to the centre of town, The Dell or to Portswood, where they could find the trouble they were seeking. Secondly, they had neglected to take into consideration the invention of the telephone. Local residents phoned the police, who quickly rounded them up and took them into custody.

The *Echo* 'understood the 60 yobs were hardcore members of the notorious 6.57 Crew, a gang who travel to away games to cause mayhem.' The report quoted one elderly resident of St Denys as saying she was 'terrified.' It was indeed a glorious episode in the annals of the 'notorious 6.57 Crew', who, while they totally failed to make it anywhere near The Dell – or, indeed, confront their deadliest enemies in what they refer to as 'the town we do not name' – did manage to terrify one little old lady. Awesome!

The game those arrested missed was nothing to write home about, although the score was certainly one to celebrate in the pubs, clubs and homes of Portsea Island. Bob Brunskell described it, in the *Echo*, as 'a strangely low-key affair, lacking the passion and sparkle expected from such an occasion.' Under the headline, POMPEY STRIKE AS SAINTS AGONISE OVER MISSED CHANCES, he reported that

> Saints were in a derby daze… Their forwards slumbered, their backs fumbled and Pompey were gifted three points. Pompey manager Alan Ball wasn't complaining. In contrast to their Solent neighbours, they finished economically, capitalised on good fortune and then rubbed salt into the Saints' wounds by toying with them in the closing stages.

Brunskell calculated that, on the chances afforded, Southampton should have won 6–3: 'with Pompey often vulnerable at the back, Colin Clarke and Danny Wallace should have had a field day.' Wallace should have had a couple, while Clarke, who 'needed a hat-trick to complete a century of League goals, … should have collected,' twice missing opportunites provided by Glenn Cockerill and once planting 'a tame six-yard shot into Knight's hands.'

Pompey, meanwhile, snapped up two of their three chances. It took them only 23 minutes to 'establish a two goal bridgehead,' after which the Saints 'were chasing the game desperately.' Steve Baker's 'agonising afternoon' began when Vince Hilaire beat him to a Clive Whitehead cross and set up Barry Horne for the opener on 15 minutes. Eight minutes later Baker 'failed to control the ball out on Pompey's left flank,' allowing Mick Quinn to square to Terry Connor, who 'finished brilliantly, curling a sweet right-footer' past Burridge.

And that was it. Case and Graham Baker never managed to take control of midfield. It was claimed that they were carrying strains from the previous game on QPR's artificial pitch at Loftus Road but, even if Horne, Dillon and Kennedy were having an easy ride, they never let it go to their heads. Horne, especially, caught the eye of the Southampton supporters – and management.

Too late in the game, Chris Nicholl introduced the precocious talents of Rodney Wallace and Matthew Le Tissier, but neither possessed the experience seriously to challenge Pompey's edge and Southampton suffered their first League defeat by Portsmouth since 1964.

Running tally:	Pompey	94	Saints	77	Drawn	33

Last Word

The result at The Dell came close to being significant for both sides. For Pompey, it was their second away win of the season – and brought high hopes that they could emerge unscathed from the relegation ruck. For the Saints, it meant they were in imminent danger of dropping into it, unless there was a major return to form.

In fact, Southampton pulled comfortably clear of the drop-zone, starting with a 2–0 victory at Old Trafford in their next League outing and finishing the season in 12th place. Alan Shearer had by then made his debut, although it would not be until 1989-90 that he'd become the fulcrum of Nicholl's exciting attacking formation with Le Tissier and Rod Wallace.

Pompey had less luck. Attendances had failed to reach anything like expected and financial vultures were circling Fratton Park – not least the Inland Revenue, who had brought a High Court winding-up petition against the club. Kennedy's game against the Saints was his last for Portsmouth, before he was transferred to Bradford City. The finances were further enhanced by an FA Cup run that ended in the quarter-finals at Luton. Soon after that, Ian Baird, who had been less than sensational in Pompey blue, was transferred back to Leeds, at a loss of £100,000.

Portsmouth finished the season 19th, in the third automatic relegation place.

1988to 1996

In the summer of 1988, John Deacon sold Pompey to former Queen's Park Rangers chairman, Jim Gregory, who began his reign with a much-needed refit of Fratton Park. And, with the threat of liquidation now off the agenda, Alan Ball was able to invest in fresh talent.

The return on those investments did not impress the Chairman who replaced Ball with coach, John Gregory, in January 1989. A year later, Gregory made way for Frank Burrows to have a second spell as Portsmouth's manager. He lasted until the following March, when assistant manager Tony Barton – the former Portsmouth full-back and then player-coach who had returned to Fratton Park, via managerial posts that included three seasons as Nicholl's assistant at The Dell – was made caretaker-manager.

But he didn't get the job full-time – in the summer of 1991, Jim Smith, who had managed QPR for Jim Gregory, took his turn at Fratton Park. It was under Smith that Pompey found themselves, at the start of the 1992-93 season, in the First Division again – by dint of having been a Division II club when the FA Premier League was inaugurated. The Saints, accordingly, became a Premiership team, much to the *chagrin* of those in the national press who believed this breakaway competition should have been restricted to 'big clubs'.

Meanwhile, at The Dell – where managerial stability was a byword – Chris Nicholl was sacked at the end of the 1990–91 season and replaced by former Dell coach and Reading manager Ian Branfoot. He lasted two-and-a-half unhappy seasons, before Lawrie McMenemy returned to the club as 'Director of Football', an appointment that was quickly followed by the departure of Branfoot and the arrival, from Exeter, of Alan Ball.

If this appointment left some of the national press bemused – Ball's record as a manager had been less than spectacular – it was widely welcomed by supporters:

at least Ball was popular, whereas Branfoot – and, in particular, his devotion to the long-ball game – never had been. The Saints avoided the drop on the last day of the season. Le Tissier, who had struggled to impress Branfoot, had more than returned Ball's unblinking faith in him. He had saved the season with 25 goals, including eight in his last five games, climaxing in a spectacular contribution to a 3-3 draw at West Ham on the final day.

Tuesday 10 May 1994 **Alan Knight Testimonial**

Portsmouth 1 Southampton 5

Knight	Kuhl	Andrews	Allen (Hughes)
Swain	Kristensen	Dodd	Magilton (Ball)
Blake	Anderton	Monkou	Maddison (Bennett)
Gilbert	Walsh	Charlton (Kenna)	Dowie (Banger)
Russell	Hateley	Benali	Le Tissier (Beasant)
Chamberlain		Widdrington (Maskell)	

Subs used: Creaney, Whittingham, Tait, Barry Horne, Brian Horne, Burns, Hilaire, Dillon, Sandford, Aspinall

Fratton Park

Referee: Mr M. Pierce (Portsmouth) **Attendance:** 16,831

Three days after their 'Great Escape', Southampton went to Fratton Park to play a side that was not so much Portsmouth as an Alan Knight XI (or XXI, if you count the substitutes).

It didn't matter to Mike Neasom of the *News* that this 'vast array of those that have come and gone' lost 5-1 to Alan Ball's in-form side: the fact that Ball and McMenemy had brought that side along, in 'response to Alan Knight's invitation, … showed the respect [they] hold for their host' (a sentiment roundly restated by Alan Ball in his foreword to this book).

Almost 17,000 wanted to join in that response and those of them willing to view the entertainment through unbiased eyes were treated to a luxuriant feast of Le Tissier's skills. Neasom applauded his 'exceptional talent,' while noting that his failure to score 'delighted those who preferred to abuse him, but he did everything else.'

Iain Dowie opened the scoring in the 16th minute, with a looping header, then Maddison 'poked in a second, after Knight had saved well from Simon Charlton.' Pompey, clearly on the defensive, came up with a brilliant tactical plan 10 minutes into the second half, taking a man off, and replacing him with two substitutes. Once this oversight had been rectified, Maskell 'slammed home' Banger's cross. After 65 minutes, Jeff Kenna's floated cross 'drifted over Knight

and in off the far post.' Banger set up David Hughes for Saints' fifth with 10 minutes to go.

Knight had by then left the field, after a lap of honour and a standing ovation – and scoring! Benali had 'fouled' Guy Whittingham – and the Portsmouth referee, Mick Peirce, awarded what the *Echo* thought a 'diplomatic penalty.' Knight was able to 'crown his big night by racing the length of the field to send Ian Andrews the wrong way from the spot.'

Knight had been replaced by Brian Horne and Ball had brought on himself and Dave Beasant, the latter  replacing Le Tissier, although he 'played to the gallery' and kept his goalkeeping gloves on.

A good time was had by all. Even 'the mindless minority' was able to get into the act, by steaming onto the pitch at the final whistle in an attempt to confront the 'gleeful' visiting Saints' supporters. They were 'foiled' by the police.

Alan Knight

Running tally:	**Pompey**	**94**	**Saints**	**78**	**Drawn**	**33**

Southampton   3   Portsmouth   0

Beasant	Venison	Knight	Simpson
Dodd	Magilton	Pethick	Durnin
Neilson	Heaney (McDonald)	Gittens	Wood (Carter)
Monkou	Shipperley	Butters	Walsh
Charlton	Watson (Maddison)	Stimson	Hall (Burton)
Le Tissier		McLaughlin	

The Dell

Referee: Mr M. Bodenham (Cornwall)

Attendance: 15,236

Another season, another manager's name on the Southampton FC stationery. Dave Merrington had succeeded Alan Ball, who had been lured to Maine Road. Merrington was a popular figure at The Dell, having been the Youth team coach who developed the Wallace brothers, Matt Le Tissier and Alan Shearer.

The esteem in which his protégés held him has been well-charted and Le Tissier literally gave his mentor the shirt off his back, when he presented him with his first England shirt. But Merrington's ability as a Youth coach did not translate into first-team success – well, not fast enough for the Southampton board.

Meanwhile, Terry Fenwick was at the helm at Fratton Park. Martin Gregory, who had succeeded his father as Chairman, was anxious to unload the club, there was precious little money for transfers and Portsmouth were struggling to stay in Division I. The good news was that, after some wheeling and dealing, Paul Walsh had returned to Pompey – he was one of those players who could make all the difference.

When the two clubs were again drawn against each other in the FA Cup, after a gap of a mere 12 years, the Saints had home advantage, so places were at a premium. Only 1,500 tickets would be allocated to Portsmouth supporters, as The Dell's enforced all-seater capacity was

Paul Walsh
was back for Pompey
and could perhaps
'make all the difference'.

by now a little over 15,000. The kick-off was again switched to Sunday at noon, and a giant, 20ft x 30ft, video screen was installed at Fratton Park so the regulars could watch the action from the discomfort of the South Stand. Rumours circulated that Pompey's hooligan element would be booking into the bed & breakfast hotels around The Dell on Saturday night, to enjoy an evening and morning of pandemonium in Southampton.

This did not come to pass.

While the *Echo* and the *News* were more restrained, in their build-up, than they had been in 1984, some of the nationals again went overboard. Martin Thorpe previewed the game for the *Guardian*:

The domestic game is home to many local derbies, yet one of the most fiercely contested is a match which, because the combatants have long inhabited different divisions, rarely gets played. This Sunday rival communities will offer up a Solent prayer for victory… Entertainment is probably the wrong word. The last time the two teams met, in May 1994, there was crowd trouble – and that was just for a testimonial game.

Indeed. And, as we have just seen, the last competitive derby match before that had been Pompey's win at The Dell in 1988.

Discussing the Pompey T-shirts, bearing the legend 'January 3, 1988', commemorating that win, Thorpe reminded his readers that

Pompey eventually went down from the old First Division that season. 'But it didn't matter,' says Paddy Thomas, chairman of the Portsmouth Supporters' Club. 'It was worth it just to win at The Dell.'

Not the first or last time the claim would be made and an example of the 'stupidly intense' expressions of 'rivalry' that Thorpe was looking for. Moreover, he continued, 'at Fratton Park any visiting former Southampton player is likely to be greeted by cries of "scummer" each time he touches the ball.'

Actually, Thorpe missed a trick here, because the situation had become so banal that Saints supporters were now chanting 'scummer' at ex-Pompey players, including the former Bitterne Park schoolboy, Darren Anderton, and some of them were claiming that they had coined the term – another cause for acrimony.

When the big show started, Steve Bone, writing from the perspective of the *blue few* in the *News* on Monday, captured the atmosphere better than the sports journalists:

Even the build-up lacked much anticipation.
Fans arrived, queued and took their seats much as they would have done at any other game against any opposition. Of course there was the chanting and counter-chanting between the Pompey fans in the East Stand and their opposite numbers in the Archers Road end. But it took the lone bellowing of 'Southamp-ton' to spark off the inevitable anti-Southampton chants, and it continued on much the same level from there.
It was never very fierce; never very original.

Paul Weaver was at the match for the *Guardian*. Ignoring such frivolities as the Alan Knight testimonial to which his colleague Adam Thorpe had referred – or, indeed, any of the titanic derby

League games before 1921 – he concluded that there was 'no rivalry in English football more intense than that between these two Hampshire clubs, and the relative infrequency of their meetings – this is only the 29th, and the first for eight years – adds piquancy.'

Yet, while 'there was no lack of competitiveness' and there were eight bookings that said so, 'the derby frenzy failed to disguise,' Weaver argued, 'the difference in quality between the two sides... Portsmouth were no match for the superior finishing and better-organised defending of the Premiership club.'

Matthew Le Tissier was undoubtedly the man of the match, spraying the ball about in his usual insouciant manner. He had no part in the first goal, though. The Saints broke out of their own penalty area, following appeals for a foul against Walsh. With the Pompey defenders in disarray, Jim Magilton 'bundled' the ball in, after Gordon Watson's cross had been half-cleared by Jon Gittens and Knight had 'palmed the ball off the line.' It had taken 12 minutes.

Matthew Le Tissier, 'undoubtedly the man of the match,' leaves John Durnin standing and Fitzroy Simpson on the deck.

Magilton struck again 50 seconds into the second half. Le Tissier collected the ball in his own half, from Dave Beasant's throw, advanced 'deep into enemy territory and… tested Knight with a curling drive.' The 'keeper parried the shot to Magilton, who 'contrived a simple volley.' The third came in the 81st minute, Shipperley converting a Le Tissier cross.

Steve Bone was not a happy man: 'all of us knew Southampton had won because they were the better team and Pompey couldn't raise their game to cancel out their superiority. And yes, it hurt. It hurt then and it still hurts now.'

Terry Fenwick put it to the *Guardian* that 'three goals flattered Southampton but we saw the difference between the sides in the penalty areas.'

And that was it. But the next Cup-tie was only eight seasons away.

Neil Shipperley (*left*) has a simple tap-in for Saints' third goal.

| Running tally: | Pompey | 94 | Saints | 79 | Drawn | 33 |

Final Word

The 1996 Cup result brought almost as much relief to Southampton *aficionados* as that of 1984 - though without anything like the trauma. Defeat seems to have been taken more phlegmatically in Portsmouth, too, compared with the reaction in '84. It has to be said that Pompey supporters were almost certainly more preoccupied by who was going to end up owning their club, as Martin Gregory continued to look for a buyer, than with another Cup exit at the hands of what Colin Farmery termed 'their bitter rivals'.

The fact is that both clubs had gone into a decline since 1984. Pompey did not have the stability - or, for that matter, the drive - at Board level, to build on their support, while the Saints - with the capacity of The Dell reduced, after the *Hillsborough* reports, to just over 15,000 - did not have the financial wherewithal to sustain a top-flight squad of players.

For the time being supporters, in both cities, would have to content themselves with survival.

READ ON: The comments from Guy Askham are from a 2003 interview for this book, while Colin Farmery's verdict on John Deacon's spending and his thoughts on the 'bitter' rivalry are from his *Tindall to Ball*. John Mortimore has revealed, in *Dell Diamond*, why he opted for Portsmouth in 1973, while David Peach assessed Ivan Golac's attacking qualities in an interview for that book. Verdicts on Dave Merrington as a Youth coach are to be found, for instance, in Alan Shearer's biography and Matthew Le Tissier's testimonial programme. See 'Sources'.

Chapter 13
1996-2004: Premiership-mates

There was a gap of seven seasons before the two clubs and their fans were united again. Portsmouth had remained in the new Division I, while Southampton had remained in the Premier League – just.

The Saints' status during this time was often precarious, but they looked more likely to stay up than Pompey ever looked like joining them in, or leapfrogging them into, the top flight – until 2003.

The 2002-03 season was an *annus mirabilis* for both clubs. After an unprecedented turnover of managers, Gordon Strachan led Southampton to their best League season since 1990, finishing eighth in the Premiership and reaching the FA Cup Final at The Millennium Stadium in Cardiff – where they may have lost 1-0 to Arsenal, but the fans had a great day out.

And Portsmouth had their best season since … well, opinions differ on this, but they ran away with the First Division Championship and the prospects of staying up looked a whole lot more promising than in their previous return to the top flight in 1987.

Since that 1996 FA Cup-tie, there had been a lot of changes at Fratton Park and The Dell; especially at The Dell, which was now being re-developed as a residential estate – and if Fratton Park was still Pompey's home ground, after flirtations with relocation, there were, at long last, concrete plans to transform it into a modern stadium. Which would, of course, be bigger and better than Southampton's new ground. Meanwhile, in October 2004, an *Observer* poll to find the 'crappiest football ground' in England and Wales ranked Fratton Park at No.5 – and that only because a biased Sports Editor had rigged the results to keep it out of the top three.

Southampton's 50-year struggle to leave The Dell ended in 2001, when they moved to the Friends Provident St Mary's Stadium in Northam, on the site of the old gas works. It was a state-of-the-art footballing arena, 10 minutes stroll from the centre of town. Its 32,000-odd capacity made Southampton the first club in the modern era to build a new ground capable of accommodating a record home gate – perhaps as much an indictment of The Dell's limitations than an indication of the Board's outrageous ambitions.

The Northam site had been secured under the leadership of new chairman Rupert Lowe, who had been head-hunted by the club, to guide its transformation into a plc. He was an intriguing choice of chief executive: he had never seen a game of professional football until he came to The Dell in October 1996.

Yet despite presiding over constant managerial change (most infamously the defection of Glenn Hoddle to Tottenham in March 2001), he has certainly shown himself to be more than capable in the job – while amply proving the old adage that 'you can't please all of the Saints' supporters all of the time.'

Southampton had a torrid time attempting to secure their first win at St Mary's and the story that a Pompey shirt (or shirts) had been slipped into the structure during the cement-pouring (the best place for it, according to many) got quite a lot of publicity.

So did the activities of a pagan priestess invited by the media to exorcise the spirits of the Anglo-Saxon graveyard beneath the pitch, immediately after which the first home win was secured – against Charlton on 24 November 2001.

Meanwhile, Jim Gregory's son, Martin, was looking for a buyer and/or a manager who could build a team that would attract enough paying customers to make Portsmouth FC a going concern. Among his less successful gambits was to invite Terry Venables to take a hand in matters.

We will leave the details for the Pompey historians, but it was not the happiest of decisions, and the episode ended in tears for all concerned, except perhaps Mr Venables. Manager Terry Fenwick departed at the same time as Venables, making way for the second coming of Alan Ball, while Gregory was negotiating to sell the club to American millionaire Vince Wolanin and rock star, Brian Howe.

Wolanin's bid failed, but Ball did manage to keep Portsmouth up, in their centenary season. Ironically,

Manchester City, the club Ball had left Saints to manage, dropped into Division II. But the financial situation remained precarious and, amid much drama, including renewed interest from Wolanin and moves by a consortium formed by Warren Smith, Portsmouth went into administration in February 1999.

By some miracle – and the genius of Alan Ball – they avoided the drop by virtue of goals scored and in April the club and the administrators eventually found their white knight and financial saviour in the American-based, Serbian businessman Milan Mandaric, assisted by a former director, David Deacon, son of John Deacon.

Harry Redknapp   Jim Smith

Cost: £4.5 million. Half the price, as Graham Hiley sadistically observed in the *Echo*, that Southampton had recently received from Blackburn for Kevin Davies.

Mandaric promised Premiership football in three years. It took four, and a quick turnover of managers, but he found the right man in Harry Redknapp, who in turn hired former Pompey manager, Jim Smith, as his assistant.

Portsmouth were back in the top flight. It was just like the good old days – 1927 to, say, the mid-1950s – save that, this time around, Southampton were already there, waiting to contest a couple of hot derby games.

Tuesday 2 December 2003   **Carling Cup**

Southampton 2 Portsmouth 0

Niemi	Delap	Srnicek	Smertin
Dodd	Telfer	Zivkovic (Foxe)	Faye (Sherwood)
Lundekvam	Marsden (Prutton)	Stefanovic	Berger
M. Svensson	Beattie	De Zeeuw	Sheringham
Higginbotham	Ormerod (Delgado)	Taylor	Yakubu
Fernandes		Stone	

Referee: Mr G. Poll

St Mary's
Attendance: 29,201

It transpired that there would be three 'hot derbies' to contend in 2003-04, as Pompey were drawn to play at St Mary's in the Fourth Round of the Carling Cup (the League Cup smelling as sweet by another name), the first time the two Solent clubs had met in the competition and only the fourth occasion, you'll have noticed, in which they had met in any national knock-out competition.

A tasty little entrée, then, for the clubs' first meeting in the FA Premier League, in 19 days' time, and an excuse for plenty of foaming at the mouth in the press. Both the *News* and the *Echo* were concerned to stress that rivalry can be fierce and friendly, Everton and Liverpool being held up as an example of riveting – but generally bloodless – encounters. As the *Echo*'s Simon Carter saw it, the two clubs had 'the chance – twice over – to show national audiences that it IS possible to have passion and a keen rivalry without it exploding into trouble, gruesome headlines and subsequent FA charges and fines.'

Harry Redknapp opted for the under-dog role: Gordon Strachan was doing a 'great job', he told the *Echo*, and it had been 'a fantastic achievement' to reach the Cup Final and finish eighth: 'but Gordon has got a much stronger squad than I've got. He's got a lot of options – I only had 13 players training this morning.'

Portsmouth did indeed have a long injury list and, after a bright start – which had seen them briefly topping the table – had fallen away. They had failed to score in four of their previous five matches; but, then, Southampton had failed to score in eight of their last 10.

The game kicked off 15 minutes late, 'traffic delays' being blamed over the public address system. It was a lot more dramatic than that, as Harry Redknapp told the press: the driver of the team's bus had performed

a miracle. We were just bombing along [the M27, when] the cars in front of us all smashed into each other. We were about to plough over the top of the lot of them, we could all see it coming, we'd have gone right over the top of the cars, there's no doubt of that... how we swerved the coach over the road to miss them, I'll never know.

So it was that the driver, Mick Pullen, became Pompey's man of the day.

This was not the most ideal preparation for an important fixture. Neither was what happened as the players came onto the pitch – which upset any hopes the *Echo* and *News* harboured regarding the possibility of a passionate but keen rivalry, 'without it exploding into trouble, gruesome headlines and... ,' even if we were spared the FA charges and fines.

A one-minute silence had been scheduled to honour Ted Bates, who had died on 27 November. Somewhat predictably, there were individuals among the visiting supporters who appreciated what a man who had done so much for Southampton FC over 66 years – as player, coach, manager, executive and president – meant to the home crowd and who deliberately set out to sabotage the tribute.

It was so predictable that there were those, including Mary Bates, Ted's widow, who felt the minute's silence should have been held over until the Premiership visit of Charlton, five days later; and some even rationalised the argument by contending that tradition demanded a tribute at the next *League* home game. But Rupert Lowe considered this Cup-tie to be 'the appropriate game' and was not prepared to be 'knocked off course by a lunatic fringe.'

That fringe was duly addressed in the evening's programme – which they would obviously buy and read contemplatively before the game – with a plea that Ted Bates's 'gentlemanly nature' would 'be reflected' during the silence.

The club solemnly expressed its confidence that 'the Pompey supporters will pay their respects as solemnly as the Southampton fans did when Aaron Flahavan [Portsmouth's Southampton-born goalkeeper] was killed in a car crash'.

The Southampton players pay their respects to Ted Bates.
(*Left to right*) Fernandes, Niemi, Telfer, Beattie, Ormerod, Lundekvam, Dodd, Delap, M. Svensson, Marsden, Higginbotham.
For a fuller view of the on-pitch tribute, including the Portsmouth players, see the back cover.

Indeed, the Chairman of the Pompey Supporters Club had written (in a letter reproduced in the matchday programme of 25 August 2001) to thank those fans for 'the immaculate and dignified tribute they gave Aaron'. The Portsmouth Chairman Milan Mandaric gave notice, elsewhere in the programme of 2 December 2003, that he 'would find it very difficult to believe and accept if any of our fans did not give proper respect but I am confident they will behave with the correct dignity'.

The hopes of the two Chairmen were shattered. The referee's whistling for silence provoked jeering and the jeering provoked booing from among the home fans. There was plenty of shushing from the real Pompey supporters, which appeared to be having an effect – until one, very sad, individual loudly articulated the word 'SCUM!' which reverberated around the now silent ground and sparked renewed booing and jeering. Graham Poll blew his whistle rather than carry on with this pitiable and ungracious demonstration of callousness that was duly disowned by the 'silent majority' of Portsmouth fans, to whom a page of the programme for the Premiership game of 21 December was given over.

They used words like 'disgraceful', 'disgusting', 'despicable', 'mindless' and 'moronic' to describe the behaviour of the vocal few.

So it was with a bad taste in just about everybody's mouth that the Cup-tie kicked-off.

It was not a scintillating exhibition of the footballing arts. The Saints' recent inability to find each other with the ball was manifest, but they were quick to regain possession and Pompey looked the less composed of the two teams from the start – perhaps discomforted by the near miss on the motorway and/or the behaviour of some of their fans, or simply disorientated by the enforced changes in the line-up?

Perhaps all of these factors contributed, athough Mark Storey, of the *News*, thought Pompey had the best of the opening half-hour and, 'on possession, attacking intent and sharpness, ... should have taken the lead.' They even had 'a decent-looking penalty claim' when Teddy Sheringham 'went down under Jason's Dodd challenge,' but Mr Poll was unmoved.

The Saints went ahead on 33 minutes, however, when Ormerod laid the ball out to Marsden. He 'superbly picked out Beattie,' who in turn impressed the *Echo*'s Adam Leitch with his 'neat' finish. Beattie celebrated by running around the back of the goal with his hand clamped over his mouth. For Steve Bone, providing the fan's perspective in the *News*, 'the wind had been taken out of our sails – and the 4,200 Pompey fans present went unusually quiet for the rest of the night.'

Above: Beattie's 'neat' finish

Right: His injury-time penalty

With five men strung across mid-field, Portsmouth appeared clueless at to how to respond, the Saints always looking the more assured side. Which is not to say they were assured – just more assured than their opponents, who rarely stretched the home back four, never mind Antti Niemi.

The longer it went on, the quieter the Pompey contingent became. Indeed, the loudest crowd reaction of the second half came when the St Mary's faithful greeted the introduction of Agustin Delgado, the most elusive player in the Premier League, for a five-minute cameo – until one minute into injury time, when Beattie 'burst into the area and was brought down by a clip from De Zeeuw.' This time, Graham Poll did point to the spot and dismissed the Pompey defender, whereupon Beattie 'stepped up and duly dispatched the spot kick to send St Mary's wild again.'

If it had been a 'far from a classic performance,' for Adam Leitch, 'and not even the kind of blood and thunder derby many had predicted,' Mark Storey was less generous: 'OH, WHAT A SORRY NIGHT' ran the *News* headline over his report.

From the disgrace of the morons failing to observe Ted Bates' minute's silence to James Beattie's injury-time penalty, it was a night to forget at St Mary's.

Aftermath

The *News* had more to lament than the result. The next day's page three headline read

BLACK DAY FOR THE BLUES
AS YOBS TARNISH CUP DERBY.

Four features of 'Portsmouth's evening of shame' were listed:

- Hundreds of fans hurling objects at officers and rival fans
- Mobs of Pompey fans trying to storm city centre pubs
- Yobs terrorising residents in the street as they fought pitch battles
- Supporters trying to goad opposition fans into violence after the game.

There followed a sorry catalogue of incidents, also logged in the *Echo.*. Home supporters had been denied their pre-match pint because most of the city-centre pubs were closed, yet a reported 200 of Portsmouth's bravest, boldest and drunkest clashed with Saints' supporters in St Mary Street, which ended up with the Pompey 'fans' firing missiles at police, including bottles, pieces of wood 'and even a bike.' Two windows were broken in a second hand shop and a police vehicle was damaged.

Sixteen of the arrests were made at the game and there were five ejections. Later on, there was an arrest as 'Saints fans attempted to taunt and rub salt into the wounds as the dejected Pompey supporters' were waiting, under police supervision, at Central Station.

The *News* editorial could not have been easy to write:

All too predictably, the game was accompanied by the worst violence a senior officer has seen in years of policing such occasions, and by the deliberate ruination of a silent tribute to one of Southampton's – no, one of football's – all time greats.

So instead of talking about Pompey's need to rediscover their form on the field, we have to condemn the minority of thugs and idiots who again besmirched the name of the club and the city. Many Pompey fans last night held their heads in their hands as a minority interrupted the minute's silence. But none can have felt the shame more acutely than chairman Milan Mandaric, who had to sit through the experience in the director's box with his Southampton counterpart.

They will be hoping that somehow, in the brief time before the clubs' first Premiership match, the men of mindless malevolence can be brought to heel. Police cannot do it by themselves. We desperately need the good people of Portsmouth to play their part.

That means that anyone who boasts at work or in the pub that he was involved in the St Mary's mayhem must receive no plaudits. He (or she) must be treated with disdain, ignored, isolated.

Such people thrive on the oxygen of their peers' applause. Deprive them of that, and they will shrink as bullies.

In short, another defeat by the Saints and dishonoured by poltroons: it wasn't a good night to be from Portsmouth. And, to paraphrase Al Jolson, *we hadn't seen nothing yet!*

Running tally:	**Pompey**	94	**Saints**	80	**Drawn**	33

Southampton   3   Portsmouth   0

Niemi	Prutton	Wapenaar	Sherwood
Dodd	Marsden (Baird)	Primus	Hughes (Yakubu)
Lundekvam	Pahars (McCann)	Foxe	Taylor
M. Svensson	Ormerod (Phillips)	Stefanovic	Sheringham
Higginbotham	Beattie	Schemmel (Zivkovic)	Roberts
Telfer		Smertin	

St. Mary's

Referee: Mr J. Winter (Cleveland)   **Attendance:** 31,697

Another one for the history books, the first-ever Premiership fixture between the two clubs and only their third meeting in the top flight.

On both current League form and precedent, the points were a doddle for the Saints, who were seventh in the Premiership, nine points ahead of Pompey, in 17th place, and were well ahead on League wins over their neighbours.

Then again, the only top-flight match played between the two sides in Southampton to date had ended in that Portsmouth win of 'January 3, 1988' T-shirt fame.

Then again… the statistics and the portents could be shuffled to suit either side – though Pompey's injury plague continued.

The game, on the advice of the Hampshire Constabulary, was scheduled for noon on a Sunday – so again, no pre-match drinks for the Southampton supporters. Which meant there was much muttering in the city's hostelries to the effect that they were being deprived of their usual pint – or glass of wine, G & T, whatever – because certain elements on the other side of Spit Head couldn't hold their lager.

It was another under-dog day for Harry Redknapp. 'It's going to be tough for us,' he told the *Observer*.

> They're in good form and while we've played well enough, we've made a lot of individual errors that have cost us games. But it's particularly difficult for me, losing six of my best starting eleven, it's too many. You can get away with one or two, but when you start losing six… If you took six out of [Gordon Strachan's] team he'd struggle.

Then again, Harry had thrown a side together that had won the First Division championship the previous season, so it shouldn't have been beyond him to chuck one together to beat Saints – who, despite their relatively lofty position and a recent win at Anfield, still weren't passing the ball well.

The good news for Pompey was that Richard Hughes was back, making his first start in 15 months, after injuries and suspensions. The good news for the Saints was that Marian Pahars was considered fit enough to play, albeit wide left rather than as Beattie's striking partner, where Brett Ormerod was preferred to Kevin Phillips, yet to find his scoring touch after the summer's big transfer from Sunderland.

Again, Pompey strung five across midfield and frustrated the Saints' attempts to keep possession but, while the home team found it hard to get forward in numbers, Pompey's game-plan saw them restricted, predominantly, to their own half. So while Southampton's scoring opportunities were hard come by, Portsmouth rarely threatened.

When the visitors' system broke down in the 34th minute, there was a considerable amount of ill luck involved – you might even say slapstick.

Jason Dodd's corner from the left eluded Wapenaar and was curling into the top right-hand corner of the goal, when it ricocheted off the head of Schemmel, onto the bar, down onto the back of Schemmel's head and into the net. Dodd admitted there was an element of the fluke about it: 'there was a bit of wind out there, but it was only supposed to be a cross - it wasn't meant to go in,' he told the *News*. 'I didn't really feel like celebrating. It was a bit embarrassing, to be honest.' The dubious-goals panel relieved him of any lasting embarrassment by declaring it a Schemmel own goal.

Still, they all count, as Harry Redknapp would probably have said had Pompey scored from a similar

Jason Dodd (*below*) had an eventful afternoon, appearing to score the first goal and setting up the third.

Above: His in-swinging corner from the left has gone over goalkeeper Wapenaar and into the net, off the head of Schemmel, the defender on the post. It would eventually be deemed an own goal.

Marian Pahars scored the second.

Right: He releases a 'beautiful curling shot'.

Bottom: The photogenic dive of Wapenaar cannot stop it.

effort. And, as in the Carling Cup game, Pompey rarely looked dangerous thereafter and their more vocal supporters all but disappeared into their shells – going through the motions of defiance rather than trying to gee their side up. That didn't last, though. Reviewing the fans' behaviour for the *News*, Neil Allen explained how 'it took a while for both sets of fans to get their voices back [in the second half], but soon the volume was cranked up. It generated the best atmosphere of the game, irrespective of who was making the noise, as songs echoed from both ends of the ground. But when Saints grabbed a second goal, the visiting fans were silenced.'

Pahars did the damage in the 67th minute, with a strike that recalled his pre-injury form of two seasons before.

Running onto a pass from Chris Marsden (*right*), he 'turned outside and then cut inside between two Pompey defenders before picking his spot in the far corner with a beautiful curling shot.' Or so claimed Adam Leitch in the *Echo*. According to Mark Storey of the *News*, the goal had come, like the first, from a defensive mistake: Boris Zivkovic, a second-half substitute for Schemmel, should not have allowed Pahars to 'skip inside him' like that.

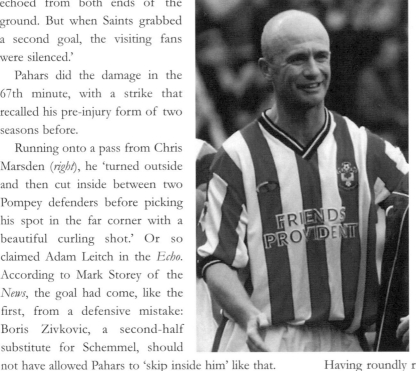

By then, Redknapp had brought on Yakubu Ayegbeni as an extra striker, but to no avail. Beattie again added insult to injury-time. Chris Baird 'flicked the ball' to Phillips, a fellow-substitute, who in turn found Dodd, 'whose first-time cross was met by the flying Beattie.'

It cannot be claimed that the Saints scintillated but, as Jeremy Wilson put it, in the *Echo*, they had no need to: 'it was a bit like watching Audley Harrison comfortably dispatch an opponent who half expected to lose before he climbed in the ring.'

Mark Storey's headline was a wide-screen epic of dissatisfaction: 'It hurts to say it, but let's admit it. Pompey are listless and rudderless, floating back weakly towards the Nationwide with their heads bowed.' It had been for him

easily the bleakest day of the season. Not the worst performance, but the most joyless experience. The question is: how many of the players realise that?

And how many will be looking around to jump ship if Pompey go down?

Harry Redknapp was quick to point out – again – that he had six first choice players out. 'We're disappointed, it is not easy. I've got a small squad and we're decimated by injuries and suspensions. If you took as many players out of Gordon Strachan's team it would be difficult for them to cope.'

If that reads like a replay of his pre-match comments to the *Observer*, well, he was just drawing breath. A fired-up photograph of him appeared in the *News*, beside the headline 'XMAS? I WON'T BE JOINING IN NOW' and above his protest that 'I won't eat my Christmas dinner… I'm going to be the most miserable person you've ever seen in your whole life, I swear to God. My wife's Christmas isn't going to be worth bothering about.'

Having roundly rubbished the Saints' goals, he again lamented that he 'came here with no team.' And yet he 'came in at half-time wondering how we were 1-0 down. They were poor but we weren't any better. If we'd got the next goal there would have been something in the game.'

With the Saints now in fourth place, and in running for the European Champions League, it was looking as though Mrs Strachan might at least have a tolerable Christmas.

Jeremy Wilson was quite carried away by it all: 'Pompey did brilliantly to gain promotion to the Premiership, but the Saints have also moved up a level in the past year. As such, a fairly sizeable gap still exists between the two clubs.' Really?

| Running tally: | Pompey | 94 | Saints | 81 | Drawn | 33 |

Portsmouth 1 Southampton 0

Hislop	Faye	Niemi	Telfer
Pasanen	Smertin	Dodd	A. Svensson (Prutton)
Primus	Taylor	Lundekvam	McCann (Pahars)
De Zeeuw	Sheringham	Higginbotham	Phillips
Stefanovic	Yakubu (Lua Lua)	Crainey (Fernandes)	Beattie
Stone		Delap	

Fratton Park

Referee: Mr M. Halsey

Attendance: 20,140

The editor of the *News* 'would have liked nothing better' than to fill the next day's front page with a photo of 'Yakubu's beaming smile after his goal won three crucial Premiership points for Pompey. Instead we have to splash an image of mounted police dealing with a small minority of thugs who were bent on causing trouble and brought shame on the whole of Portsmouth.'

Indeed, there can't have been a greater anti-climax for Pompey supporters than having the glory of the most gratifying result of the season – or perhaps the last three

The front page the editor of the *News* wished he had not needed to publish.

centuries, if we can trust the *News* on this – snatched from the headlines by a herd of yahoos.

The build-up to the game was dominated by managerial changes, most especially the vitriolic reaction in some Saintly quarters to the possibility of Glenn Hoddle returning to Southampton – a situation shamelessly exploited and exacerbated by the *Echo*. Gordon Strachan had announced in January that he was not going to renew his contract when it expired in the summer; but then, a month later, amid all the Hoddle hoo-ha, he decided to go early. Former Pompey player Steve Wigley was promoted from 'Director of Youth' to 'caretaker', which prompted no great change to the indifferent form of the team.

After two games under Wigley, both draws, Paul Sturrock, who had successfully steered Plymouth Argyle from the depths of Division III to Division II promotion contenders, was recruited and celebrated his appointment with a somewhat flattering 2–0 home win over Liverpool, a week before Fratton Park's first derby for 16 years.

Meanwhile, Pompey were still in the relegation zone, two points behind 17th-placed Leicester City and 12 behind mid-table Saints – who, it was apparent, hadn't 'moved up a level in the last year,' after all. A win was more vital for hopes of Premiership survival than for local bragging rights – although there were still those (we are assured) who would sacrifice the former for the latter.

The kick-off time was set for 4.00 pm, to suit the Sky TV schedules, pubs around Fratton Park ignored police advice to close and so there was plenty of time for certain local personalities to take on ample quantities of Dutch courage. Predictably, there were

Yakubu Aiyegbeni 'gloriously' beats Niemi, with Dodd stranded.

skirmishes between police and poltroons before the Saints fans arrived and bricks and planks were thrown at them when they did – even as they were being escorted by police from Fratton Station to the ground.

The visitors are due a word of sympathy here, because it was not a nice day weather-wise either; and the away-end at Fratton Park has remained uncovered. *News* columnist Steve Bone set the scene:

> HAIL SOUTHAMPTON. That was the headline we all dreaded.
> But it was HAIL ON SOUTHAMPTON, which was much funnier.
> The pre-match storm, a lightning bolt and all, couldn't have been better timed.
> It proved not only that there is a God, but also that he lives in the heavens above Portsmouth and supports his local team.
> From having to stand there and get stung and drenched as the hail and rain came down, through seeing their average (at best) team getting played off the park by their deadliest rivals, it must have been hell.
> And aren't we glad.

Ah well, no sympathy there then, but Mr Bone should be advised that there are those Saints fans for whom Pompey are not the 'deadliest rivals', that place in their heart being reserved for the likes of Spurs – especially after Hoddle's perfidious jumping of ship, followed by the nicking of Dean Richards – and even Leeds, whose

6-1 defeat by Pompey probably upset fewer Southampton supporters than Bone might imagine.

Both sides were disrupted just before the kick-off. Matt Taylor replaced ex-Southampton midfielder, Eyal Berkovic, who reported being 'unwell' and then, as the teams were warming up, Michael Svensson pulled a calf muscle – an injury that would see him miss the rest of the season and selection for Sweden in Euro 2004. Danny Higginbotham moved over from left-back and former Celtic defender, Stephen Crainey, was given his second start since joining the Saints in January.

As for the game itself, the *News* and the *Echo* agreed that the Saints just weren't up for it. They were outplayed in midfield, where Jon Brodkin of the *Guardian* found Alexei Smertin 'full of energy'. And, if Amdy Faye 'was sometimes let down by his distribution,' Pompey were generally responsible for 'almost all the decent passing.' All of which meant that James Beattie and Kevin Phillips lacked support and 'were largely ineffectual,' while Portsmouth were creating more chances than they appeared capable of converting: Yakubu Aiyegbeni was 'twice wasteful, which hardly constituted a surprise. Finishing is not [his] strong point.'

But, as the photo demonstrates, Yakubu won the game with a shot that had no need to be 'strong' – just balletic. It came in the 68th minute, when Smertin found Stone. Mark Storey of the *News* takes up the story:

Stone, instinctively, hit his cross low and hard across the face of goal. Three Southampton shirts couldn't reach it, but Yakubu did, gloriously shooting home from inside the six-yard box. Fans broke free from the stands and hugged the Yak. The stewards meant to stop them probably wanted to do the same.

The Saints supporters had a split second of hope as the clock ticked down to a Pompey victory, when Beattie's knock-down allowed Phillips to unleash what Adam Leitch described as a 'brilliantly acrobatic flying scissor kick.' It beat Shaka Hislop, but 'smashed the inside of the post and came out.'

We might feel short-changed that, after gloating about the drenching Saints' supporters received, Steve Bone did not feel disposed, or was not allocated the space, to mention that bottles and coins had been thrown at them or to comment on what happened after the game, as 400 police officers struggled to hold back a horde of what the media described as 'yobs' and 'hooligans'.

As in 1984, visiting fans were kept in the ground – this time for two hours. Simon Walters of the *Echo* admired their 'dark humour' on this 'Black Sabbath if there ever was one': as they were held there 'until afternoon turned into night,' they serenaded the empty seats with *You're Not Singing Anymore* and *You're Supposed To Be At Home.*

They were being kept away from 'officers with shields and batons and police on horseback [charging] fans in a bid to disperse them' and from a further series of charges with police dogs that 'sent yobs running down side streets and alleyways.'

Yet the fun was far from over. Police car windscreens were smashed, private vehicles damaged and garden walls 'wrecked'; the windows and doors of several shops were staved in; equipment from a building site was thrown at passers-by and police; and the staff in the *John Jacques* public house cowered in the dark as the disturbances outside prompted the landlord to switch all the lights off and stay closed.

It transpired that the police operation that night cost £105,000, and we have yet to come up with a figure for the damage to private and business property. There were four arrested during the game on such charges as drunk and disorderly, racist chanting and provocative behaviour and five arrests made during the street disturbances.

Chief Superintendent Dan Clatcher told Tuesday's press of the police's 'determination to identify every person involved in these ugly acts of violence… These were mindless acts of hooliganism and those responsible have no place in football.' He 'expected up to 100 further arrests.'

It emerged that many of those waiting outside Fratton Park, attempting to get on terms with the visitors, had not been to the game at all.

The *News* revealed that the 'hooligans used mobile phones to co-ordinate attacks on police and rival supporters' and that, before the skirmishing, 'there were a number of people in different parts of the city communicating with each other about what they were going to do.'

One has to ask: with supporters like these, who needs visiting hooligans? Which begs a further question: why all the talk in the local media about animosity towards Southampton? After all, it isn't Southampton's yobs who have made a tradition of smashing Portsmouth up and terrifying its inhabitants after derby games.

Study of CCTV film led to further arrests, trials and successful prosecutions. One 14 year-old girl was caught on camera, throwing at least 16 missiles at police. She created a new record: the youngest-ever female to be banned from football matches.

Fans invaded the pitch and 'hugged the Yak'.

| Running tally: | Pompey | 95 | Saints | 81 | Drawn | 33 |

Final Word

The dunderheads apart, it wasn't such a bad result for either side. Pompey had won a game that, as was made evident in the *News,* was bigger than beating Arsenal, Manchester United and Chelsea all at the same time, while Saints supporters minded to aggregate were able to chant, '5-1, we beat you 5-1.' So honour was perhaps satisfied and it seems to be generally agreed that it was this win that sparked a revival that saw Pompey burst free from the clutches of relegation.

And further, just to emphasise that boorish behavior at, and around, football matches is not confined to Portsmouth, the *Echo*'s front page of 8 May carried one of the more pathetic stories of the season: seven 'Southampton football thugs' had been convicted, for up to four years, for partaking in a pre-planned confrontation at Maze Hill Station with a group of London's toughest hooligans from... err Charlton.

It was no joking matter either, three Saints fans being left unconscious and needing hospital treatment. The *Echo* didn't clarify whether they were part of the fearsome *crew* or poor unfortunates unwittingly caught up in the fighting. Whatever, it must have come as much as a surprise to Charlton supporters, as it did to those of Saints, that they had a hard-core hooligan element in their midst.

But we have devoted enough space to this element for the moment – we shall return to the matter in the last three chapters, which include a Pompey perspective – so let us get back to the football.

Not that the football was that great in 2003-04, even if it did leave our respective favourites in the Premier League with just two points between them: the closest they had finished since the 1960s in the Second Division.

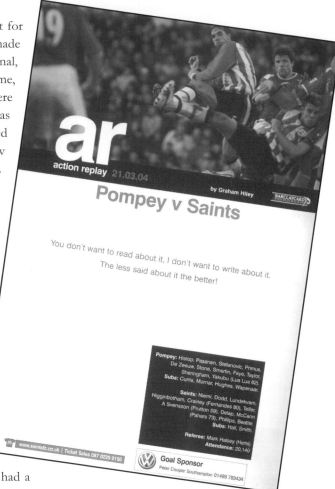

ar action replay 21.03.04

by Graham Hiley

Pompey v Saints

You don't want to read about it, I don't want to write about it. The less said about it the better!

Pompey: Hislop, Pasanen, Stefanovic, Primus, De Zeeuw, Stone, Smertin, Faye, Taylor, Sheringham, Yakubu (Lua Lua 82). **Subs:** Curtis, Mornar, Hughes, Wapenaar.

Saints: Niemi, Dodd, Lundekvam, Higginbotham, Crainey (Fernandes 80), Telfer, A Svensson (Prutton 59), Delap, McCann (Pahars 73), Phillips, Beattie. **Subs:** Hall, Smith.

Referee: Mark Halsey (Herts)
Attendance: 20,140

www.saintsfc.co.uk | Ticket Sales 087 0220 0150

Goal Sponsor
Peter Cooper Southampton 01489 783434

The last word on all of this should perhaps go to Graham Hiley, writing in the Saints' matchday programme on the 209th derby game – although, as his full-page report (reproduced *above*) shows, he was not minded to take it.

Very droll, but it is as well that those deputed to report on the previous 208 encounters didn't feel that way.

READ ON: The *Observer* poll results were compiled by Gemma Clarke. The timing of the tribute to Ted Bates was defended by Rupert Lowe in the special, commemorative edition of *Dell Diamond.* See 'Sources'.

Part II

Neighbours and Rivals

This part of the book mainly moves out of the derby scene and into aspects of the Saints-Pompey relationship that might at times be sub-titled 'rivalry, *what* rivalry?'

Chapters 14-15 catalogue men who have played for both clubs, in peace-time or war-time, respectively. The latter chapter also charts the coming-together, in a common team, of players from the two clubs.

Chapter 16 features the fans – *not* a representative sample but a few volunteers, recruited by word-of-mouth or the internet. Most of them are 'two-timers', Saints fans who admit to having watched football at Fratton Park, even when their side was not playing there. If that appears to hard-core loyalists to be unspeakable behaviour, we dread to think what they might make of the handful who confess to having 'come over', in that they've transferred their allegiance from Pompey to the Saints.

Whichever group they fall into, their experiences have given many of these fans perspectives on the 'rivalry'. These form the second part of this chapter: why has the rivalry been 'unrelenting', as our sub-title puts it, if our two clubs have met so seldom in recent years? And why do some football fans find it so odd that anybody can not only watch, but even 'support', more than one team in Hampshire?

Chapters 17-18 take up such themes, among others. Barry Bendel offers a Pompey perspective on it all – the results and the rivalry – and Dave Juson sweeps up on the nature of the relationship between friends and rivals who have been the county's top two these past 105 years.

Chapter 14
Played for Both

Clay Aldworth and Gary Chalk

This chapter is about men who have served both clubs. It is in three parts:

A   Men who have played for both clubs in one or more of three Leagues: Southern League, Football League and Premiership. This means that it excludes unofficial war-time appearances that are the subject of the next chapter.

The playing statistics in this first part are for 'League' appearances and goals in those three Leagues, up until the end of the 2003-04 season. So Peter Crouch is simply credited with having made his debut for Southampton.

B   Players who never made it into 'League' football, thus defined, with one club but did with the other.

C   Nine men who, although they never played for both, have served both clubs in some permutation of player, coach and/or manager.

A: Played 'League' football for both

John BAINBRIDGE				Forward
Born:	Seaham, April 1880	League Appearances	League Goals	
Died:	January 1960			
Signed for Pompey:	May 1906	25	4	
Signed for Saints:	May 1907	84	20	

Came to The Dell in the summer of 1907, having had considerable Southern League experience with Reading and then a season with Portsmouth. A reliable performer, his right-wing partnership with Frank Jefferis drew favourable comparisons with the famed duo of Wood and Arthur Turner, seven years earlier. Ill health ended his Dell career and he returned to his native North East where, after playing briefly for Hartlepool, he reverted to his original occupation of coal miner.

Ian BAIRD				Forward
Born:	Southampton, 1 April 1964	League Appearances	League Goals	
Signed for Saints:	July 1980	22	5	
Signed for Pompey:	June 1987	20	1	

An England Schoolboy international who quickly developed into a strong bustling centre-forward. He made a big impact in the Saints Reserves but struggled to do the same for the first team, so two loan spells with Cardiff City and Newcastle United were followed by a £100,000 transfer to Leeds United. Having moved to Fratton Park, where Alan Ball was trying to bolster Pompey's attack in preparation for their return to Division One, he was beset by injury and disciplinary problems and rejoined Leeds in March 1988.

Dave BEASANT
Goalkeeper

Born:	Willesden, 20 March 1959	League Appearances	League Goals
Signed for Saints:	4 November 1993	88	0
Signed for Pompey:	9 August 2001	27	0

'Lurch', as he was affectionately known, was Saints Player of the Year in 1995-96 when he kept an impressive 13 clean sheets. But when new manager David Jones brought a 'keeper (Paul Jones) with him in 1997, Dave found himself down the pecking order and moved to Nottingham Forest, initially on loan but then permanently. At the age of 42, he moved to Portsmouth. He started and finished the 2001-02 season as first choice, having had a spell as unused cover at Tottenham. Latterly goalkeeping coach at Fulham and for the Northern Ireland team.

William BEAUMONT
Centre-half

Born:	Lancashire, October 1883	League Appearances	League Goals
Died:	19 November 1911		
Signed for Pompey:	September 1907	70	2
Signed for Saints:	October 1910	27	0

Cost Pompey £75 when he joined from Swindon Town. He was on the verge of retiring from the game in 1910 when Saints offered him another life. He accepted, carried on his full-time trade in Portsmouth, trained every night at Fratton Park and made contact with his team-mates only on match days. Never a brilliant player, he was, nonetheless, versatile and could operate anywhere in the half-back line. Having retired, for real, in the summer of 1911, he died within months from pneumonia

John BERESFORD
Full-back

Born:	Sheffield, 4 September 1966	League Appearances	League Goals
Signed for Pompey:	23 March 1989	108	8
Signed for Saints:	6 February 1999	17	0

A left-sided defender or midfield player capped by England at School, Youth and 'B' levels. Cost Pompey £300,000 from Barnsley. After three good years with them, he moved to Newcastle for £650,000 and then on to Saints for £1.5m, towards the end of the 1997-98 season. Only seven minutes into the next season, however, he badly damaged his cruciate knee ligaments. Made only three more appearances as sub before retiring.

Robert BLYTH
Forward

Born:	Muirkirk, 2 June 1900	League Appearances	League Goals
Died:	Southwark, 1956		
Signed for Pompey:	April 1921	8	2
Signed for Saints:	January 1922	8	0

Arrived at The Dell after making 10 Southern League appearances for Pompey and another couple in the Cup. He had a brief run in Saints first team when Charles Brown was injured. He had left the club by the end of the 1922-23 season for a brief career in the United States. His uncle William had played for Pompey, while his father, Bob, had been a player, manager, director and chairman.

Tommy BOWMAN
Half-back

Born:	Tarbolton, 26 October 1873	League Appearances	League Goals
Died:	27 August 1958		
Signed for Saints:	May 1901	88	2
Signed for Pompey:	May 1904	85	3

Scottish born, Tommy came to The Dell as a reputed centre-half. Played in the 1902 Cup Final and was ever-present in the Championship side of 1904. Having missed only five League games in three years, he moved to Pompey in 1904. Dropped out of first-class football to join Eastleigh Athletic in 1909. A boiler scaler by trade, he later worked for many years in Southampton Docks.

Arthur BROWN
Goalkeeper

Born:	Cowes, July 1888	League Appearances	League Goals
Died:	not known		
Signed for Saints:	January 1906 & 1910	39	0
Signed for Pompey:	April 1907	9	0

Signed for Saints while still a student at Hartley College. After subsequent spells at Cowes and Pompey, he again registered with Southampton, where he made the goalkeeper's jersey his own. Was Great Britain's reserve goalkeeper in the Stockholm Olympics of 1912. Soon after that, he emigrated to Canada, where he became the chief civil engineer on a dock scheme in Halifax, Nova Scotia.

Arthur CHADWICK
Centre-half

Born:	Church, July 1875	League Appearances	League Goals
Died:	Exeter, 21 March 1936		
Signed for Saints:	May 1897	81	6
Signed for Pompey:	May 1901	43	9

A powerful and efficient defender for whom the season of 1899-1900 climaxed in two England caps, followed by an FA Cup runners-up medal with the Saints. Although never capped again, he won further honours with Pompey – the Southern League Championship of 1901-02 – before moving to Northampton in 1904. Returned to The Dell in 1925, as the first ex-player to become Southampton manager and soon enjoyed another Cup run – to the 1927 semi-final.

Mike CHANNON
Forward

Born:	Orcheston, 28 November 1948	League Appearances	League Goals
Signed for Saints:	March 1964 & September 1979	510	185
Signed for Pompey:	August 1985	34	6

Made his debut for Saints Reserves in September 1964, aged 15yrs 10 months, to break the club record. He won the first of his 46 England caps (45 as a Saint) in October 1972. The scorer of 20 international goals, he was coveted by top clubs. Having stayed loyal despite relegation, he was rewarded with an FA Cup winners' medal in 1976. Joined Pompey in 1985 at the age of 37, signed by his former team-mate Alan Ball. He made his 700th League appearance at Grimsby Town. Remains Southampton's leading goalscorer.

Colin CLARKE — Forward

Born:	Newry, Northern Ireland, 30 October 1962	League Appearances	League Goals
Signed for Saints:	July 1986	82	36
Signed for Pompey:	May 1990	85	18

Chris Nicholl paid £400,000 to bring Colin to The Dell just days after he had returned from the World Cup in Mexico. Having scored a hat-trick on his debut – the first-ever Saint to do so – he ran up 20 goals in his first season and 16 in the next, establishing himself as a striker of international repute. Yet, as quickly as he had won the fans' esteem, he fell from grace with a series of transfer requests and talk of a move to a 'bigger' club. Pompey broke their transfer record when they paid QPR £450,000 for him in 1990. Latterly coaching in the United States.

Eamonn COLLINS — Midfield

Born:	Dublin, 22 October 1965	League Appearances	League Goals
Signed for Saints:	December 1981	3	0
Signed for Pompey:	May 1986	5	0

A protégé of Alan Ball, who gave Eamonn his Blackpool debut when he was only 14 and then brought him to The Dell as an apprentice. A light midfielder, he played regularly for the Reserves but lacked the muscle to force himself into the first team. So it was no surprise when he followed his mentor, first to Pompey and then to Colchester. Latterly manager of St Patricks Athletic in Ireland.

Andy COOK — Full-back

Born:	Romsey, 10 August 1969	League Appearances	League Goals
Signed for Saints:	June 1987	16	1
Signed for Pompey:	December 1996	9	0

Andy took the place of full-back Mark Dennis for the opening two games of the 1987-88 season, but his promise was eclipsed by the arrival of Derek Statham. Having featured on the left-wing for the Youth team and also played at times in midfield, he perhaps suffered from not truly settling into any one position. His versatility on the left-hand side of the pitch appears, however, to have impressed Alan Ball, who signed him twice, first for Exeter City and then for Pompey.

Peter CROUCH — Forward

Born:	Macclesfield, 30 January 1981	League Appearances	League Goals
Signed for Pompey:	July 2001	37	18
Signed for Saints:	July 2004	debut August 2004	-

This 6 ft 7ins centre-forward had a fine season at Fratton Park, showing better ball control than is usually expected of tall strikers and an ability to run at and beat defenders. Although sold to Aston Villa towards the end of that season, he was nevertheless voted Pompey's 'Player of the Season'. His arrival at Southampton raised questions – was Paul Sturrock planning a long-ball game and where was Beattie going? – but the manager soon departed with those questions unanswered.

Ron DAVIES   Forward

Born:	Ysol Basing, Holywell, 25 May 1942	League Appearances	League Goals
Signed for Saints:	August 1966	240	134
Signed for Pompey:	April 1973	59	18

 Having being capped five times by Wales, Ron joined Saints for a club record fee of £55,000. In his first season, he scored 43 goals from 47 appearances and was leading goalscorer in the First Division. The following season, his League tally of 28 made him joint-top goalscorer with George Best. When he scored all four goals in Saints' 4-1 win at Old Trafford, Matt Busby declared him the best striker in Europe. Ron would have joined United 'at a heart-beat' but did so only after a spell with Pompey, where he scored 16 goals in his first season. After which, he played and coached in the USA.

C.B. FRY   Full-back

Born:	Croydon, 25 April 1872	League Appearances	League Goals
Died:	7 September 1956		
Signed for Saints:	December 1900	16	0
Signed for Pompey:	December 1902	2	0

The complete all-round sportsman, Charles Burgess Fry excelled at athletics, rugby, football and in particular cricket. Although registered as a Saints player in 1898, his many commitments with the Corinthians delayed his Southern League debut until December 1900. He gained an England cap the following year and was a member of the Cup Final side beaten by Sheffield United. His limited availability frustrated the club and he was allowed to move to Portsmouth, where an injury promptly caused him to retire from the game, while continuing to run up 94 first-class centuries and to captain England, for whom he would make 26 Test appearances.

Paul GILCHRIST   Forward

Born:	Dartford, 5 January 1951	League Appearances	League Goals
Signed for Saints:	March 1972	107	17
Signed for Pompey:	March 1977	39	3

Bought as a forward by Ted Bates, Paul adapted to playing in midfield for Lawrie McMenemy. During the 1976 FA Cup run he showed he had not lost his eye for goal when he scored two memorable goals, a spectacular over-the-shoulder shot against West Bromwich Albion and a 25-yarder against Crystal Palace in the semi-final. In the team only because of an injury to Hugh Fisher, Paul perhaps tends to be the forgotten man when fans recall the Cup-winning side, probably because he made only two more appearances before moving to Fratton Park.

Mervyn GILL   Goalkeeper

Born:	Exeter, 13 April 1931	League Appearances	League Goals
Signed for Pompey:	September 1953	6	0
Signed for Saints:	December 1955	1	0

Represented the RAF while doing his National Service at Thorney Island and was on Portsmouth's books as an amateur, getting six games in 1953-54. Briefly with Woking before signing amateur forms with Saints. Demobbed in April 1956, he signed professional but a 3-1 victory at Walsall was to be his only game. From December 1962 until retiring in 1990, he worked for English China Clay Quarries.

Jon GITTENS — Centre Half

Born:	Moseley, Birmingham, 22 January 1964	League Appearances	League Goals
Signed for Saints:	October 1985 & March 1991	37	0
Signed for Pompey:	August 1993	83	2

A raw but fast centre-half when Saints signed him, Jon had the chance to learn from playing alongside Kevin Bond or Mark Wright. A free agent in the summer of 1987, he refused a new contract and signed for Swindon Town, with a tribunal fixing the fee at £40,000. Chris Nicholl raised a few eyebrows by spending £400,000 to bring him back to The Dell, a day before the 1991 transfer deadline. After a spell at Middlesbrough, he returned to the South Coast for three seasons with Pompey. Still lives in the area, where he is involved in non-league football.

Alex GLEN — Forward

Born:	Kilsyth, 11 December 1878	League Appearances	League Goals
Died:	Not known		
Signed for Saints:	May 1906	29	10
Signed for Pompey:	May 1907	7	1

Glen was a dexterous, elegant dribbler and, being a tall man, swerved and weaved with devastating effect. He formed a strong right-wing partnership with Frank Jefferis for the Saints until the last two months of the 1906-07 season when his discipline deserted him dramatically. Whereupon he moved to Pompey for a season, before finishing his career with Brentford.

Ivan GOLAC — Full-back

Born:	Kuprivnica, Yugoslavia, 15 June 1950	League Appearances	League Goals
Signed for Saints:	August 1978 & March 1984	168	4
Signed for Pompey:	January 1985	8	0

He had won four caps for Yugoslavia when Lawrie McMenemy brought him to The Dell, where his ferocious tackling and surging, flamboyant style made him a huge favourite with the fans, who voted him Player of the Year in 1981. He realised his dream of playing at Wembley by appearing in the 1979 League Cup Final. Having failed to agree terms, he left in November 1982 but returned in March 1984, via AFC Bournemouth, Manchester City and Yugoslavia. He is not alone in thinking he should have played in the 1984 semi-final, in place of the injured Steve Williams. Portsmouth took him on loan for four months, since when he has coached across Europe, from Belgrade to Dundee.

Willie HAINES — Forward

Born:	Warminster Common, 14 July 1900	League Appearances	League Goals
Died:	Frome, 5 November 1974		
Signed for Pompey:	December 1922	164	119
Signed for Saints:	May 1928	70	47

'Farmer's Boy' Haines was something of a legend at Fratton Park, where Pompey fans would often voice their approval of his forward play with a rendition of 'To be a Farmer's Boy'. He was certainly a centre-forward with a style of his own. You were never likely to see him dashing around the field and he seldom, if ever, tried to hit the ball hard, preferring instead to place it with tantalising precision. In his four years at The Dell, he was twice top scorer, combining well with another ex-Pompey forward, Jerry Mackie. In 1960, he became the President of the Portsmouth Supporters Club.

Trevor HEBBERD — Midfield

Born:	Alresford, 19 June 1958	League Appearances	League Goals
Signed for Saints:	September 1974	96	8
Signed for Pompey:	September 1991	4	0

'Smiler', as he was known, first appeared for Saints' Reserves at the age of 16. Playing in a variety of positions, he was a valuable squad-member, without fully asserting himself. Sold to Oxford in a deal that brought Mark Wright and Keith Cassells to The Dell, he had six successful seasons there, with a League Cup Winners' medal in 1986 to show for it. On loan to Pompey from Derby County in October 1991, he made one full appearance, plus three as sub.

Scott HILEY — Full-back

Born:	Plymouth, 27 September 1968	League Appearances	League Goals
Signed for Saints:	August 1998	32	0
Signed for Pompey:	December 1999	75	0

A versatile full-back, signed by David Jones, he could play in either full-back position, sometimes partnering Dodd on his right, though mainly Benali or Colleter to his left. But he never made either position his and moved to Pompey, signed by Alan Ball for the third time. Within days of Scott's arrival at Fratton Park, Ball was sacked. Not figuring much under new manager, Tony Pulis, he was re-introduced when Steve Claridge took over and was named Pompey Player of the Year for season 2000-01.

Barry HORNE — Midfield

Born:	St. Asaph, Denbighshire, 18 May 1962	League Appearances	League Goals
Signed for Pompey:	July 1987	70	7
Signed for Saints	March 1989	78	5

 Starting out at Wrexham, he moved south to join Alan Ball's Pompey for £60,000. If he was not expected to be a regular choice, once given his chance, he was never out of the side. Voted Player of the Year, he scored three goals, one being the first in Pompey's 2-0 win at The Dell in 1988. When he joined the Saints, he became their most expensive signing at £700,000.

Ted HOUGH — Full-back

Born:	Walsall, 4 December 1899	League Appearances	League Goals
Died:	Birmingham, 3 September 1978		
Signed for Saints:	October 1921	175	0
Signed for Pompey:	May 1931	1	0

It was fortunate that the Saints director who was sent to a Walsall Works team to secure Ted's services had his wallet with him, as they agreed to release him only if the director stood a round of drinks. This unusual transfer fee — said to have ended up as 52 pints' worth — was beer money well spent, as Ted remained with Saints for a decade. Moving to Pompey for a fee of £200, he played only one game before a transfer to Bristol Rovers. Ted later returned to Portsmouth to work at the local power station as a fitter's mate.

Bert HOULKER — Half-back

Born:	Blackburn, 27 April 1872	League Appearances	League Goals
Died:	Blackburn, 27 May 1962		
Signed for Pompey:	May 1902	23	1
Signed for Saints:	May 1903	59	3

Having won his first England cap two days before he left Blackburn Rovers for Pompey, 'Kelly' was awarded his second when England played Wales at Fratton Park the next season. One cap later, he was on his way to The Dell, where he was twice more capped and won a Southern League Championship medal, as well. Tenacious and strong, rather than clever, he was immensely popular at all of his clubs and, although he intended to retire from the game in 1906, Blackburn tempted him back for one more season. He ran a coal and haulage firm until he retired in 1947, aged 75.

Bill KENNEDY — Half-back

Born:	Saltcoats, Ayrshire, 2 February 1912	League Appearances	League Goals
Died:	Southampton, 12 December 1989		
Signed for Pompey:	March 1932	1	0
Signed for Saints:	August 1936	43	0

A junior at Fratton Park in 1932, he joined Saints in 1936. A reliable centre-half, there were times, during the 1936-37 season, when he formed a settled half-back line with Cyril King and Bill Kingdon, but he spent much of the next season in the Reserves. He refused terms in May 1938 and moved north of the border to Hamilton but, after the war, returned to Southampton to serve aboard the Queen Mary. When he retired from the sea in 1962, he continued to live in the city, working at Mullards.

George LAWRENCE — Forward

Born:	Kensington, London, 14 September 1962	League Appearances	League Goals
Signed for Saints:	September 1980 & December 1984	80	12
Signed for Pompey:	February 1993	14	0

Spotted by Southampton's London scouting network, he was once described by Lawrie McMenemy as 'Slinky'. George brought added meaning to the word 'unpredictable'. He could, when remembering to take the ball with him, completely perplex opposing defenders and cause havoc in the penalty area. Having signed for Portsmouth in 1993, he played in the final 11 League matches as a sub and then came off the bench against Leicester City in the play-offs.

John LEWIS — Forward

Born:	Aberystwyth, August 1881	League Appearances	League Goals
Died:	Burton-on-Trent, 12 September 1954		
Signed for Pompey:	May 1900	21	7
Signed for Saints:	August 1907	24	10

Having started his League career with Bristol Rovers, he joined Pompey for the 1900-01 season. He arrived at The Dell six years later from Brighton, after another spell with Bristol Rovers, with whom he won his one Welsh cap. John was a clever little forward and, although his size could be a handicap against burly opponents, he formed a useful partnership with Fred Harrison in his one season as a Saint.

Alex McDONALD   Forward

Born:	Greenock, 12 April 1878	League Appearances	League Goals
Died:	Bonness, 1949		
Signed for Saints:	May 1901	5	5
Signed for Pompey:	March 1902	7	7

A first-rate marksman, Alex McDonald had scored one of the Everton goals that knocked Saints out of the FA Cup in 1901. He joined Southampton later that year and made an explosive start to the next season by scoring five goals in as many games. But in competition with the wealth of excellent forwards on the club's books, he soon found himself in the background. That did not match his ambitions and by mid-season, he had left for West Ham. His stay there was also short and he was at Fratton Park before the season was out. Never a regular there either, he was soon on his travels again.

John McILWAINE   Centre-half

Born:	Falkirk, 12 June 1904	League Appearances	League Goals
Died:	Bellodyke, 24 April 1980		
Signed for Pompey:	February 1928	56	5
Signed for Saints:	June 1930 & August 1933	117	18

 His transfer from Falkirk to Pompey caused a sensation in the football world. One of the outstanding centre-halves in Scotland and much sought after by many a top English club, he chose to join a struggling First Division club, instead. He cost Pompey a club record £5,000 and captained them to the FA Cup Final at Wembley in 1929. Came to The Dell for another club record, £2,650, before spending two years with Llanelli. He then returned to Southampton where, in his final (1935-36) season, he combined the roles of assistant manager, coach and team captain.

Jerry MACKIE   Forward

Born:	Motherwell, 1 January 1894	League Appearances	League Goals
Died:	Chichester, 5 January 1959		
Signed for Pompey:	May 1920	247	78
Signed for Saints:	March 1928	81	24

James Mackie – always known as 'Jerry' – featured in Pompey's promotion-winning sides of 1924 and 1927. He was their first-choice inside-right for close on six years until, with manager Jack Tinn building for the future, he was sold to Saints for £1,000. Scored six goals in seven games, including a hat-trick on his home debut, and generally enjoyed a 'swansong' two seasons alongside former Pompey team-mate, Willie Haines, during which he scored his 100th league goal in 1931.

Alan McLOUGHLIN   Midfield

Born:	Manchester, 20 April 1967	League Appearances	League Goals
Signed for Saints:	December 1990	24	1
Signed for Pompey:	February 1992	309	54

An apprentice who never made it at Old Trafford, Alan got his break with Swindon Town in 1986. Having been brought to The Dell by Chris Nicholl for a club record of £1m, he played in all 22 of their remaining games. But he failed to start the next season under Ian Branfoot and moved to Pompey, initially on loan, in 1992, appearing in the FA Cup semi-final against Liverpool and the Division I play-off against Leicester City. Shortly before he was sacked, Alan Ball sold him to Wigan Athletic for £300,000. He is latterly on the staff of Forest Green Rovers.

Steve MIDDLETON — Goalkeeper

Born:	Portsmouth, 28 March 1953	League Appearances	League Goals
Signed for Saints:	July 1970	24	0
Signed for Pompey:	July 1977	26	0

Having managed only one decent run for Saints at the beginning of the 1975-76 season, he went on loan to Torquay, whence Jimmy Dickinson signed him for Pompey. He expressed himself delighted to join his home-town club, having been unhappy with Lawrie McMenemy's policy of signing ageing stars. He started well but, after a mistake in a cup-tie against Swindon Town, he conceded 12 goals in three games and was out of favour. He returned for a second run but his football career was over.

George MOLYNEUX — Full-back

Born:	Liverpool, July 1875	League Appearances	League Goals
Died:	Rochford, 14 April 1942		
Signed for Saints:	May 1900	142	0
Signed for Pompey:	May 1905	23	0

Secured on a free transfer, George was a fine, quick-tackling full-back, who made his first appearance for England at Ibrox in April 1902 when 25 people were killed and the game was expunged from the records. He duly made his debut in the restaged game and won three further England caps while at The Dell. He also picked up three Southern League Championship medals before joining Pompey in 1905, where he remained for one season.

Harry PENK — Forward

Born:	Wigan, 19 July 1934	League Appearances	League Goals
Signed for Pompey:	September 1955	9	2
Signed for Saints:	July 1960	52	6

Henry Penk – always known as 'Harry' – joined Pompey in September 1955 from his home-town club, Wigan Athletic, then a non-league side. Although he had a run at outside-left at the end of 1955-56, he barely featured the following season and moved on to Plymouth. Ted Bates brought him from there as cover while John Sydenham was doing his National Service. But the end of Sydenham's Army days virtually spelled the end of Harry's first-team days.

Matt REILLY — Goalkeeper

Born:	Donnybrook, Ireland, 22 March 1874	League Appearances	League Goals
Died:	Dublin, 9 December 1954		
Signed for Saints:	December 1895	2	0
Signed for Pompey:	July 1899	138	0

Gunner Reilly became a local legend in Portsmouth, keeping goal for Royal Artillery, and was able to play a couple of Southern League games for the Saints before the RA joined that competition. His service career ended at the time Portsmouth FC were assembling their team and manager Frank Brettell lost no time in signing him up for 'the Professionals'. Reilly's reputation, as well as his popularity, grew while with Pompey, where he soon won the first of his two caps for Ireland. He joined Dundee in 1904, before retiring as a publican.

Matthew ROBINSON
Full-back

Born:	Exeter, 23 December 1974	League Appearances	League Goals
Signed for Saints:	July 1993	14	0
Signed for Pompey:	February 1998	69	1

Although he made 14 appearances for Saints, Matt started in only three of them. In February 1998, he became Alan Ball's second signing of his second managerial spell at Fratton Park and went straight into Pompey's side at left-back. He enjoyed further long runs in the first team but soon after Tony Pulis succeeded Alan Ball as manager, he was sold to Reading, where he was serenaded with a variation on the refrain from *The Graduate* – 'Here's to you, Matthew Robinson …'

Bill ROCHFORD
Full-back

Born:	Newhouse, Scotland, 23 May 1913	League Appearances	League Goals
Died:	Bishop Auckland, 9 March 1984		
Signed for Pompey:	August 1931	138	1
Signed for Saints	July 1946	128	0

A member of Pompey's FA Cup-winning side of 1939, whose first run-out had been against Saints in the Rowland Hospital Cup in 1932. Made his full debut a year later at right-back and, by 1936, was representing the English League. Moved to left-back in 1937 and stayed there, following up his Wembley appearance with a further 206 games for Pompey during the War. Joined Saints in 1946 for £550 and captained them until 1950, latterly as player-coach. Hugely admired for his tactical nous – especially at offside – he failed, to the surprise of his disciples, to get the manager's job when Bill Dodgin left in 1949.

Bobby STOKES
Forward

Born:	Portsmouth, 30 January 1951	League Appearances	League Goals
Died:	Portsmouth, 30 May 1995		
Signed for Saints:	February 1968	216	40
Signed for Pompey:	August 1977	24	2

A promising Portsmouth schoolboy, Bobby was 14 when Pompey abandoned their Youth team in 1965 and he needed a good home to go to. Southampton offered him one, straight from school, the next summer, and he soon won an England Youth cap. After scoring twice on his Easter 1969 debut, he had to wait until 1971-72 for a regular spot. It was said of him that 'you could wind him up in August and he would still be running in May.' In 1976, he needed to keep running until 1 May and to remain wound-up until the 83rd minute at Wembley. Then all that remained was to slot the ball past Manchester United's Alex Stepney, to win the Cup, and his special niche in Saints' history was assured. Yet he would start only eight more games for Southampton before ending his Football League career at Pompey. He died prematurely of broncho-pneumonia.

Played for Both

Isaac TOMLINSON — Forward

Born:	Chesterfield, 16 April 1880	League Appearances	League Goals
Died:	Bournemouth, 24 August 1970		
Signed for Saints:	May 1905	29	8
Signed for Pompey:	May 1906	5	0

An extremely speedy winger, Ike was considered, with his accurate shooting, to be the double of former Saint, Joe Turner. Unfortunately, he had an excitable temperament and, suffering from nerves, particularly in away games, often failed to deliver the goods. His nerves were sometimes so bad that before important games he preferred to walk around the ground rather than sit in the dressing room. A move to Pompey did not improve his disposition and, after only five games in 1906-07, he moved to Scotland.

Malcolm WALDRON — Centre-half

Born:	Emsworth, 6 September 1956	League Appearances	League Goals
Signed for Saints:	September 1974	178	10
Signed for Pompey:	March 1984	23	1

Spotted while playing for Havant and Hampshire School teams, he was snapped up by Saints, while Pompey dallied over offering terms. He established himself at the beginning of the 1976-77 season, where his speed and heading ability often paid dividends. Saints' Player of the Year in 1979, he gained England honours when selected for a 'B' international against New Zealand that same year. Cost Pompey £45,000 when he joined from Burnley and scored his only goal in a 4-4 draw with Fulham.

John WARNER — Full-back

Born:	Preston, 1883	League Appearances	League Goals
Died:	Preston, 16 May 1948		
Signed for Saints:	May 1905	17	0
Signed for Pompey:	May 1906	227	10

With speed one of his main assets, he was considered more than a match for any forward. He could also use the ball well and would have probably remained at The Dell for some considerable time had it not been for the directors' mistaken impression that one of his knees was unsound. He was allowed to move to Fratton Park where he made 227 Southern League appearances, proving the Southampton board wrong. He remained at Pompey as a player until 1915 and later became their trainer.

Ernest WILLIAMS — Forward

Born:	Ryde, Isle of Wight 1882	League Appearances	League Goals
Died:	Portsmouth, 5 August 1943		
Signed for Pompey:	December 1906	32	5
Signed for Saints:	October 1912	1	0

Played for Ryde before joining Portsmouth in December 1906. An amateur throughout his career, he played over 30 Southern League matches. In five seasons at Fratton Park, he won two England amateur caps in 1910-11. Having then moved to Chelsea but failed to make their first team, he joined Saints in 1912. After making only one appearance on the left-wing, he gave up football to concentrate on a teaching career.

B: Players on the books of both clubs

This category includes two players — Frank Moore, seemingly the first man to play for both, and Bert Youtman, each of whom appeared in Southern League football for Portsmouth, but in a lesser League for Southampton — and half-a-dozen amateurs who never made it at one club (Pompey, save in one case) but made the League grade at the other.

Edward BELL			League Appearances	League Goals
				Forward
Born:	Gibraltar, 1886			
Died:	Somme, 24 March 1918			
Signed for Saints:	March 1907		4	0
Signed for Pompey:	February 1911		0	0

As the son of a soldier in the 7th Regiment, he played his early football at Arthur Turner's old club, South Farnborough. Like Arthur a right-winger, he was not, however, in the same class. Had brief spells as an amateur with Crystal Palace and Portsmouth before signing for Saints in March 1907. Twice awarded the Military Cross during the Great War, he lost his life in 1918.

Billy BEVIS			League Appearances	League Goals
				Forward
Born:	Warsash, 29 September 1918			
Died:	Warsash, 22 August 1994			
Signed for Pompey:	February 1934		0	0
Signed for Saints:	June 1937		82	16

Having joined Pompey as a 15 year-old amateur, but failed to make an impression, he had his career revived by Tom Parker. The Saints manager's faith in him was quickly justified as Billy made 68 pre-war League appearances, the highlight being a hat-trick at Swansea in April 1939. A petty officer gunner in the merchant navy during the war, he was torpedoed three times and mined once. Returning to The Dell on demob, he played only 14 more games for Saints before quitting League football.

Bill BUSHBY			League Appearances	League Goals
				Half-back
Born:	Shildon, 21 August 1914			
Died:	25 December 1997			
Signed for Pompey:	June 1939		0	0
Signed for Saints:	September 1946		2	0

Brought from Southend United as cover for Pompey captain, Jimmy Guthrie, badly injured in a car crash. The outbreak of war, followed by Guthrie's full recovery, meant he never played officially for Portsmouth. Worked at Folland Aircraft during the War and played in their star-studded side. So did Bill Dodgin, who signed him for Southampton after the War. After one season and only two games for Saints, he retired into local football, while again working at Follands.

David GUNTER
Full-back

Born:	Portsmouth, 4 March 1933	League Appearances	League Goals
Signed for Pompey:	1952	0	0
Signed for Saints:	June 1954	7	0

The brother of Phil Gunter, the Pompey full back (1951-1963), David never progressed beyond the amateur ranks at Fratton Park. On moving to The Dell, he retained that status in his first year. Signing professional in 1955, he became one of the most regular members, over the next two seasons, of the Combination side – save on those occasions when he deputised for left-back Tommy Traynor in the first team. Released in May 1956, he joined the non-league circuit and later became a police officer in Portsmouth, retiring in 1998.

Bernard HARRISON
Forward

Born:	Worcester, 28 September 1934	League Appearances	League Goals
Signed for Pompey:	October 1952	0	0
Signed for Saints:	August 1959	3	0

An England Schoolboy international, Bernard is probably better remembered for his exploits for Hampshire County Cricket Club than for his games for Pompey and Saints. Although he played only 14 times for Hants between 1957 and 1962, scoring one century, that is considerably more than his professional football appearances in the county – none for Pompey, where he failed to progress beyond amateur status, and three for Saints in their Third Division Championship season of 1959-60.

Maurice LEATHER
Full-back

Born:	Eastleigh, 9 November 1929	League Appearances	League Goals
Signed for Saints:	1945	0	0
Signed for Pompey:	January 1950	18	0

An England Youth international, despite being on the short side, at 5ft 7ins, for a goalkeeper. Maurice was an amateur at The Dell, where he managed one game for the Reserves, in a side that included Ted Bates and Bill Ellerington, in September 1947. As an understudy to Ernie Butler at Portsmouth, he occasionally had his first-team moments.

Mick MILLS
Full-back

Born:	Godalming, Surrey, 4 January 1949	League Appearances	League Goals
Signed for Pompey:	May 1964	0	0
Signed for Saints:	November 1982	103	3

An apprentice at Pompey when the club abandoned the Youth and Reserves sides in 1965, Mick was released and moved to Ipswich Town. In 17 years at Portman Road, he won many of the game's top honours, before signing for Lawrie McMenemy during the 1982-83 season. Taking over as captain in March 1984 from the injured Steve Williams, he guided Saints to runners-up in Division I. Awarded the MBE the same year, Mick had one more season left in him, when he was ever-present at 36 years-old.

Frank MOORE — Forward

Born:	Cowes	League Appearances	League Goals
Signed for Pompey:	December 1899	2	0
Signed for Saints:	June 1900	0	0

A well-known Isle of Wight footballer of his day, Frank joined Pompey during their initial season in the Southern League but was unable to gain a regular place in the side, owing to the outstanding form of regular outside-left, Nobby Clarke. During the following close season, he moved to Southampton, thus becoming the first player to move between the two clubs. He made one Western League appearance before he returned to his first love, Cowes, where he continued to give sterling service.

Alf RAMSEY — Full-back

Born:	Dagenham, 22 January 1920	League Appearances	League Goals
Died:	Ipswich, 28 April 1999		
Signed for Pompey:	January 1940	0	0
Signed for Saints:	October 1943	90	8

As centre-half in an Army XI defeated 10-3 by the Saints in August 1943, Sergeant Ramsey was 'bewildered' by the 'speed and movement' of his opponents. But not disgraced – Southampton duly signed the Pompey amateur and played him not only as a centre-half but as a centre-forward. It was at right-back, however, that he enjoyed a post-war run at The Dell, during which he won his first England cap. Having lost his place to Bill Ellerington, he demanded a transfer. He moved to Tottenham and established himself for England – although his finest hour will always be remembered, surely, as when he managed his country to the World Cup win of 1966.

Derek REEVES — Forward

Born:	Parkstone, 27 August 1934	League Appearances	League Goals
Died:	Bournemouth, 22 May 1995		
Signed for Pompey:	1951	0	0
Signed for Saints:	December 1954	273	145

First came to the notice of Portsmouth in 1951 while playing for Bournemouth Gasworks in the Hampshire League. Although he was on Pompey's books, National Service took him into the Dorset Regiment in 1952 and, on completing his term of service, he was snapped up by Southampton. He quickly became the scourge of Third Division defenders and was the club's top scorer for four seasons, climaxing in the 1959-60 promotion campaign, when his 39 goals created not only a Division III record but a Saints record that stands to this day. Second Division defences afforded him fewer opportunities, but he did score a famous five against Leeds United in a memorable League Cup-tie in December 1960. He finished his League career at Bournemouth.

Bert YOUTMAN — Forward

Born:	Southampton, 1 June 1893	League Appearances	League Goals
Died:	not known		
Signed for Saints:	July 1913	0	0
Signed for Pompey:	March 1920	1	0

Progressed through the Southampton minor leagues before signing amateur forms for Saints. A regular in their reserves, he made his only first-team appearance in a Southern Alliance match against Brighton in November 1913. His only appearance for Pompey was at outside-left in the club's fourth match in the Football League when he replaced regular left-winger Willie Beedie.

C: Men who otherwise served both clubs

You may have noticed that, of those who played for both clubs, a handful – Chadwick, Warner, McIlwaine and Rochford – also coached or managed at one or the other. We have identified a further nine professionals, none of whom played for both Saints and Pompey but who have been associated with the two clubs in some permutation of playing, coaching and/or managing.

Seven of them played for one or the other team, the exceptions being John Mortimore and Frank Burrows. Since retiring in 2002, Mortimore has continued to be associated with Southampton FC, initially as Vice-President and then succeeding Ted Bates as President in January 2004.

We have not included scouts, since it is unlikely that every example of a scout is on the record. We are aware, for instance, that Tony Barton remained at Fratton Park as Chief Scout for a while between playing and coaching, but we have not included that in his record below. Nor have we listed the likes of ex-Saint Ted MacDougall, who was scouting for Pompey in the late 1990s.

Name	SOUTHAMPTON			PORTSMOUTH		
	Player	Coach/Asst-Manager	Manager	Player	Coach/Asst-Manager	Manager
Alan BALL	12/76-05/78 03/81 - 10/82		01/94 - 07/95		c.s. 98 - 05/84	05/84 - 01/89 01/98 - 12/99
Tony BARTON		09/85 - 05/86		12/61 - 05/66	05/67 - 80 1989 - 02/91	02/91 - 05/91 (C)
Kevin BOND	09/84 - 08/88				05/98	
Frank BURROWS		08/83 - 86			1978-79 09/89 - 01/90	05/79 - 03/82 01/90 - 02/91
Jimmy EASSON		07/51 - 02/53		02/29 - 03/39	09/45 - 07/50 09/57 - 58	
John MORTIMORE		04/68 - 05/71 06/79 - 05/84 02/89 - 05/02				05/73 - 09/74
Peter OSGOOD	03/74 - 12/77				06/86 - 06/88	
Steve WIGLEY		07/01 - 02/04 03/04 - 08/04	02/04 - 03/04 (C) 08/04	03/89 - 08/93		
Harry WOOD	05/98 - 05/05				1905-12	

Notes:

We have used the coaching/managerial labels as follows:

Manager — First-team manager (incl 'head coach'). A 'caretaker' spell is indicated, where this is known, by (C).
Coach/Asst Mgr — This embraces all manner of coaching (incl Reserves and Youth teams) and the various roles performed by 'Assistant Managers', some of which chores would have fallen to 'trainers' in the days of Harry Wood.

We have included, where known, the month of coming or going. Otherwise, we have indicated close season (c.s) or have stated just the year.

Chapter 15
United in War

David Bull

Whether you perceive Pompey's parade of the FA Cup around The Dell, as war beckoned (see Chapter 10), as being neighbourliness or one-upmanship, there is no gainsaying that the two clubs would become sharing neighbours during the War. The Saints' use of Fratton Park for a 1941 Cup-tie is an almost incidental example, compared with the way in which several players turned out for both clubs and/or played together for a 'works team'.

Such 'guesting' was not, of course, a new phenomenon: Dave Juson recorded in Chapter 6 how Saints and Pompey each had guests during the First World War and how some Southampton players were appearing more often for one of the shipyard sides (Thornycrofts or Harland and Wolff) in the last two war-time seasons than for the Saints themselves.

There were also a few examples of players who turned out for both Southampton and Portsmouth during that war. Eric Tomkins of Northampton Town, a regular guest at The Dell, made a couple of War League appearances for Portsmouth, while Saints' Porter and Pompey's Lee had a few League games for each, Porter formally transferring to Portsmouth a week before the armistice.

Then there were three League regulars – Saints' Jewett and Kimpton; and Pompey's Priestley – who played the odd friendly for the other side, while a handful of others ran up a dozen games between them, mostly friendlies, across the two clubs.

Although we have a photo (see page 87 above) of the Harland and Wolff side that had acquired so many Southampton players, our knowledge of such sharing during the 1914-18 War is inevitably confined otherwise to the bare statistics.*

It is possible, however to draw, in respect of the Second World War, upon direct evidence, notably the testimonies of four men – two from each club – who played for Folland Aircraft[†].

This chapter starts by identifying the men who turned out during the 1939-45 War for both Saints and Pompey. There were 22 of them, of whom 14 made just the one-off appearance for one of these teams, while playing anything from a single game to 149 for the other.

One promiscuous guest, Chelsea's Peter Buchanan, got into double figures for both sides. And he was one of those players (the interviews have yielded the names of eight, but perhaps there were more) who appeared not only for both clubs but who also found time to turn out for Follands – mainly a combined Saints-Pompey XI, with a dash of Chelsea, to which the second part of this chapter is devoted.

Played for Both

The previous chapter identified 45 men who 'played for both', in the sense that they made 'official' first-team appearances, at different stages in their careers, for both Pompey and Saints.

Oddly enough, not one of that band appeared for both clubs during the War – although the war-time experiences of one of them, Bill Rochford, constitute an interesting transition from one club to the other.

Having played 140 times for Portsmouth pre-war – including the 1939 Cup Final – Rochford would play another 206 games for them during the War. While he would not find time to play for Saints, he would sometimes turn out for Follands, where he appears to have impressed team-mate Bill Dodgin – so much so

---

* This impressive evidence has been compiled by Gary Chalk and will be marshalled for the 'prequel' to *In That Number*.
[†] Ted Bates, Bill Bushby and Bill Dodgin were interviewed for *Dell Diamond*, along with Mary Bates, who was secretary to the Buyer at Follands, while Bert Barlow relived his days of playing there with George Summerbee, for Colin Shindler's study of the Summerbee dynasty.

that, when the latter became Saints' manager, he would sign Rochford and make him the captain (in his 134 appearances) of the side that would take the club to unprecedented heights – albeit over-shadowed, of course, by the fantastic achievements of his old club.

Nor does the list include an ex-Saint – Ted Drake, who guested once for Pompey (scoring four times) – or a future Saint: Charlie Wayman, whose seven appearances for Portsmouth in 1944-45, while serving in the navy, included the September 1944 match against Southampton, reported in Chapter 10, when his performance led Saints' defender, Bill Dodgin, to ear-mark him as a goalscorer he would later sign.

Of those who did contrive to play for both sides during the war, only five played for one or the other in peace-time (Tables 1-2). Jimmy Allen and Jock Anderson had each won Cup Final medals with Portsmouth: the former in 1934, before he moved to Aston Villa (where he became a cigarette card celebrity, *above*); the latter in 1939 – and, as we shall see, both would play for Follands, too.

Conversely, Reg Tomlinson had come to The Dell in 1938 and been the regular centre-forward in the last pre-war season, when his 13 goals included Saints' consolation effort at Chelmsford – when you consider that Southampton's most humiliating-ever FA Cup defeat occurred in the season that Portsmouth won the thing, it is perhaps as well, for the Saints fans of the day, that the 'rivalry' between the two clubs was so benign.

By joining the local police force – as opposed to the likes of Follands – Tomlinson had to commit to playing most of the time for a formidable Police side, which could have fielded 11 ex-Saints (as identified in *Dell Diamond*).

Jimmy Guthrie is chaired from the Wembley pitch by a group of celebrants that includes three of his future team-mates at Follands: **1** Parker, **2** Anderson and **3** Morgan.

So he was available to play only twice for Southampton and once for Portsmouth.

The other two in this category were Stan Clements (*right*) and Bill Bushby. Clements, from Gosport, was only 16 when the War broke out. He signed for Saints in 1944, had half a dozen games spread between them and Pompey, and then had a post-war career at The Dell, mainly as an understudy at centre-half. By contrast, Bushby was signed, in the 1939 close season, specifically as a stand-in – to the Pompey captain, Jimmy Guthrie, who had been injured in a car-crash. While the outbreak of War prevented an official appearance for his new club, Bill played 77 war-time games for Pompey and one for Saints. But he was another member of the Follands side who was wooed, like Rochford, to The Dell – albeit, in his case, for just two peace-time appearances in 1946-47.

The remaining 17, who played officially for neither team, fall into two categories: those who were on the books of one of the sides but never appeared for them

in peace-time; and players from clubs elsewhere who were in the area for some war-connected reason and who managed to turn out on each side of Spit Head (see Tables 3-4).

Hence five Southampton youngsters – Alan Dempsey, Charles Lonnon, Jock Salter, Les Laney and Tom Hassell – each limited their 'big-time' football to the War. The first three were bit-players, making only eight appearances between them for one side or the other. The last two were among those local lads who had a reasonable war-time career at The Dell, both as wingers, without ever wearing first-team colours afterwards. Laney (55 appearances, plus one for Pompey) would never play League football at all, but Hassell (112 + 1) would make 125 League appearances, most of them for Aldershot.

The Pompey amateur who played for both clubs is a different case altogether. The story of how the 19 year-old Walley Barnes and his brother John rejected 'attractive' professional terms from Southampton in 1938, and signed amateur forms for Portsmouth instead, is told – with some wild inaccuracies – in the former's autobiography and is repeated (with most of the errors corrected, I hope) in *Dell Diamond* – fully enough for it to be skimmed over here. Suffice it to note that Barnes, stationed at Blandford, went to watch Saints lose at Bournemouth in 1941-42 – something they did three times that season – and met Tom Parker, the Southampton manager. He decided he'd play for Saints after all and did so on 32 occasions (compared with just the one appearance, like his brother, for Pompey).

In 1943, Mr Parker fell out with the Board and arranged for Barnes to move to Arsenal. On Easter Saturday 1944, however, he returned to The Dell when Southampton were entertaining Portsmouth in a friendly. As noted in Chapter 10, he'd asked in vain for a game for the visitors, but turned out for Saints as his second choice.

Of the remaining 11, who guested for both clubs while signing officially for neither, it can be seen from Table 3 that John Harris and George Summerbee were the main players. Saints' reputation for bringing on youngsters during the War, under the tutelage of a guest or two, was mentioned in Chapter 10 (and is addressed, in more detail, in *Dell Diamond*). Thus the 22 year-old Harris came from Wolves to play senior pro to the likes

of Hassell and Laney – until he defected to Chelsea amid a dispute over bonus payments. The converse of his 121 games for Saints and one for Pompey was George Summerbee's record of 1:149.

Each of them played for Follands. The story of how Winchester-born George came down from Preston North End, in 1940, to guest for Portsmouth is told by Colin Shindler: the Portsmouth director who bade him return south undertook to secure him a job at Follands: and Preston duly gave their permission for him to play for Folland Aircraft.

As can be seen from the table, three Follands team-mates, Peter Buchanan, Harold Pond and Bert Tann, each played an aggregate of around 40 games for the two clubs. Buchanan, a Scottish international winger, is perhaps the most famous of these – thanks, not least, to Saints' celebrated 7-0 win over Chelsea on 29 December 1945, when he arrived at The Dell as the visitors' 12th man, only to be loaned to their hosts.

The 1943 programme reproduced here illustrates the phenomenon: the Southampton side included four 'played-for-both' guests (Tann, Pond, Harris and Barnes), of whom the first three also turned out, along with Bates,

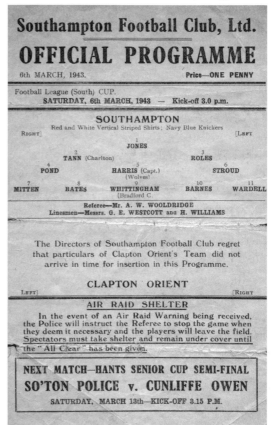

for Follands. Incidentally, Southampton won 1-0 with a goal from Whittingham of Bradford City..

Folland Aircraft FC

Unlike the two shipyard sides that were in the same South Hants War League as Saints and Pompey during World War I, Follands played in the Hampshire League, where they finished second, in 1940-41, to Pompey Reserves. For good measure, they also won four local cups that season, including both the Hampshire, and the Southampton, Senior Cups. In 1941-42, they reversed the tables on Portsmouth by winning that League but lost in the Final of the Hants Senior Cup.

As indicated earlier, it has been possible to identify, in the text above and/or in the tables overleaf, eight players who managed to play for Saints, Pompey and Follands. The Portsmouth-Southampton membership of this side did not stop there, though. Apart from Anderson and Rochford, already noted, at least four other members of the FA Cup-winning side – Bert Barlow, Cliff Parker, Lew Morgan (*right*) and captain Jimmy Guthrie – all played for Pompey and Follands, as did Guthrie's understudy, Bushby, of course.

Barlow attributed this concentration to the friendship between the two managers, Jack Tinn of Portsmouth and 'Tubby' Wiseman of Folland Aircraft.

Not that this prevented a few Saints players joining in. Apart from Dodgin and Bates, already identified, there was trainer Jack Scott. When he became 'fed up' with the

War Reserve police force that he had joined at the start of the War, Bates reasoned that 'if you could play football, you could usually get a job somewhere.' So it was that he joined Follands, less for the job than the football. In 1941-42, indeed, he played entirely for Follands and was a member of the side which surrendered the Hampshire Senior Cup to a Southampton Police team that included eight ex-Saints.

Of the eight League players in their Final line-up, six – Bates, Dodgin, Allen, Anderson, Bushby and Tann – have already been mentioned above. The other two were the Bateses' Netley landlord, Dick Foss from Chelsea (who would go on to be the Chelsea Youth coach revered by the likes of Greaves and Venables) and Michael Brannan, the Notts County 'keeper.

Their achievements in terms of Cups and Leagues won or lost are not, however, the issue here. The point is that, in Folland Aircraft's works-team, Saints and Pompey were united. And this was, it would seem, the crucible where Bill Dodgin played with Bushby and Rochford, whom he would sign from Portsmouth in his first year as Southampton's manager (to say nothing of Parker, who later declined to join this westward flow).

Bushby may have played but two games for Dodgin but Rochford would become his formidable captain, would nurture Alf Ramsey and, more especially, Bill Ellerington and would be among the most important of all the 'played-for-both' footballers identified in the previous chapter.

The Follands team – with manager Tubby Wiseman (*seated, left*) and Mr Folland (*standing, right*) – that lost to the Borough Police in the Hampshire Senior Cup Final of 1942.

Back row (left to right): Dodgin (Saints), Townsend (local), Brannan (Notts County), Tann (Charlton), Allen (Aston Villa), Bushby (Pompey).

Front row: De Lisle (local), Anderson (Pompey), Ryans (local), Foss (Chelsea), Bates (Saints).

Table 1: Played pre-war for Pompey (P) or Saints (S)

Player	"Official" career		War-time appearances		Played for Follands (F)
	Years	Appearances	Pompey	Saints	
Jimmy ALLEN (P)	1930-34	132	7	8	F
Jock ANDERSON (P)	1933-46	84	94	3	F
Reg TOMLINSON (S)	1938-39	37	1	2	-

Table 2: On the books of either Pompey (P) or Saints (S) and would play for Saints after the War

Player	"Official" career for Saints		War-time appearances		Played for Follands (F)
	Years	Appearances	Pompey	Saints	
Bill BUSHBY (P)	1946-47	2	77	1	F
Stan CLEMENTS (S)	1947-55	120	2	4	-

Table 3: Guests who never played officially for either

Player	Club	War-time appearances		Played for Follands (F)
		Pompey	Saints	
Peter BUCHANAN	Chelsea	28	11	F
Jock DAVIE	Brighton	4	9	-
Reg HALTON	Bury	5	6	-
John HARRIS	Wolves	2	121	F
Harold POND	Carlisle	1	34	F
George SUMMERBEE	Preston	149	1	F
George SWINDIN	Arsenal	1	1	-
John SYKES	Millwall	1	1	-
Bert TANN	Charlton	7	36	F
George TWEEDY	Grimsby	1	8	-
Steve WALKER	Exeter	1	13	-

Table 4: Played officially for neither but on books of either Pompey (P) or Saints (S) during the War

Player	War-time appearances	
	Pompey	Saints
Walley BARNES (P)	1	32
Alan DEMPSEY (S)	1	1
TOM HASSELL (S)	1	112
Les LANEY (S)	1	55
Charles LONNON (S)	1	1
Jock SALTER (S)	3	1

READ ON: Much of this chapter is derived from interviews for *Dell Diamond*, where several of the events are discussed in more detail. It draws also on Walley Barnes's *Captain of Wales* and upon Colin Shindler's *Fathers, Sons and Football*, in which the Folland days of George Summerbee and others are recalled by Bert Barlow. See 'Sources'.

Chapter 16
Two-Timing & Coming Over
David Bull

When Portsmouth beat Huddersfield to reach the FA Cup Final in 1939, it meant that a referee in line to officiate at Wembley that year would be denied the opportunity: Salisbury referee, George Searle, was ruled out as being resident in the Fratton catchment area.

It's odd, that. Born in Salisbury a few months after Pompey's FA Cup triumph, I grew up thinking of Portsmouth as a foreign country. Weaned on Western League football in Salisbury, the *only* Football League side I could possibly support was Southampton: baptism, Christmas 1948.

That said, I confess I twice ventured to Fratton Park as a schoolboy in the 1950s.

You won't need reminding (and you can skip back to Chapter 11 if you do) that the exciting Saints side to which I was introduced had failed to make it to the First Division, which Pompey had been winning twice. So going all the way to Portsmouth to watch them play Spurs at that exalted level – I think it must have been in November 1951 – was doubtless a treat to be savoured, even if the massive frame of visiting 'keeper Ted Ditchburn is all I can remember of it.

By the time we moved to Camberley in 1954, the Saints were in Division III. And I could now get the train to Waterloo and take my pick of Division I football. Even so, I could hardly resist the invitation from the Physics master and his son to go watch Portsmouth v Manchester United one April evening in 1958. I could from time to time see the Saints at Aldershot and Reading – and once or twice at Brentford – but by boarding the Waterloo train, I could reach for the stars.

This chapter was originally to be given over to my generation of star-chasers who, Saints fans to the core, nevertheless travelled from Southampton to Portsmouth on alternate Saturdays during the first 10 seasons or so after the War, in order to watch superior fare. Many of

their stories were solicited on the 'SaintsList' (the Saints Internet chat-room), on which they (OK, we) are known as SOGs, an abbreviation (for Sad Old Gits) that it will occasionally suit me to adopt here.

But a subsequent thread on this List – somebody innocently asked whether any Listees ever went to matches as a neutral when they couldn't watch Saints – flushed out a confession or two from younger fans who'd visited Fratton in recent years. That prompted me to wonder whether any Listees wanted to 'come out' with any other kind of explanation for two-timing. My enquiry effectively unearthed two further kinds of adventurer: those with a compelling family reason for going to Fratton; and a few true (well, not so true) blues who have transferred their affections to the Saints.

If, as I suggest below, switching allegiances tends to be seen as the ultimate betrayal by a football fan, those in the other three categories have done something that many a self-righteous 'true fan' would consider unthinkable: they have set foot in the home-ground of a

"TURF" CIGARETTES

TED DITCHBURN
TOTTENHAM HOTSPUR
& ENGLAND

50 FAMOUS FOOTBALLERS Nº 16

rival neighbour, an action strictly to be reserved for those occasions when their team are the visitors. This chapter will touch only occasionally on Saints supporters following their team at Fratton Park: those games have been amply covered in Part I of this book. We shall, however, learn from fans in each of these four categories how their various experiences have helped to shape their view of the Saints v Pompey rivalry.

The massive frame of Spurs' Ted Ditchburn was all a young Saints fan could remember of his first visit to Fratton Park.

We shall be hearing, then, from the following, in turn:

- The young star-chasers who went to Fratton in those early post-war years.
- Latter-day neutrals – more recent examples of going to watch Pompey on a 'free' Saturday.
- Family matters – fans for whom going to both grounds met some kind of family obligation.
- Deserters – the ultimate confessors: Portsmouth fans who have 'come over'.

I shall then attempt to draw out, as I say, how these fans have come to view the Saints v Pompey rivalry.

The star-chasers of the early post-war years

War-time football had brought the likes of Arsenal to Southampton – to say nothing of Aldershot, with such guests as Frank Swift and Tommy Lawton, let alone a few star guests for the Saints.

This had given **Herbie Taylor** such a 'taste for watching the better players in action' that, as a post-war teenager, he felt he 'had to go to Fratton Park' to keep up the habit.

In contrast, **Stan Edwardson** – by six years Herbie's senior and old enough to remember being in The Dell's record FA Cup crowd in January 1937 – felt he had been 'starved of football' for seven years and was ready to see

more of the real thing than he could get on a fortnightly basis at The Dell.

So he, too, would have to head for Portsmouth every other Saturday – in his case with his mother and two brothers, plus his father when he was not at sea, in the family's 'old pre-war car'. Parking 200 yards from the ground would not be a problem, as most of the crowd – often 40,000 or more – would have come by bus or train (or the Isle of Wight ferry). For the rest of our star-chasers, the train to Fratton was the only real option but this in itself was 'an adventure for a young lad' like **Norman Hull**, after war-time travel restrictions. What awaited him at the other end was a bonus: watching all those stars in such a massive crowd was 'a bit special'.

It wasn't that you never saw stars in those Second Division days at The Dell. **Barrie Bedford** thinks back to Charlie Wayman's debut against Birmingham City in November 1947, when the two goals conceded by England goalkeeper Gil Merrick included a late penalty that 'almost decapitated him as Alf Ramsey's rocket shot went in off the underside of his cross-bar'. And when Eddy Brown arrived in a trade for Wayman in September 1950, he faced John Charles of Leeds on his first outing.

Relegation to Division II need not mean losing your stars. Thus Tom Finney remained with Preston and played at The Dell in March 1951, when a draw secured North End's return to the top flight. But if you believed

Pompey's Championship side of 1948-1949, as autographed for David Hutchinson:

Back row (*left to right*): Hindmarsh, Yeuell, Butler, Dickinson, Ferrier.

Middle row: Bob Jackson (manager), Scoular, Barlow, Flewin, Rookes, Reid, Jimmy Stewart (trainer).

Front row: Harris, Parker, Clarke, Phillips, Froggatt.

that you couldn't have too much of a good thing, then Fratton Park was where you could regularly count on seeing not just the odd visiting celebrity but a near pitch-full of stars in the home side – including Jack Tinn's emerging internationals, much discussed in Chapter 10 and at the start of Chapter 11.

It would be superfluous to list the galaxy of visiting stars who attracted these '*football* supporters' – as **Jim Whitfield** emphatically, and aptly, labels his ilk – but when he went to Portsmouth to watch Stanley Matthews play for Blackpool, Jim reckons he was enjoying 'probably the two most attractive teams in the country.'

Indeed. Barrie Bedford was there for Blackpool's early-season visit in 1949 when they beat the League Champions 3-2 to end Pompey's unbeaten home run that stretched back to Christmas 1947. But, then, you *had* to be there, seeing them 'in the flesh', as he puts it, or you wouldn't see their likes at all. Many an SOG will tell you that his TV baptism was, like mine, the 'Matthews Final' of 1953, when *Match of the Day* was still a dozen seasons away.

Young fans knew their heroes from cigarette cards, *Charles Buchan's Football Monthly* (from 1951) and whichever annual we'd landed for Christmas, essential sources of coloured photos for autograph-hunters to get signed.

If acquiring the top signatures of the day was one of your purposes in pre-pubescent, or even adolescent, life, you would need frequently to travel to Portsmouth. That was not an option for me from Salisbury but I was fortunate to have a lazy alternative: all I had to do was to sit next to Ian Dunlop for my school dinner.

If memory serves, his granddad was on the Board at Fratton Park and Ian's sweet tooth enabled me to trade my dessert, on a regular basis, for autographs and programmes galore.

If, however, you were a genuine face-to-face collector, then Southsea on a Saturday morning was the place to be. Barrie Bedford would often be part of a small group assembled by mid-morning outside whichever Southsea hotel the visiting team was staying at.

David Hutchinson especially remembers loitering outside the *Beach* and the *Queens* – although Manchester United always stayed at the *Melville*.

His gang liked to 'walk along the front with our heroes,' but Barrie and his mates would bide their time:

When the players had all gone out for their walk on Southsea Common, often we would cross to the car-parking area – it's still there – opposite the *Beach Hotel* and play our own soccer matches with a small ball. Portsmouth and Southampton boys would 'pick up' sides and the game would flow until the professionals re-appeared for another signing session. Word would be passed between the autograph hunters, no matter whether they were Saints or Pompey supporters, of the details of the visiting team's departure arrangements after the match, our last opportunity for gathering those signatures: would it be Fratton or Portsmouth Station; from which level; and at what time?

For **Rob Holley**, autograph-hunting was essentially a post-match activity. Coming home to Millbrook from war-time evacuation in 1945, he had acquired an instant Dell hero in Don Roper. But Fratton Park was the place to catch the international stars and, if he used his bike instead of the train, Rob reckoned not only to minimise the cost but to maximise the time he could linger for signatures afterwards.

Which was all very well until you had a puncture – as he did when a friend and he cycled down to watch Pompey's first home match of 1949-50, an evening game against Manchester City (and the last match in that unbeaten run that Barrie Bedford would see broken by Blackpool three days later). Rob and his friend were 'about a couple of miles from the ground' when he punctured 'but, determined not to miss the start, I pedalled on regardless.' That only postponed the problem, of course:

After the game my front tyre was a sorry sight. With no money and no way of phoning home – nobody we knew had a phone in 1949 – there seemed no alternative but to walk home. My friend stayed with me until I reached the floating bridge at about 7.00 a.m and I arrived home around nine o'clock, by which time I was plodding. I will draw a veil over what my father said but he had actually *gone to the police* to report me missing and had *not gone to work*. Two unheard of things for Holley père and I was never allowed to forget it.

The only time Rob can remember taking the train was in the February snow of 1948. After his cousin and he had queued for an hour outside the ground, the game against Arsenal was called off. So they 'trudged back to Fratton Station in a blizzard, to be met by a very dislocated train service.' Which meant that they got home about 6.00 p.m, snatched an evening's sleep and then set off to The Dell to join another queue – for tickets for the Saints' FA Cup quarter-final against Spurs: 'the snow had stopped but it was a perishing night.' Ah! The trials of trying to have it both ways! Yet what innocent fun it all was:

> There was *never* any trouble that I remember, even when we made it obvious we were Southampton supporters by cheering when the half-time scores were posted on the *Football Mail* scoreboard and we saw Saints were doing better than we expected. There was always some good-natured joshing but never more: we even took pint glass bottles of *Tizer* in with us and handed them round the dockyard mateys at half-time, although that seems very difficult to believe now.

J. MILBURN
(Newcastle U.)

The autographed photo of Jackie Milburn, to get which David Hutchinson sacrificed his place in the school team.

from his 'meagre' first wages to go and stand on the Fratton Park terraces, 'filled with a cross-section of supporters, many of them naval personnel.' He assumes that, like his, their support lay elsewhere: they were there 'mainly to enjoy the football.'

Herbie Taylor elaborates on this last point:

> I did not go to watch Portsmouth, I went to watch a good game of football with teams littered with players I had seen only on cigarette cards. But I did want Pompey to win – after all, they were a fellow-Hampshire team – but if they didn't, somehow it just did not matter.
> Whenever Saints lost, it hurt. If Pompey lost… nothing.

But it was like that among the autograph-hunters, too. Such was 'the lack of animosity between us and the Pompey lads,' David Hutchinson recalls, that he befriended one of the Portsmouth collectors, Frank Hulse, and they would stay at each other's homes in their quest to fill their books. And such was his determination to secure the autograph of his hero, Newcastle's Jackie Milburn, that he cried off from a Saturday game for Itchen Grammar School to be in Southsea: 'the sports master found out why I didn't play and never picked me again, but I did get a lot of stars' signatures because of his cussedness.' And all of this was facilitated by 'players who were proud to sign their autographs – and you could read them.' How impossible it would all be today, David feels, with 'security at hotels, teams with minders, players reluctant to sign and, if you are lucky enough to get some autographs, you cannot read most of them.'

'Happy days', he concludes.

Quite so – yet **Mike Graham** has difficulty in persuading younger subscribers to the SaintsList that SOGs like him had 'some great times at Portsmouth.' After all, following Saints away was not then a realistic option. **John Warren** would have liked to do so occasionally but it was beyond his means, so he saved

Rob Holley felt a similar loyalty to the county: although 'jealous' of Pompey's success, he 'actively wanted them to win the Championship – because I distinctly recall a feeling of pride that an unfashionable Hampshire side could put it over those London snooties.' Such sentiments seem to have been widely shared.

Pete Seddon even admits to having a Pompey 'idol' in Peter Harris – a rather more elegant winger, it must be said, than his Dell favourite, Billy Wrigglesworth.

Pete joined the Southampton-to-Fratton train at Bitterne. So did Barrie Bedford, while Herbie Taylor got on at St Denys.

Pete Seddon's hero, Peter Harris, who signed for David Hutchinson.

The half-price return fare from Bitterne was 1s.11d (9½p in today's currency). For Jim Whitfield, boarding at Woolston, it was only 1s.6d (7½p). **Ray Terris** and a school-mate wangled an even lower fare: 'we would go to Central Station and buy a platform ticket for a penny and jump on a Portsmouth train. When we got there, we would look for a large group of Pompey fans and mix with them as they left the station. We were never asked for our tickets.' So they 'saw some of the best players of the day at a very good price,' he reckons. Indeed, it cost only 9d (3¾p) to go through the boys' turnstiles at Fratton Park, Jim Whitfield recalls, compared with a shilling (5p) to watch Second Division football at The Dell.

Even so, Barrie Bedford's 'pocket money didn't allow Portsmouth trips often enough.' When Saints were away and he couldn't afford to go to Fratton, he had to settle for the vicarious thrill of seeing the jam-packed 'one o'clock Pompey' train – visible from his garden in Bitterne Park – taking lucky Southamptonians to the top football of the day.

Latter-day neutrals

If those SOG memories are essential to the Saints v Pompey folklore – as much a feature of the Age of Austerity, for those young star-chasers, as food rationing and clothing coupons – there has been little point, these last 40-odd years, in any Southampton fans making the pilgrimage to Fratton, in order to watch second-class football – at best!

Notwithstanding, three Saints fans here explain why they have been there in recent years, in one case to watch Nationwide First Division fare and, in each of the others, for an FA Cup-tie against lower-division visitors.

For **Martyn Moody** and **Richard Ember**, it was all about friendship. In August 1998, the fixture list offered Martyn the perfect chance to entertain an old school friend for the weekend and to accompany him to Fratton Park on the Saturday where Ipswich, the friend's team, were the visitors. Saints were away to Charlton that day and it had not been announced, when the old boys' reunion was being fixed, that action from The Valley would be shown on the big screen at The Dell.

It was 11 seasons since Southampton had played at Fratton Park and Martyn had not 'realised how just how big the rivalry had become between Saints and Pompey.'

And he certainly wasn't giving it a thought as he – neutral and surely anonymous – accompanied his partisan friend to the away end. What he hadn't reckoned on was having to endure three cheers for Charlton – a cheer for each time the score at The Valley was announced on the PA or the scoreboard. The final cheer – and last laugh, to boot – came at the final whistle. After the scoreboard had 'flickered into action, before cutting out' – they know how to keep you in suspense at Fratton Park – the PA cut in with the top news of the day: Charlton 5 Southampton 0. The cheers from three sides of the ground were 'massive' and, even at the Ipswich end, Martyn felt as though 'everyone one was looking at me and I had a big finger over my head pointing at me. I can't think of a worse place to be after such a heavy defeat.'

Richard Ember had an altogether less humiliating experience, even though he was among home supporters. One of them was a work-mate, a Pompey fan who had accompanied him to St Mary's a couple of times. A regular away-tripper, Richard doesn't have that many empty Saturdays, but Saints' FA Cup Third Round mauling by Newcastle United left him free to accept his friend's invitation to watch Pompey v Southend United in the Fourth Round on 24 January 2004.

Taken into the Supporters Club for starters, he was publicly introduced as 'my Scummer mate'. This set the tone for a 'hospitable' reception which continued during the match, when he blatantly sat out, amid 'some good banter', choruses of *Stand Up if you Hate the Scum*. There was more such singing during the post-match drinking session which involved some of the 'Pompey Hardcore', including John Westwood, acclaimed, in the 6.57 book, as 'Pompey's No.1 Fan' (as recorded on camera, *overleaf*).

Yet Richard never felt 'threatened or intimidated'. It 'saddens' him and his friend 'that we cannot have a beer together, before and after a derby game, because of the lunatics in each camp.'

Rut Harwood and his mates decided not to test the mood of the locals when they drank, *incognito*, in the railway club between Fratton station and the ground. A fanatical Saints-away follower, Rut was destined for Millmoor on 5 January 2002. But when Saints' Third Round FA Cup-tie was frozen off, he fancied a pay-on-the-day outing to Pompey's tie against Third Division Leyton Orient. With the odds on an Orient win at 6/1, Rut 'popped in the bookies' on his way to the station and

On the occasion of his visit to Fratton Park as a neutral, Saints supporter Richard Ember (*left*) has been kitted out as a true blue by 'Pompey's No. 1 Fan,' John Westwood.

Family matters

Whenever the subject of football fans' loyalty is being debated and the view that *nothing* can justify changing clubs is being stridently aired, I like to pose the dilemma for the parent who leaves the town where his or her football loyalties were formed, who remains faithful (of course) to that first love through thick and more often thin, but whose children then opt to support *their* home-town team: what do Mum and Dad do about that, especially if the children require parental supervision at their local ground?

Alan McDougall found the perfect solution, having been born in Havant in 1960 to a Southamptonian father who worked in Portsmouth but still supported Saints. It was, of course, the time when the fortunes of Saints and Pompey were starting to cross and, by the time Alan was old enough to accompany his father to The Dell, Southampton were a Division I side, while Second Division Portsmouth had had a season in Division III. But 'everybody else at school was Pompey' so, as soon as he could be trusted to go to Fratton Park with some of those boys from school, he did.

This 'comfortable life' – the Archers Road end with his dad one Saturday; the Fratton end with his mates the next – worked well until the early 1970s. Alan doesn't 'suppose it was any coincidence that around this time football hooliganism started for real':

> I could have potentially become a target.
> Fortunately, my mates were still my mates and,
> as I still went with them occasionally to Fratton Park,
> I was one of the crowd.

When Saints were relegated in 1974, though, this changed his relationships at school – 'the atmosphere became decidedly chilly' – and Frattonising with his mates became even less frequent. **Malcolm Ross** likewise experienced this 1974 watershed. He had been brought up a Saints supporter like his father before. But after a couple of seasons of going to The Dell with his

wagered £10, 'to add extra interest.' He noted 'a few Pompey fans' boarding the train at Southampton Central – yes, there are Portsmouth fans living in Southampton (and *vice versa*, as we shall see). To his surprise, two of his Saints friends joined the train at Woolston and the three of them decided, as I say, on a pre-match drink in the thick of things: 'luckily, nobody in the place tried to engage us in conversation about Pompey's chances of winning the Cup this year, or else we might have given the game away with our uncontrollable fits of laughter.'

Which is just as well perhaps, given the outcome of the postponed tie at Rotherham. But he did have a laugh, that afternoon at Fratton Park, at the antics of Portsmouth's Japanese goalkeeper, Yoshikatsu Kawaguchi, right in front of him at the away end. Leading by a 'lucky' first-half goal, Pompey conceded four without reply in the second half. 'This is the one and only time,' Rut reflects, 'that I've ever sung another team's songs. I go home smiling, £60 in profit, and get to see myself jumping about on *Match of the Day*.'

You just *know* that none of the star-chasers would have engaged in such partisan singing. Even if they had, they'd never have bet on the beneficiaries of their choral efforts; and nor would they have been able to hear themselves on *Sports Report*.

Two-timing & Coming Over

dad, his parents separated in 1969 and he now saw his non-custodial father only on Saturdays:

> the only thing we had in common was footie so to replace the void of a Saturday without Saints, we would go to see the Skates. I quite liked going down there for a Second Division game and sometimes didn't mind them winning. That all changed in 1974.

When Pompey came to The Dell for a Second Division game in September 1974, Malcolm 'couldn't believe the hate channelled towards me and other Saints fans from this lot a few miles down the road and about whom I didn't really have any thoughts one way or another. I didn't understand why.'

For the return fixture at Fratton Park on Boxing Day, Alan McDougall went in the away end with his father and the other members of the family who had become Saints fans. Having savoured that end, he 'drifted back' there when teams he 'knew' were playing Portsmouth until 'gradually, I realised that temporarily supporting the opposition at Fratton Park gave me an emotional involvement in the game.' He would occasionally switch ends and go with his mates,

> though that was more for the thrill of being part of the crowd. I cheered for Pompey but it wasn't for real. There was nothing to cheer with Pompey: they were in terminal decline and Saints had all the stars.

David Reynolds similarly alternated his Saturdays between the two grounds from his home in Langstone Harbour: a lad at Fratton one week; to The Dell with Dad the next. But his father was not at his side: he was in the Saints' goal.

When he signed for Southampton in 1960, Ron Reynolds carried on living in his native Haslemere. But, with a business interest in Havant, he moved the family down there in 1962. David recalls his first day at school in Warblington: 'the son of the Saints goalkeeper in a hotbed of fanatical Pompey supporters – imagine the confrontation I experienced!' He was 'quickly accepted and absorbed,' though, 'when they realised I could play a bit' – much as it later helped Alan McDougall to have the physique that went with being in the rugby team.

David kept goal not only for the school but at representative level. That meant meeting up a lot with Bobby Stokes in regular training and coaching sessions at Fratton Park. He jokes about that being the 'enemy camp' but, as a supporter standing on the Milton End terrace, he could watch, among others, two of his father's friends: Jimmy Dickinson and Ron Tindall.

He was sitting in the stand, though, in September 1963, when he saw his father led from the field, 'his shoulder obviously completely detached, to the extent that he appeared to be cradling the arm from falling off. It was a sickening sight.' Ron Reynolds's career was over (see the match report in Chapter 11). The family moved back to Haslemere, where Ron died on his 71st birthday in 1999. David still lives there and I've seen him a few times at St Mary's, on one occasion accompanied by a son who has contrived to become an Arsenal supporter.

When Alan McDougall went away to teacher training college in 1978, 'any elastic that was left with Pompey was well and truly broken.' But he returned to Portsmouth 10 years later, where he began to teach in 1993:

> I kept my allegiances to myself for a while, but they gradually came out and, despite my original fears, I had absolutely no trouble whatsoever – mainly because I showed Pompey fans respect and I could recount tales of the good old days with the best of them. I was usually described as a 'scummer', but a good lad really.

David Reynolds would go one week to watch his dad, Ron (*left*) in the Saints' goal and to Fratton Park, the next week, to see his dad's friend, Ron Tindall (*right*), playing for Pompey.

He nowadays teaches at a different school – on the A3. He's still in the Fratton Park catchment area, but there are many Saints fans at his school who 'proudly wear their shirts: there may be hope after all.'

Coming over to the Saints

If switching your allegiance to another club is something that no 'true' fan is permitted to do, then what price abandoning the club of your childhood for its near-neighbour? Which here means 'coming over' from Pompey to Saints. Consider, if you will, the confessions of half a dozen Portsmouth fans who now consider Southampton their team and, in most cases, exclusively so.

Born in Southsea, **Gerry Dunger** was a 'natural' Pompey fan and can remember going to Fratton Park, a 15-20 minutes' walk away, from about the time he first saw them in the 1934 Cup Final. His family background gave him a strong 'neutral' interest in football, though. His step-grandfather, 'Bertie' Cowles, was the secretary of the Norfolk FA* and this enabled young Gerry to go to Wembley every year, where his father was a stadium usher. In 1939, of course, his team were back there, this time to win. Then, after the War, he had those wonderful seasons of Champion football that young lads from Southampton were so keen to go and see. From 1953 to 1967, he was practising medicine out of the country but his brother and he watched every home League game, in 1967-68, standing on the open terrace at the north-west corner of the ground.

Fratton Park

MY brother and I have regularly attended the games at Fratton Park this season, but not having had any opportunity to acquire tickets for next Saturday's show, I am wondering how many other regular supporters like ourselves will not be there.

The ticket distribution, as usual, favours the ticket touts, the physically robust, and the young with the underlying principle of first come first served on the Sabbath.

Last Saturday's programme explained unconvincingly why 31,000 cup-tie tickets could not be issued as vouchers to the 27,000 supporters present; the chief consideration seemed to be the extra ten thousand mythical non-regulars that might turn up.

Each faithful supporter was offered the dismal prospect of queueing for hours in competition with non-supporters and touts.

No consideration for out-of-town supporters, except in the Isle-of-Wight; no consideration for the Sunday worker; the non-Christian; the older and not so robust supporter that feels he cannot queue; the family man whose wife and children cannot spare him for two days of the week-end.

I am not so embittered to neglect to hand out some common sense to the Fratton Park management; issue vouchers long before the cup games loom to supporters who attend the least fashionable fixtures on the wettest and coldest days. Alternatively, issue season tickets for terraces to those who want them.

Gerald T. Dunger.
Chandler's Ford.

Their 'loyalty was not rewarded,' however, when it came to the sale of tickets for that season's FA Cup Fifth Round against West Bromwich Albion. It had looked as though this could be the first Pompey-Saints Cup-tie for 62 years, but a West Brom side with a full-back as a makeshift goalkeeper contrived to win a Fourth Round replay at The Dell. To say that Gerry was not pleased with Portsmouth's arrangements for selling tickets – 'two per person, at 9.00 a.m on Monday to a queue of overnight campers' – would be an under-statement. Working a night shift as casualty officer to the Royal South Hants Hospital in Southampton, he 'had no opportunity to join the queue' and was 'enraged to think that tickets were probably sold to people who had never watched a league game, while regular supporters went ticketless.' His letter of protest to the Portsmouth *Evening News* produced a 'kind benefactor': the principal of a Portsmouth school for blind boys sent him a couple of spare tickets behind the Milton Road goal, from which he watched West Brom triumph 2-1 on their way to winning the Cup.

Gerry Dunger was not just writing a letter of protest to the local 'paper. He was withdrawing his 'custom' and switching brands - something put-upon football fans are not supposed to do.

---

*The part played by Bertie Cowles in the discovery of Ted Bates is told in the latter's biography (for which Gerry Dunger's family cuttings were a valuable source).

His protest did not stop there, though. Although his brother and he saw out the season on the terraces, they felt 'sufficiently aggrieved' to withdraw their support thereafter. Gerry switched his allegiance to Southampton – 'a move that offered a marked reduction in match-day travelling time' from his home in Chandlers Ford – while his brother stopped going to football altogether.

David Gosling's switch likewise had its origins in a policy decision by Portsmouth FC. In his case, it was the abandonment, in 1965, of the Reserves. Portsmouth-born, David had seen his first game at Fratton in 1945 – a 5-0 win against Reading – and, as he liked to watch a game every Saturday, he regularly followed the Reserves. He would 'very infrequently' venture along the coast to Southampton – or even to Bournemouth or Brighton – to see a game; but the basic menu, week-in, week-out, was Pompey and Pompey Reserves.

When he completed his National Service in 1956 and had access to a car, he became a little more adventurous – a few more visits per season to The Dell, up to Aldershot and even to Reading – in his quest to 'see a football match every week: I would never be without a game on a Saturday.' It stayed that way for another nine years – until 1965, when Portsmouth's Reserves were removed from the equation (as discussed in Chapter 11). This meant that he was 'free' to watch the Saints 'more and more regularly,' starting with their tense promotion season and continuing into Division I. He would still watch Pompey but, 'as the quality of the football dropped off' at Fratton Park, he found himself becoming a Southampton supporter – and on the way to being the St Mary's season ticket-holder that he is today.

So might he now contemplate going back to Premier League Portsmouth? 'Good Heavens, No! The allegiance to Saints came and the allegiance is still very strong.'

Frank Russell was much younger when he changed his allegiance. His dad and he had been 'staunch Pompey fans' when his father's work as an engineer with *Esso* caused the family to relocate to Hythe. Frank was 11. With no motorway, nor even a Marchwood by-pass, Fratton Park was now two hours or so away by motorbike-and-sidecar – a prospect dismissed as 'almost impossible: it was a terrible wrench for Dad and me.' It was the 1958-59 season. Pompey were still in the First Division (just) and Ted Bates was trying to build a side that would lift Saints out of the Third. So father and son were in no hurry to drop in at The Dell. When, after a year or so, they did so, Frank felt he was visiting impoverished neighbours:

> The Dell was a scruffy, dirty and distinctly poor ground. To an 11 year-old, Fratton Park was large and vibrant and I particularly remember being impressed by the mock-Tudor frontage of the main entrance. Even their kit seemed better. The blue shirts, white shorts and red socks always looked fantastic – and so much better than the red-and-white shirts and hooped socks, which made the players look very short and stocky, I always thought.

But by the time Saints had won promotion and Ted Bates was building his Cup-running side of 1963, 'Pompey were in free-fall.' Frank can remember many a match at this time when 'Saints would score a hatful of goals at The Dell and watching them was a joy.' The Russells' perceptions were changing – and their loyalties with it. It wasn't many more seasons before 'The Dell got a lick of paint and new seats, while Fratton got tattier and tattier.'

Jim Wilson's conversion followed a fallow, football-free, period. He was 10 when his Auntie's boyfriend first took him to Fratton Park in 1971 – from Gosport, whither his family had arrived from Australia the previous year. It was 'a dour 0-0 draw', though not dour enough to put him off, and when his family moved to Portsmouth in 1976, he became a regular. That lasted another five years, until he 'married, started a family, moved to an SO postcode for work reasons and simply stopped going to football.'

Yes, *stopped!* Reading the messages on the SaintsList, I sometimes feel that younger fans have no concept of supporters opting out – because of some permutation of job, relocation and domesticity – for a chunk of their life, only to reappear when circumstances permit. When Jim Wilson made his re-entry midway through the 1994-95 season, however, it was at The Dell, where a colleague had a season ticket along with his dad and other family members. When the father died, Jim accepted an invitation to 'take over a dead man's ticket – about the only way to get into The Dell, with its small capacity.'

After a break of 14 years, going into a football ground again was a revelation: 'I realised how much I enjoyed the occasion that is a live professional game. Of course, this was now the Premier League, so my "reincarnation" match was a better quality of 0-0 draw.' Jim is nowadays a regular at St Mary's. So are **Robert Pearson** and his

20 (h) Stoke C	W 2-0 Paine 2		18,298	10							6	9	5	8	7	
	App		32	6	3	4	6	6	2	38	33	42	42	42		
	Goals		14	1							13	1	22	10		

Sean O'Sullivan converted to the Saints in time to watch an unchanged side (*right*) in their exciting Cup-run of 1963.

Author's confession : these autographs were obtained not by queueing outside hotels but by visiting the players 30-odd years later.

Back row (left to right): S.Williams, T.Traynor, K.Wimshurst, R.Reynolds, T.Knapp, C.Huxford.
Front row: T.Paine, G.O'Brien, G.Kirby, D.Burnside, J.Sydenham.

wife, even though Portsmouth-born Robert was first taken to Fratton Park as a five year-old in the early 1950s, another 'natural' Pompey fan standing, on the box his father had taken along for him, 'on the first row of steps near the corner flag on the north side.' His dad died in 2000, a year before the Pearsons, by now living in the New Forest, decided that a new stadium offered them a chance to become season-ticket holders at their nearest League ground.

Robert is confident that 'Dad would not turn in his grave' at this move because, 'staunch Pompey supporter' that Mr Pearson, Senior was, 'he, like me, wanted all southern clubs to succeed and that included Saints, Brighton, Bournemouth and Reading.' So there is no contradiction, for Robert, in wishing his father 'could have lived to see his beloved Pompey achieve Premiership status (and retain it for more than one season'); in wanting Saints to win 36 of their Premiership fixtures; and in feeling that his only 'problem' arises from the meetings of the south's top two, when 'you could say a draw would be the best result.'

David Gosling had a similar experience with his father, who 'didn't worry one way or the other' about his son's transfer of allegiance: he was another who 'liked football but he didn't worry who he watched.' On the other hand, an uncle, 'a very strong Portsmouth supporter,' would call him a 'turncoat' and he had 'quite a few arguments' with his sons, one of whom is a Fratton regular with his own son. His family have lately become less troubled by his desertion, though, 'with Pompey doing a bit better.'

Jim Wilson feels similarly relaxed about those relatives who are still living in Portsmouth:

They don't give me any grief for 'turning'. In fact, I get more stick from Saints fans who know of my Pompey background – although it's mostly in good humour, with a running joke about the Pompey crest rumoured to be tattooed on a hidden part of my anatomy. It doesn't exist – honest!

Sean O'Sullivan's family likewise indulged his fickleness, although his was a childhood thing. Born in Plymouth to an Argyle-supporting father, Sean was 11 when the Royal Army Pay Corps transferred his dad to Worthy Down in 1958. The family settled in Winchester, where 'the local butcher corrupted a poor 11 year-old boy into supporting Pompey.' The butcher continued to escort Sean to Fratton Park even after he had started at St Mary's College in Bitterne the following year. But then his father took him to The Dell on the opening day of

1961-62 to watch Argyle – another game in which Ron Reynolds was seriously injured – and Sean discovered where the quality stuff could be found on the south coast: 'I was taken by the sort of football Saints played and was converted on the spot. I took a lot of ribbing from Dad but he was good enough to take me to all the games in the 1962-63 Cup-run.' Sean has moved around a bit since then, including three spells overseas, but has remained a Southampton fan – on the principle that he was old enough, at 14, to know the difference between right and wrong.

Frank Russell's family has been considerably less forgiving than those of Jim and Sean. Even though he converted more than 40 years ago, he reckons that 'almost all' of his family in Portsmouth, most of them born since he left there, 'cannot find it in their hearts to give Southampton Football Club one ion of praise.' Which brings me to my ultimate question of how the above experiences have shaped the contributors' views of the rivalry between Saints and Pompey fans.

Perspective on the rivalry

Frank Russell imagines that he is 'in a unique position to comment' on 'the startling animosity between the two sets of supporters – or some of them,' but we have seen that his experience has been shared at least by Jim Wilson – and goodness knows how many other converts who might not have been so willing, if invited, to 'put their heads above the parapet' (says Jim, questioning his own folly). I want to suggest here, though, that other forms of two-timing we have encountered in this chapter have also caused those involved to have views on – and maybe explanations for – the increased intensity of football 'rivalry' across the Solent.

Let's start with the SOGs. As I intimated earlier, Mike Graham has a tough time, explaining why he has retained a 'soft spot' for Pompey and stoutly defending his continuing capacity to 'love them as a Hampshire club' – a sentiment expressed earlier by Herbie Taylor. Barrie Bedford likewise intends to 'go on wishing Portsmouth success in *all* their matches – except when their opponents are the Saints and provided they are not in the same league and threatening to finish higher,' while Gerry Dunger feels that his 'Saturdays are only blissful when all three southern Hampshire teams [including Bournemouth] record a win.'

Perhaps all this says is that, if you've happily co-existed as friendly neighbours, it's hard to acquire anything like the hatred that younger fans have grown up with. Herbie Taylor sombrely puts this into perspective:

> I *hated* the bloke who dropped a bomb on our
> house while I was in the air-raid shelter, blowing
> the roof off, shattering all the windows and destroying
> all our possessions. I had no hatred left for
> fellow-football fans who happened to be rooting
> for a different team than the one I was supporting.
> I had, and still have, *no* reason to 'hate' them.

None of this should be taken to imply, however, that younger Saints supporters cannot be well-disposed towards Portsmouth and their fans, wanting them to be promoted in 2003 and glad that they stayed up in 2004 – even if such goodwill needed to be reined in a little, for the reasons expressed by Barrie Bedford, when it looked as though their late burst might propel them up the table, beyond Saints. That's if such sentiments hadn't been totally shattered already by the outlandish behaviour of a Pompey minority – first during the one minute's silence for Ted Bates in December and then at Fratton Park in March – as described by Dave Juson in Chapter 13.

Jim Wilson, now in his mid-40s and coming from a quite different angle from Barrie, echoes him when he claims not to 'harbour any animosity' to the club he forsook for Saints and insists that he doesn't 'begrudge the Fratton Park faithful any success.' As we saw earlier, though, he has been a more fortunate convert than Frank Russell, even though Frank came over all those years ago. Frank regrets to say so, but

> I really do think that the *intense* stuff comes from the
> Pompey side and comes from one thing only – envy.
> My wife and I recently attended a family party, where
> we met a Portsmouth guy of about 40 years-old who had
> so tainted his 10 year-old son that the boy simply refused
> to speak to me, just because I was a 'scummer'.
> This wasn't in jest; it was really meant and very, very
> hurtful. It's all so very sad. When you try to defend Saints'
> magnificent record of simply surviving with the 'Big Boys'
> for so long – something you think they would admire
> and want to copy – you are met with ignorance and denial.

Alan McDougall comes to a similar conclusion about *envy*, a conclusion that he reaches in insightful stages. As we saw earlier, he felt there was no 'aggro' before 1972 but then 'young lads at school, my age ironically, got caught up in the whole hooligan scene.' This was fuelled in 1974 – and we saw how both Malcolm Ross and he felt this – not by Saints' superiority but by their decline to Pompey's diminished level and the opportunities this afforded for that aggro to be better targeted. But then Southampton won the Cup; Portsmouth went all the way down to Division Four, while Saints returned to the First Division; and then, as Malcolm observes, Kevin Keegan arrived 'and resentment grew almost daily.' Even so, returning to Portsmouth in 1988, after 10 years away, Alan was 'shocked by the sheer venom that existed among the locals for Southampton.'

It was the same for Pete Seddon, in 2004, after a longer gap. He had stopped going as a neutral in the 1950s but had seen most of the derbies in the 1960s when, as he recalls, 'there was nothing nasty, just banter, really.' So, now living in Portsmouth and having borrowed the Fratton Park season-ticket of 'a very good friend,' he ventured to the ground's first Premiership derby in March 2004. He was surprised by what he witnessed from the home fans:

> It was the worst display of vile, obscene, non-stop abuse I have ever encountered at a football match, or anywhere else, directed not only at the Southampton players but at the subs warming up, the match officials – in fact, anything other than their team. The hatred here in Portsmouth towards *anything* from Southampton just has to be seen – and heard – to be believed.

Yet does it cut both ways? More than it used to, it seems. When Mick Channon moved to Fratton Park in 1985, he found it was difficult for an ex-Saint 'to be accepted by the Portsmouth people. I'm sure a lot of them hated me when I first went there… I have noticed there is a terrible hatred in a lot of Portsmouth people for folk from Southampton… But funnily enough, it doesn't seem to work the other way.'

That was then. But now? Having observed, 'with some sadness,' the revived opportunities, in 2003-04, for match-day expressions of the rivalry, Alan McDougall felt that 'Saints fans were now returning the abuse with as much venom as it is given and the sheer hatred is almost laughable.' Gerry Dunger sensed that at St Mary's on the occasion of the first Premiership derby in December 2003, as he 'watched a smiling, smartly dressed father, singing *We hate Pompey*, while standing beside his young son, making sure that indoctrination starts at an early age.'

Robert Pearson similarly objects to this chant and I must say that, of all the nonsense I've heard at football matches, the *Pompey Scum* song ranks among the silliest. I say 'silly' rather than vicious, because I'm disinclined to take 'hate' chants too seriously: I can remember when we sang *We hate Nottingham Forest*, not because Brian Clough's lads had done anything to upset us, but because the line required a five-syllable ending and Crewe Alexandra didn't quite fit the bill. Moreover, Gerry remembers that derby game for when he shared a 'mixed' table in a hospitality suite, where the home win was 'greeted by handshakes all round.'

This sheer variety of experiences, even at the same game, makes it difficult to generalise, but there seems to be a degree of consensus emerging – albeit within a small, self-selected line-up of witnesses – that envy has built up the hatred on one side (Pompey's) and periodic equality of status has given those fans a chance to express it. Some seem to feel that when equality was restored in 2003-04, the hatred was still mainly one-sided – although Alan McDougall, Gerry Dunger and Robert Pearson are less sanguine.

But suppose Pompey were to become top-dogs again in the coming years – what then? Would envy grip the embittered Saints fans? Or would they be hopping onto trains like the star-chasers of the Austerity Years to go and watch their betters? This latter question has been posed by a couple of SOGs, one of whom has attempted to answer it. Herbie Taylor doesn't think he would resume the pilgrimage: 'I would not feel comfortable any more. It seems you have to support one team or the other these days. No one is a neutral any more.'

I calculate that I've watched football as a neutral on 27 League grounds, on three of which I've never seen Southampton play. I kicked that habit, though, in the late 1980s. I had become, in my late 40s, no longer a football fan; only a Saints fan. I tended to view that as matter of ageing rather than as a sign of the times: I'd simply grown out of dispassionate spectatorship. Yet, when I think about it, Herbie has a point: neutrality ain't what it used to be. The reason is simple: all-ticket matches and the segregation that goes with it has taken so much of the *fun* out of being a neutral.

As Alan Rogers (No.11) walks away, Steve Moran (No.8)
celebrates the famous goal (as seen on page 198)
that prompted a Saints fan on the North Bank
to tuck his scarf well into his parka.

Where does a neutral sit at today's segregated ground? I've never been one for going behind the goal if I could help it and could not see myself doing what Rut Harwood did at Fratton Park (although perhaps I might for the sake of a friend, the way Martyn Moody did). Even when I'm an away fan, I've always preferred to stand on the half-way line with the home crowd.

Jim Whitfield harks back to his 'favourite match' at Fratton Park when Saints won 5-2 in February 1966 and he invites us to 'imagine being able now to stand on the North Bank terrace among the Pompey crowd and cheer on your own team in a local derby.'

Well, I was determined, Jim, to do just that for the 1984 Cup-tie. After all, it was one of *the* great side-line terraces to stand on – on a par, say, with the Kippax at Maine Road, if not quite in the same class as that

towering bank at The Valley. A couple of 40-somethings in our red-and-white scarves, we strolled onto the North Bank, amid some tolerably aggressive banter – although my female companion said she had no idea that young men would 'use such language to a mature woman' – and we lived to tell the tale.

I must admit that I tucked my scarf well into my parka when Steve Moran scored. Yet our experience hardly matches the 6.57 recall of that day, when the Pompey 'firm' had its 'biggest-ever' turn-out, with 2,000 of them on the North Bank alone, ready to 'kill' a visiting 'mob of 200 frightened rabbits.'

The point is that football has always been tribal – you have only to read Dave Juson's accounts, in Part I, of Victorian derbies between Saints and Pompey to see that – but we have been able to enjoy both tribalism *and* camaraderie.

A perverse effect of segregating in the name of safety has been to nurture a possessive territorialism – witness the ridiculous fury when an away goal is celebrated by somebody sitting in one of *our* seats – and consorting with the enemy has become so much more difficult. It's all so sad.

A Pompey perspective?

We have not gone in search of Portsmouth fans with matching stories to tell – notably of visits to The Dell when that was where the top south coast football was being played – but there are a few clues to be found in the 6.57 book.

But Barry Bendel, our 'resident' Pompey fan, describes, in the next chapter, how he rejected a prior opportunity to support Saints. It makes you wonder how fortuitous it may have been for many a youngster along the south coast to become a supporter of one side or the other. His tale is another example of the *fragile* basis on which an allegiance can be formed, but then held with utter *conviction* for life. Rob Silvester, the Portsmouth author of the 6.57 story, had already been to White Hart Lane with his father, when he moved to Portsmouth, aged six, and likewise became a Pompey fan for life.

Yet none of this helps us to understand why most of the contributors to this chapter – and most of its readers, I imagine – have stuck with their childhood choice, while others have found it possible to switch allegiances, even between neighbouring rivals.

We are assured by Rob Silvester that, in the 1970s and 1980s, Pompey fans came to matches in Southampton 'by the trainload'. But the notion of watching a better quality of football seems not to have been among the objectives: rather were their motives to enjoy supporting Saints' opponents or to seek 'a punch-up'. As an example of the latter, the 6.57 writers twice cite an invasion, at the Archers Road end in January 1977, when Pompey's game at Swindon was called off and three coach-loads of 'Pompey boot boys' came to The Dell for a round or two of 'seventies terrace fighting at its best.' *

That is a defiantly offensive approach compared with the heads-down strategy adopted by Rut Harwood and his mates in 2002. But, then, the 6.57 claim to be 'THE football fans of the South' is based on their fighting abilities, while Southampton supporters boast no such active 'major crew' and therefore 'never get mentioned in any book about football violence'. Indeed, they are mentioned only reluctantly in the 6.57 book, none of the interviewees for which 'could bring themselves to even mention the words Southampton Football Club.'

That echoes chillingly the sentiments of Jim Wilson's family. For those of us who believe it possible to have both rivalry *and* camaraderie – such as Richard Ember has experienced as recently as January 2004 – Jim's story of a 10 year-old seemingly bred to hate is disturbing,

indeed. It will be even more disturbing if, as Alan McDougall concludes, Southampton fans are beginning to reciprocate.

Far from challenging the assertion that emerges from this chapter – that the venom has come mainly from Pompey fans – the 6.57 writers champion that claim with pride. If you overlook, as they do, Saints' FA Cup history from 1898 to 1927 and start the clock with Portsmouth's first Final in 1929, then the 6.57 image of Pompey, from then into the 1950s, as 'unrivalled by any on the south coast' cannot be disputed (even if their triumphalist litany neglects the 1934 Cup Final but invents, by way of compensation, a 1950 Wembley appearance). The loss of that supremacy 'may be to blame', they suggest, for the unilateral hatred, as 'a once great Pompey football team [went] tumbling down to the depths of the Fourth Division, while its much reviled neighbour, a comparatively small club, has kept itself in the top flight.'

So long as that resentment remained one-sided, with few opportunities for it to be articulated at derby games, then Southampton fans could afford to smile at the idea of being the 'small club' and not worry desperately about their non-appearance in books on violence.

Let's hope that Alan McDougall's prediction, based on observing young people at the chalk-face, is wrong and that retaliation is not bursting out all over.

READ ON: Rob Holley's discovery of Don Roper is reported in *Match of the Millennium*, while Bertie Cowles's role in the discovery of Ted Bates is explained in *Dell Diamond*.. Mick Channon's Pompey memories are from his *Man on the Run*. Rob Silvester's 6.57 book is co-authored by Cass Pennant. See 'Sources'.

---

* The match between Southampton and Millwall is twice described as an FA Cup-tie in 1978 – a confusing way of referring to this 1977 League game. But, to be fair, the 6.57 writers do not purport to report, accurately or otherwise, on football matches, only on the behaviour of Pompey's 'legendary fans'.

Chapter 17
A Pompey Perspective

Barry Bendel

There has long been a misconception among Pompey fans, misled by historians, that competitive games between our two clubs comprise a mere 30 or so League matches over a period of 105 years.

I fear that this distortion of the facts may have contributed, at least in part, to the festering hatred for Southampton Football Club. In reality, it is a feeling based on envy and ignorance.

If this book had been available before now, it might have contributed nothing to eradicating the more extreme behaviour of the violent few, but it would have enlightened those who believe that history matters and who were willing to listen.

The trouble has been that, for much of the past 40 years, there have been too few opportunities to 'get even' and, besides, Southampton were in a different League to us. Yet, for anyone who believed that Saints' superior recent history was the total picture, the way in which Part I of this book has chronicled the 209 games between our two sides should do something to redress the balance.

Having been invited to contribute a Pompey perspective to this study, I started by reading the match reports, anecdotes and statistics for all of those games. Following that, I feel confident that I can persuade even the most fanatical Portsmouth supporter that there is no need to envy Southampton: the evidence contained in Part I of this book tells us that, historically, Saints fans have much more to envy us for – and a long way to go to catch us up.

This book will stand as the definitive record of footballing competition between the two giants of South Coast football. From a Pompey fan's point of view, the prospect of *regular* competition should be something to relish. Apart from believing that most people would prefer the rivalry between our clubs to take place on the pitch rather than in the streets, I think the Premiership has been dominated by Northern and London clubs for far too long. Two strong local teams is a healthy state of affairs and keen competition can only help both of them to succeed and prosper in the world's best League.

Local derbies have been around ever since football was first played. Alan Ball has referred in his foreword to some of those he has personally experienced in Liverpool, Manchester and North London and, having lived in Italy, I have seen at close quarters the rivalry of AC v Inter in Milan and of Roma v Lazio in Rome. If you take those five examples, there is an obvious difference from our situation here on the Solent, in so far as each of those pairings is located within a common city boundary.

The closest I can think of to Southampton and Portsmouth are Newcastle and Sunderland – or maybe Derby and Nottingham Forest? But my impression of these rivalries is that feelings towards the 'enemy' tend to be expressed only during matches between them. At Fratton Park, anti-Saints chants are part of the song-sheet irrespective of whom Pompey are playing. A chorus of *If you hate the scum, stand up* will be repeated at intervals throughout the match, its frequency depending on how boring the game is. If it's a really dire affair, a more obscene rendering can be expected, to the tune of *She'll be coming round the mountain*.

I gather – from the previous chapter – that the converse is true at St Mary's, with the equally indiscriminate singing of their *Pompey Scum* chant. Why are we also 'scum'? Having striven to find something really nasty to call us like 'skates', Southampton fans seem to have found the term unworkable and, adopting the old adage of 'if you can't beat them…,' have decided to call us what we call them. So we're all scummers now. This could eventually lead to an identity crisis, but it's still early days.

When I watched Pompey during the 1940s and 1950s, such publicly-expressed animosity didn't exist and fans of both teams would stand together on the terraces and merely exchange a bit of rude but harmless banter, as illustrated, in the previous chapter, by the experiences of Saints fans who unashamedly travelled to Fratton Park for a better class of football.

How different it has become. I felt ashamed and angry, in December 2003, when some of the Portsmouth contingent screamed obscenities at the start of what was intended to be a minute's silence for the Saints legend, Ted Bates. As detailed in the Chapter 13, plenty of Pompey fans wrote to St Mary's to express their disgust. Showing a little respect was surely not too much to ask – anymore than we expect, and get, respect from visiting fans during our own silent tributes to departed heroes.

Come March 2004, it was clear that there was something much more seriously wrong when, after a keenly-contested game at Fratton Park, Pompey secured their first win over Southampton for 16 years. Instead of smiling faces, there were masks of burning hatred outside Fratton Park, as those visiting supporters who hadn't been locked in attempted to leave.

People were injured. And the violence was directed not only at Saints fans or the police. Take John and Katherine Winter and their son Max. The *News* reported how these non-football fans had gone to collect a take-away pizza, when their car was surrounded by the mob and they had to endure 10 minutes of hell as the vehicle was pounded with bricks and stones.

It was impossible to see any sign of celebration anywhere near Fratton Park. Hard to understand, considering the widespread agreement that the 1-0 victory was the catalyst that got the team back to winning ways and, most importantly, to staying in the Premiership. As I read some of the horrible details about the riots, I asked myself '*who* exactly are the Scum?'

It was particularly sad to see that some of the mob were no more than children. The police are well aware that much of the extreme behaviour of the adults is fuelled by drink – as reported in Chapter 13, there were people who had stayed in nearby pubs drinking throughout the match – and, in some cases, by drugs, too: it is quite common to see so-called supporters sniffing 'crack' in the streets around the ground, psyching themselves up for the battle. If only we could depend upon the large number of convictions and sentences bringing an end to this madness.

Now that we can meet at least twice in a season, perhaps the bitterness will die down. In the early days, both clubs shared the same struggle for financial survival, as well as the ignominy of being spurned by the northern-dominated Football League. The positive outcome of this shared isolation was an incredible number of games played between the two clubs.

Magic (and less-than-magic) moments

More than three-quarters of those encounters took place before I was born, so nearly all of the accounts in Part I come as new to me as to a teenager.

My experience of reading them has thrown up many surprises, a few of which I'd like to pick up as I go through the highlights, from the perspective of a Pompey fan, of our 209 meetings.

Here, then, are my Top Twenty moments:

1 If today's 'style' of chanting had been in vogue in 1899-2000, Portsmouth fans would have been entitled to voice a few rounds of *You're supposed to be the Champs*. There were the Saints, winners of the Southern League for the past three seasons, losing four of their first five meetings with the new kids from Portsmouth. A convincing early 'lead' for Pompey, then, in the accumulative total of wins and losses that you can follow in the summary charts on pages 264-267.

2 Around the third anniversary of the first game, the two sides met for the 15th time and Pompey's wins went into double figures. They were outscoring the Saints – hats off to Danny Cunliffe for the first derby goal and many more to come! – while Matt Reilly, who had had a couple of games for the Saints, had become a local hero in the Portsmouth goal.

3 By 1904, the two sides had won a few Championships between them. In 1903, Pompey had won the Western League for the third season in a row, having won the Southern League in 1902. But the Southern League Championship remained mainly a Southampton preserve: their 1904 title was their sixth in eight seasons. And they were much doughtier FA Cup performers, reaching the Final in 1900 and 1902. Pompey would take a long time to master Cup football.

4 The calendar years 1903 to 1905 saw the Saints catching up, when they completed successive Southern League 'doubles' over Pompey and went ahead in games won for the first time. It would take Portsmouth eight years to regain that lead, after which it would change hands once or twice until Pompey's win in the 97th derby meeting on 1 April 1918 would give them a lead that they have never since surrendered. Not that either side had as yet established the edge in these matters: an impartial observer would have been hard-pressed to say which had been the better team over the first 100 or so meetings.

5 During World War I, sparse crowds turned out to see sides that were often missing their star players – but were able, conversely, to field guests. As discussed in Chapter 15, a few players even turned out for both clubs. The isolation of Southampton and Portsmouth from London was intensified by two war-time developments: the local media was at odds with the antagonism of the national press to playing football at all during the War; and when War Leagues were formed, they mostly kept Saints and Pompey out of the capital. The outcome was that they played each other more often than ever, eight times during the 1917-18 season alone.

6 Permitted to play in the Football League at last, by the creation of a new Third Division in 1920, the two clubs took no time at all to climb up to Division II, the Saints leading the way in 1922, followed by Pompey in 1924. The fans of each side clearly respected the achievements of the other. Thus, in 1922, after the annual Pickford Cup game on the last day of the season, Pompey supporters applauded the Southampton players; and, two years later, at the same fixture at Fratton Park, the Saints fans returned the compliment – it was good news that their old rivals were to join them in the same division once more.

7 But the next promotion was of a different order. When Pompey went up to Division I, who'd have thought that they would not meet the Saints in a League match for another 33 years? What's more,

Portsmouth, hitherto the FA Cup duffers, reached three Finals between 1929 and 1939, while Southampton won only one FA Cup-tie between their quarter-final of 1927 and their Third Round win in 1946. As the title of Chapter 9 puts it, Pompey were 'on another planet'.

8 The Bendel family contact with both clubs began during the 1930s. My father, who was living in Hammersmith, was more of a sports-goer than a football fan. Having befriended some Fulham supporters at the Stamford Bridge dog-track, he would go to Craven Cottage, where he took a shine to the Pompey side that won an FA Cup-tie there in 1931. Ever the champion of the underdog, though, he also developed quite a soft-spot for the Saints after seeing them lose 4-2 to Fulham in 1932 and subsequently followed their Second Division visits to the Cottage. He wasn't one to rush into allegiances, though, so when his landlady's influenza enabled him to use her ticket at Wembley in 1934, he went with an open mind. When Jimmy Allen was injured, it was Pompey's turn to appeal to his sympathy for the afflicted. I mention this as a prelude to explaining, below, my own loyalties: if my father was going to support anybody, it could so easily have been Saints – or, even moreso, Fulham.

9 And what more needs to be said about Pompey's next visit to Wembley in 1939? The *Echo* cartoon on page 136 acclaims it as a triumph for Hampshire and you can readily see, from Chapter 9, how that theme of county neighbours had continued across the inter-planetary divide.

10 During the War, Saints and Pompey again met often – 21 times from the Jubilee match on the eve of hostilities to their last War League game in 1945 – and shared rather more players than they had during the Great War. And when The Dell was bombed in 1940, obliging Southampton to play all their League matches away from home, they staged a 'home' Cup-tie at Fratton Park – a most generous act of neighbourliness as their hosts provided not only a ground but several hundred fans who turned out to support them.

On Barry Bendel's first visit to The Dell, Charlie Wayman (*above*) did not meet expectations, but Spurs' goalkeeper, Ted Ditchburn, made an impression - even if Ted Bates outjumped him on this occasion.

11 When the League programme started again in 1946, both clubs did reasonably well in their respective divisions. For four seasons, Southampton were in the top four in Division II but these achievements were somewhat eclipsed by Pompey's two successive Championships of 1949 and 1950. Dave Juson has paid repeated tributes, in Chapter 10 and again at the start of Chapter 11, to those achievements and there is perhaps no need to crow about them here. As Jack Tinn's young discoveries blossomed, two of Saints' young hopefuls – Alf Ramsey, previously released from his amateur terms with Pompey, and Don Roper – departed for North London .

12 There was no disputing who was now top dog. I can recall, from as early as 1947, the patronising way in which my school-friends and I discussed Southampton, who were so clearly a lower-class side. I must have taken this prejudice along with me when I went to watch a football match for the very first time. After pleading with him to take me from our Bognor home to football at Fratton Park, my dad instead carted me off to The Dell on 28 February 1948, to see an FA Cup Sixth Round tie between Saints and Spurs. It was quite like old times: Southampton in the quarter-final, while Portsmouth had been knocked out in the Fourth

Round – and were without a game that day, their scheduled League opponents being in Cup action. Perhaps I was negative about the whole experience because I had wanted to watch Pompey play? Or perhaps I was disappointed by Saints losing 1-0 to Spurs – especially after Dad's build-up about what Charlie Wayman was going to do. I shall never know. In fact, the only thing I can remember about this game is how impressive Ted Ditchburn was in the Spurs' goal. David Bull and I have discussed the strange coincidence that the only thing either of us can recollect about our first visit to the other's ground is Tottenham's goalkeeper. But maybe it's not such a coincidence: Ditchburn had the frame to make quite an impression.

13 So like my father in the early 1930s, I could easily have become a Southampton fan. But I didn't. Three weeks later, I was at Fratton Park when Portsmouth beat Manchester City 1-0. And that's where my loyalty has remained ever since.

14 Between 1945 and 1960, the two clubs met only four times, mostly trying out their new floodlights. A win each and a couple of draws – one of which I saw at Fratton Park in 1953 (*see line-ups opposite*) – were the only times opposition fans ever saw each other. In those days, I believed – along with most of their supporters, I imagine – that Pompey's lofty status would remain for ever and, even when Southampton were relegated to Division III (South) soon after that floodlit game of 1953, I hardly gave it a second thought. Yet we now know that Southampton were experiencing the shock of relegation only six years before we did.

15 It was easy to develop an ostrich mentality if you were a Pompey fan at that time. I remember that, even when we started to struggle in 1957, I still had faith that they would survive. The trouble is, things can change – and they did.

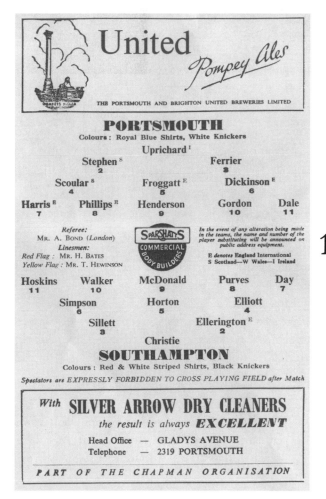

No matter that the first floodlit match at Fratton Park ended in a draw, the line-ups show the difference in quality between the two sides. Portsmouth could boast seven internationals (indicated by the letters 'E' for England, etc), while Southampton fielded only Ellerington of this ilk.

16 All the time the Saints were inhabiting the lower reaches of football, I don't think very many people in Portsmouth even mentioned them. But when Division II proved unexpectedly hard, it was a bitter pill to swallow when Southampton won the Division III Championship in 1960 to achieve parity with their old rivals for the first time since 1927. Pompey had become so weak, with the able assistance of Freddie Cox (*above*), that it didn't feel much like parity when the two sides met at The Dell in the third game of the 1960-61 season. Saints thrashed us 5-1. At Fratton Park, we held them to a 1-1 draw but, after we were relegated that season, it was not lost on some sulking Pompey fans that those three points surrendered to Southampton would have saved us.

17 The demise of Portsmouth Football Club coincided with the abolition of National Service, which was, in my opinion, a contributory factor in the increased violence in our society. Young male football fans, denied this channel for natural energy and aggression, found an outlet in opposing fans. Not all of them, of course, but I really do believe that, without two years' National Service, potentially aggressive young men missed the discipline imposed by a higher authority. The Swinging Sixties increased this freedom still further and it was understandable when violence, on a minor scale initially, started to erupt at stadiums all over the country. It took most of the 1960s for this to become a really serious matter and, when Pompey bounced back as Division III champions in 1963, any bitterness towards their neighbours remained largely below the surface. For four seasons, Saints v Pompey was a mouth-watering fixture.

18 It lasted for only four seasons, though. In February 1966, Southampton took their leave of Fratton Park with a 5-2 win, on their way to winning promotion, that season, to the top flight for the first time in their history. They were runners-up to Manchester City, the side Pompey had so narrowly pipped to achieve that status a whole 39 years earlier. Now, though, the Saints were top dogs again. And they let us know it, the evening after they virtually clinched promotion, to the tune of 6-1, in John Hollowbread's testimonial.

Steve Wigley, in the days when he reminded Barry Bendel of Peter Harris.

Steve Wigley has added another entry to the interesting list, as recorded in Chapter 14, of those we have shared. Steve was extremely popular during his three seasons as a player at Fratton Park and, for us older fans, he was a reminder of the style and stature of our legendary outside-right, Peter Harris.

19 The worm had truly turned. From then on, Saints won the lion's share of their infrequent meetings. Just to rub a little more salt into the wound, Portsmouth-born Bobby Stokes – who would surely have been a Portsmouth player had the club not abandoned Youth and Reserves football in 1965 – scored the only goal, to defeat Manchester United in the 1976 FA Cup Final and to establish himself as a Southampton legend. This also meant that the two clubs were level again in the Cup Final stakes: three appearances and one win apiece. That said, it's about time that Pompey won a major Cup-tie against the Saints, but the opportunities have been all too rare. I was at The Dell for the last of our three FA Cup meetings in January 1996. Saints outplayed us to the tune of 3-1 and, with the match being beamed to Portsmouth, their fans were able to gloat: *Are you watching, Fratton Park?*

20 And so to parity renewed in 2003. The consequent derbies, with a Carling Cup bonus thrown in, were overshadowed, alas, by the dreadful events for which I expressed my contempt earlier in this chapter. Having changed their managers between the two Premiership meetings, Southampton have since done it again. The promotion, to manager, of

Conclusion and confession

I have to confess that I have never felt the slightest animosity towards Southampton, yet I do understand why a lot of Pompey fans have – even though I have no time, you'll have gathered, for those who express their feelings physically. When I started supporting Pompey, there was no negativity of any kind. Working abroad, I didn't see many games at Fratton Park during the 1960s and 1970s; but I imagine it must have felt rather like seeing the poor people down the road win the lottery and move into a mansion, when you've fallen on hard times and are having to live in a small room at your mother-in-law's with your wife and two kids.

After reading this book, most Pompey fans ought to feel a lot more positive: they can rest assured that our account is comfortably in the black. The bottom line on page 267 reads:

Matches played	209	
Saints wins	81	goals 354
Pompey wins	95	goals 399

In future, if Southampton happen to beat Arsenal or Chelsea or Manchester United, maybe some of us will give them a small cheer. It goes without saying that when Saints play us, we want only one result and, when that happens, I sincerely hope we will celebrate in *style*.

Chapter 18
Friends, Rivals & Countymen

Dave Juson

'Although I would sooner any other team beat us than Southampton
- this for merely sentimental reasons...'

Thus Sentinel to his *Football Mail* readers, after a Pompey defeat in 1920. A phrase that echoes down the decades. But these days, alas, sentiment has little to do with it.

Indeed, reference to the *Daily Echo* and the *News* during the 2003-04 season reveals an alarming decline in the intellectual toughness of football journalists since the 1960s. Back then, your side lost a game, you picked yourself up, you brushed yourself down and you started all over again; there was always the next game and there was always the next season; or the one after that. Now, it would seem, lives are ruined by results. Defeat is unforgivable. Losers are inconsolable.

All of which is, I suggest, the result of too much empathy with the wrong sort of fans, a fair few of whom display a worrying lack of the mental and moral fortitude that it takes to be a real supporter. And by being a 'supporter', I mean somebody who can get behind their team when the going is tough, not those who make threatening gestures and scream insults at opposition fans when their team goes one down (or even before) and then sink into a sulk when they go two down – which appears to be the rule among the more excitable elements at St Mary's and Fratton Park, these days. And we have said enough already, in Part II of this book, about those twits who believe that just hurling abuse is not enough to demonstrate their loyalty to the cause.

And as for the football, 2003-04 – while it did bring Saints and Pompey together again – was not a classic season. Even the most dispassionate, and circumspect, of neutrals would have to agree that, as examples of the noble art of football, none of the derbies was much to enthuse about.

And there were a good many dispassionate neutrals watching the three games, all of which were broadcast by satellite television. We had the opportunity to impress a world-wide audience and what we gave them was two evidently mediocre football teams playing below their modest potentials and two sets of 'fans' hurling vitriol and foul-mouthed abuse at each other.

A great advert for the region.

Still, one duff season over 105 years and 209 games proves little. If Part I of this book has established anything it is that we are fortunate to have two very resilient football clubs, with a tradition of entertaining football and, on both sides, philosophically-inclined supporters inured against the worst the Fates can throw against them – even if, when it comes to derbies, they can be somewhat over-sensitive in defeat, or more exuberant in victory, than their rivals might consider seemly.

It wasn't always like that. One of the major joys in researching this book has been reading the colourful description of the 'animated' crowds that embroidered the opening of the match reports (a few of which have managed to escape the editorial chain-saw). And it is apparent that, on the whole, people went to games determined to enjoy themselves – win or lose – and, on the whole, they evidently did just that.

This is not to say that there was not crowd trouble between 1899 and 1927, when the Saints-Pompey rivalry was at its most competitive, because there were incidents at games and the local press were quick to pick up on it. In the *Football Mail* of 19 October 1912, the editor fulminated on the behaviour of the crowd, which had used 'filthy language and abuse' during Pompey's recent visit to Millwall's East Ferry Road Ground, in contrast to the Fratton Park crowd that was often complimented on its sportsmanship.

And that appears to have been true of The Dell, too: the reasons that there are no reports of crowd disruption in this book – before the 1960s, at least – is that there were none. Or, at least, none worthy of note in the local press. We may assume that two drunks slogging it out on the pavement was far too common a sight in both towns (judging from the magistrates' court reports) for anybody to be interested in the cause of it, whether it be footer or not.

As we have seen, there were individual lapses – such as when a spectator was 'admonished' by the referee during the November 1903 derby at Fratton Park for using 'bad language' to Kelly Houlker: did he call him a 'scummer', I wonder? But they appear to have been rare and the near riot at The Dell, after Harland & Wolff had defeated Pompey in March 1919, was, judging from the reaction of the press in Southampton and Portsmouth, unprecedented; and it is significant that the *Evening News* was quick to dissociate Pompey's regular adherents from the incident, identifying the miscreants as young servicemen.

As for any general impression of ill-will between the two cities, I am among those who feel it is somewhat exaggerated; but I am disinclined to launch into an analysis of, let alone a diatribe on, why and how what hostility that does exist emerged, though I will venture that many aspects of it are as worrying as they are silly – and note that trouble between the less mature natives of neighbouring towns seems not to be that uncommon, especially when their respective football teams are playing each other. It can even happen at derby games between Dorchester and Weymouth. And if many youths are disposed to congregate and pick fights with their contemporaries in neighbouring streets, we shouldn't wonder at their behaviour at football matches.

Sadly, it has to be conceded that the match-day, especially the derby-day, experience is not the joyful experience it was in days of yore. Why? We could write another book on that, but so much has changed since football hooliganism became fashionable in the 1960s: crowd segregation has certainly taken the brake off the behaviour of a lot of the more stupid spectators. Yet, for some reason, the result seems now to have become more important than the spectacle and we supporters – and I stress *we*; most of us anyway, I would hazard – are no longer as generous, in defeat or in victory, as we were, and… the list is endless. And that's *before* we discuss the Saints-Pompey rivalry – which has now evolved into something daunting, some would say a matter of life and death. Bill Shankly, were he still with us, would quip 'it's more important than that.' But he would be joking.

My point is, that we are no longer cheering our respective sides on for the pure fun of doing just that. As Herbie Taylor, the most traditional and upstanding of supporters, pointed out in Chapter 16, even he has lost the knack of it. Many of us have never had it. At least Herbie knows what he is missing.

But it is not all doom and gloom. The vast majority of Saints' fans came home exultant, after a great day out giving their best at the 2003 FA Cup Final in Cardiff, despite the defeat. And millions of television viewers admired the sporting support given their side by the Fratton Park crowd as Arsenal ripped Pompey apart in the FA Cup in 2004.

You see, demonstrable proof that we have the pure spirit of sporting enthusiasm within us when the occasion demands. And there is no bigger, more demanding, occasion than a derby in the Premier League – except perhaps a derby game in Europe?

And Europe is the next target for both clubs. Local bragging rights over the last League game are for losers; the Saints and Pompey have the potential to be competing for a place at the next level. And better than elbowing each other for a place in that particular sun – which would be exciting enough to be going on with – there exists the possibility of Pompey and Saints competing with each other at that level.

Quite how you overturn the hegemony of the billionaires of Old Trafford, Highbury, Stamford Bridge *et al* in a climate of 'money gets all' is, admittedly, problematical, but if Manchester United, Arsenal, Chelsea and the giants of former years really were as eternally invincible as the media 'experts' will always lead us to believe, we and all the other clubs would have wound up our/their affairs, sold off the players and grounds and paid off the shareholders decades back.

So, into Europe, in good time, and – who knows? – we could be buying each other drinks in the street cafés of Paris, Rome or Milan, prior to a European Championship Final, in the not too distant future.

But let's leave the yahoos back home!

Statistics

The next six pages consist of three tables:

Table 1 is a complete check-list of the 209 games played, from 1899 to 2004, between the first teams of Southampton (indicated as 'SFC') and Portsmouth (PFC).

The last three columns show the accumulative tally of wins by each side, with draws shown as 'D'.

Other abbreviations used surely require no explanation, especially since everything is set out fully enough at the head of each match report in Part I of this book.

The 64 first-class fixtures among the 209 games are shown in bold type.

Table 2 is a summary of the results shown in Table 1, categorised by the nature of the competition, if any. While football statisticians will continue to debate such distinctions, we have used a three-fold classification:

- First-Class
- Other 'official' competitions (that 'count' in less restrictive classifications of appearances)
- 'Unofficial' first-team matches that tend not to be counted in players' appearances.

Table 3 is a season-by-season check on how each side fared in first-class competitions.

Table 1: The derby games, match by match

	Date		Venue	Score SFC	PFC	Competition	Games Won SFC	PFC	D
	1899-00								
1	06-Sep	1899	Fratton Park	0	2	Friendly	0	1	0
2	18-Oct	1899	Fratton Park	1	5	S District Combination	0	2	0
3	02-Apr	1900	The Dell	1	0	S District Combination	1	2	0
4	14-Apr	1900	The Dell	0	2	**SL Division I**	1	3	0
5	16-Apr	1900	Fratton Park	0	2	**SL Division I**	1	4	0
	1900-01								
6	22-Sep	1900	Fratton Park	0	0	**SL Division I**	1	4	1
7	06-Mar	1901	The Dell	0	4	Western League	1	5	1
8	20-Mar	1901	Fratton Park	1	2	Western League	1	6	1
9	06-Apr	1901	The Dell	2	0	**SL Division I**	2	6	1
	1901-02								
10	04-Sep	1901	Fratton Park	0	1	Western League	2	7	1
11	11-Sep	1901	The Dell	1	3	Western League	2	8	1
12	12-Oct	1901	Fratton Park	2	2	**SL Division I**	2	8	2
13	02-Nov	1901	The Dell	3	4	**SL Division I**	2	9	2
	1902-03								
14	01-Sep	1902	The Dell	3	1	Western League	3	9	2
15	10-Sep	1902	Fratton Park	1	4	Western League	3	10	2
16	27-Sep	1902	The Dell	1	1	**SL Division I**	3	10	3
17	10-Jan	1903	Fratton Park	3	0	**SL Division I**	4	10	3
	1903-04								
18	02-Sep	1903	Fratton Park	2	1	Western League	5	10	3
19	07-Sep	1903	The Dell	5	2	Western League	6	10	3
20	21-Oct	1903	Fratton Park	5	4	Southern Charity Cup	7	10	3
21	28-Nov	1903	Fratton Park	1	0	**SL Division I**	8	10	3
22	26-Mar	1904	The Dell	2	0	**SL Division I**	9	10	3
23	13-Apr	1904	Fratton Park	2	4	Friendly	9	11	3
	1904-05								
24	01-Sep	1904	The Dell	2	2	Western League	9	11	4
25	07-Sep	1904	Fratton Park	2	0	Western League	10	11	4
26	26-Nov	1904	The Dell	1	0	**SL Division I**	11	11	4
27	25-Mar	1905	Fratton Park	2	1	**SL Division I**	12	11	4
	1905-06								
28	06-Sep	1905	Fratton Park	2	0	Western League	13	11	4
29	11-Sep	1905	The Dell	5	2	Western League	14	11	4
30	01-Nov	1905	Fratton Park	0	1	Hants Benevolent Cup	14	12	4
31	13-Nov	1905	The Dell	4	2	Southern Charity Cup	15	12	4
32	25-Nov	1905	Fratton Park	0	1	**SL Division I**	15	13	4
33	13-Jan	1906	The Dell	5	1	**FA Cup**	16	13	4
34	31-Mar	1906	The Dell	1	2	**SL Division I**	16	14	4
	1906-07								
35	19-Sep	1906	The Dell	2	3	Western League	16	15	4
36	26-Sep	1906	Fratton Park	2	3	Western League	16	16	4
37	20-Oct	1906	The Dell	2	0	**SL Division I**	17	16	4
38	14-Nov	1906	Fratton Park	2	0	Southern Charity Cup	18	16	4
39	23-Feb	1907	Fratton Park	2	1	**SL Division I**	19	16	4
40	08-Apr	1907	The Dell	0	1	Hants Benevolent Cup	19	17	4
	1907-08								
41	28-Sep	1907	Fratton Park	0	3	**SL Division I**	19	18	4
42	04-Dec	1907	Fratton Park	2	0	Western League	20	18	4
43	16-Dec	1907	The Dell	0	1	Western League	20	19	4
44	25-Jan	1908	The Dell	1	0	**SL Division I**	21	19	4
	1908-09								
45	26-Sep	1908	The Dell	2	0	**SL Division I**	22	19	4
46	30-Sep	1908	Fratton Park	2	4	Western League	22	20	4
47	28-Oct	1908	The Dell	4	1	Western League	23	20	4
48	30-Jan	1909	Fratton Park	0	3	**SL Division I**	23	21	4
49	22-Feb	1909	The Dell	1	0	Southern Charity Cup	24	21	4
50	10-Mar	1909	Fratton Park	1	1	Hants Benevolent Cup	24	21	5
51	15-Mar	1909	The Dell	1	2	Southern Charity Cup	24	22	5
52	19-Apr	1909	The Dell	4	3	Hants Benevolent Cup	25	22	5
	1909-10								
53	20-Sep	1909	The Dell	3	2	Southern Charity Cup	26	22	5
54	06-Nov	1909	Fratton Park	1	1	**SL Division I**	26	22	6
55	29-Nov	1909	The Dell	2	3	Hants Benevolent Cup	26	23	6
56	19-Mar	1910	The Dell	1	2	**SL Division I**	26	24	6
	1910-11								
57	10-Sep	1910	The Dell	3	0	**SL Division I**	27	24	6
58	30-Nov	1910	Fratton Park	1	2	Hants Benevolent Cup	27	25	6
59	07-Jan	1911	Fratton Park	1	0	**SL Division I**	28	25	6

	Date		Venue	Score		Competition	Games Won		
				SFC	PFC		SFC	PFC	D
	1911-12								
60	18-Sep	1911	The Dell	2	1	Eastham Benefit	29	25	6
61	27-Sep	1911	Fratton Park	1	1	Friendly	29	25	7
62	25-Oct	1911	The Dell	5	1	Hants Benevolent Cup	30	25	7
63	24-Feb	1912	Fratton Park	0	2	Friendly	30	26	7
	1912-13								
64	28-Sep	1912	The Dell	2	3	**SL Division I**	30	27	7
65	16-Oct	1912	Fratton Park	0	2	Hants Benevolent Cup	30	28	7
66	06-Nov	1912	The Dell	0	3	Southern Alliance	30	29	7
67	20-Nov	1912	Fratton Park	0	2	Southern Alliance	30	30	7
68	25-Jan	1913	Fratton Park	0	2	**SL Division I**	30	31	7
	1913-14								
69	17-Sep	1913	Fratton Park	1	3	Southern Alliance	30	32	7
70	24-Sep	1913	The Dell	1	0	Southern Alliance	31	32	7
71	08-Oct	1913	The Dell	0	1	Hants Benevolent Cup	31	33	7
72	25-Dec	1913	Fratton Park	0	2	**SL Division I**	31	34	7
73	26-Dec	1913	The Dell	4	3	**SL Division I**	32	34	7
	1914-15								
74	25-Dec	1914	Fratton Park	1	0	**SL Division I**	33	34	7
75	26-Dec	1914	The Dell	4	3	**SL Division I**	34	34	7
76	28-Apr	1915	Fratton Park	0	2	Hants Benevolent Cup	34	35	7
	1915-16								
77	11-Sep	1915	Fratton Park	2	2	Friendly	34	35	8
78	02-Oct	1915	The Dell	1	2	Friendly	34	36	8
79	25-Dec	1915	Fratton Park	1	1	Friendly	34	36	9
80	27-Dec	1915	The Dell	2	1	Friendly	35	36	9
81	05-Feb	1916	Fratton Park	2	2	Friendly	35	36	10
82	11-Mar	1916	The Dell	4	2	Friendly	36	36	10
83	08-Apr	1916	The Dell	2	3	Hants Benevolent Cup	36	37	10
84	08-Apr	1916	Fratton Park	0	7	Hants Benevolent Cup	36	38	10
85	21-Apr	1916	Fratton Park	2	0	South West Combination	37	38	10
86	24-Apr	1916	The Dell	3	0	South West Combination	38	38	10
	1916-17								
87	04-Nov	1916	Fratton Park	1	0	London Combination	39	38	10
88	27-Jan	1917	The Dell	1	0	London Combination	40	38	10
89	03-Mar	1917	Fratton Park	0	1	London Combination	40	39	10
90	14-Apr	1917	The Dell	2	1	London Combination	41	39	10
	1917-18								
91	01-Sep	1917	The Dell	3	2	Friendly	42	39	10
92	08-Sep	1917	Fratton Park	4	4	Friendly	42	39	11
93	03-Nov	1917	Fratton Park	0	3	Friendly	42	40	11
94	25-Dec	1917	Fratton Park	1	1	Friendly	42	40	12
95	26-Dec	1917	The Dell	2	3	Friendly	42	41	12
96	29-Mar	1918	Fratton Park	2	4	South Hants War League	42	42	12
97	01-Apr	1918	The Dell	0	4	South Hants War League	42	43	12
98	20-Apr	1918	The Dell	2	3	Friendly	42	44	12
	1918-19								
99	07-Sep	1918	Fratton Park	2	5	Friendly	42	45	12
100	14-Sep	1918	The Dell	1	1	Friendly	42	45	13
101	25-Dec	1918	Fratton Park	1	5	South Hants War League	42	46	13
102	26-Dec	1918	The Dell	3	6	South Hants War League	42	47	13
103	18-Apr	1919	Fratton Park	1	1	South Hants War League	42	47	14
104	21-Apr	1919	The Dell	9	1	South Hants War League	43	47	14
	1919-20								
105	26-Jly	1919	Fratton Park	3	5	Friendly	43	48	14
106	18-Oct	1919	Fratton Park	1	5	**SL Division I**	43	49	14
107	28-Feb	1920	The Dell	0	0	**SL Division I**	43	49	15
108	15-May	1920	The Dell	2	0	Hants Benevolent Cup	44	49	15
	1920-21								
109	11-Sep	1920	The Dell	2	0	**FL Division III**	45	49	15
110	18-Sep	1920	Fratton Park	1	0	**FL Division III**	46	49	15
111	11-May	1921	Fratton Park	0	1	Hants Benevolent Cup	46	50	15
	1921-22								
112	10-Oct	1921	The Dell	4	0	Arnfield Benefit	47	50	15
113	16-Nov	1921	Fratton Park	0	1	Unemployed Fund	47	51	15
114	18-Mar	1922	Fratton Park	2	0	**FL Division III (S)**	48	51	15
115	25-Mar	1922	The Dell	1	1	**FL Division III (S)**	48	51	16
116	08-May	1922	The Dell	3	1	Hants Benevolent Cup	49	51	16
	1922-23								
117	04-Dec	1922	The Dell	1	3	McIntyre Benefit	49	52	16
118	16-Apr	1923	Fratton Park	2	1	Hospital Cup	50	52	16
119	23-Apr	1923	The Dell	2	2	Hants Benevolent Cup	50	52	17

	Date		Venue	Score		Competition	Games	Won	
				SFC	PFC		SFC	PFC	D
	1923-24								
120	14-Nov	1923	The Dell	0	2	Lee Benefit	50	53	17
121	05-May	1924	The Dell	2	3	Hospital Cup	50	54	17
122	07-May	1924	Fratton Park	0	2	Hants Benevolent Cup	50	55	17
	1924-25								
123	27-Sep	1924	The Dell	0	0	**FL Division II**	50	55	18
124	29-Nov	1924	Fratton Park	1	1	**FL Division II**	50	55	19
125	04-May	1925	Fratton Park	0	2	Hospital Cup	50	56	19
126	06-May	1925	The Dell	1	1	Hants Benevolent Cup	50	56	20
	1925-26								
127	05-Sep	1925	The Dell	1	3	**FL Division II**	50	57	20
128	23-Sep	1925	Fratton Park	3	0	Warner Benefit	51	57	20
129	16-Jan	1926	Fratton Park	2	1	**FL Division II**	52	57	20
130	03-May	1926	The Dell	2	4	Hospital Cup	52	58	20
131	05-May	1926	Fratton Park	1	5	Hants Benevolent Cup	52	59	20
	1926-27								
132	28-Aug	1926	Fratton Park	1	3	**FL Division II**	52	60	20
133	15-Jan	1927	The Dell	0	2	**FL Division II**	52	61	20
134	09-May	1927	The Dell	4	1	Hants Benevolent Cup	53	61	20
135	11-May	1927	Fratton Park	1	5	Hospital Cup	53	62	20
	1927 to 1939								
136	07-May	1928	Fratton Park	1	6	Benevolent/Hospital Cups	53	63	20
137	06-May	1929	Fratton Park	2	1	Hospital Cup	54	63	20
138	08-May	1929	The Dell	3	2	Hants Benevolent Cup	55	63	20
139	05-May	1930	Fratton Park	0	0	Hants Benevolent Cup	55	63	21
140	07-May	1930	The Dell	0	2	Hospital Cup	55	64	21
141	04-May	1931	The Dell	0	4	Hants Benevolent Cup	55	65	21
142	06-May	1931	Fratton Park	2	2	Hospital Cup	55	65	22
143	18-Apr	1932	The Dell	1	0	Hants Combination Cup	56	65	22
144	09-May	1932	The Dell	2	2	Hospital Cup	56	65	23
145	11-May	1932	Fratton Park	1	5	Hants Benevolent Cup	56	66	23
146	05-Oct	1932	Fratton Park	0	6	Hants Combination Cup	56	67	23
147	03-May	1933	Fratton Park	0	5	Benevolent/Hospital Cups	56	68	23
148	22-Nov	1933	Fratton Park	0	1	Hants Combination Cup	56	69	23
149	07-May	1934	The Dell	1	4	Benevolent/Hospital Cups	56	70	23
150	08-May	1935	Fratton Park	0	1	Benevolent/Hospital Cups	56	71	23
151	27-Apr	1936	The Dell	1	2	Hants Benevolent Cup	56	72	23
152	20-Aug	1938	Fratton Park	2	4	FL Jubilee	56	73	23
	1939-40								
153	19-Aug	1939	The Dell	0	3	FL Jubilee	56	74	23
154	23-Sep	1939	Fratton Park	3	2	Friendly	57	74	23
155	02-Dec	1939	Fratton Park	1	4	FL South B	57	75	23
156	20-Jan	1940	The Dell	2	0	FL South B	58	75	23
157	23-Mar	1940	Fratton Park	1	3	FL South C	58	76	23
158	24-Apr	1940	The Dell	1	0	FL South C	59	76	23
	1940-41								
159	25-Dec	1940	Fratton Park	2	1	S Regional Lge	60	76	23
160	08-Feb	1941	Fratton Park	2	5	S Regional Lge	60	77	23
161	15-Mar	1941	Fratton Park	0	6	S Regional Lge	60	78	23
162	02-Jun	1941	Fratton Park	1	8	Hants Combination Cup	60	79	23
	1941 to 1943								
163	25-Dec	1942	Fratton Park	3	2	League South	61	79	23
164	26-Dec	1942	The Dell	0	2	League South	61	80	23
165	24-Apr	1943	Fratton Park	0	0	Friendly	61	80	24
	1943-44								
166	25-Dec	1943	The Dell	6	3	League South	62	80	24
167	27-Dec	1943	Fratton Park	2	4	League South	62	81	24
168	08-Apr	1944	Fratton Park	1	2	Friendly	62	82	24
169	15-Apr	1944	The Dell	3	0	Friendly	63	82	24
	1944-45								
170	30-Sep	1944	Fratton Park	1	3	League South	63	83	24
171	13-Jan	1945	The Dell	2	4	League South	63	84	24
172	07-Apr	1945	Fratton Park	4	7	Friendly	63	85	24
	1945-46								
173	08-Sep	1945	Fratton Park	2	3	League South	63	86	24
174	15-Sep	1945	The Dell	3	1	League South	64	86	24
	1946 to 1960								
175	22-Oct	1951	The Dell	2	2	Hants Combination Cup	64	86	25
176	02-Mar	1953	Fratton Park	1	1	Friendly	64	86	26
177	07-Mar	1955	The Dell	1	3	Friendly	64	87	26
178	16-Feb	1957	The Dell	3	1	Friendly	65	87	26

	Date		Venue	Score		Competition	Games	Won	
				SFC	PFC		SFC	PFC	D
	1960-61								
179	27-Aug	1960	The Dell	5	1	**FL Division II**	66	87	26
180	31-Dec	1960	Fratton Park	1	1	**FL Division II**	66	87	27
	1961 to 1963								
181	12-Aug	1961	The Dell	0	2	Friendly	66	88	27
182	13-Oct	1962	Fratton Park	1	1	**FL Division II**	66	88	28
183	02-Mar	1963	The Dell	4	2	**FL Division II**	67	88	28
	1963-64								
184	28-Sep	1963	Fratton Park	0	2	**FL Division II**	67	89	28
185	08-Feb	1964	The Dell	2	3	**FL Division II**	67	90	28
	1964-65								
186	12-Sep	1964	Fratton Park	3	0	**FL Division II**	68	90	28
187	16-Jan	1965	The Dell	2	2	**FL Division II**	68	90	29
	1965-66								
188	28-Aug	1965	The Dell	2	2	**FL Division II**	68	90	30
189	05-Feb	1966	Fratton Park	5	2	**FL Division II**	69	90	30
190	10-May	1966	The Dell	6	1	Hollowbread Benefit	70	90	30
	1966 to 1974								
191	11-Mar	1967	Fratton Park	2	2	Friendly	70	90	31
192	20-Apr	1970	The Dell	2	4	Sydenham Benefit	70	91	31
193	05-May	1972	Fratton Park	7	0	Milkins Benefit	71	91	31
194	03-May	1974	Fratton Park	0	0	Neave Benefit	71	91	32
	1974-75								
195	14-Sep	1974	The Dell	2	1	**FL Division II**	72	91	32
196	26-Dec	1974	Fratton Park	2	1	**FL Division II**	73	91	32
197	06-May	1975	Fratton Park	1	2	Hiron Benefit	73	92	32
	1975-76								
198	27-Sep	1975	The Dell	4	0	**FL Division II**	74	92	32
199	06-Apr	1976	Fratton Park	1	0	**FL Division II**	75	92	32
	1976 to 1987								
200	16-May	1980	Fratton Park	4	2	Reid Benefit	76	92	32
201	22-Dec	1981	Fratton Park	1	2	Hants Professional Cup	76	93	32
202	28-Jan	1984	Fratton Park	1	0	**FA Cup**	77	93	32
	1987-88								
203	22-Aug	1987	Fratton Park	2	2	**FL Division I**	77	93	33
204	03-Jan	1988	The Dell	0	2	**FL Division I**	77	94	33
	1988 to 2003								
205	10-May	1994	Fratton Park	5	1	Knight Benefit	78	94	33
206	07-Jan	1996	The Dell	3	0	**FA Cup**	79	94	33
	2003-04								
207	02-Dec	2003	St Mary's	2	0	**Carling Cup**	80	94	33
208	21-Dec	2003	St Mary's	3	0	**Premiership**	81	94	33
209	21-Mar	2004	Fratton Park	0	1	**Premiership**	81	95	33
			Goals	354	399				

Table 2: The derby results in summary

Full Results By Competition	PLD	RESULTS			GOALS	
		SAINTS	POMPEY	DRAWS	SAINTS	POMPEY
'FIRST-CLASS' COMPETITIONS						
Southern League	32	15	12	5	43	43
Football League	26	12	6	8	47	33
Premiership	2	1	1	0	3	1
FA Cup	3	3	0	0	9	1
League Cup	1	1	0	0	2	0
TOTAL	64	32	19	13	104	78
OTHER 'OFFICIAL' COMPETITIONS						
Southern District Combination	2	1	1	0	2	5
Western League	18	8	9	1	36	34
Southern Alliance League	4	1	3	0	2	8
Other official cups	48	14	29	5	66	110
TOTAL	72	24	42	6	106	157
ALL OFFICIAL COMPETITIONS	136	56	61	19	210	235
Unofficial cups	1	0	0	1	1	8
War Leagues	27	12	14	1	53	64
Testimonials & Friendlies	45	13	20	12	90	92
ALL MATCHES	209	81	95	33	354	399

Table 3: How they fared in first-class competition, season by season

SAINTS				POMPEY		
League/Division	Place	FA Cup	Season	League/Division	Place	FA Cup
SL Division I	3	Rd 1	1894-95			
SL Division I	3	Rd 1	1895-96			
SL Division I	Champs	Rd 2	1896-97			
SL Division I	Champs	**S-F**	1897-98			
SL Division I	Champs	Q-F	1898-99			
SL Division I	3	**R-Up**	1899-00	SL Division I	R-up	Rd 1
SL Division I	Champs	Rd 1	1900-01	SL Division I	3	Qual
SL Division I	3	**R-Up**	1901-02	**SL Division I**	Champs	Q-F
SL Division I	Champs	Rd 1	1902-03	SL Division I	3	Rd 1
SL Division I	Champs	Rd 2	1903-04	SL Division I	4	Rd 1
SL Division I	3	Q-F	1904-05	SL Division I	8	Rd 2
SL Division I	R-up	Q-F	1905-06	SL Division I	3	Rd 1
SL Division I	11	Rd 2	1906-07	**SL Division I**	R-up	Rd 2
SL Division I	11	**S-F**	1907-08	SL Division I	9	Rd 3
SL Division I	3	Rd 1	1908-09	SL Division I	4	Rd 2
SL Division I	5	Rd 2	1909-10	SL Division I	6	Rd 2
SL Division I	17	Rd 1	1910-11	SL Division I	Relg 20	Rd 1
SL Division I	16	Rd 1	1911-12	**SL Division II**	R-up	Rd 2
SL Division I	17	Rd 1	1912-13	SL Division I	11	Rd 1
SL Division I	11	Rd 1	1913-14	SL Division I	9	Rd 1
SL Division I	6	Rd 3	1914-15	SL Division I	7	Rd 1
War Competitions			1915-19			
SL Division I	8	Rd 1	1919-20	**SL Division I**	Champs	Rd 1
FL Division III	R-up	Rd 3	1920-21	FL Division III	12	Rd 1
FL Division III (South)	Champs	Rd 2	1921-22	FL Division III (South)	3	Rd 1
FL Division II	11	Q-F	1922-23	FL Division III (South)	7	Rd 1
FL Division II	5	Rd 3	1923-24	**FL Division III (South)**	Champs	Rd 1
FL Division II	7	**S-F**	1924-25	FL Division II	4	Rd 2
FL Division II	14	Rd 3	1925-26	FL Division II	11	Rd 3
FL Division II	13	**S-F**	1926-27	**FL Division II**	R-up	Rd 4
FL Division II	17	Rd 3	1927-28	FL Division I	20	Rd 3
FL Division II	4	Rd 3	1928-29	FL Division I	20	**R-Up**
FL Division II	7	Rd 3	1929-30	FL Division I	13	Rd 4
FL Division II	9	Rd 3	1930-31	FL Division I	4	Rd 5
FL Division II	14	Rd 3	1931-32	FL Division I	8	Rd 5
FL Division II	12	Rd 3	1932-33	FL Division I	9	Rd 3
FL Division II	14	Rd 3	1933-34	FL Division I	10	**R-Up**
FL Division II	19	Rd 4	1934-35	FL Division I	14	Rd 4
FL Division II	17	Rd 3	1935-36	FL Division I	10	Rd 3
FL Division II	19	Rd 3	1936-37	FL Division I	9	Rd 3
FL Division II	15	Rd 3	1937-38	FL Division I	19	Rd 4
FL Division II	18	Rd 3	1938-39	FL Division I	17	**WINNERS**
War Competitions			1939-45			
War League		Rd 4	1945-46			Rd 3
FL Division II	14	Rd 4	1946-47	FL Division I	12	Rd 4
FL Division II	3	Q-F	1947-48	FL Division I	8	Rd 4
FL Division II	3	Rd 3	1948-49	**FL Division I**	Champs	**S-F**
FL Division II	4	Rd 3	1949-50	**FL Division I**	Champs	Rd 5
FL Division II	12	Rd 4	1950-51	FL Division I	7	Rd 3
FL Division II	13	Rd 3	1951-52	FL Division I	4	Q-F
FL Division II	Relg 21	Rd 5	1952-53	FL Division I	15	Rd 3
FL Division III (South)	6	Rd 1	1953-54	FL Division I	14	Rd 5
FL Division III (South)	3	Rd 2	1954-55	FL Division I	3	Rd 3
FL Division III (South)	14	Rd 2	1955-56	FL Division I	12	Rd 4
FL Division III (South)	4	Rd 3	1956-57	FL Division I	19	Rd 4
FL Division III (South)	6	Rd 2	1957-58	FL Division I	20	Rd 4
FL Division III	14	Rd 3	1958-59	FL Division I	Relg 22	Rd 5
FL Division III	Champs	Rd 4	1959-60	FL Division II	20	Rd 3

SAINTS					POMPEY			
League/Division	Place	FA Cup	FL Cup		League/Division	Place	FA Cup	FL Cup
FL Division II	8	Rd 4	Rd 5	1960-61	FL Division II	Relg 21	Rd 3	Rd 5
FL Division II	6	Rd 3	Rd 1	1961-62	FL Division III	Champs	Rd 1	Rd 3
FL Division II	11	S-F	Rd 2	1962-63	FL Division II	16	Rd 4	Rd 4
FL Division II	5	Rd 3	Rd 1	1963-64	FL Division II	9	Rd 3	Rd 4
FL Division II	4	Rd 4	Rd 3	1964-65	FL Division II	20	Rd 3	Rd 3
FL Division II	R-up	Rd 3	Rd 3	1965-66	FL Division II	12	Rd 3	Rd 3
FL Division I	19	Rd 4	Rd 3	1966-67	FL Division II	14	Rd 4	Rd 2
FL Division I	16	Rd 4	Rd 2	1967-68	FL Division II	5	Rd 5	Rd 3
FL Division I	7	Rd 4	Rd 5	1968-69	FL Division II	15	Rd 4	Rd 2
FL Division I	19	Rd 4	Rd 2	1969-70	FL Division II	17	Rd 3	Rd 1
FL Division I	7	Rd 5	Rd 2	1970-71	FL Division II	16	Rd 4	Rd 3
FL Division I	19	Rd 3	Rd 3	1971-72	FL Division II	16	Rd 5	Rd 1
FL Division I	13	Rd 3	Rd 3	1972-73	FL Division II	17	Rd 3	Rd 2
FL Division I	Relg 20	Rd 5	Rd 4	1973-74	FL Division II	15	Rd 5	Rd 2
FL Division II	13	Rd 3	Rd 4	1974-75	FL Division II	17	Rd 3	Rd 2
FL Division II	6	WINNERS	Rd 2	1975-76	FL Division II	Relg 22	Rd 4	Rd 2
FL Division II	9	Rd 5	Rd 2	1976-77	FL Division III	20	Rd 3	Rd 1
FL Division II	R-up	Rd 4	Rd 3	1977-78	FL Division III	Relg 24	Rd 2	Rd 3
FL Division I	14	Q-F	R-up	1978-79	FL Division IV	7	Rd 2	Rd 1
FL Division I	8	Rd 3	Rd 3	1979-80	FL Division IV	promo 4	Rd 3	Rd 1
FL Division I	6	Rd 5	Rd 2	1980-81	FL Division III	6	Rd 1	Rd 4
FL Division I	7	Rd 3	Rd 2	1981-82	FL Division III	13	Rd 1	Rd 2
FL Division I	12	Rd 3	Rd 4	1982-83	FL Division III	Champs	Rd 2	Rd 1
FL Division I	R-up	S-F	Rd 3	1983-84	FL Division II	16	Rd 4	Rd 2
FL Division I	5	Rd 5	Rd 4	1984-85	FL Division II	4	Rd 3	Rd 2
FL Division I	14	S-F	Rd 4	1985-86	FL Division II	4	Rd 3	Rd 5
FL Division I	12	Rd 3	S-F	1986-87	FL Division II	R-up	Rd 4	Rd 3
FL Division I	12	Rd 4	Rd 2	1987-88	FL Division I	Relg 19	Q-F	Rd 2
FL Division I	13	Rd 3	Rd 5	1988-89	FL Division II	20	Rd 3	Rd 2
FL Division I	7	Rd 5	Rd 5	1989-90	FL Division II	12	Rd 3	Rd 2
FL Division I	14	Rd 5	Rd 5	1990-91	FL Division II	17	Rd 5	Rd 3
FL Division I	16	Q-F	Rd 4	1991-92	FL Division II	9	S-F	Rd 3
Premiership	18	Rd 3	Rd 3	1992-93	New Division I	3	Rd 3	Rd 3
Premiership	18	Rd 3	Rd 2	1993-94	Division I	17	Rd 3	Rd 5
Premiership	10	Rd 5	Rd 3	1994-95	Division I	18	Rd 4	Rd 3
Premiership	17	Q-F	Rd 4	1995-96	Division I	21	Rd 3	Rd 1
Premiership	16	Rd 3	Rd 5	1996-97	Division I	7	Q-F	Rd 2
Premiership	12	Rd 3	Rd 4	1997-98	Division I	20	Rd 3	Rd 1
Premiership	17	Rd 3	Rd 2	1998-99	Division I	19	Rd 4	Rd 2
Premiership	15	Rd 4	Rd 4	1999-00	Division I	18	Rd 3	Rd 2
Premiership	10	Rd 5	Rd 3	2000-01	Division I	20	Rd 3	Rd 2
Premiership	11	Rd 3	Rd 4	2001-02	Division I	17	Rd 3	Rd 1
Premiership	8	R-up	Rd 3	2002-03	Division I	Champs	Rd 3	Rd 2
Premiership	12	Rd 3	Rd 5	2003-04	Premiership	13	Q-F	Rd 4

Key to Table 3

'R-up' = runners-up, whether in League or Cup.

The League columns – for the Southern League (SL), Football League (FL) and Premiership – indicate promoted ('promo'), where that is not obvious from being 'Champs' or 'R-up', and relegation ('relg').

The Cup columns show the Round (Rd) reached, including semi-final (S-F).
The FA Cup columns also show quarter-finals (Q-F: Third Round until 1905, then Fourth Round until 1925, and Sixth Round thereafter).
The phrase 'quarter-final' tends not be used for the Fifth Round of the FLC (*League Cup*), so we have not imposed it here.
'Qual' indicates being knocked out in the FA Cup Qualifying rounds.

Sources

The bulk of this book is dependent upon articles and reports from contemporary newspapers, at Portsmouth City Library, Southampton Central Library and the British Newspaper Library at Colindale. We are grateful to Editor Ian Murray for permission to use the *Southern Daily Echo* archives.

The principal newspapers consulted are:

The Athletic News, Manchester; *Football Chat & Athletic World*, London; *The Hampshire Advertiser*, Southampton; *The Hampshire Independent,* Southampton; *The Evening News* (later *The News*), Portsmouth; *The Football Echo & Sports Gazette* (and variations, latterly *The Pink*), Southampton; *The Football Mail* (with several variations of title), Portsmouth; *The Football News & Southern Sport*, Portsmouth; *The Portsmouth Times; The Southampton Pictorial; The Southampton Times & Hampshire Express; The Southern Daily Echo.* All quotations from national newspapers are attributed in the text.

Portsmouth FC :

There are some fine works on Portsmouth FC. We have drawn upon the following:

Barry Bendel, *The Pride of Pompey,* self-published, 2003.
Colin Farmery, *Portsmouth Champions of England, 1948–49 & 1949–50*, Desert Island Books, 2002 edn.
Colin Farmery, *Portsmouth: from Tindall to Ball, a complete record,* Desert Island Books, 1999
Roger Holmes, *Pompey Players 1920-2001,* Bishops Printers, 2001.
Peter Jeffs, *Pompey's Gentleman Jim*, Desert Island Books, 1988.
Peter Jeffs, Colin Farmery, Richard Owen, *Portsmouth Football Club: 1898–1998: the Official Centenary History*, Bishops Printers, 1998
Mike Neasom, Mick Cooper & Doug Robinson, *Pompey: the History of Portsmouth Football Club*, Milestone, 1984.

Southampton FC:

All Hagiology titles owe a debt of gratitude to the researches and collations of Duncan Holley and Gary Chalk:

Saints: a Complete Record of Southampton Football Club, 1885–1987, Breedon Books, 1987.
The Alphabet of the Saints: a complete who's who of Southampton FC, ACL & Polar, 1992.
In That Number: a post-war chronicle of Southampton FC, Hagiology Publishing, 2003.

We have also referred to 'the prequel' to *In That Number*, scheduled for publication in or after 2007, and to three other Hagiology Publishing titles already in print:.

David Bull, *Dell Diamond: Ted Bates's 66 seasons with The Saints,*1998 (pbk edn, 2004)
David Bull & Bob Brunskell (eds), *Match of the Millennium: The Saints' 100 Most Memorable Matches*, 2000.
Dave Juson & David Bull, *Full-Time at The Dell: from Watty to Matty 1898–2001*, 2001

Works of reference:

The other reference books on which we have constantly drawn have been those dependable annuals – the *News Chronicle Football Annual* (up to season 1960-61), the *News of the World Football Annual* (from 1961-62) and the *Rothmans Football Yearbook* (reconstituted as the *Sky Sports Football Yearbook* from 2003-04) – along with four other invaluable sources:

Mike Collett, *The Guinness Record of the FA Cup*, Guinness Publishing, 1993.

Barry J. Hugman (ed.), *The PFA Premier & Football League Player's Records 1946-1998,* Queen Anne Press, 1998.

Jack Rollin, *Rothmans Book of Football Records,* Headline, 1998

Dennis Turner & Alex White (eds.), *The Breedon Book of Football Managers*, 1993

We have also drawn, without specific reference in the text, upon the following:

Leigh Edwards, *The Official History of the Southern League, 1894–1994,* Paper Plane, 1993

C.B. Fry, *Life Worth Living: some phases of an Englishman*, Eyre & Spottiswoode, 1939

Geoffrey Green, *The Official History of the FA Cup*, Naldrett, 1949

Simon Inglis, *League Football and the men who made it*, Willow Books, 1988

Lawrie McMenemy, *The Diary of a Season*, Arthur Barker, 1979

Jack Rollin, *Soccer at War, 1939–45*, Willow Books, 1985

Geoffrey Stavart, *A Study in Southsea, the unrevealed life of Doctor Arthur Conan Doyle*, Milestone, 1986

Anthony Trigg, *Portsmouth Past and Present*, Milestone, 1984

Martin Tyler, *Cup Final Extra! A Celebration for the 100th FA Cup Final – How the Finals Were Reported 1874–1980*, Hamlyn,1980

Cited sources:

Otherwise, the books and articles to which we have specifically referred in the text are:

Books and Articles

Walley Barnes, *Captain of Wales,* Stanley Paul, 1953.

Bryon Butler, *The Official History of the Football Association,* Queen Anne Press, 1991.

Mick Channon, *Man on the Run: an autobiography*, Arthur Barker, 1986

Gemma Clarke, 'Simply the worst,' *Observer* Sport, 10 October 2004.

Rev. J. Silvester Davies, *A History of Southampton*, 1883 (facsimile edition, Hampshire Books, 1983)

Daniel Defoe, *A Tour Through The Whole Island of Great Britain, 1724-26,* Penguin edn, 1971

Sir Arthur Conan Doyle, *Memories and Adventures*, Hodder and Stoughton, 1924

Alfred Gibson & William Pickford, *Association Football and the men who made it* (four volumes), Caxton, 1905–06

Geoffrey Green, *Soccer in the Fifties,* Ian Allan, 1974.

Frank Keating, 'If football is war with rules, why not play on?' *Guardian*, 10 September 2004.

A. Temple Patterson, *Portsmouth: a history*, Moonraker Press, 1976

Cass Pennant & Rob Silvester, *Rolling with the 6.57 Crew: the true story of Pompey's legendary football fans,* John Blake, 2003.

William Pickford, *The Hampshire Football Association Golden Jubilee Book*, Hampshire FA, 1937

Colin Shindler, *Fathers, Sons and Football*, Headline, 2001.

Kevin Smith, *Glory Gunners: The History of Royal Artillery (Portsmouth) FC*, Board Books, 1999

Jason Tomas, *The Goal Machine: portrait of a football superstar,* Mainstream Publishing, 1997.

Iain Wilson, *C.B. Fry: an English hero*, Richard Cohen Books, 1999.

Programmes and Fanzines

It is obvious throughout the book where we have drawn, for text and/or illustration, upon matchday programmes (or the Matthew Le Tissier testimonial programme) and the occasional fanzine, so we have not thought it necessary to log them here.

Presentations & Subscribers

Authors

CLAY ALDWORTH – First match, 11 December 1971 v West Ham, 3-3. A Millbrook Secondary School trip to Belgium in May 1976 meant he missed a certain game at Wembley that year. The party was arriving back in England on the Saturday afternoon, everyone listening to the game on the radio. When Bobby Stokes scored, the whole bus erupted – some shock for the driver! Following in his father's footsteps, he went to work in Southampton Docks. Having joined Whitbread in Romsey in 1988, he is still in the beer trade with Tradeteam at Totton. Starting out in the Chocolate Boxes at The Dell, he purchased his first season ticket, at 15, in 1978 (East Stand bench seats) for the grand sum of £40. Now a season ticket-holder in the Northam Stand at St Mary's (for quite considerably more), he is currently working on interactive CD Rom sporting titles, including Saints Year Discs and Formula One.

BARRY BENDEL – First match 1948: Saints v Spurs. First Pompey game, 20 March 1948: Pompey 1 Manchester City 0. First remembered details of a game: 27 November 1948, when Pompey celebrated their Golden Jubilee with a spectacular 4-1 win against Arsenal at Fratton Park in front of 43,000 spectators. Emigrated to the USA in 1957 and, on his return to England two years later, attended St Martin's Art School in London. Worked as an Art Director in Advertising for about 40 years and in tourism for another four. He was separated from Portsmouth for about 10 years, while working overseas, but has not missed a home League match since 1989. In 2003, he wrote, designed and published his first book, *The Pride of Pompey*. Many of the caricatures for that book have been reproduced in this one, on which he has thoroughly enjoyed working.

DAVID BULL – Soon after seeing his first game at The Dell in 1948 – the one at which the photo of Charlie Wayman on page 258 was taken – he left his native Salisbury to be a Camberley teenager, an Exeter student and a university teacher, latterly in Bristol. A barrister occasionally chairing appeal tribunals in his 'retirement', he fears the history of Southampton FC has become his day-job. Writing on football, in the Saints matchday programme or the odd fanzine, was supposed to be for fun – or for charity, as in editing a couple of collections of fans' memories, on behalf of the Child Poverty Action Group. But since he completed *Dell Diamond* in 1998, he has been involved in Hagiology Publishing's further titles (*as listed opposite*), causing the publication of *Constant Paine* to be re-scheduled more often than Saints' Saturday 3.00 p.m kick-offs.

GARY CHALK – A native of Eastleigh, attending Chamberlayne Primary and later Alderman Quilley Schools, he saw his first match on 28 October 1967 v Burnley, 2-2. Has been employed at the town's Alstom Railway Works as a coppersmith for the past 30 years. Co-author, with Duncan Holley, of *Saints: a complete record* (1987), *Alphabet of the Saints* (1992) and, latterly, *In That Number* – an encyclopaedic history of Southampton FC from 1946 to 2003, the 'prequel' to which (1885-1946) he is now working on (*see opposite*). Has collaborated with Leigh Edwards, and latterly Dave Juson, on the compilation of historical series in the Saints matchday programme. An original Hagiologist and something of a librarian to the collective, he has a large number of items in his reference collection.

DAVE JUSON – Author, with David Bull, of *Full-Time at The Dell* and contributor to *Match of the Millennium*, he was born and mostly bred in Southampton. He saw his first Saints-Pompey derby in March 1963. His connections with Portsmouth are numerous: his Dad was in the Fleet Air Arm; he enjoyed memorable excursions to Billy Manning's Fun Fair and HMS Victory, as a lad; and, for a while, he worked in Southsea. An historian – he studied at Ruskin College, Oxford and the University of Leicester – he has continued to visit Portsmouth, because the museums are impressive, the natives are friendly and it has some cracking pubs.

Hagiology Publishing

Formed in 1998, Hagiology Publishing is a collective of Saints fans committed to the collection and dissemination of accurate information on the history of Southampton FC.

Its first publication, in 1998, was *Dell Diamond,* the story of Ted Bates's first 60 seasons with the Saints (republished in commemorative, paperback edition in 2004, with a special, new chapter honouring Ted's last six seasons).

Each of its next three publications, *Match of the Millennium* (2000), *Full-Time at The Dell* (2001) and *In That Number* (2003), was generously promoted by Matthew Le Tissier. In gratitude for his efforts as our "Patron Saint", we were pleased to present him with a framed copy of his memorable "Great Escape" free-kick at Upton Park in 1994:

Matthew accepts the token of gratitude from (*left to right*) Duncan Holley, Dave Juson, David Bull and Gary Chalk.
Insets: Clay Aldworth (*left*) and Barry Bendel, who have joined us in the production of this fifth book, **SAINTS v POMPEY**.

This latest venture is Hagiology Publishing's fourth publication within an agreement with Southampton FC and the *Southern Daily Echo* regularly to produce books on aspects of Saints' history. The next books in the pipe-line are:

CONSTANT PAINE – a biography of Terry Paine (Autumn 2005)
and, of course, the 'prequel' (1885-1946) to *In That Number.*

Enquiries about SAINTS v POMPEY should be addressed to the appropriate member of the Hagiology collective as indicated below:

Individual (incl mail-order) enquiries:
Dave Juson
The Flat, 44 Shirley Road,
Freemantle, Southampton, SO15 3EU
Tel: 023(80) 221410
davejuson@hagiography.fsnet.co.uk

All retail and review enquiries:
David Bull (Editor)
170 Westbury Road
Bristol BS9 3AH
Tel: 0117 962 2042
bull.hagiology@blueyonder.co.uk